Nietzsche's *On the Genealogy of Morals*

Critical Essays on the Classics
Series Editor: Steven M. Cahn

The volumes in this series offer insightful and accessible essays that shed light on the classics of philosophy. Each of the distinguished editors has selected outstanding work in recent scholarship to provide today's readers with a deepened understanding of the most timely issues raised in these important texts.

Plato's *Republic*: Critical Essays
   edited by Richard Kraut
Plato's *Euthyphro, Apology*, and *Crito*: Critical Essays
   edited by Rachana Kamtekar
Aristotle's *Ethics*: Critical Essays
   edited by Nancy Sherman
Aristotle's *Politics*: Critical Essays
   edited by Richard Kraut and Steven Skultety
Augustine's *Confessions*: Critical Essays
   edited by William E. Mann
Aquinas's *Summa Theologiae*: Critical Essays
   edited by Brian Davies
Descartes's *Meditations*: Critical Essays
   edited by Vere Chappell
The Rationalists: Critical Essays on Descartes, Spinoza, and Leibniz
   edited by Derk Pereboom
The Empiricists: Critical Essays on Locke, Berkeley, and Hume
   edited by Margaret Atherton
The Social Contract Theorists: Critical Essays on Hobbes, Locke, and Rousseau
   edited by Christopher Morris
Kant's *Groundwork on the Metaphysics of Morals*: Critical Essays
   edited by Paul Guyer
Kant's *Critique of Pure Reason*: Critical Essays
   edited by Patricia Kitcher
Kant's *Critique of the Power of Judgment*: Critical Essays
   edited by Paul Guyer
Mill's *On Liberty*: Critical Essays
   edited by Gerald Dworkin
Mill's *Utilitarianism*: Critical Essays
   edited by David Lyons
Mill's *The Subjection of Women*: Critical Essays
   edited by Maria H. Morales
Nietzsche's *On the Genealogy of Morals*: Critical Essays
   edited by Christa Davis Acampora
Heidegger's *Being and Time*: Critical Essays
   edited by Richard Polt
The Existentialists: Critical Essays on Kierkegaard, Nietzsche, Heidegger, and Sartre
   edited by Charles Guignon

Nietzsche's *On the Genealogy of Morals*

Critical Essays

Edited by
Christa Davis Acampora

ROWMAN & LITTLEFIELD PUBLISHERS, INC.
Lanham • Boulder • New York • Toronto • Oxford

To My Students

ROWMAN & LITTLEFIELD PUBLISHERS, INC.

Published in the United States of America
by Rowman & Littlefield Publishers, Inc.
A wholly owned subsidiary of The Rowman & Littlefield Publishing Group, Inc.
4501 Forbes Boulevard, Suite 200, Lanham, Maryland 20706
www.rowmanlittlefield.com

PO Box 317
Oxford
OX2 9RU, UK

British Library Cataloguing in Publication Information Available

Library of Congress Cataloging-in-Publication Data

Nietzsche's On the genealogy of morals : critical essays / edited by Christa Davis
Acampora.
    p.   cm.— (Critical essays on the classics)
    Includes bibliographical references and index.
    ISBN-13: 978-0-7425-4262-4 (cloth : alk. paper)
    ISBN-10: 0-7425-4262-9 (cloth : alk. paper)
    ISBN-13: 978-0-7425-4263-1 (pbk. : alk. paper)
    ISBN-10: 0-7425-4263-7 (pbk. : alk. paper)
    1. Nietzsche, Friedrich Wilhelm, 1844–1900. Zur Geneologie der Moral.
2. Ethics.   I. Acampora, Christa Davis, 1967–   II. Series.
B3313.Z73N55   2006
170—dc22   2006009324

Printed in the United States of America

♾ ™ The paper used in this publication meets the minimum requirements of American
National Standard for Information Sciences—Permanence of Paper for Printed Library
Materials, ANSI/NISO Z39.48-1992.

Contents

Acknowledgments   vii

Abbreviations, Citations, and Translations of Nietzsche's Works   xi

Introduction

In the Beginning: Reading Nietzsche's
On the Genealogy of Morals from the Start   1
Christa Davis Acampora

Part I. On Genealogy

1   A "Dionysian Drama on the 'Fate of the Soul' ": An Introduction to
Reading *On the Genealogy of Morality*   19
    Keith Ansell Pearson

2   Nietzsche, Re-evaluation, and the Turn to Genealogy   39
    David Owen

3   The Genealogy of Genealogy: Interpretation in Nietzsche's Second
Untimely Meditation and in *On the Genealogy of Morals*   57
    Alexander Nehamas

4   Nietzsche's Style of Affirmation: The Metaphors of Genealogy   67
    Eric Blondel

5   Nietzsche and the Re-evaluation of Values   77
    Aaron Ridley

6   Genealogy, the Will to Power, and the Problem of a Past   93
    Tracy B. Strong

**Part II. Reading Nietzsche's *Genealogy*—Focused Analyses
of Parts and Passages**

7   Slave Morality, Socrates, and the Bushmen: A Critical
Introduction to *On the Genealogy of Morality, Essay I*   109
    Mark Migotti

8   Lightning and Flash, Agent and Deed (*GM* I:6–17)   131
      Robert B. Pippin

9   On Sovereignty and Overhumanity: Why It Matters
      How We Read Nietzsche's *Genealogy* II:2   147
      Christa Davis Acampora

10 Finding the *Übermensch* in Nietzsche's
      Genealogy of Morality   163
      Paul S. Loeb

11 The Genealogy of Morals and Right Reading: On the Nietzschean
      Aphorism and the Art of the Polemic   177
      Babette E. Babich

12 "We Remain of Necessity Strangers to Ourselves": The Key Message
      of Nietzsche's *Genealogy*   191
      Ken Gemes

13 Nihilism as Will to Nothingness   209
      Wolfgang Müller-Lauter

Part III. Critiquing *Genealogy*

14 The Entwinement of Myth and Enlightenment   223
      Jürgen Habermas

15 Translating, Repeating, Naming: Foucault, Derrida,
      and the Genealogy of Morals   233
      Gary Shapiro

16 Nietzsche, Deleuze, and the Genealogical Critique of Psychoanalysis:
      Between Church and State   245
      Alan D. Schrift

Part IV. On Politics and Community

17 Nietzsche's Genealogy: Of Beauty and Community   259
      Salim Kemal

18 Nietzsche and the Jews: The Structure of an Ambivalence   277
      Yirmiyahu Yovel

19 Nietzschean Virtue Ethics   291
      Christine Swanton

20 How We Became What We Are: Tracking the "Beasts of Prey"   305
      Daniel W. Conway

Bibliography   321

Index   327

About the Contributors   335

Acknowledgments

I am grateful to Steven Cahn for suggesting I consider the project, to Eve DeVaro for her reception to the idea, and, especially, to Tessa Fallon and Emily Ross for assistance with a variety of technical questions and tasks. Frank Kirkland made possible some administrative assistance during various stages of manuscript preparation, and Nathan Metzger provided early research assistance and collection of materials that proved very helpful. Special thanks are owed to Ben Abelson, Brian Crowley, Adele Sarli, and Catherine Schoeder, who read most if not all of the nearly one hundred articles and book chapters that were considered for possible inclusion in the book. My weekly discussions with them were always informative and interesting. Brian Crowley and David Pereplyotchik graciously aided with the preparation of the index. Persons too numerous to name generously discussed the book's contents and arrangement with me over the past year, most notably Keith Ansell Pearson. Several contributors took additional time to edit their essays for publication here. I am particularly grateful for the assistance of Keith Ansell Pearson, Babette E. Babich, Dan Conway, Ken Gemes, Paul Loeb, Mark Migotti, David Owen, Alan Schrift, Gary Shapiro, and Tracy B. Strong. Finally, I wish to thank my family for patiently listening to my nearly daily recounting of both thrilling insights and complaints about permissions editors. To those not responsible for the latter, I extend my sincere gratitude.

All of the material presented in this volume has been edited. In many cases, previously published pieces were edited and/or revised by the authors. In the acknowledgements below, I indicate whether contributions were excerpted and edited and/or revised by the author. Contents not listed below are now published for the first time.

"Nietzsche, Re-evaluation, and the Turn to Genealogy," David Owen. Edited by the author after its original publication in *European Journal of Philosophy* 11:3 (2003): 249–72. Reprinted with permission of Blackwell Publishing, Ltd.

"The Genealogy of Genealogy: Interpretation in Nietzsche's Second *Untimely Meditation* and in *On the Genealogy of Morals*," Alexander Nehamas. Excerpted from *Literary Theory and Philosophy*, edited by Richard Freadman and Lloyd Reinhardt (London: Macmillan, 1991), 269–83. Reproduced with permission of Palgrave Macmillan.

"Nietzsche's Style of Affirmation: The Metaphors of Genealogy," Eric Blondel. Excerpted from *Nietzsche as Affirmative Thinker*, edited by Y. Yovel (The Hague: Martinus Nijhoff Publishers, 1986), 136–46. Excerpt reprinted with permission of Springer.

"Nietzsche and the Re-evaluation of Values," Aaron Ridley. Edited by the author after its original publication in *Proceedings of the Aristotelian Society* 105 (2005), 171–91. Reprinted by courtesy of the Editor of the Aristotelian Society, copyright 2005.

"Slave Morality, Socrates, and the Bushmen: A Critical Introduction to *On the Genealogy of Morality, Essay I*" Mark Migotti. Revised and excerpted by the author after its publication in *Philosophy & Phenomenological Research* 58:4 (December 1998): 745–80.

"Lightning and Flash, Agent and Deed (*GM* I:6–17)," Robert B. Pippin in *Friedrich Nietzsche, Genealogie der Moral*, edited by Otfried Höffe (Berlin: Akademie Verlag, 2004), 47–63. Reprinted with permission of the author.

"On Sovereignty and Overhumanity: Why It Matters How We Read Nietzsche's *Genealogy* II:2," Christa Davis Acampora. Revised by the author from its original publication in *International Studies in Philosophy* 36:3 (Fall 2004): 127–45.

"Finding the *Übermensch* in Nietzsche's *Genealogy of Morality*," Paul S. Loeb. Excerpted and revised by the author from its original publication in *Journal of Nietzsche Studies* 30 (Autumn 2005): 70–101. Reprinted with permission of the Pennsylvania State University Press.

"Nihilism as Will to Nothingness," Wolfgang Müller-Lauter. In *Nietzsche: His Philosophy of Contradictions and Contradictions of His Philosophy*, written by Wolfgang Müller-Lauter and translated by David J. Parent (Chicago: University of Illinois Press, 1999), 41–49. Reprinted with permission of the University of Illinois Press.

"The Entwinement of Myth and Enlightenment," Jürgen Habermas. Excerpted from *The Philosophical Discourse of Modernity*, written by Jürgen Habermas and translated by Frederick Lawrence (Cambridge, MA: MIT Press, 1987), 120–30. Excerpt published here with the permission of the author, MIT Press, and Polity Press.

"Translating, Repeating, Naming: Foucault, Derrida, and the Genealogy of Morals," Gary Shapiro. Excerpted by the author from its original publication in *Nietzsche as Postmodernist: Essays Pro and Con*, edited by Clayton Koelb (Albany, NY: State University of New York Press), 39–55. Reprinted with permission of SUNY Press.

"Nietzsche, Deleuze, and the Genealogical Critique of Psychoanalysis: Between Church and State," Alan D. Schrift. Edited and revised by the author after its original publication as "Between Church and State: Nietzsche, Deleuze, and the Critique of Psychoanalysis" in *International Studies in Philosophy* 24:2 (Summer 1992): 41–52. Reprinted with the permission of the publisher.

"Nietzsche's Genealogy: Of Beauty and Community," Salim Kemal in *Journal of the British Society for Phenomenology* 21:3 (October 1990): 234–49. Reprinted with the permission of the journal editor.

"Nietzsche and the Jews: The Structure of an Ambivalence," Yirmiyahu Yovel in *Nietzsche and Jewish Culture*, edited by Jacob Golumb (New York: Routledge, 1997), 117–34. Reprinted with permission of Routledge.

"Nietzschean Virtue Ethics," Christine Swanton in *Virtue Ethics: Old and New*, edited by Steven M. Gardiner (Ithaca, NY: Cornell University Press, 2005), 179–92. Reprinted with permission of the author and Cornell University Press.

"How We Became What We Are: Tracking the 'Beasts of Prey,'" Daniel Conway. Revised by the author from its original publication in *A Nietzschean Bestiary: Becoming Animal Beyond Docile and Brutal*, edited by Christa Davis Acampora and Ralph R. Acampora (Lanham, MD: Rowman & Littlefield Publishers, Inc., 2004), 156–77. Published with permission of the author and publisher.

Abbreviations, Citations, and Translations of Nietzsche's Works

ABBREVIATIONS AND CITATIONS

The essays that follow have been edited so as to use the same citation format throughout. References are given in the body of the book. Redundant references to the German texts for Nietzsche's published writings have been deleted, since these are easily identifiable in the now standard editions. References to Nietzsche's unpublished writings have been standardized, whenever possible, to refer to the most accessible edition of Nietzsche's notebooks and publications, the *Kritische Studienausgabe* (*KSA*), compiled under the general editorship of Giorgio Colli and Mazzino Montinari. References to the edition of letters in this collection are cited as *KSAB*.

Roman numerals denote the volume number of a set of collected works or standard subdivision within a single work, and Arabic numerals denote the relevant section number. In cases in which Nietzsche's prefaces are cited, the letter "P" is used followed by the relevant section number, where applicable. When a section is too long for the section number alone to be useful, the page number of the relevant translation is also provided. In the cases in which the *KGW* and *KSA* are cited, references provide the volume number (and part for *KGW*) followed by the relevant fragment number and any relevant aphorism (e.g., *KSA* 10:12[1].37 refers to volume 10, fragment 12[1], aphorism 37). The following abbreviations are used for citations of Nietzsche's writings.

A = *The Antichrist*
AOM = *Assorted Opinions and Maxims*
BGE = *Beyond Good and Evil*
BT = *The Birth of Tragedy*
CW = *The Case of Wagner*

D = *Daybreak*
DD = *Dionysian Dithyrambs*
DS = *David Strauss, the Writer and Confessor*
EH = *Ecce Homo* [sections abbreviated "Wise," "Clever," "Books," "Destiny"].
  Abbreviations for titles discussed in "Books" are indicated instead of "Books"
  where relevant (e.g., *EH* "GM").
FEI = "On the Future of Our Educational Institutions"
GM = *On the Genealogy of Morals*
GS = *The Gay Science*
HC = "Homer's Contest"
HCP = "Homer and Classical Philology"
HH = *Human, All Too Human*
HL = *On the Use and Disadvantage of History for Life*
IM = "Idylls from Messina"
KGW = *Kritische Gesamtausgabe*
KSA = *Kritische Studienausgabe*
KSAB = *Kritische Studienausgabe Briefe*
LR = "Lectures on Rhetoric"
NCW = *Nietzsche Contra Wagner*
PN = *Portable Nietzsche*
PTAG = *Philosophy in the Tragic Age of the Greeks*
RWB = *Richard Wagner in Bayreuth*
SE = *Schopenhauer as Educator*
TI = *Twilight of the Idols* [sections abbreviated "Maxims," "Socrates," "Reason,"
  "World," "Morality," "Errors," "Improvers," "Germans," "Skirmishes,"
  "Ancients," "Hammer"]
TL = "On Truth and Lies in an Extra-moral Sense"
UM = *Untimely Meditations* (when referenced as a whole)
WP = *The Will to Power*
WPh = "We Philologists"
WS = *The Wanderer and His Shadow*
Z = *Thus Spoke Zarathustra* [References to *Z* list the part number and chapter title
  followed by the relevant section number when applicable.]

TRANSLATIONS

The following translations of Nietzsche's works are utilized in this volume. Authors
acknowledge the relevant translators as occasions require. In cases in which no translation is indicated, the author has supplied his or her own translation.

The Antichrist (written in 1888). In *The Portable Nietzsche*. Ed. and trans. Walter
  Kaufmann. New York: Viking Press, 1968. Also translated as *The Anti-Christ*. In

Twilight of the Idols/The Anti-Christ. Trans. R. J. Hollingdale. New York: Viking Penguin, 1968.

Assorted Opinions and Maxims (1879). Vol. 2, part 1 of *Human, All Too Human.* Trans. R. J. Hollingdale. Cambridge: Cambridge University Press, 1986.

Beyond Good and Evil: Prelude to a Philosophy of the Future (1886). Trans. Walter Kaufmann. New York: Vintage Books, 1966. Also trans. R. J. Hollingdale. London: Penguin Books, 1990. Also trans. Judith Norman. Ed. Rolf-Peter Horstmann and Judith Norman. Cambridge University Press, 2002.

The Birth of Tragedy, Or: Hellenism and Pessimism (1872). In *The Birth of Tragedy* and *The Case of Wagner.* Trans. Walter Kaufmann. New York: Vintage Books, 1967. Also *The Birth of Tragedy.* Trans. Francis Golffing. New York: Anchor Books, 1956. And *The Birth of Tragedy.* Trans. Shaun Whiteside. London: Penguin Books, 1993.

Daybreak: Thoughts on the Prejudices of Morality (1881). Trans. R. J. Hollingdale. Cambridge: Cambridge University Press, 1982.

Ecce Homo: How One Becomes What One Is (written in 1888). In *On the Genealogy of Morals* and *Ecce Homo.* Trans. Walter Kaufmann. New York: Vintage Books, 1969.

The Gay Science: With a Prelude in German Rhymes and an Appendix of Songs (1882 and 1887 [Book V added]). Trans. Walter Kaufmann. New York: Vintage Books, 1974. Also trans. Josefine Nauckhoff and Adrian Del Caro. Ed. by Bernard Williams. Cambridge: Cambridge University Press, 2001.

David Strauss: The Writer and the Confessor (1873). Trans. by R. J. Hollingdale. Cambridge: Cambridge University Press, 1983.

"Homer's Contest" (written in 1871). Trans. Christa Davis Acampora. *Nietzscheana* 5/6, 1996. Excerpts also translated as "Homer's Contest." In *The Portable Nietzsche.* Ed. and trans. Walter Kaufmann. New York: Viking Press, 1968.

Human, All Too Human: A Book for Free Spirits, Vol. 1 (1878). Trans. R. J. Hollingdale. Cambridge: Cambridge University Press, 1986.

On the Genealogy of Morals (1887). In *On the Genealogy of Morals* and *Ecce Homo.* Trans. Walter Kaufmann and R. J. Hollingdale. New York: Vintage Books, 1969. Also *On the Genealogy of Morality.* Trans. Carol Diethe. Ed. by Keith Ansell-Pearson. Cambridge: Cambridge University Press, 1994; revised edition forthcoming, 2006. Also *On the Genealogy of Morality.* Trans. Maudemarie Clark and Alan J. Swensen. Indianapolis, IN: Hackett Publishing Company, Inc., 1998.

"On Truth and Lies in a Nonmoral Sense" (written in 1873). In *Philosophy and Truth: Selections from the Notebooks of the 1870s.* Trans. Daniel Breazeale. Atlantic Highlands, NJ: Humanities Press, 1979.

On the Use and Disadvantage of History for Life (1874). In *Untimely Meditations.* Trans. R. J. Hollingdale. Cambridge: Cambridge University Press, 1983.

Richard Wagner in Bayreuth. (1875) Trans. Richard T. Gray. In *The Complete Works of Friedrich Nietzsche, Volume 2: Unfashionable Observations.* Stanford: Stanford University Press, 1995.

Schopenhauer as Educator (1874). In *Untimely Meditations*. Trans. R. J. Hollingdale. Cambridge: Cambridge University Press, 1983.

Thus Spoke Zarathustra (1883 [Parts 1–2]; 1884 [Part 3]; 1885 [Part 4]). In *The Portable Nietzsche*. Ed. and trans. Walter Kaufmann. New York: Viking Press, 1968.

Twilight of the Idols (written in 1888). In *The Portable Nietzsche*. Ed. and trans. Walter Kaufmann. New York: Viking Press, 1968. Also *Twilight of the Idols: Or How to Philosophize with a Hammer*. Trans. Duncan Large. Oxford: Oxford University Press, 1998. Also trans. in *Twilight of the Idols/The Anti-Christ*. Trans. R. J. Hollingdale. New York: Viking Penguin, 1968.

The Wanderer and His Shadow (1880). Vol. 2, part 2 of *Human, All Too Human*. Trans. R. J. Hollingdale. Cambridge: Cambridge University Press, 1986.

The Will to Power (selected notes from 1883–1888). Ed. Walter Kaufmann. Trans. Walter Kaufmann and R. J. Hollingdale. New York: Vintage Books, 1967.

Nietzsche's Works in German

Kritische Studienausgabe. Ed. Giorgio Colli and Mazzino Montinari. Berlin and New York: Walter de Gruyter, 1967–1988.

Kritische Studienausgabe Sämtliche Briefe. Ed. Giorgio Colli and Mazzino Montinari. Berlin and New York: Walter de Gruyter, 1986.

Kritische Gesamtausgabe, Ed. Giorgio Colli and Mazzino Montinari. Berlin and New York: Walter de Gruyter, 1967–.

Werke in drei Bänden. Ed. Karl Schlechta. 3 vols. Munich: Carl Hanser, 1954–1956.

Introduction

In the Beginning
Reading Nietzsche's *On the Genealogy of Morals* from the Start

Christa Davis Acampora

"Let us start again, from the beginning"

(*GM* III:1)

Right from the start, Nietzsche's *On the Genealogy of Morals* presents us with some intriguing questions. Simply considering its title—and the choices that translators have made in rendering it into English—opens a number of them. Although several essays in this volume discuss these issues, I shall briefly mention them here because they raise concerns that from the outset will direct readers down different paths. At stake is Nietzsche's general task, how it stands in relation to what might be considered related works or approaches, and how it has been appropriated (and might be extended in the future) in philosophy, political theory, history, and the other related areas of inquiry that have taken to the notion of "genealogical" investigation. So, we shall begin with that very beginning.

The original German title reads: *Zur Genealogie der Moral: Eine Streitschrift*. The German preposition *zur*—a contraction of *zu* and the article *der*—is common enough. It can mean "toward the" or "on the." In a helpful article annotating the *Genealogy*, David S. Thatcher recounts Walter Kaufmann's reasons for preferring "on" in the translation he completed with R. J. Hollingdale[1]—a survey of other uses of *zur* by Nietzsche suggests he does not use it to intend "toward"—and other translators have followed this lead.[2] I do not find this to be conclusive evidence, though, and it does make a difference whether Nietzsche thought he was contribut-

1

ing *to* (a body of work on) genealogy, whether he was writing *on* (but not himself doing) genealogy from which he was distancing himself, or whether he thought he was *leading us toward* something that we are not yet in a position to do or to see. These are not mutually exclusive goals and, regardless of the precise translation upon which we settle, it is appropriate to see Nietzsche as having each of these aims. He is contributing to a certain body of work devoted to determining the development of human beings such that they became social creatures who developed what we today call "morality." And he is distancing himself from particular ways in which some of his contemporaries have endeavored to do this, as I mention briefly below.

But it is also clear that Nietzsche thinks he is leading us or preparing us for something we have not yet been able to do, to begin a new inquiry, namely, to understand something about ourselves in terms of what we are now and what our future possibilities might be, and perhaps also to exhibit a *way* of investigating a variety of facets of human existence and how those features have acquired their meanings. Any doubt that Nietzsche's aims include being *on the way toward* something, should be dispelled when we read the very first lines of the book: Nietzsche, evoking a line from one of his favorite philosophers, Heraclitus, tells us that, "We are unknown to ourselves," suggesting that part of his enterprise involves helping us, as readers, to become less of "strangers to ourselves" (an idea Ken Gemes discusses at length in his "Strangers to Ourselves" in this volume).[3] We are so because "we have never sought ourselves."

Heraclitus is reported to have made the uncanny claim, "I went seeking myself."[4] This thought is *uncanny* because it would seem that nothing is closer, and perhaps least in need of being sought, than ourselves. Faith in the transparency of the self seems to be one of the key ideas in modern philosophy—consider, for instance, the grist of self-knowledge in Descartes' *Meditations*. Gemes explores what is uncanny or, in the German *unheimlich*—literally "un-home-ly"; we might also think of it as "unsettling," "disturbing," or "uprooting"—about Nietzsche's project in *On the Genealogy of Morals*.

The *Genealogy* is supposed to be about *us*, about drawing us into a project aimed at knowing ourselves better, as Gemes elaborates in detail, and Robert B. Pippin and Tracy B. Strong treat in their essays. Pippin's "Lightning and Flash" explicates the curious passage in the first essay where Nietzsche seems to deny that we are "selves" at all (*GM* I:13). Strong, in his "Genealogy, the Will to Power, and the Problem of a Past" describes how "weak" and "strong" wills relate to the degree to which one manages to listen to "knowing conscience" and "become the one you are" (*GS* 270).

Nietzsche's opening indicates that the story of the book might resonate in some way with the story of ourselves. The same paragraph continues with a citation from the first book of the New Testament, Matthew 6:21: "Where your treasure is, there will your heart be also." In other words, your highest aims (i.e., what you treasure) will direct your desires (i.e., what you pursue and how you go about it). Many of Nietzsche's books aim to call our attention to asking the question of what our highest aims are and how we might produce (by artistically creating visions of) that to which a human life might vibrantly aspire. But although Nietzsche cites the book of Matthew here, he does not simply reiterate its answer. Nietzsche's "good news," we must imagine, will involve a transformation or a revaluation of what are identified as the *treasure* and the *heart* of Christianity (that is, it involves a deep exploration of what is *prized* or valued most highly and the desire or *passion* that motivates the pursuit of such).

Nietzsche's *Genealogy* constitutes a new beginning, some kind of seeking; it *is* on the way toward something, perhaps the discovery of a new "treasure." And, in case we need further convincing of this point, at the end of the second essay of the *Genealogy*, following Nietzsche's account of the development of modern morality and what he calls "the bad conscience," he evokes the image of "the man of the future, who will redeem us" from the mess he has just described, and he ties this redemptive image to the name of his Zarathustra (*GM* II:24 and 25). Paul S. Loeb in his "Finding the Übermensch in Nietzsche's *Genealogy of Morality*" goes to great lengths to show how this is so and the difference it makes for how we think about what is the future alternative for which Nietzsche argues. All of this is followed by an elaborate analysis, specifically an *exegesis* of the nature of ascetic ideals (about which Wolfgang Müller-Lauter sheds considerable light in his "Nihilism as Will to Nothingness"). And that discussion concludes with consideration of whether (and, if so, how) it is possible to generate meaning and significance in any way other than through ascetic practices, which Nietzsche considers to be destructive and ultimately self-undermining. So, it is clear that Nietzsche's project is on its way toward somewhere but that it does not ultimately reach its conclusion. This is not Nietzsche's last word on the matter, and he does not consider his account complete.

There is no disagreement among translators about the translation of *Genealogie*, naturally, but as one can see when reading the essays collected here, the relation of genealogy to history, to the "English psychologists" Nietzsche dismisses in his preface and first essay, to the work of his former friend Paul Rée, and to "genealogy" as practiced by those inspired by Michel Foucault are considerably contentious issues. Numerous authors included here treat facets of these concerns (e.g., Alexander Nehamas in "The Genealogy of Genealogy: Interpretation in Nietzsche's Second *Untimely Meditation* and in *On the Genealogy of Morals*," Gary Shapiro in "Translating, Repeating, Naming: Foucault, Derrida, and the Genealogy of Morals," and Alan D. Schrift in "Nietzsche, Deleuze, and the Genealogical Critique of Psychoanalysis: Between Church and State").[5] How does this influence the reader from the very start? The matter concerns what counts as a "start," because there is considerable variation in how certain key words relating to beginnings and origins in *Zur Genealogie der Moral* are translated. These words give us some clues about just what Nietzsche intends by "genealogy" and whether and how he is practicing or applying it (and there is disagreement about whether genealogy is a method or an interpretative activity that one practices in an exemplary fashion—see Babette E. Babich, "The Genealogy of Morals and Right Reading: On the Nietzschean Aphorism and the Art of the Polemic" on this point).[6]

The problematic words in question are *Herkunft*, *Ursprung*, and *Entstehung*, and their compounds. Roughly, these words could be translated as "descent," "origin," and "emergence" in that order. How we think about Nietzsche's use of these words is related to what we consider his project to be in *On the Genealogy of Morals*.[7] Is Nietzsche providing us with his own view of the "descent of man" in the form of a developmental story that is similar to or at odds with the "descent of man" as provided by Charles Darwin and other evolutionary theorists? Is Nietzsche offering a story about an "original condition," something like the "state of nature" that early modern philosophers provided in their political philosophies? Is he endeavoring to disclose the "true origins" of morality in order to show that religious morality, particularly, is not what we think it is? Is he tracing the emergence of nobility (and/or slavishness) in the manner of a pedigree? Is he giving us a naturalistic account of the emergence of morality among human beings? Is genealogy chiefly critique, and is it supposed to be different from (and more effective than) making a logical argument against that which is criticized? And if the latter, is there any way to legitimately make judgments about the superiority of differing genealogical critiques, if universal reasoning about these matters has been undermined? These are questions that we confront when we consider *from the beginning* what Nietzsche intends by "genealogy."

The first section of this volume addresses the nature of Nietzsche's genealogical project. Keith Ansell Pearson's "A 'Dionysian Drama on the "Fate of the Soul"'; An Introduction to Reading *On the Genealogy of Morality*" addresses many of the questions raised above, providing a far-reaching but specific scope through which to consider how Nietzsche envisions the incorporation of knowledge with the love of our fate. Of particular interest are Ansell Pearson's discussion of the soul, bad conscience, and guilt, in which he describes how Nietzsche retains a conception of soul as "a system of valuations and value-affects," how bad conscience is *fated* as the internalization of the "'instinct for freedom'" and "will to growth," and how guilt is the idealized moralization of the debtor-creditor relation that affords a particularly intense manifestation of cruelty turning back on itself. The drama of the soul, then, is the pressure and play of these affects, which is the source of our undoing as well as our possible creativity. In the second chapter, "Nietzsche, Re-evaluation and the Turn to Genealogy," David Owen describes how Nietzsche's turn to genealogy is motivated, in part, by his concern to provide a naturalistic account of our valuing of truth. Owen provides an especially compelling account of how this problem develops for Nietzsche, dating back to his earlier reflections on morality in *Daybreak*. It is this account of the value of truth, Owen argues, that provides Nietzsche's rationale for why we should abandon Christianity. Alexander Nehamas, in "The Genealogy of Genealogy," ties genealogy to Nietzsche's earlier views on history to show how genealogy aims at an interpretation that creates a new relationship to the past. This new relation does not necessarily involve a *falsification* of that past. Moreover, Nehamas argues, such interpretative activity is tied to how phenomena acquire meaning and significance at all (on this latter point especially, compare the concerns of Habermas). Eric Blondel, in his "Nietzsche's Style of Affirmation: The Metaphors of Genealogy," argues that Nietzsche's genealogy endeavors to bring forth relations between body, language, and world to provide a bodily basis of meaning. Nietzsche's genealogy, Blondel argues, constitutes a *symptomatology* of morality, which also considers the conception of the body that issues from and appears within the set of signs that constitutes morality. Aaron Ridley's "Nietzsche and the Re-evaluation of Values" shows how Nietzsche's genealogy is bound up with a project of re-evaluating intrinsic values *as intrinsic*. This project links genealogy with an effort to authoritatively re-evaluate the values of traditional morality in a way that does not itself depend upon the authoritative origins (God, pure reason, etc.) of traditional morality. And, in a new work, Tracy B. Strong articulates the project of genealogy as reflecting the desire to "transform the present by changing the past." To explain how this seemingly impossible task might be plausible, Strong discusses Nietzsche's conception of will, its directions (or *Wohins*), and how such directions affect the qualities of will in terms of their relations to themselves and their pasts. Of particular interest is Strong's distinction of slavish and noble types in terms of their relations to their past, how their *genealogies* affect and effect their activity in the present and the future toward which they strive.

Nietzsche's preface and the beginning of his first essay help us to discern what it is that he is doing, but a review of the different translations most commonly available to readers of English shows how difficult it is to map these points to translation of the three problematic words pertaining to origins described above. It is clear that there is at least one kind of "genealogy" that Nietzsche is *not* practicing, namely, whatever it is that he associates with "English psychologists." But here Nietzsche's targets are not completely transparent, because he does not identify them by name, except to tell us that his former friend Paul Rée (himself *not* an Englishman) has written a book that closely resembles, and by Nietzsche's estimation is far too influenced by, the works of these people.[8] We certainly have some clues as to their identity, and the matter is clearly related to how Nietzsche thinks about Darwin, those he influenced (such as Herbert Spencer), those who embrace a utilitarian view (such as John Stuart Mill), and those associated with a certain kind of empiricism (such as John Locke and David Hume; see Ansell Pearson in this volume). So, *if* Nietzsche is involved in a naturalistic project, it is certainly *somehow* different from that in which he considers these figures to be involved. Anyone arguing that Nietzsche is giving us that kind of story of *descent* must satisfactorily address this problematic matter.

Moreover, it appears that Nietzsche is not offering us a genetic account of morals, at least not in the manner of tracing them to a specific, singular origin whose value endures or inheres in our current morals and practices.[9] Nietzsche's *GM* II seems to make this clear in his discussion of the purpose of punishment. There, Nietzsche is considering the relation between punishment and the development of morality. He advises that we cannot read these purposes off the particular morals and sanctions we have today—tracing them back in time is not as simple as tracing a family tree.

Purposes do not evolve in a particular direction over time, rather they can be (slowly or quickly) redirected, reorganized, absorbed into something that we consider to be completely different or new, and so forth:

> The cause of the origin of a thing [*die Ursache der Entstehung*] and its eventual utility, its actual employment and place in a system of purposes, lie worlds apart; whatever exists, having somehow come into being, is again and again reinterpreted to new ends, taken over, transformed, and redirected by some power superior to it; all events in the organic world are a subduing, a *becoming master*, and all subduing and becoming master involves a fresh interpretation, an adaptation through which any previous "meaning" and "purpose" are necessarily obscured or even obliterated. (*GM* II:12)

And what accounts for these changes, what is meant by "becoming master"? Tracy B. Strong elaborates an approach in his account of the masterful relation to oneself that constitutes "becoming what one is," Daniel Conway describes the evolutionary development (and demise) of the masters throughout Nietzsche's text, and Christine Swanton explores how "mastery" might be a component of a kind of virtue theory. Answering this question sheds light on translation of the final word in the main title of Nietzsche's text—*Moral*—because what Nietzsche in *GM* II:12 describes as "becoming master" refers to a basic idea that unites the three different essays of the book and pinpoints Nietzsche's general interest in the whole process of development and change in moral values, that is, *morality as such*.

Another way of describing that which drives such change in morality is to call it, with Nietzsche, *will to power*. In *GM* I, he provides an account of mastery and power that considers a distinctively human capacity for achieving power, for becoming master, through the process of valuation. In *GM* II, Nietzsche considers how that particular feature of human existence has focused on a specific kind of mastery of the affects and the physiological organizations they express. And in *GM* III, Nietzsche considers the way in which the ascetic ideal is the general form of the kind of mastery that the first essay identified as characteristically human, namely, the creation of meaning through valuation and revaluation. The ascetic ideal is an expression of "becoming master" insofar as it reflects an attempt to achieve mastery through dominating and suppressing some aspect of existence in pursuit of something supposedly "higher"—what is "higher" is considered so and acquires its value through destruction of what presently is. What Nietzsche calls "will to power" can be seen as characteristic of this process—there is not some *thing* that is *willing* power *behind* this activity. Rather, the general phenomenon itself is, as Nietzsche continues in the passage with which we began this line of consideration, "a succession of more or less profound, more or less mutually independent processes of subduing, plus the resistances they encounter" (*GM* II:12). All events in the organic world unfold thus, and in *On the Genealogy of Morals* Nietzsche endeavors to highlight how such can be seen in the case of the human animal.

In this respect, Nietzsche is clearly seeking to contribute to a naturalistic account of the phenomenon of morality. It is common now for those discussing Nietzsche's ideas about will to power to link them with his understanding and critique of then-contemporary evolutionary biology and to situate this concern in the context of various theories of natural forces and/or psychological drives.[10] This way of characterizing Nietzsche's naturalism equates it, not without some tension, with a kind of scientism. The "tension" to which I allude refers to the fact that Nietzsche is explicitly critical of science. Indeed, as Gemes outlines and Ansell Pearson mentions in this volume, Nietzsche argues in the third essay of the *Genealogy* that the scientific enterprise, which would appear to be a good opponent of the Christian ascetic ideal Nietzsche so vociferously and polemically rails against, turns out to be the most recent manifestation of the *very same ideal*, particularly in its commitment to truth. So those who argue that Nietzsche's project is to provide a naturalistic account of morality or our moral psychology (as Owen, Ridley, and Swanton do) have to reconcile this idea with Nietzsche's criticism of science (on naturalism in Nietzsche, see also Pippin's essay in this volume).

One way of resolving the tension between Nietzsche's naturalism and his critique of science is to say that while Nietzsche might be critical of science earlier in his career, he changes his mind in his "mature writings" (generally thought to be those following *Thus Spoke Zarathustra*, sometimes reaching back a bit earlier). This is the approach of Brian Leiter in his Routledge Guidebook *Nietzsche on Morality*, where he claims that "The *Genealogy*, and Nietzsche's mature philosophy generally, proposes a *naturalistic* explanation, that is, an explanation that is continuous with both the results and methods of the sciences."[11] Since Leiter appears to think that appreciation of Nietzsche's aesthetic interest is appropriate only for consideration of the *literary* (and hence nonphilosophical) aspects of Nietzsche's work, he virtually ignores it in his interpretation of the *Genealogy*.[12] This leads him to largely ignore what Nietzsche has to say about interpretation in the *Genealogy* and to limit discussion of creativity to consideration of how (rare human psychological) types have certain creative capacities of discovery (of truths consistent with and in accordance with the methods of the physical sciences).

Other readers of Nietzsche endeavor to show how a different (i.e., nonscientistic) naturalism emerges when Nietzsche's aestheticism is taken seriously.[13] This is not to say that Nietzsche rejects science or a standpoint in which science is given priority over other perspectives, but rather that Nietzsche recognizes all human knowing is not only partial but also an act of creativity.[14] This last notion is intricately linked to genealogy by Salim Kemal in his chapter "Nietzsche's Genealogy: Of Beauty and Community," which appears in the final section of this volume. Nietzsche's concern in the *Genealogy* is with the phenomenon of morality as such and not simply particular moral views. It unfolds in a context that is naturalistic but which highlights the (natural) aesthetic powers of human beings. Thus, my own view is to side with those who translate the German *Moral* as "Morality," although this book uses the title most familiar to English-speaking audiences from Kaufmann and Hollingdale's rendering it as "Morals."

Finally, we should consider the subtitle to the book. It also strikes a bell-tone that should reverberate through one's reading of Nietzsche's text. Nietzsche tells us from the very beginning that what he is presenting is provocative—*Eine Streitschrift*, appropriately translated "a polemic," literally "fighting writing." Why would one write a polemical treatise on the topic of morality? What makes it so controversial? What, precisely, does it attack? What *constitutes* its attacking? And how does Nietzsche see his book as playing a role in a larger contest? These interesting questions are raised and explored in greater detail in several of the chapters that follow. For example, Shapiro takes notice that in titling his work thus, Nietzsche might be indicating not only that he is initiating an *agon* or contest with those "outside" the text but also within it, that the book constitutes a *dialogue* rather than a diatribe; and Babich explains how this reflects Nietzsche's involvement of his readers, baiting them to follow him and personally bringing them into the genealogical project.

Where do these considerations of genealogy and polemicizing about morality lead? As noted above, the essays in the first section of this book, "On Genealogy," consider what it means to engage in *genealogy* as a philosophical practice and to reconcile what it means to practice genealogy with Nietzsche's ideas about truth, perspectivism, art, science, and history. Some consider how genealogy might be thought to be an alternative not only to other kinds of scientific approaches but also to other philosophical methodologies, such as dialectic (e.g., Migotti). Some consider how genealogy stands in relation to "gay science" and what light it sheds on thinking about Nietzsche's kind of philosophical thinking, ourselves as readers of Nietzsche, and philosophical practices we might wish to develop and exercise in the future (e.g., Owen).

The second part of this volume, "Reading Nietzsche's *Genealogy*," provides readers with focused analyses of specific passages in the *Genealogy*. Mark Migotti in his "Slave Morality, Socrates, and the Bushmen: A Reading of the First Essay of *On the Genealogy of Morals*" elaborates Nietzsche's discussion of the slave revolt in morality as described in *GM* I and considers how it could be possible that it could have been successful. Through consideration of Nietzsche's views of Socrates, Migotti deepens our understanding of what Nietzsche considers "masterful" and "slavish," and he offers some fascinating discussion of the plausibility of Nietzsche's view as an empirical hypothesis. In his extensive discussion of *GM* I:13, Robert B. Pippin also considers the slave revolt in morality described in the first essay but focuses on a particular feature of this revolt—namely the creation of a subject, lying behind and thus capable of responsibility for its actions, a separation Nietzsche likens to separating lightning from its flash. Pippin elaborates an expressivist concept of subjectivity that facilitates resolving a dilemma that arises when considering Nietzsche's "anti-agent" view in *GM* I:13 and the conception of agency that forms the basis of his critique of slave morality in the first place.

Discussion of *GM* II opens with a focus on the neglected first two sections of the text. Christa Davis Acampora reconsiders Nietzsche's reference to "the sovereign individual" in *GM* II:2 in her "On Sovereignty and Overhumanity: Why It Matters

How We Read Nietzsche's *Genealogy* II:2," arguing that contrary to the dominant currents in Nietzsche studies (reflected in several essays in this volume, including Ridly, Strong, and Gemes), Nietzsche's reference to the sovereign individual signals his rejection and the self-overcoming of an ideal he thinks we already hold. In his "Finding the *Übermensch* in Nietzsche's *Genealogy of Morality*," Paul S. Loeb argues for the significance of Nietzsche's *Zarathustra* in understanding his *Genealogy*. Loeb's position has significant implications for how we are to take Nietzsche's remark about the "sovereign individual," discussed in the previous essay, how this relates to Nietzsche's overhuman ideal suggested at the end of *GM* II, and how this latter ideal reflects some unappreciated views Nietzsche has about memory, history, and time. More specifically, Loeb offers analysis of what "overcoming" involves, providing a unique interpretation of eternal recurrence as the overcoming of "mere animal" forgetting, such that we remember all of our past lives that are buried deep in our subconscious. This yields what Loeb calls a "second forgetting" that is part of the new kind of conscience that further develops the capabilities that came with the invention of "bad conscience" described in *On the Genealogy of Morals*. In this respect, readers might compare Loeb's vision of the future (or further possibilities) with the views presented by Ansell Pearson and Conway.

Babette E. Babich in "The Genealogy of Morals and Right Reading" introduces us to the third essay of the *Genealogy* in her focus on what she describes as both the readerly and writerly aspects of the aphorism. Obviously, reading an aphorism requires a certain kind of practice. As Babich notices, the aphorism is both uniquely accessible and difficult. Its brevity and memorable relation of ideas makes it easy for most to get *something* (if only half) from it. But because the aphorism is a distillation of a complex set of relations that the author is arranging and transforming, appreciating the aphorism in its fullness, particularly when authored by a master, is rather difficult. And, as Babich illustrates, it is potentially quite painful, for the aphorism is barbed like a hook. It is intended to bait and then catch its audience. To illustrate this feature, Babich applies an art of interpretation to an analysis of the first essay of the *Genealogy*, which reveals its deeply *anti*-anti-Semitic intentions. Such a reading compares interestingly with Yirmiyahu Yovel's chapter included in the volume, since Yovel highlights this facet of Nietzsche's writings but has a rather different interpretation of the nature of his remarks about the ancient (pre-Second Temple) period.

Two further points from Babich's essay are worth noting here, since they are relevant to reading not only Nietzsche's book but also this one. Throughout her essay, Babich increasingly provides a greater sense of what is meant by the *writerly* aspect of philosophical reading in which writer and reader are not so distinct. Reading is not simply a matter of receiving the message or communicative intent of the author, who is the creator or cause of such a message. Instead, readers are involved in the work of the aphorism insofar as reading involves a kind of writing, too. That is to say that all reading involves both a rewriting of the text in the process of recreating for oneself the organization of ideas presented and an artful appropriation of such ideas. This, Babich claims, is what it means for an aphorism to be learnt by heart, harkening back to Nietzsche's preface to *On the Genealogy of Morals*, and it is related to what it means to write in blood, harkening back to the section of *Thus Spoke Zarathustra* from which the *epigraph* to *GM* III is drawn.

Babich applies her reading of the aphorism to the dispute in the secondary literature about whether it is the epigraph or the first section of the third essay for which the remainder of the essay is to serve as an exegesis as Nietzsche directs his readers in *GM* P:8. She reaches the same conclusions as John Wilcox and Maudemarie Clark (simultaneously advanced on different grounds by Christopher Janaway).[15] These parties agree on an important fact that Wilcox and Clark establish on empirical grounds and Babich and Janaway establish largely on interpretative or hermeneutic grounds. Does it make any difference how they got there, given that both reached the same truth? Babich offers a tremendous example of how it does, and the comparison with Janaway puts this in even greater relief than her modest endnote on the matter. Certainly, historical knowledge (which might be taken to be of an empirical sort—that is a knowledge of the existence of such persons as Hippocrates and their development of such rhetorical mnemonic and therapeutic devices such as the aphorism) plays a role in Babich's ability to *recognize* the aphorism and to not mistake an epigram for an aphorism. But her essay is more than an application of this prior historical knowledge or a building upon the historical facts—her view is further developed through an application of an art of interpretation that allows her to illuminate the complex facets of the aphorism (to not simply get the *easy* half) and to see how these are reflected not only in the third essay of Nietzsche's *GM* but in the book as a whole, including the interesting account of the *work* of the first essay as it ensnares the anti-Semite. The discovery of materials in an archive does not accomplish or even properly prepare one for this *philosophical* work. A similar critique might be charged against Janaway's essay—while Janaway does a good job of showing how the interpretative error of past commentators led them to some torturous efforts to explain how the third essay could possibly be an *exegesis* of the epigraph from *Zarathustra*, he concludes that Nietzsche's original claim about this matter from the preface ultimately is fairly straightforward or that it is not "as radical" as Nietzsche's readers have taken it to be. Having properly *identified* the aphorism through reasonable practices of interpretation, Janaway has *understood* at most only half. Finally, in Babich's emphasis on the work of the aphorism and its readerly and writerly characteristics, her interpretative exposition allows her own readers to see for themselves (she does not do all of the work for them) both that *GM* III is clearly an exegesis of what is numerically designated as the first section and why the epigraph is *apt*.[16]

Thus, Ken Gemes is somewhat distinctive among interpreters of *GM* III in that he begins his "'Strangers to Ourselves': The Key Message of Nietzsche's *Genealogy*" not with the epigraph or even the first section of the essay but rather with Nietzsche's important preface and the opening of the book as a whole. Gemes's guiding concern is to elaborate how our being "strangers to ourselves" is revealed in the third essay where Nietzsche shows how the contemporary embrace of the scientific viewpoint, which we consider to supersede if not reject the religious perspective Nietzsche criticizes, is actually the ultimate embodiment of the ascetic ideal. And it is a highly influential elaborate account of the ascetic ideal and its relation to nihilism that concludes the second part of this volume: Wolfgang Müller-Lauter's, "Nihilism as Will to Nothingness," which is reprinted here in its entirety. Müller-Lauter focuses on the conceptions of will and power that shape Nietzsche's discussion of asceticism and ascetic ideals in *GM* III. More specifically, Müller-Lauter describes Nietzsche's conception of the rough distinction between weak and strong wills (granted that characterizing things in this way is "crude" and that Nietzsche's view is more subtle), and the "disgregation" that is characteristic of the weak's decadent nihilism. Müller-Lauter's discussion has been highly influential in interpretations of Nietzsche's idea of will to power and bad conscience (see, for example, Tracy B. Strong, in this volume), and he provides a particularly helpful account of what it would mean to "will nothingness."[17]

The third and fourth parts of this volume treat prominent criticisms and applications of genealogy, including the relevant aesthetic, political, and ethical dimensions of Nietzsche's work. In the third part titled "Critiquing *Genealogy*," Jürgen Habermas argues in an excerpt from "The Entwinement of Myth and Enlightenment" that genealogy aims to be critical in a complete or total way. It is thus that the *Genealogy* provides the model for Theodor W. Adorno and Max Horkheimer's later *The Dialectic of Enlightenment*. But such a radical critique undermines even the norms of rational discourse and thereby leaves genealogy's adherents resorting to mythology rather than reason. Gary Shapiro distinguishes genealogy from the practice of tracing a family tree, but sees it as related to recognition of what Wittgenstein would later describe as "family resemblances" insofar as the project of uncovering the various historical layers involves identifying and listening to the multiple voices one finds in a text. Shapiro challenges Habermas's reading of Nietzsche and illustrates how Foucault and Derrida appropriate genealogy in their own works. Through an ingenious analysis of Derrida's writing on Claude Lévi-Strauss, Shapiro illuminates the ways in which Derrida engages in "repeating the genealogy of morals" (*Of Grammatology*) through a self-critique of science that is similar to that found in Nietzsche's *Genealogy* (particularly *GM* III). Alan Schrift continues the discussion of those influenced by Nietzschean critique in his "Nietzsche, Deleuze, and the Genealogical Critique of Psychoanalysis." Schrift argues that the analytic critique of Gilles Deleuze and Felix Guattari's *Anti-Oedipus* follows that of Nietzsche's *GM* insofar as Deleuze's psychoanalyst is the most recent version of Nietzsche's priest, and the methods of analysis share a logic of productive desire that organizes the diagnosis of disorder and its therapies. Readers might compare Schrift's account of the Oedipal drama at the center of psychoanalysis's effort to produce a need for the solution it offers with Ansell Pearson's account of Nietzsche's Dionysian drama of the soul.

The fourth and final part, "Of Politics and Community," commences with Salim

Kemal's "Nietzsche's Genealogy: Of Beauty and Community." Kemal focuses on the particular kind of creativity that constitutes genealogy, and he reveals how genealogical interpretation—rather than being solipsistic or particularlistic—actually supplies the basis for the creation of a communal sense of identity and the exercise of communal judgment. He thus explains how a community of creators might be possible, something that critics of Nietzsche's apparent individualism deny. His discussion of resentment and rules is particularly illuminating in this regard. Insofar as creative activity is inherently not conservative, Kemal thinks Nietzsche's sense of beauty is necessarily progressive. This stands in sharp contrast with Yirmiyahu Yovel, who argues in his "Nietzsche and the Jews: The Structure of an Ambivalence" that Nietzsche's "pro-Jewish attitude" comes "from the right" since it is "antiliberal." Yovel explains how Nietzsche's deeply ambivalent views about Jews do not simply reflect conflicting or contradictory positions but rather stem from a coherent conception of history in which Nietzsche distinguishes the ancient Jews (whom he admires), the Jewish priests associated with the period of "the Second Temple" (whom he condemns), and the modern Jews of the Diaspora (whom Nietzsche admires, in part because they did not follow the path charted by the second group, which ultimately became Christian). Yovel argues that Nietzsche is critical of the "revolution" ignited by Christianity and that he advocates a return to the aristocratism and virtues of the ancient Jews, traces of which are found in (seeming progressive) resistance from Jews in the modern diaspora.

Nietzsche's interest in and relevance for a theory of virtue is the topic of Christine Swanton's "Nietzschean Virtue Ethics." In an argument that might be compared with Müller-Lauter's (and Strong's) discussion of "weak" and "strong" wills, Swanton distinguishes "undistorted" from "distorted" will to power. Such distortions, malformations, or the lack thereof characterize the "healthy" and the "sick," respectively (and this way of thinking about sickness and health might also be compared and contrasted with Blondel's *symptomological* approach). From this, Swanton considers the possibilities for *Nietzschean* virtue ethics as she argues against the idea that Nietzsche is an immoralist,[18] claiming that his work supplies material for an ethics of self-improvement, and she helpfully situates this discussion in the context of recent work on perfectionism in ethics.

Finally, Daniel Conway, in his "How We Became What We Are: Tracking the 'Beasts of Prey,'" provides a novel account of both origins and future direction. Conway reconstructs a fascinating account of Nietzsche's philosophical anthropological developmental that lies behind the genealogies he offers in *GM* I and *GM* II, including Nietzsche's account of human domestication. Of special interest is his discussion of the origins of the social and political orders Nietzsche describes. This sheds important new light on Nietzsche's infamous "beast of prey" and his conceptions of "predation" and "cultivation." Drawing on this significant background, Conway is able provide a new account of "artistry" in Nietzsche's text, particularly as it contrasts with the asceticism of the priests in *GM* III. Conway concludes his chapter and the volume with a masterful illumination of Nietzsche's conception of the possible metamorphosis of the human animal. While artistic, this process is also thoroughly natural.

The bibliography at the end of the book is arranged according to the general organizing themes of this volume, providing suggestions for further reading on the topic of the nature of genealogy, analyses of particular passages, critical applications of Nietzsche's genealogy, and issues of politics and community that Nietzsche's *Genealogy* raises. I have annotated that portion of the bibliography to indicate the relevance of the entry to the area of inquiry. Bibliographies for more general works on moral philosophy and psychology and Nietzsche's *Genealogy* follow. The bibliographic references provide direction for navigating the vast sea of monographic literature that is not included in this volume. Works appearing in journals and in collections of essays that are more difficult to access were given priority in my selection process. Some of the discussions here are classics that have defined the terms on which Nietzsche is still read today (e.g., Nehamas, Blondel, Müller-Lauter, and Habermas). Others treat some of the most prominent and thorniest issues in Nietzsche interpretation (e.g., Ansell Pearson, Owen, Migotti, Pippin, Acampora, Loeb, and Gemes). Some elaborate how Nietzsche's views are relevant to contemporary discussions in ethical and political theory (e.g., Ridley, Strong, Yovel, Swanton, and Conway). And still others address broad concerns about how Nietzsche's views have been applied and how such applications might influence how we read Nietzsche in the future (e.g., Babich, Shapiro, Schrift, Yovel, and Kemal). There are many other interesting works that might have been included here, but for reasons of space and production cost could not be accommodated between these covers. My hope is that as direction for reading Nietzsche's *On the Genealogy of Morals* this book marks a genuine starting point—not just for beginners but also for those who, endeavoring to "practice reading as an art" (*GM* P:8), begin again and again (*GM* III:1).

NOTES

1. Note that this same translation is commonly attributed solely to Kaufmann, including in some of the essays collected here, but the translation was completed by both men; Kaufmann is the general editor of the volume in which the translation appears. I rely upon this translation in my introduction.

2. David S. Thatcher, "*Zur Genealogie der Moral*: Some Textual Annotations," *Nietzsche-Studien* 18 (1989): esp. 598–99. Keith Ansell Pearson, editor of the edition of *GM* translated by Carol Diethe (Cambridge University Press, 1994), does not *simply* follow Kaufmann's lead. In an earlier work, Ansell Pearson claims that he prefers what he calls the "'innocence' of 'On the . . .'" as a translation of this first term in Nietzsche's title. See his *Nietzsche Contra Rousseau* (Cambridge: Cambridge University Press, 1991), 251 n26.

3. Heraclitus is not explicitly named at this point in the preface of *On the Genealogy of Morals*, which likely accounts for why so few commentators take much notice of Nietzsche's paraphrase. Heraclitus is mentioned elsewhere in the book—see the references at the follow-

ing crucial points: *GM* II:16, *GM* III:7, and *GM* III:8. In *Ecce Homo* (*EH* "BT" 3), Nietzsche associates Heraclitus with "tragic wisdom" and Dionysian philosophy, ideas discussed in this volume by Keith Ansell Pearson.

4. Diels-Kranz fragment 101. An excellent discussion of Heraclitus, the fragments attributed to him, and their context is provided by Charles Kahn, *The Art and Thought of Heraclitus: An Edition of the Fragments with Translation and Commentary* (New York: Cambridge University Press, 1979). See also Hermann Diels and Walther Kranz, *Die Fragmente der Vorsokratiker* (Berlin: Weidmann, 1903). Nietzsche's interest in this idea of not knowing ourselves because we have never sought ourselves is surely related to his fascination with the Pindaric maxim "Become who [or what] you are," and readers should recall that one of the inscriptions at the temple of the Delphic oracle is "Know thyself." (The other is "Nothing in excess.") Literature specifically devoted to discussion of the maxim includes Alexander Nehamas, "'How One Becomes What One Is,'" *Philosophical Review* 92 (1983): 385–417; Brian Leiter, "The Paradox of Fatalism and Self-Creation in Nietzsche" in *Willing and Nothingness: Schopenhauer as Nietzsche's Educator*, edited by Christopher Janaway (Oxford: Oxford University Press, 1998); Babette E. Babich, "Nietzsche's Imperative as a Friend's Encomium: On Becoming the One You Are, Ethics, and Blessing," *Nietzsche-Studien* 33 (2003): 29–58; David Owen and Aaron Ridley, "On Fate," *International Studies in Philosophy* 35:3 (2003): 63–78; and Tracy B. Strong's and Babette E. Babich's contributions to this volume.

5. On Paul Rée, see Robin Small's introduction to his translation of Rée's *The Origin of the Moral Sensations* and *Psychological Observations* (Paul Rée, *Basic Writings*, edited and translated by Robin Small [Urbana and Chicago: University of Illinois Press, 2003]); Robin Small's *Nietzsche and Rée: A Star Friendship* (Oxford: Oxford University Press, 2005); Lou Salomé's *Nietzsche*, edited and translated by Siegfried Mandel (Urbana: University of Illinois Press, 2001); and Jacqueline Stevens, "On the Morals of Genealogy," *Political Theory* 31:4 (2003): 558–88.

6. Also see Salim Kemal, "Some Problems of Genealogy," *Nietzsche-Studien* 19 (1990): 30–42. An interesting article that treats genealogy as a method, one related to Hume's "experimental reasoning" is David Couzens Hoy's "Nietzsche, Hume, and the Genealogical Method" in *Nietzsche as Affirmative Thinker*, edited by Yirmiyahu Yovel (Dordtrecht: Martinus Nijhoff Publishers, 1986): 20–38.

7. Tracing Nietzsche's use of these terms is virtually impossible to do in English translation, since the words are variously translated within most editions, and differently translated across editions. As one example, consider a passage from the fourth section of the preface, which Jacqueline Stevens (op. cit.) discusses. In *GM* P:4 Nietzsche is describing his work in relation to Rée's and the development of his own *Human, All Too Human*, which he claims is where he introduced some of the key ideas of *GM*. In describing what he is doing, he calls his work "Herkunfts-Hypothesen," which is translated as "genealogical hypotheses" by Kaufmann, "hypotheses on descent" by Diethe, and "hypotheses concerning origins" by Clark and Swenson. Ansell Pearson catalogues uses of *Herkunft*, *Ursprung*, and *Entstehung* in his *Nietzsche Contra Rousseau* (Cambridge: Cambridge University Press, 1991), 252 n51. See also Shapiro in this volume, and consult the bibliography section titled "Critiquing Genealogy."

8. During the eighteenth and nineteenth centuries, a good number of writers published works on histories of morals and their evolutionary development, and their relations to civil institutions, particularly law. As David Thatcher observes, W. E. H. Lecky's *History of European Morals* (1869) was a work in this vein, which Nietzsche owned and annotated exten-

sively. Its first chapter, titled "The Natural History of Morals" mentions Bain, Bentham, Hartley, Hobbes, Hume, Hutcheson, Locke, Mandeville, Mill, Paley, Shaftesbury, Adam Smith, Spencer, and others (Thatcher, *"Zur Genealogie der Moral*: Some Textual Annotations," 588). For discussion of Nietzsche's reading, appropriation, and disagreements with some of these figures, particularly Spencer, see Gregory Moore's excellent *Nietzsche, Biology, Metaphor* (Cambridge: Cambridge University Press, 2002).

9. Raymond Geuss argues that Nietzsche's genealogy is decidedly *not* about providing a pedigree: the genealogy he provides is not oriented upon grounding a sense of entitlement or birthright, but rather is intended to trace the multiple, diverse, separate, and historically contingent lines of development of Christian morality ("Nietzsche's Genealogy," *European Journal of Philosophy* 2:3 [1994]: 274–92.) Paul S. Loeb argues that Nietzsche's use of "genealogy" *is* an attempt to supply a pedigree as characterized by his aristocratic point of view ("Is There A Genetic Fallacy In Nietzsche's *Genealogy of Morals?*" *International Studies in Philosophy* 27:3 [1995]: 127; see also Loeb's discussion of *Herkunft* [126ff]).

10. As a most recent example, see John Richardson's *Nietzsche's New Darwinism* (Oxford: Oxford University Press, 2004). Richardson's earlier work on Nietzsche also provides an interesting account of will to power as it relates to Nietzsche's power ontology (John Richardson, *Nietzsche's System* [Oxford: Oxford University Press, 1992]). On Nietzsche's reception of his contemporary evolutionary theory, see Moore, *Nietzsche, Biology, Metaphor.*

11. Brian Leiter, *Nietzsche on Morality* (New York: Routledge, 2002), 11.

12. For a prominent account of the relevance of the literary form of *GM* as it relates to its philosophical content and intent, see Arthur Danto, "Some Remarks on *The Genealogy of Morals,*" *International Studies in Philosophy* 18:2 (1986): 3–15.

13. A different take on Nietzsche's naturalism and Nietzsche's potential contribution to this general trend in philosophy today is provided by Bernard Williams. In his "Nietzsche's Minimalist Moral Psychology," Williams focuses on what he describes as Nietzsche's "method of suspicion," which has the effect of reducing illusory concepts that hinder progress toward providing "a more realistic moral psychology" (*European Journal of Philosophy* 1:1 [1993]: 1–14). In his "Naturalism and Genealogy," Williams considers what is *wanted* in a naturalistic account of moral psychology and suggests that fictional stories such as those told in *GM* might play a role in advancing such goals (*Morality, Reflection and Ideology*, edited by Edward Harcourt [Oxford: Oxford University Press, 2000]: 149–61).

14. On Nietzsche's naturalism as it relates to his aestheticism, see Christoph Cox, *Nietzsche: Naturalism and Interpretation* (Berkeley: University of California Press, 1999) and Hans Seigfried, "Nietzsche's Natural Morality," in *The Journal of Value Inquiry* 26 (1992): 423–31. See also Richard Schacht, "How to Naturalize Cheerfully: Nietzsche's *Fröhliche Wissenschaft,*" in *Making Sense of Nietzsche: Reflections Timely and Untimely* (Urbana: University of Illinois Press, 1995), 187–205; and Richard Schacht "Of Morals and *Menschen*: Nietzsche's *Genealogy* and Anthropology," in *Nietzsche, Genealogy, Morality*, edited by Richard Schacht (Berkeley: University of California Press, 1994), 427–48.

15. For the time being, Janaway's article is probably the best known and heretofore provides the best balance of advancing the argument on both *internal evidence* and publication records ("Nietzsche's Illustration of the Art of Exegesis," *European Journal of Philosophy* 5:3 (1997): 251–68). He also reviews some of the most significant contributions to the literature that begin with (or at least give prominent place to) the mistaken assumption that the epigraph, rather than the first section, is the aphorism to which Nietzsche refers. Taking guidance

for interpretation from Nietzsche's own instructions on this matter—"I have offered in the third essay of the present book an example of what I regard as 'exegesis' in such a case—an aphorism is prefixed to this essay, the essay itself is a commentary on it"—and comparing that with the compositional history of the text, Janaway decisively demonstrates how the first section of the third essay (*GM* III:1) is the aphorism on which Nietzsche performs his exegetical work and how this reflects Nietzsche's views about interpretation generally. See also John Wilcox, "What Aphorism Does Nietzsche Explicate in *Genealogy of Morals* Essay III?" *Journal of the History of Philosophy* 35:4 (October 1997): 593–610 (published the same time as Janaway's original article) and Maudemarie Clark's "From the Nietzsche Archive: Concerning the Aphorism Explicated in *Genealogy* III" in *Journal of the History of Philosophy* 35:4 (October 1997): 611–14.

16. Readers eager to continue reflection might consider how it is that Janaway swallows one-half of the aphorism while Arthur C. Danto swallows the other. To appreciate this, consider Danto's own discussion of the barbed character of the aphorism as it relates to involving the reader. See his "Some Remarks on *The Genealogy of Morals*," *International Studies in Philosophy* 18:2 (1986): 3–15.

17. Müller-Lauter's treatment of how the reversal of values becomes *bound* to what it reverses resembles, although it occurs in a very different analytical framework, Judith Butler's discussion of bad conscience in her *The Psychic Life of Power: Theories in Subjection* (Stanford, CA: Stanford University Press, 1997), 63–82. A different but influential interpretation of willing nothingness is found in Arthur C. Danto's "Some Remarks on *The Genealogy of Morals*," *International Studies in Philosophy* 18 (1986): 3–15. Nehamas, in this volume, discusses Danto's reading as it relates to the coherency of Nietzsche's views about interpretation and meaning.

18. Thus, Swanton is arguing directly against Philippa Foot's now classic "Nietzsche's Immoralism," which first appeared in the *New York Review of Books* (38, no. 11 [June 1991]: 18–22) and was later republished in Richard Schacht's *Nietzsche, Genealogy, Morality*. Since Foot has very little to say about Nietzsche's *Genealogy* (and makes few direct references to *any* of Nietzsche's works) her discussion is not reprinted in this volume.

I

ON GENEALOGY

1

A "Dionysian Drama on the 'Fate of the Soul'"

An Introduction to Reading *On the Genealogy of Morality**

Keith Ansell Pearson

The genius of the heart, a heart of the kind belonging to that secretive one, the tempter god and born Pied Piper of the conscience whose voice knows how to descend into the underworld of every soul, who does not utter a word or send a glance without its having a crease and aspect that entices, whose mastery consists in part in knowing how to seem—and seem not what he is, but rather what those who follow him take as one *more* coercion to press ever closer to him, to follow him ever more inwardly and completely: the genius of the heart that silences everything loud and self-satisfied and teaches it how to listen . . . ; that smoothes out rough souls and gives them a taste of a new longing . . . the genius of the heart, from whose touch everyone goes forth the richer, neither reprieved nor surprised, nor as if delighted or depressed by another's goodness, but rather richer in themselves, newer than before, opened up, breathed upon and sounded out by a warm wind, more unsure, perhaps, more brooding, breakable, broken, full of hopes that still remain nameless, full of new willing and streaming, full of new not-willing and back-streaming . . . but my friends, what am I doing? Who is it that I am telling you about? Have I forgotten myself so much that I have not even told you his name? Unless, of course, you have already

---

*This essay draws on some material presented in my editor's introduction to the second, revised edition of *On the Genealogy of Morality*, trans. Carol Diethe (Cambridge: Cambridge University Press, 2006). Citations from *GM* are drawn from this edition.

guessed who this questionable spirit and god may be, who demands this kind of *praise*.

Nietzsche, *Beyond Good and Evil*, 295

The day we can say, with conviction: "Forwards! Even our old morality would make a *comedy!*" we shall have discovered a new twist and possible outcome for the Dionysian drama of the "fate of the soul" (*Schicksal der Seele*).

Nietzsche, *On the Genealogy of Morality*, Preface

Fate [late Middle English] *Fate* is from Italian *fato* or (later) from its source, Latin *fatum* "that which has been spoken," from *fari* to speak. The primary sense of the Latin *fatum* was "doom or sentence of the gods"; this changed to "one's lot."

Oxford Dictionary of Word Histories

INTRODUCTION

Although it is now prized as his most important and systematic work, Nietzsche conceived *On the Genealogy of Morality* (1887) as a "small polemical pamphlet" that might help him sell more copies of his earlier writings.[1] It clearly merits, though, the level of attention it receives and can justifiably be regarded as one of the key texts of European intellectual modernity. For shock value, no other modern text on the human condition rivals it. Nietzsche himself was well aware of the character of the book. There are moments in the text where he reveals his own sense of alarm at what he is discovering about human origins and development, especially the perverse nature of the human animal, the being he calls "the sick animal" (*GM* III:14): "There is so much in man that is horrifying! . . . The world has been a madhouse for too long!" (*GM* II:22). In *Ecce Homo*, Nietzsche discloses that an "art of surprise" guides each of the essays that make up the book and admits that they merit being taken as among the "uncanniest" things ever scripted. He then stresses that his god, Dionysus, is also "the god of darkness" (*EH* "GM"). Indeed, *On the Genealogy of Morals* is one of the darkest books ever written. However, it is also, paradoxically, a book full of hope and expectation. Not only does Nietzsche provide us with a stunning story about humanity's monstrous moral past (the deformation of the human animal through Christian moralization), he also wants us, his readers, to read the text of our past in such a way that it becomes possible to discover "a new twist and possible outcome for the Dionysian drama of the 'fate of the soul' " (*GM* P:7).

In this essay I attempt to open up this neglected aspect of Nietzsche's text. I first provide some essential information about the book. I then begin my analysis by treating the significance of the concept of the "Dionysian," followed by discussion of the importance of the question of "fate" and Nietzsche's characterization of the "soul" and its fate. Crucial to this analysis is Nietzsche's treatment of the bad con-science in the Second Essay of *On the Genealogy of Morals*, which I discuss at some length. Finally, I argue that the doctrine of the eternal return of the same works as a new, experimental way of living and knowing that seeks to replace an interpreta-tion of existence as guilty with a recognition of error and the need for human beings to now attempt to incorporate truth and knowledge.

Nietzsche's exercise in historical genealogy is informed by some basic but none-theless crucial questions. How and why does one engage with the past? What are one's hopes for the future? Is there a future? How does one come to live in time? How does one overcome the past and build on one's inheritance—Does one seek to accuse and blame the past or does one recognize its formative character? Is there a debt to be paid off? Is the debt one we owe to ourselves and our right to a future? Do we transform the debt into a gift we give to ourselves and to new life? In short, how does one become what one is?

For Nietzsche the issue of how we human beings have become what we are is to be posed in terms of a "drama." How are we to hear the significance of this word in his writing? In a note Nietzsche gives in *The Case of Wagner* (1888), he states that it has been a major misfortune for aesthetics that the word "drama" has always been translated as "action." He then states: "Ancient drama aimed at scenes of great *pathos*—it precluded action (moving it *before* the beginning or *behind* the scene). The word *drama* is of Doric origin, and according to Doric usage it means 'event,' 'story'—both words in the hieratic sense. The most ancient drama represented the legend of the place, the 'holy story' on which the foundation of the cult rested (not a doing but a happening: *dran* in Doric actually does not mean 'do')" (*CW* 9). In other words, drama concerns events that are undergone, suffered, and endured. In *GM* II Nietzsche attempts to show that the acquisition of the bad conscience was not an *option* for the human animal; rather, it became the chance and the possibility it is by an ineluctable leap, a catastrophe, and a fate. To relate the development of the bad conscience is thus to tell the fateful story of the human animal. From an exalted perspective one can attain, it becomes possible to see it is the form of con-science that has shaped man to date in terms of his greatest affliction—injurious psychic masochism—and yet contains within it the human's great promise, that of overcoming himself. The question of "fate" pertains to the meaning of the past and the sense and direction of the future; fate is a determination to be interpreted or deciphered as both necessity and possibility.

NIETZSCHE'S POLEMIC: THE APPEARANCE OF NEW TRUTHS BETWEEN THICK CLOUDS

In *Ecce Homo* Nietzsche describes *On the Genealogy of Morals* as consisting of "three decisive preliminary studies by a psychologist for a re-evaluation of values." The first essay probes the "psychology of Christianity" and traces the birth of Christianity out of a *particular* kind of spirit, namely, of *ressentiment*; the second essay provides a "psychology of the conscience," where it is conceived not as the voice of God in man but as the instinct of cruelty that has been internalized after it can no longer discharge itself externally; the third essay inquires into the meaning of ascetic ideals, examines the perversion of the human will, and explores the possibility of a counter ideal. Nietzsche says that he provides an answer to the question of whence comes the power of the ascetic ideal, "the *harmful* ideal *par excellence*"—to date it has been the only ideal; it has been without a competitor, no counter ideal has been made available "*until the advent of Zarathustra.*"

Nietzsche further tells us that each essay that makes up the book contains a beginning calculated to mislead, which intentionally "keeps in suspense"; this is followed by disquiet, "isolated flashes of lightning" with "very unpleasant truths" making themselves audible "as a dull rumbling in the distance"; then, at the conclusion of each essay, and "amid dreadful detonations," "a *new* truth" becomes "visible between thick clouds." Each essay begins coolly and scientifically, even ironically, but at the end of each a reckoning is called for, and this demand concerns the future. At the very end of *GM* I, for example, Nietzsche says that questions concerning the worth of morals and different tables of value can be asked from different angles, and he singles out the question "value *for what?*" as being of special significance. The task of these different sciences of knowledge is to "prepare the way for the future work of the philosopher": solving the "problem of values" and deciding on their hierarchy. He advises that we need to transform the "suspicious relationship" that has hitherto been posited between philosophy, physiology, and medicine "into the most cordial and fruitful exchange" (*GM* I:17n). At the end of *GM* II, Nietzsche appeals to "the man of the future" who will redeem humanity from the curse of its reigning ideal and from all those things that arise from it, notably nihilism and the will to nothingness (*GM* II:24). In the penultimate section of *GM* III, Nietzsche hints at a new direction for the "will to truth," arguing that as this will becomes "conscious of itself as a problem in us" there will follow the destruction of Christian morality, and this is a "drama" that will be "the most terrible and questionable" but also "the one most rich in hope" (*GM* III:27). Moreover, a new "will" is to be uncovered and posited in an effort to sublimate the principal ideal that has hitherto reigned on earth (*GM* III:28). All of this should indicate that Nietzsche's "critique" of morality, as well as his inquiry into the human and his moral past, is developed from a specific but curious place: "a premature-born" and as yet "undemonstrated future" (*GS* 382; see also *EH* "Z" 2). Although *Thus Spoke Zarathustra* is a text that many of Nietzsche's commentators find alien to their philosophical taste, it is clear that as far as Nietzsche himself is concerned the meaning of his critique of morality and attempted overcoming of man are to be found, largely, in that work.

In *Beyond Good and Evil* and *On the Genealogy of Morality*, Nietzsche sets out to present his readers with a set of unpleasant and uncomfortable truths. Some of these are "truths" of culture that modern humans have forgotten and repressed, and one of the tasks of genealogy is to remind us of them.[2] They include: what we call "high culture" is based on a deepening and spiritualization of cruelty—European humanity has not killed off the "wild beast" (*BGE* 229); what we take to be "spirit" or "mind," distinguishing the human animal from the rest of nature, is the product of a long constraint, involving much violence, arbitrariness, and nonsense (*BGE* 188); and modern European morality is "herd animal morality," which considers itself as defining morality and the only morality possible or desirable (*BGE* 202). Nietzsche argues that in their attempts to account for morality, philosophers have not developed the suspicion that morality might be "something problematic"; in effect what they have done is articulate "an erudite form of true *belief* in the prevailing morality" and, as a result, their inquiries remain "a part of the state of affairs within a particular morality" (*BGE* 186). Nietzsche seeks to develop a genuinely critical approach to morality, in which all kinds of novel, surprising, and daring questions are posed. He does not inquire into a "moral sense" or a moral faculty[3]—a common intellectual practice in the work of modern moralists and humanists, such as Francis Hutcheson, David Hume, and Immanuel Kant, for example—but rather sets out to uncover *the different senses* of morality, that is, the different "meanings" morality has acquired in the history of human development. His attempt at a critique involves developing a knowledge of the conditions and circumstances under which values emerged, giving us an appreciation of the different "senses" of morality: as symptom, as mask, as sickness, as stimulant, as poison, and so on.

In *On the Genealogy of Morals* Nietzsche is motivated to uncover "morality" and subject it to "critique"—it is to be viewed as the "danger of dangers" because its prejudices contribute to the situation in which the present is lived at the expense of the future (*GM* P:6). Nietzsche's concern is that the human species may never attain its *"highest potential and splendor."* In Nietzsche's hands, history becomes the story of the deformation and perversion of culture, conceived as species activity aimed at the production of sovereign individuals. Culture both disappeared a long time ago and has still to begin: "Species activity disappears into the night of the past as its product disappears into the night of the future."[4] If the aim and meaning of culture is "to breed a tame and civilized animal, a *household pet*, out of the beast of prey 'man'" (*GM* I:11), then today, Nietzsche says, we see the extent to which this process has resulted in a situation where man strives to become "better" all the time, "more comfortable, more mediocre, more indifferent, more Chinese, more Christian" (*GM* I:12). This, then, is the great danger of culture as civilization: it will produce an animal that takes taming to be an end in itself, to the point where the freethinker will announce that the end of history has been attained (for Nietzsche's criticism of the "freethinker" see *GM* I:9). Nietzsche argues that we moderns are in danger of being tempted by a new European type of Buddhism, united in our belief in the supreme value of a morality of communal pity, "as if it were Morality itself, the summit, the *conquered* summit of humankind, the only hope for the future, comfort in the present, the great redemption from all past guilt" (*BGE* 202).

Nietzsche opens the preface of *On the Genealogy of Morals* on a striking note, claiming that we moderns are knowers who are, in fact, *unknown* to ourselves. Nietzsche contends that if we don't search for ourselves then we will never "find" ourselves. To search for ourselves requires that we have the stern discipline of a "will to knowledge," and for this we need preparation to step outside of the all-too timely frame of the present. Because they are too caught up in "merely 'modern' experience," the moral genealogists—Nietzsche has in mind those he calls the "English psychologists" and the work of his former friend Paul Rée—are altogether lacking in knowledge; they have "no will to know the past, still less an instinct for history" (*GM* II:4). For Nietzsche, the moral past presents itself as a "long, hard-to-decipher hieroglyphic script" (*GM* P:7). He offers his own text, with its three inquiries, as a "script" (*GM* P:8): it is thus a work of interpretation that demands an art of interpretation be brought to bear on its own eventful reading of the past. In this way Nietzsche implicates the reader's own fateful becoming in his Dionysian drama on the fate of the soul.

THE DIONYSIAN PHENOMENON
AND CHEERFULNESS

When Nietzsche first introduces the figure of Dionysus in his work in 1872, it is associated with states of intoxication and rapture, entailing the breakdown of our ordinary, empirical forms of cognition. Dionysus virtually disappears from Nietzsche's writings after this point until he makes an important reappearance in *BGE* (especially 295), as well as *GS* 370, and then *TI* "Ancients" 4 and 5. In his later writings Nietzsche equates the Dionysian with an exuberant "Yes to life" that offers the highest and profoundest insight into reality, one which is to be "*confirmed and maintained by truth and knowledge*" (*EH* "BT" 3, my emphasis). In *Twilight of the Idols*, Nietzsche stresses that the Hellenic instinct, its will to life, finds expression in the "Dionysian mysteries" and the "psychology of the Dionysian state." What is guaranteed in these mysteries is "*Eternal* life, the eternal return of life," in which the future is heralded and consecrated in the past and there is a "triumphant yes to life over and above death and change" (*TI* "Ancients" 4). These insights, which are subject to a practice of truth and a passion of knowledge, inform Nietzsche's project of inquiry in the genealogy of morality, and at the deepest level.

In *Ecce Homo*, Nietzsche tells us that he is a disciple of the philosopher Dionysus who has "the right" to understand himself as "the first *tragic philosopher*" (*EH* "BT" 3). In *BGE* 295, Nietzsche admits that it is something new and strange, something not without its dangers, to be told that Dionysus is a philosopher and that gods philosophize. He calls upon Dionysus as the voice of philosophy's untimely bad conscience (see also *CW* P). This, we might say, is the "greatest" conscience, as when Nietzsche says that the philosopher is the figure who has "the most wide-ranging responsibility, whose conscience encompasses mankind's overall development" (*BGE* 61). Where we moderns feel sure of the universal validity and consummate nature of our values and virtues, to the point of self-satisfaction, the philosopher, inspired by the god of darkness will plant seeds of doubt, anxiety, and contempt. Nietzsche's philosopher is "*necessarily* a man of tomorrow and the day after tomorrow" who exists "in conflict with his Today"; the "ideal" of "today" is his enemy (*BGE* 212). Indeed, he takes modern empiricism, with its "doltish mechanistic ideas," to task because it displays only a "plebeian ambition" (*BGE* 213), and accuses the "English"—Hobbes, Hume, and Locke, for example—of devaluing the concept "philosopher" (*BGE* 252). The philosopher's task, Nietzsche writes in another place, is to deprive stupidity of its good conscience (*GS* 328). For Nietzsche, the problem is that we believe we know what Socrates confessed he didn't know, namely, what is good and what is evil, that is, *what morality is* (*BGE* 202); while Christianity can fairly be considered to be "the most disastrous form of human presumption yet" (*BGE* 62). This is why Nietzsche speaks, in the preface to *On the Genealogy of Morals*, of discovering the vast, distant, and concealed land of morality *for the first time*.

Although Nietzsche is making a novel contribution to the so-called "science of morality," a science he considers to be at a clumsy and crude state of development (*BGE* 186), he holds that there is no European thinker who is prepared to entertain the idea that moral reflection can be carried out in a dangerous and seductive manner, "that it might involve one's *fate!*" (*BGE* 228). He acknowledges the extent to which the *immoralist* is a duty-bound person, called upon to both fear and love the invisible and inaudible world of morals—of subtle commanding and obeying—occasionally dancing in his chains and yet impatient on account of "the secret hardness" of his fate (*BGE* 226). Nietzsche wants his readers to appreciate, above all, that our attempts at knowledge have the character of fate. It is in terms of fate that Nietzsche wishes us to engage with history; only in this way can we incorporate the past into ourselves and earn an exalted right to the future. In an aphorism on "the great health" Nietzsche posits the "the ideal of a spirit" that plays "naively," from "overflowing power and abundance," with everything that has been hitherto "called holy, good, untouchable, divine," which he says is an ideal "of a human, superhuman well-being and benevolence" that will appear *inhuman* when it stages an encounter with "all earthly seriousness" to date (*GS* 382). Nietzsche wants us to overcome "man" and "morality" in a spirit of serenity; in this way we will "cheerfully" pay off our debts to the past and free ourselves for new modes of existence. This also involves the "tragic" because it entails our own undoing as we face the seriousness and responsibility of our task, that of creating a future for ourselves. The "free spirit" knows what kind of "you shall" he has obeyed and, in so doing, "he also knows what he now *can*, what only now he—*may* do" (*HH* P).

Nietzsche often draws attention to the halcyon tone of his writing: "It is the stillest words which bring the storm, thoughts that come on doves' feet guide the world" (*EH* P:4). For Nietzsche, we need to learn how to *dance* over our problems, including the problem of morality. Having "the most fearful insight into reality" and undergoing "the 'most abysmal thought'" does not mean one finds an objection to existence, not "even to the eternal recurrence of existence," but rather one more reason to be "the eternal Yes to all things." If we are able to declare that into every abyss we bear the blessing of our affirmations, then this is to repeat, once more, "*the concept of Dionysos*" (*EH* "Z" 6). To speak in terms of the "halcyon element" is, for Nietzsche, to approach the problems of existence in terms of a "sunny brightness, spaciousness, breadth, and certainty" (*GM* P:8). In the book's preface, then, Nietzsche discloses that his script becomes comprehensible only in terms of the *joyful* science. The knowledge of the past he seeks will not blame the past or incite revenge against it; rather, it will construe it as both necessity and self-overcoming, and it will do so by opening up a sunny spaciousness amongst dark clouds, including the dark cloud that hovers over man himself.

Indeed, in *GM* P:7, Nietzsche refers to his conception of knowledge or science (*Wissenschaft*) as "la gaya scienza." This science consists in taking delight in the problem of life and entails a highly spiritualized thinking that has conquered fear and gloominess. Nietzsche's cheerfulness stems from his experiences of knowledge, including the experience of disillusionment and despair that can result from the practice of the love of knowledge, which is a long pressure that needs to be resisted. Nietzsche speaks of gay or joyful science as a reward, for example, "a reward for a long, brave, diligent, subterranean seriousness." He conceives knowledge in terms of a "world of dangers and victories in which heroic feelings . . . find places to dance and play." He posits as a principle, "*Life as a means to knowledge*," in which the pursuit of knowledge is not to be conducted in a spirit of duty or as a calamity or trickery (*GS* 324). He speaks of the human intellect as a "clumsy, gloomy, creaking machine" and of how the human being always seems to lose its good spirits when it thinks by becoming too serious (*GS* 327). He wants to teach the intellect how it does not have to be such a machine and to challenge the prejudice that would hold that where laughter and gaiety inform thinking it is good for nothing. Nietzsche continues to speak of his cheerfulness (*Heiterkeit*) in later works. In *Ecce Homo*, for example, he speaks of being "cheerful among nothing but hard truths" (*EH* "Books" 3). As Nietzsche reminds his readers in the "Self-Criticism" he penned in *The Birth of Tragedy* (1886), Zarathustra is a figure who proclaims laughter to be something holy (*BT* "Self-Criticism" 7). We can best free ourselves for our own tragedy—the seriousness of our own down-goings and goings-over—by liberating ourselves from what most oppresses us, for example, the past and inherited nature, through the cultivation of a spirit of gaiety and securing a cheerful disposition.

The theme of cheerfulness runs throughout Nietzsche's writing. In his "Untimely Meditation" of 1874 on Schopenhauer, he argues that there are different types of cheerful thinkers. The true thinker always cheers and refreshes, whether he is being serious or humorous; he expresses his insights not with trembling hands and eyes filled with tears, but with courage and strength, and as a victor. Such a cheerful thinker enables us to "behold the victorious god with all the monsters he has combated" (*SE* 2). By contrast, the cheerfulness of mediocre writers and quick thinkers makes us feel miserable; this is because they do not actually see the sufferings and monsters they purport to combat. The cheerfulness of shallow thinkers needs to be exposed because it seeks to convince us that things are easier than is actually the case. For Nietzsche, there is little point in a thinker assuming the guise of a teacher of new truths unless he has courage, is able to communicate, and knows the costs of what has been conquered.

Nietzsche was highly conscious of what he calls, in a letter to his friend Paul Deussen, his "whole *philosophical heterodoxy*": he does not simply present his reader with problems concerning existence and knowledge but dramatizes them through parables, thought-experiments, imagined conversations, and the like. His aim is always to energize and enliven philosophical style through an admixture of aphoristic and, broadly speaking, "literary" forms. His stylistic ideal, as he puts it on the title page of *The Case of Wagner* (parodying Horace), is, paradoxically, "ridendo dicere *severum*" ("saying what is *somber* through what is laughable"), and these two modes, the somber and the sunny, are mischievously intertwined in his philosophy, without the reader necessarily being sure which one is uppermost at any one time. The tone of the texts from the late period, which include *GM*, is that "of gay detachment fraught with a sense of destiny."[5]

NIETZSCHE AND FATE

Nietzsche is occupied with questions of fate from the very beginning of his writing. In "Fate and History" (*Fatum und Geschichte*, 1862), the young Nietzsche pondered the problem of how to best develop a critique of religion and Christianity that would be appropriate for the time. Influenced by the great American writer Ralph Waldo Emerson (1803–1882), Nietzsche appeals to history and natural science as a possible secure foundation upon which to build the tower of new speculation: they are the wonderful legacy of our past and the harbingers of the future. For Nietzsche, fate is necessity. We are not "autonomous gods," Nietzsche insists, but rather fundamentally heteronomous in our being, that is, we are determined by all kinds of external influences and impressions; and, world history is more than "a dreamy self-deception." Without fate—necessity, including the passive contraction of fundamental habits—freedom of the will is an aimless spirit. Fate prescribes the principle: "Events are determined by events."

In another essay written at the same time entitled "Freedom of Will and Fate,"[6] Nietzsche argues that absolute freedom of the will would make man into a god, whilst the fatalistic principle, if that's all there was, would make him a mere automaton. The human being is a *spiritual* automaton (he converts and transforms energy but in ways that do not obey prescribed laws of nature; this is what Nietzsche considers "the dangerous health"). Although fate is nothing other than a chain of events, as soon as we act we create our own events and come to shape our own fate. Nietzsche also realizes once we appreciate the extent to which the "activity of the soul" (the tendency of our "will") can proceed intelligently without the need for conscious control and direction, then the strict distinction between fate and freedom of the will proves untenable and both notions come to fuse with the idea of individuality. Nietzsche notes that fate appears to a person in the mirror of his or her own personality, so that people who believe in fate are "distinguished by force and strength of will," while those who let things happen, "allow themselves, in a degrading manner, to be presided over by circumstances."

What is it, though, supposing we are well-disposed toward it, that enables us to receive fate? Is there a voice in us that awakens us to our desire? Is this what we call, conveniently, "conscience"? All of the doctrines we associate with the later Nietzsche are responses to these questions: Dionysus, the eternal recurrence of the same, and the will to power. In short, they are different ways of thinking fate and freedom in terms of our dual nature as creatures and creators: "In the human being, *creature* and *creator* are united: the human being is matter, fragment, excess, filth, nonsense, chaos; but the human being is also creator, sculptor, hammer-hardness, observer-divinity, and the Seventh Day—do you understand this opposition?" (*BGE* 225). This is the "opposition" Nietzsche is working through in the entirety of his writings, beginning in the early 1860s and culminating in the late works such as *Beyond Good and Evil* and *On the Genealogy of Morality*. We only have to think, for example, of the demonic voice that inspires the thought of eternal recurrence in *GS* 341: "do you desire this once more and innumerable times more?" in which we are not sure whether the "this" refers to what has happened and will happen again and again (fate), or whether it refers to what we will make happen, transforming fate into a task (freedom), willing it to return again and again as the object of our desire. Nietzsche wants us to see it as *both* fate and freedom.[7] The task is to be become well-disposed toward life and ourselves—toward their material, natural, and historical conditions.

In *Beyond Good and Evil* Nietzsche criticizes the way we think of free will in a superlative metaphysical sense. To posit the will as a miraculous *causa sui* is to abstract it from its material conditions, with the result that freedom becomes impossible to conceive since there is nothing to work on and sculpt (*BGE* 21). Such a positing reflects the desire of a "half-educated" spirit to bear "complete and ultimate responsibility for one's own actions and to relieve God, the world, one's ancestors, coincidence, society from it." This is tantamount to the self dragging itself by its hair out of the "swamp of nothingness and into existence." The idea of the "unfree will" is equally implausible, Nietzsche stresses, since it amounts to a misuse of cause and effect. Ultimately, it is "only a matter of *strong* and *weak* wills." Such wills reveal themselves in how they respond to the problem of "constraint" (which is part of what makes our acceptance of fate a "power" of necessity). Nietzsche's treatment of this issue closely echoes the remarks he makes in the essays of his youth. On the one hand, the strong type (vain and noble) holds that it has a "personal right" to take credit for its actions and will not readily relinquish responsibility (it is what gives him belief in himself and his power). On the other hand, there is a "fatalism of the weak-willed" in which the assumption of responsibility for oneself is cast off and one can be "free" to be "responsible for nothing."

Nietzsche wants the moral philosopher to arrive at an appreciation of the fecund economy of life that can only thrive through an abundance of different types of existence: "We do not readily deny; we seek our honour in being *affirmative*" (*TI* "Morality" 6). He wants us to reject the claim that an individual "should be such and such." This is because it is necessary to appreciate that the individual itself is *a piece of fate*, "one more law, one more necessity for all that is to come and will be." He argues that notions of free will, of a "moral world order," of "guilt and punishment," need to be eliminated and psychology, history, nature, social institutions, and sanctions purified of them (*TI* "Errors" 7). Nietzsche posits his fundamental teaching in the following terms:

> What alone can *our* doctrine be?—That no one *gives* man his qualities, neither God, nor society, nor his parents and ancestors, nor *man* himself—the nonsense of the last idea rejected here was taught as "intelligible freedom" by Kant, perhaps already by Plato, too. *No one* is responsible for simply being there, for being made in such and such a way, for existing under such conditions. . . . The fatality (*Fatalität*) of one's being cannot be derived from the fatality of all that was and will be. *No one* is the result of his own intention, his own will, his own purpose. . . . One is necessary, one is a piece of fate (*Verhängniss*), one belongs to the whole, one *is* in the whole. . . . That no one is made responsible any more, that a kind of Being cannot be traced back to a *causa prima*, that the world is not a unity . . . this *alone is the great liberation*—this alone re-establishes the *innocence* (*Unschuld*) of becoming. . . . We deny "God," we deny responsibility in God: *this* alone is how we redeem the world. (*TI* "Errors" 8)

Nietzsche is arguing that we go wrong in our thinking about self and world when we try to identify an ultimate *source* of responsibility (a "first cause," for example). He is not denying that there are conditions in the world for the assumption of meaningful responsibility to take place, which is why in the same text he states that freedom means "Having the will to be responsible to oneself" (*TI* "Skirmishes" 38). This freedom, however, consists in acts and tasks of overcoming, including overcoming one's own self: "The free man is a *warrior*." For Nietzsche, the idea of "intelligible freedom" provides us with the wrong idea of endowment (fate) since it means "freedom" is either simply prescribed ahead of our actual empirical existence and so cannot become a genuine task, as in the case of Schopenhauer, or it is a posited ideal requiring a practice of sublime cruelty toward our heteronomous natures, as in the case of Kant (for Nietzsche's criticism of Kant see also *GS* 335 entitled "Long Live Physics"). Such a "freedom" operates behind our backs, as it were, and comes to us as a voice from *beyond* the world, one that either condemns us to become what we are or that makes such a task impossible to realize.

We might suppose that the fundamental question posed to us by the eternal return, a question posed of our will and desire (will to power), is one that is addressed to us from the mysterious depths of our being. However, these depths are, in fact, those of our cultural formation and it is the buried and repressed labor of culture that Nietzsche sets out to uncover in *On the Genealogy of Morals*. The text can be read as nothing other than an attempt to address "conscience" as an issue of fate that is to be uncovered by means of a probing historical inquiry into the culture of the human.

THE FATE OF BAD CONSCIENCE

In *Beyond Good and Evil* Nietzsche seeks to purify our notion of the "soul" and reinstates its rights in science. The idea that the soul denotes something eternal and indivisible, such as an atom or a monad, is to be rejected. However, we do not need to go as far as those Nietzsche calls "bungling naturalists" who would do without the notion altogether. Rather, the way is now clear, Nietzsche suggests, for reutilizing this venerable hypothesis and giving it a rightful place in our science as, for example, "the mortal soul," or "soul as the multiplicity of the subject," and "soul as the social construct of drives and affects" (*BGE* 12). The "soul" then denotes a system of valuations and value-affects. Indeed, Nietzsche says that "morality" is to be understood precisely in these terms: "every act of willing is a matter of commanding and obeying, based on a social structure of many 'souls'; for this reason a philosopher should claim the right to comprehend willing from within the sphere of morality (*Moral*): morality, that is, understood as the theory of relations of domination (*Herrschafts-Verhältnissen*) under which the phenomenon of 'life' emerges" (*BGE* 19). Nietzsche's contribution to the "genealogy of morals" can be fruitfully understood as an attempt to discover how the human "soul" has been culturally and historically formed, fatefully, in terms of different systems—active and reactive—of valuations and value-affects. In *On the Genealogy of Morals* Nietzsche poses questions of freedom and fate in the context of a historical understanding of how the human has become what he is, the sick animal. The principal concept Nietzsche puts to work in the *Genealogy* is the "will to power," which denotes the animal "instinct for freedom" and a will to growth that, in the case of human beings, is fated to become internalized. This is the "origin" of bad conscience (cruelty turned back on itself, *GM* III:20). It is in *GM* II that Nietzsche's thinking on the "fate of the soul" is most dramatically put to work.

In the second essay Nietzsche develops an extraordinary story about the origins and emergence of feelings of responsibility and debt (personal obligation). He is concerned with nothing less than the evolution of the human mind and how its basic ways of thinking have come into being, such as inferring, calculating, weighing, and anticipating. Indeed, he points out that our word "man" (*manas*) denotes a being that values, measures, and weighs. Nietzsche is keen to draw the reader's attention to what he regards as an important historical insight: the principal moral concept of "guilt" (*Schuld*) descends from the material concept of "debts" (*Schulden*). In this sphere of legal obligations, he stresses, we find the breeding ground of the "moral conceptual world" of guilt, conscience, and duty (*GM* II:6). The feeling of obligation, the sense of "guilt," is linked to suffering. Nietzsche is keen to combat the pessimistic view of life and of the human animal that might arise from these insights into suffering and cruelty. He notes that what is most perturbing about suffering is not the fact it appears to be an ineradicable feature of our being, but rather that human beings have a deep need to find a meaning in it, to the point where, in the words of one commentator, we "invent or accept the most ludicrous fantasies," such as the doctrine of original sin, the theory of the transmigration of souls, and the ascription of demonic wills to imaginary gods.[8] Ascetic ideals provide such meaning even as they involve the denial and mortification of the will.[9] Nietzsche's fundamental insight is that a Christian-moral culture has cultivated a type of bad conscience in which feelings of debt and guilt cannot be relieved. This is because the bad conscience becomes attached to a set of sublime metaphysical fictions, such as eternal punishment and original sin, in which release is inconceivable.

For Nietzsche the sense of "guilt" has evolved through several momentous and fateful events in history. In the earliest societies a person is answerable for his deeds and obliged to honor debts. In the course of history this material sense of obligation is increasingly subject to moralization, reaching its summit with guilt before the Christian God. Ultimately, a person is answerable for her very existence, regardless of any of its actual conditions or responsibilities: " 'Sin'—for that is the name for the priestly reinterpretation of the animal 'bad conscience' . . . —has been the greatest event in the history of the sick soul up till now: with sin we have the most dangerous and disastrous trick of religious interpretation" (*GM* III:20).

In *GM* II:16, Nietzsche advances, albeit in a preliminary fashion, his own theory on the "origin" of the bad conscience. He looks upon it "as a serious illness to which man was forced to succumb by the pressure of the most fundamental of all changes which he experienced." This change takes place when one finds oneself "imprisoned within the confines of society and peace" (*GM* II:16). It brings with it a suspension and devaluation of the instincts. Human beings now walk as if a "terrible heaviness" bears down on them: they walk upright not only in a physical but a moral sense also. No longer can human animals simply trust their unconscious instincts in their modes of life; rather, they now have to rely "on thinking, inference, calculation, and the connecting of cause and effect," in short, their "consciousness," which Nietzsche calls the most "error-prone organ." In this completely new scenario the old animal instincts, such as animosity, cruelty, the pleasure of changing and destroying, do not cease to make their demands, but have to find new and underground satisfactions. Through the internalization of humanity, in which instincts, no longer dischargeable, turn inward, comes the invention of what is popularly called the human "soul": "The whole inner world, originally stretched thinly as though between two layers of skin, was expanded and extended itself and granted depth, breadth, and height in proportion to the degree that the external discharge of man's instincts was *obstructed*." Nietzsche insists that *this* "is the origin of 'bad conscience'." He uses striking imagery to provide us with a portrait of such a momentous development:

Lacking external enemies and obstacles, and forced into the oppressive narrowness and conformity of custom, man impatiently ripped himself apart, persecuted himself, gnawed at himself, gave himself no peace and abused himself, this animal who battered himself raw on the bars of his cage and who is supposed to be "tamed"; man, full of emptiness and torn apart with homesickness for the desert, has had to create from within an adventure, a torture-chamber, an unsafe and hazardous wilderness—this fool, this prisoner consumed with longing and despair, became the inventor of "bad conscience." (*GM* II:16)

On the one hand, Nietzsche approaches the bad conscience as "the worst and most insidious illness" that has come into being and as a sickness from which man has yet to recover, his sickness of himself. On the other hand, he maintains that the "prospect of an animal soul turning against itself" is a momentous event and a spectacle too interesting "to be played senselessly unobserved on some ridiculous planet." Nietzsche states that the bad conscience is an illness only in the sense in which pregnancy is treated as an illness (*GM* II:18). Furthermore, as a development that was *prior* to all *ressentiment*, and that *cannot* be said to represent any organic assimilation into new circumstances, the bad conscience contributes to the appearance of an animal on earth that "arouses interest, tension, hope," as if through it "something . . . were being prepared, as though man were not an end but just a path, an episode, a bridge, a great promise" (*GM* II:6). Nietzsche observes that although it represents a painful and ugly growth, the bad conscience is not simply to be looked upon in disparaging terms; indeed, he speaks of the "*active* bad conscience." It can be regarded as the "true womb of ideal and imaginative events"; through it an abundance of "disconcerting beauty and affirmation" has been brought to light. Nietzsche makes it clear that the spectacle of the bad conscience needs to be appreciated for what it is and whose end is, by no means, in sight. It is quite clear that, for Nietzsche, bad conscience constitutes humanity as we know it: it was not chosen by us, its coming into being involved a leap and a compulsion. Nietzsche wishes us to view it as an "inescapable fate" (*Verhängniss*). This is fate conceived as "doom," which is how Nietzsche almost always presents fate in his mature writings. Fate's "voice" appears to us in the form of a *curse*, one that seems to impose on us "the greatest weight" (*GS* 341); this is, in fact, the weight of ourselves.

In the course of history the illness of bad conscience reached a terrible and sublime peak. In prehistory, argues Nietzsche, the basic creditor-debtor relationship that informs human social and economic activity also finds expression in religious rites and worship, for example, the way a tribal community expresses thanks to earlier generations. Over time the ancestor is turned into a god and associated with the feeling of fear (the birth of superstition). Christianity cultivates further the moral or religious sentiment of debt, and does so in terms of a truly monstrous level of *sublime* feeling: God is cast as the ultimate ancestor who cannot be repaid (*GM* II:20). At the end of this section Nietzsche asks whether, as a result of the decline of faith in the Christian God we are now witnessing and the atheism it gives rise to, we will see a release of human beings from guilty indebtedness, thereby giving us the feeling of living a "second innocence." The problem with this supposition is that it underestimates the extent to which the concepts of debt and duty have become deeply moralized, as in the feeling of guilt before God. Nietzsche argues that the facts speak against relief from debt when the fundamental premise—belief in the creditor God—no longer applies. This is because any thought of a final payment "*is to be* foreclosed," and this reflects the fact that a terrifying pessimism has taken hold of the human psyche. The idea has been cultivated that the debtor (human beings) can never pay off the debt and so their liability or indebtedness will be eternal. Even the idea of God as creditor sacrificing himself for the guilt of man in the form of Christ does not produce human liberation but only serves to intensify the debtor's feeling of guilt. The ultimate creditor has been conceived in various ways: as the "cause" of man and the beginning of the human race, or as nature, the womb from which humankind comes into being and is viewed as diabolical, or even existence in general, which has come to be viewed as "inherently worthless" and from which the will seeks escape into nothingness, giving expression to a "nihilistic turning-away from existence." Atheistic philosophers such as Schopenhauer continue to think under the grip of a Christian metaphysics and hold existence itself to be reprehensible. We cling to guilt and want it to stick around, even after it comes unhinged from Christian theology. This is because of its efficacy in producing meaning, specifically with respect to the fact that we find living so hard on account of the suffering it causes us to undergo. Moreover, we keep it because of the sensation of power—over ourselves and others—that it affords. The essential development has taken place in terms of the human being of bad conscience seizing on religious precepts and carrying out its liking for self-torture and self-abasement with a "horrific hardness": "Alas for this crazy, pathetic beast man! What ideas he has, what perversity, what hysterical nonsense, what *bestiality of thought* immediately erupts, the moment he is prevented, if only gently, from being a *beast in deed*." (*GM* II:22). Although Nietzsche finds this development highly interesting, he also sees in it "a black, gloomy, unnerving sadness." In the case of Christianity we have a "madness of the will showing itself in mental cruelty which is absolutely unparalleled."

The second essay ends on a note of redemption. We should note: in contrast to the English word, which suggests the payment of a debt, the German word for redemption (*Erlösung*) means a setting free (cf. *Z*:II "Of Redemption"). Nietzsche's line of thought at this crucial point in the text is highly intricate and the "overhuman" future he appeals to does not suppose a simple-minded transcendence of the kind of creatures we have become. He notes that "we moderns" are the inheritors of centuries long "conscience-vivisection and animal-torture." Indeed, we have become so refined at such cruelty that we can fairly consider ourselves to be "artists in the field." Our natural inclinations are now thoroughly intertwined with the bad conscience. Nietzsche asks whether a "reverse experiment" might be possible, in which bad conscience would become intertwined with "*perverse* inclinations" and "all the ideals which up to now have been hostile to life and have defamed the world." Anyone who wishes to subscribe to such a hope will have to contend with "the *good* men." Nietzsche has in mind both those who are satisfied with humanity as it is (the lazy and the complacent) and those who impatiently wish to transcend it (the zealous). The task of envisaging a surpassing of "the human" is a "severe" and "high-minded" one; it is not a question of simply letting ourselves go. Nietzsche thus looks toward a different kind of spirit, one prepared for and by "wars and victories . . . for which conquest, adventure, danger and even pain have actually become a necessity," and in whom the practice of the "great health" has become personified. At this point Nietzsche looks ahead and outside the all-too timely frame of the present. He refers to "the *redeeming* man of great love and contempt" who will set man free from the ideal that has cursed his existence for so long, and from the nihilism and will to nothingness that arises from it. He speaks fatefully of the "decision" that will make "the will free again," give a "purpose" to the earth, and give man back his "hope."

The place from which Nietzsche issues his critique of morality may be that of a premature-born and as yet undemonstrated future, but it is also one that both relies upon our inherited emotions or affects and places them under the rule of a new practical synthesis. We see this crystallized in Nietzsche's riddle of "the Roman Caesar with the soul of Christ" (*WP* 983). Indeed, one wonders whether this might be the "spirit" that informs Nietzsche's refashioning of the genealogy of morality in terms of a "script"—a script with a cast of characters and *dramatis personae*, designed to tempt the reader into reflecting on "the fate of the soul," and that aims to teach its readers that fate is something to be *loved* (on *amor fati* see *EH* "Clever," 10).[10]

BEYOND GUILT? OR: THE ETERNAL RECURRENCE OF THE SAME?

The ending of *GM* II presents genuine difficulties for the book's readers. Is Nietzsche proposing that in the future human beings will live beyond guilt and, if he is, is this a credible and desirable thought? In proposing redemption from guilt Nietzsche is not suggesting we will no longer feel responsible for our actions or for the events of the world. His point is that a fixation on guilt serves to prohibit the search for knowledge, both of ourselves and the world, including the most difficult knowledge. This is a commitment to knowledge Nietzsche takes over from Spinoza, whom he discovered as his precursor in 1881. In a letter to his friend Franz Overbeck, Nietzsche enumerates the points of doctrine he shares with Spinoza, such as the denial of teleology, of free will, of a moral world order, and of evil, and also mentions the task of "making knowledge the most *powerful passion*." The only redemption of *noble* worth is that which sets us free from ignorance, superstition, and fear. Nietzsche's redemption doctrine does not mean that we would come to live without responsibility or that we cannot practice a good (healthy) "bad conscience." We have seen, for example, the extent to which Nietzsche's untimely philosopher weds himself to such a conscience. The intellectual conscience he is fundamentally committed to is a type of bad conscience, but one that aims to release the forces and energies of life where they have become blocked and to set them free for future growth and evolution (see *GS* 2, 335; *BGE* 230). For Nietzsche the "guilt" we have become and internalized is to be understood as a personal, abject failing that we share as human beings and that cannot be corrected by our power or any other. We are an "error"; it doesn't matter what one does, one cannot be saved; one will only repeat, again and again, the error of one's guilty existence (this is the unhealthy eternal return of the same we practice under conditions of nihilism and that expresses itself in our readiness to will nothingness rather than not will at all; we cry, "all is in vain!").

The guilt Nietzsche wishes to see disappear from the world is guilt conceived as "sin," since this supposes there is a debt that can never be paid off. It means that man's bondage to an ascetic ideal would be eternal. Even in our so-called secular, postmodern world, in which we might suppose that the theological dualism of "good and evil," as well as metaphysical notions such as sin, have been banished from our vocabulary, held to be childish, we remain firmly in the grip of a system of guilt and judgment. To see the contemporary relevance of what Nietzsche is getting at one has only to think of today's (ascetic) *ideal* of a "war on terror," which we are told may go on for some time, indeed, may last an "eternity." This binds us to an *infinite* debt and is the most terrifying fate we can imagine for the bad conscience; it is this curse imposed on life that Nietzsche's teachings aim to free us from. His "Zarathustra *event*," as he calls it, amounts to a tremendous "purification and dedication of mankind" (*EH* "BT" 4).

The fundamental challenge of Nietzsche's thinking on the "fate of the soul" is to invite us to discover new modes of feeling and thinking in which the burden of man and the curse of his fate can be lifted and transformed so that a new disposition toward ourselves and the world can come into being, taking on the force of a new habit. This is the habit of "great health," which denotes a new cognitive and affective practice of life. For the human animal there can be no purely active force; this belongs to the imaginary blond beasts of prey, and in the text Nietzsche is evidently not advocating an *ahistorical* return to a prehuman state, or to a premoral mode of existence. The bad conscience is man's *active* force. The question Nietzsche leaves us to chew is this: What is now *our* debt? This issue cannot be effectively digested without envisioning the over-human. This metaphor, I would contend, is Nietzsche's most important, his most cheerful and strongest, concept and gift. But it is also the one that is the most difficult to measure, and for good reason: Nietzsche designed it so as to challenge and put to the test the measure of humankind. Is it possible to transform the *greatest weight* (ourselves) into something light and free? Is it possible for the earth to be something other than a "madhouse"?

To approach "morality"—a system of valuations and value judgments that takes itself to be eternal, universal, and unconditional—from a Dionysian perspective is to open it up to a novel and far-reaching treatment, in which we are able to view it in terms of a semiology, a symptomatology, and a phenomenology of life (what are its various meanings and directions?). The moral valuation of life that we find in Christianity, Schopenhauer's philosophy, Plato and the whole of idealism, derives from a *"degenerated* instinct which turns against life with subterranean vengefulness" (*EH* "BT" 2). In contrast to this valuation, there is the *"supreme affirmation"* that is born out of fullness and this is "an affirmation without reservation even of suffering, even of guilt, even of all that is strange and questionable in existence." Nietzsche stresses that this "Yes to life" is both the highest and deepest insight that is "confirmed and maintained by truth and knowledge" (ibid.). It is not, then, a simple-minded, precognitive "Yes" to life that Nietzsche wishes us to practice, but one, as he stresses, secured by "truth and knowledge." The task is not to take flight from reality in the name of the "ideal," but rather to "re-cognize" it and affirm it on the basis of this recognition or knowledge (*Erkenntniss*).

For Nietzsche, "morality" represents a system of errors that we have incorporated; it is the great symbol of our profound ignorance of ourselves and the world. In *GS* 115 Nietzsche speaks of "the four errors," noting how humankind has been educated by them: we see ourselves only incompletely; we endow ourselves with fictitious attributes; we place ourselves in a "false rank" in relation to animals and nature; and, finally, we invent ever new tables of what is good and then accept them as eternal and unconditional. However, Nietzsche does not propose we should make ourselves feel guilty about our incorporated errors (they have provided us with new drives) and neither does he want us to simply accuse or blame the past. We need to strive to be more *just* in our evaluations of life and the living (for example, thinking "beyond good and evil" in order to develop a more complex appreciation of the economy of life; for Nietzsche it is largely the prejudices of "morality" that stand in the way of this; "morality" assumes a knowledge of things it does not have). The critical and clinical charge to be made against "morality" at this point in our evolution is that it has become a menacing and dangerous system that makes the present live at the expense of the future. It knows only the present and sees the future as simply an extension of the present; ours is judged to be a time that has been given for all time.

In the very first sketch Nietzsche drafted in August 1881 of his "thought of thoughts," the eternal recurrence of the same, he writes that the task is to *wait and see* to what extent truth and knowledge can stand incorporation (*KSA* 9:11[141]; see also *GS* 110). By this he means that our attempts at knowledge need to take the form of a testing, experimentation, and recognition. The task, Nietzsche says, is to demonstrate the "infinite importance of our knowing, erring, habits, ways of living for all that is to come." The question is then asked: "What shall we do with the *rest* of our lives—we who have spent the majority of our lives in the most profound ignorance? We shall *teach the teaching*—it is the most powerful means of *incorporating* [*einzuverleiben*] it in ourselves. Our kind of blessedness [*Seligkeit*], as teachers of the greatest teaching." Nietzsche believes that modern humankind, which is in the process of becoming postmetaphysical and postmoral, is being presented with what he calls "the weightiest knowledge [*Erkenntniss*]." This is a knowledge that prompts a "terrible reconsideration of all forms of life":

> [W]e have to put the past—our past and that of all humanity—on the scales and *also* outweigh it—no! this piece of human history *will* and must repeat [*wiederholen*] itself eternally; we can leave *that* out of account, we have no influence over it: even if it afflicts our fellow-feeling and biases us against life in general. If we are not to be overwhelmed by it, our compassion must not be great. Indifference needs to have worked away deep inside us, and enjoyment in contemplation, too. Even the misery of future humanity must *not* concern us. But the question is whether *we* still *want to live*: and how! (*KSA* 9:11[141])

Nietzsche has great hopes for the cultivating and incorporating thought of eternal recurrence. This "most powerful thought," he writes, uses the energy that has hitherto been at the command of other goals (*Zielen*). It thus has a "transforming effect" not through the creation of any new energy but simply by creating "new laws of movement for energy." It is in this sense that it holds "the possibility of determining and ordering individual human beings and their affects differently" (*KSA* 9:11[220]). To endure the thought of return one needs freedom from "morality" (*der Moral*) (its prejudices and presumptions), new means against the fact of pain, enjoyment of all kinds of uncertainty, and experimentalism. It is the "greatest elevation (*Erhöhung*) of the consciousness of strength (*Kraft*) of human beings" that comes into being as the over-human is created (*KSA* 11:26[283]; *WP* 1060). We need to "endure" eternal recurrence not as a fate simply given to us but as the exercise of a new freedom, one we grant ourselves a right to. This is Nietzsche's unique "Spinozism," in which an experimental practice of knowledge has become incorporated as a fundamental passion.[11] The future ones will live without metaphysical or existential guilt but not beyond responsibility (the task, Nietzsche says in *Thus Spoke Zarathustra*, is to become freely the creators, judges, and avengers of our own laws); they will cultivate a science dedicated to the incorporation of truth and knowledge but that also loves error because, being alive, it loves life (*BGE* 24). And they will bear the blessings of an affirmation of existence into their every abyss, such is their will to life and to become more—once more, and again and again. As Nietzsche argues toward the end of his great text, "self-overcoming" is the—fateful and free— law of life (*GM* III:27).

NOTES

I am immensely grateful to Christa Davis Acampora for her editorial input, and for her patience and good will.

1. Letter to Peter Gast, 18 July 1887, in *Selected Letters of Friedrich Nietzsche*, ed. Christopher Middleton (London: University of Chicago Press, 1999), 269.

2. In this way one might say that the book stages a return of the repressed. This is recognized by Debra Bergoffen in her unduly neglected article, "Why A Genealogy of Morals?" *Man and World* 16 (1983): 129–38.

3. On the idea of a "moral sense," see Francis Hutcheson, *On the Nature and Conduct of the Passions with Illustrations of the Moral Sense* (1728), annotated by Andrew Ward (Manchester: Clinamen Press, 1999).

4. G. Deleuze, *Nietzsche and Philosophy*, trans. Hugh Tomlinson (London: Athlone Press, 1983), 138.

5. Letter to Franz Overbeck, 13 November 1888.

6. The two essays from Nietzsche's youth I consider in this section can be found in *The Nietzsche Reader*, ed. Keith Ansell Pearson and Duncan Large (Oxford: Basil Blackwell, 2006), 12–17.

7. In an aphorism in *The Wanderer and His Shadow* entitled "Mohammedan fatalism" Nietzsche writes that this kind of fatalism "embodies the fundamental error of setting man and fate over against one another as two separate things," with the result that man must either resist fate or frustrate it, even though in the end it always wins. His argument that every human being is "a piece of fate," "the blessing or the curse and in any event the fetters in which the strongest lies captive," and in which "the whole future of the world of man is predetermined," is picked up and refined in the final section of "The Four Great Errors" in *TI*. It is interesting to note that in one of his earliest sketches of the eternal return of the same Nietzsche develops the thought as a response to the problem of predetermination. If all is necessity, he asks, how can I attain a degree of power of my actions? He answers as follows: "Thought and belief are a weight pressing down on me as much as and even more than any other weight. You say that food, a location, air, society transform and condition you: well your opinions do so even more, since it is they that determine your choice of food, dwelling, air, society. If you incorporate this thought within you, amongst your other thoughts, it will transform you. The question in everything that you will: 'am I certain I want to do to an infinite number of times?' will become for you the heaviest weight" (*KSA* 9:11[143]).

8. Raymond Geuss, *Outside Ethics* (Princeton: Princeton University Press, 2005), 111.

9. See Schopenhauer, *The World as Will and Representation*, Vol. I §68.

10. In his classic study of Nietzsche, Karl Jaspers correctly noted that *amor fati* is not a "passive submission to a presumably recognized necessity," but rather "the expression of free activity," such as the enjoyment of all kinds of uncertainty and experimentalism. See K. Jaspers, *Nietzsche*, trans. Charles F. Wallraff and Frederick J. Schmitz (Chicago: Henry Regnery Company, 1965), 369.

11. For some instructive insight into Nietzsche's relation to Spinoza see Yirmiyahu Yovel, *Spinoza and Other Heretics: The Adventures of Immanence* (Princeton: Princeton University Press, 1989), chapter 5, 104–36.

2

Nietzsche, Re-evaluation, and the Turn to Genealogy*

David Owen

It is a commonplace of contemporary Nietzsche scholarship to note that Nietzsche's turn to, and development of his genealogical mode of enquiry is situated within the overall project of a re-evaluation of values that begins with *Daybreak* (e.g., Geuss 1994, Ridley 1998a, May 1999, Leiter 2002). But what *specifically* motivates Nietzsche's development of genealogy? Given the continuing disagreement concerning the character of genealogy, one might suppose that an analysis of Nietzsche's reasons for developing this mode of enquiry would be subject to some scrutiny; after all, if we can get clear about Nietzsche's reasons for turning to genealogy, we will be well-placed to understand what this mode of enquiry is intended to accomplish. These disagreements range over both *what* genealogy is intended to do and for *whom* and *how* it is intended to achieve its work. Thus, for example, Leiter sees genealogy as a form of ideology-critique directed to freeing "nascent higher beings from their false consciousness" about contemporary morality in which Nietzsche's voice has authority only for those predisposed to accept his values (Leiter 2002: 176 and chapter 5, more generally; cf. Leiter 2000). Geuss, on the other hand, sees genealogy as an attempt to master Christianity by showing Christians in terms they can accept that the perspective composed by Nietzsche's values can give a better historical account of morality than the Christian perspective (Geuss 1994). Similarly Ridley and May

A version of this chapter previously appeared as "Nietzsche, Re-evaluation and the Turn to Genealogy," in *European Journal of Philosophy* 11:3 (2003): 249–72. Reprinted with permission of Blackwell Publishing, Ltd.

see genealogy as involving a form of internal criticism that, in principle, speaks to *all* of Nietzsche's contemporaries (Ridley 1998a; May 1999). However, Ridley argues that "Nietzsche cannot provide a principled method for ranking competing claims to represent our most basic interests" and so must resort to a peculiar form of flattery (Ridley 1998a: 152–53).[1] Yet what remains absent from all of these otherwise impressive accounts, and from contemporary Nietzsche scholarship more generally, is any attention to the claims of a developmental approach that, in elucidating Nietzsche's reasons for turning to genealogy, provides an interpretative basis for approaching *On the Genealogy of Morality* itself. In the light of this abiding commitment to the text of the *Genealogy*, the aim of this essay is to reconstruct the developmental context of the *Genealogy* and, in so doing, to cast some critical light on the disagreements and debates that characterize the contemporary reception of this work.

I take up this task by identifying three central problems that Nietzsche comes to recognize concerning his initial understanding of the nature and demands of the project of re-evaluation in *Daybreak*. Nietzsche's responses to these problems, I argue, provide him with both compelling reasons to develop the mode of enquiry exhibited in *On the Genealogy of Morality* and the conceptual resources necessary to do so.

I

It is in *Daybreak*, as Nietzsche tells us in *Ecce Homo*, that his "campaign against morality begins" in "a *re-evaluation of all values*" (*EH* "D" 1).[2] Whereas in *Human, All Too Human*, Nietzsche had sought to demonstrate that all moral motives (which he identified, following Schopenhauer, as unegoistic) are more or less sublimated expressions of self-interest and, thus, devalued moral values by showing that what are taken as intrinsic (i.e., independently motivating) values should be understood as instrumental values, in *Daybreak* Nietzsche admits the existence of moral motivations (no longer understood as necessarily unegoistic; cf. Clark and Leiter 1997). This development is accomplished through the proposal of an account of the origin of morality that (a) identifies moral action with conduct according to custom (*D* 9), (b) argues that customs are expressions of a community's relationship to its environment that evaluate and rank types of action in terms of their utility or harmfulness with respect to the self-preservation of the community (*D* 9; cf. *GS* 116), (c) claims the system of moral judgments that express the evaluation and ranking of types of action structure our human drives in composing a second nature characterized by a system of moral sentiments that govern our moral agency (*D* 38; cf. *D* 99), (d) suggests that early societies are characterized by superfluous customs that play the role of inculcating the rule of obeying rules (*D* 16), and (e) claims that the morality of customs is predicated on belief in imaginary causalities (*D* 10; cf. *D* 21 and 24).

This account of the origin of morality provides a way for Nietzsche to reject Schopenhauer's identification of moral action and unegoistic action as well as Kant's metaphysics of morals through an argument that looks remarkably like a naturalization of Kant's account of reverence for moral law. While Nietzsche's account of the origin of morality does not account for how we have come to be characterized by the "intellectual mistakes" that lead us to identify morality with actions performed out of freedom of will or purely altruistic motives, it supplies a basis on which such an account could be constructed once it is supplemented by the hypotheses on moral innovation,[3] on the construction of belief in a metaphysical world (e.g., *D* 33), and on the historical causes of the spread of the morality of pity (*D* 132) that Nietzsche adduces. The conclusion that Nietzsche draws from this set of arguments is presented thus:

> *There are two kinds of deniers of morality.*—"To deny morality"—this can mean, *first*, to deny that the moral motives which men claim have inspired their actions have really done so—it is thus the assertion that morality consists of words and is among the coarser or more subtle deceptions (especially self-deceptions) which men practise, and perhaps so especially in precisely the case of those most famed for virtue. *Then* it can mean: to deny that moral judgments are based on truths. Here it is admitted that they really are motives for action, but that in this way it is *errors* which, as the basis of all moral judgment, impel men to their moral actions. This is *my* point of view: though I should be the last to deny that *in very many cases* there is some ground for suspicion that the other point of view—that is to say, the point of La Rochefoucauld and others who think like him—may also be justified and in any event of great general application.—Thus I deny morality as I deny alchemy, that is, I deny their premises: but I do *not* deny that there have been alchemists who believed in these premises and acted in accordance with them.—I also deny immorality: *not* that countless people *feel* themselves to be immoral but that there is any *true* reason so to feel. It goes without saying that I do not deny—unless I am a fool—that many actions called immoral ought to be avoided and resisted, or that many called moral ought to be done and encouraged—but I think that one should be encouraged and the other avoided *for other reasons than hitherto*. We have to *learn to think differently*—in order at last, perhaps very late on, to attain even more: *to feel differently*. (*D* 103)

Thus, Nietzsche conceives of the project of a re-evaluation of values as a project in which, as the concluding sentences of this passage make clear, intrinsic values can be re-evaluated as intrinsic values (rather than as instrumental ones, say, in disguise; see Ridley 2005). On the initial understanding of this project developed in *Daybreak*, Nietzsche takes its requirements to be threefold. First, to demonstrate that Christianity is predicated on belief in imaginary causalities in order to undermine the epistemic authority of Christian morality (see *D* 13, 76–80, 86). Second, to mobilize the affects cultivated by Christian morality against that morality in order to undermine its affective power (e.g., *D* 78, 131, 199). Third, to recommend an alternative (largely Greek) morality (see *D* 556 and 199). Nietzsche takes himself to be limited to recommending an alternative ideal to that of Christianity on the grounds that while we can all agree (he thinks) that "the goal of morality is defined in approximately the following way: it is the preservation and advancement of mankind" (*D* 106), he can see no way of specifying the substantive content of this goal that is not tendentious (see *D* 106 and 139). The second and third requirements are closely related in Nietzsche's practice in that a large part of his rhetorical strategy in *Daybreak* involves exploiting the view expressed in Schopenhauer's morality of pity to the effect that suffering is intrinsically bad in order to argue that Greek morality is superior to Christian morality from this point of view. Thus, Nietzsche advances the claim that Christian morality is objectionable on the grounds that it is characterized by an interpretation of suffering—and, indeed, of existence (since suffering is an inevitable feature of it)—as punishment (*D* 13). What is objectionable about this moral interpretation of suffering is that it intensifies the suffering to which the agent is subject by treating the occasion of extensional suffering as itself a source of intensional suffering that is of much greater magnitude than the extensional suffering on which it supervenes.[4] By contrast, Greek morality allows for "pure innocent misfortune" in which the occasion of extensional suffering of the agent is precisely *not* a source of intensional suffering (see *D* 78).

The three problems that Nietzsche gradually identifies with this initial understanding of the nature and requirements of the project of re-evaluation are the following:

1. His analysis in *Daybreak* had presupposed that the loss of belief in God would lead directly to a loss of authority of Christian moral beliefs; although people would still act *as if* this morality were authoritative in that they would still, at least for a time, be characterized by the moral sentiments cultivated by Christianity, they would no longer accept the authority of the moral beliefs characteristic of Christianity. However, Nietzsche comes to see this assumption as problematic. By the time of composing book III of *The Gay Science* it appears to him that his contemporaries, while increasingly characterized by atheism, do not understand this loss of faith to undermine the authority of Christian morality. It is not that they act in accordance with morality while no longer believing in it but that they still believe in morality, that is, they take the authority of Christian morality to be unaffected by the fact that they no longer believe in God.

2. In *Daybreak*, Nietzsche had taken the authority of scientific knowledge for granted in making his case. However, he comes to acknowledge that this cannot simply be assumed given the constraint of naturalism that characterizes his project and that he requires a naturalistic account of how we come to value truth and why this should lead us to reject Christian morality.

3. The account in *Daybreak* had failed to provide any basis for re-evaluating moral values that did not simply express Nietzsche's own commitments. Nietzsche comes to see this problem as related to the inadequacy of his account

of how we come to be committed to Christian morality at all since, as he'll stress in *Beyond Good and Evil*, the establishment of Christianity promised "a revaluation of all the values of antiquity" (*BGE* 46).

Addressing these problems will lead Nietzsche to revise significantly his view of the nature and requirements of the project of re-evaluation initiated in *Daybreak*.

II

Nietzsche's perception of the first of these problems is manifest in book III of *The Gay Science* which famously opens with the announcement "God is dead; but given the way people are, there may still for millennia be caves in which they show his shadow.—And we—we must still defeat his shadow as well!" (*GS* 108)[5] The problem that Nietzsche identifies—what might be called the problem of *not inferring* (i.e., of failing to draw appropriate conclusions by virtue of being held captive by a picture or perspective)—and dramatizes in section 125 "*Der tolle Mensch*" is that while his contemporaries are increasingly coming to surrender belief in God, they do not draw the implication from this that Nietzsche insists follows. As he'll later put this implication in *Twilight of the Idols*:

> When one gives up Christian belief one thereby deprives oneself of the *right* to Christian morality. For the latter is absolutely *not* self-evident: one must make this point again and again, in spite of English shallowpates. Christianity is a system, a consistently thought out and *complete* view of things. If one breaks out of it a fundamental idea, the belief in God, one thereby breaks the whole thing to pieces: one has nothing of any consequence left in one's hands. . . .—it [the system] stands or falls with the belief in God. (*TI* "Skirmishes" 5)[6]

Nietzsche describes this phenomenon as follows:

> But in the main one may say: The event [that "God is dead"] is far too great, too distant, too remote from the multitude's capacity for comprehension even for the tidings of it to be thought of as having *arrived* as yet. Much less may one suppose that many people know as yet *what* this event really means—and how much must collapse now that this faith has been undermined because it was built upon this faith, propped up by it, grown into it: for example, the whole of our European morality (*GS* 343).

The thought is twofold. First, that the character of our morality has been shaped by our Christian faith and its authority underwritten by that faith. Second, that this is not understood by Nietzsche's contemporaries. As James Conant puts it:

> [T]hose who do not believe in God are able to imagine that the death of God marks nothing more than a change in what people should now "believe." One should now

subtract the belief in God from one's body of beliefs; and this subtraction is something sophisticated people (who have long since ceased going to church) can effect without unduly upsetting how they live or what they value (Conant 1995: 262).

Nietzsche thus recognizes the need for two related tasks. First, to provide an account of this phenomenon of *not inferring* and, second, to find a way of demonstrating that the inference that he draws is the appropriate one.

In approaching the first of these tasks, Nietzsche has in his sights the example of Schopenhauer who exhibits precisely the stance of combining "admitted and uncompromising atheism" with "staying stuck in those Christian and ascetic moral perspectives" (*GS* 357; cf. *GS* 343). Nietzsche's use of this example suggests that the problem of *not inferring* arises from the fact that his contemporaries remain commit-ted to a metaphysical stance toward the world that is "not the origin of religion, as Schopenhauer has it, but only a *late offshoot* of it" (*GS* 151). This metaphysical stance is to be understood as a product of philosophy conducted "under the seduc-tion of morality"(*D* P:3; cf. *BGE* 2 and 5) in that it is commitment to the uncondi-tional authority of (Christian) morality that finds expression in the construction of a metaphysical perspective, that is, a perspective that denies its own perspectival character.[7] We do not draw the appropriate implications from the death of God because we are held captive by a metaphysical perspective according to which the source and authority of our values is entirely independent of us.[8] In this context, Nietzsche's second task, that of showing that the death of God does have the impli-cations that he claims, requires that he provide a naturalistic account of our morality that demonstrates how we have become subject to this taste for the unconditional— "the worst possible taste," as Nietzsche calls it (*BGE* 31)—and, hence, subject to the allure of this metaphysical perspective. It also requires that he show how it has become possible for us to free ourselves from this picture (and, indeed, this taste) and why we are compelled to do so.

These latter points are closely connected to Nietzsche's engagement with the sec-ond problem that he comes to discern with his understanding of his project in *D*, namely, the need to give a naturalistic account of our commitment to the uncondi-tional value of truth.

III

Nietzsche's engagement with the topic of truth is complex but, for our purposes, the salient points are, first, that Nietzsche, at least in his mature work, is committed to the view that one can have beliefs, make statements, and so forth, that are true or false (see Clark 1990; Gemes 1992; Leiter 1994) and, second, that we are character-ized by a commitment to the unconditional value of truth. In respect of Nietzsche's perspectivism, we may merely note that this doctrine—itself a product of Nietzsche's naturalizing of epistemology—is compatible with commitment to the concept of truth: a perspective determines what is intelligibly up for grabs as true or false. Our concern, though, is with the issue raised by Nietzsche in response to the shortcomings of *D*, namely, how we come to be characterized by a commitment to the unconditional value of truth. A tentative approach to this issue is given expression in book III of *The Gay Science* in which Nietzsche suggests that the concept of knowledge arose originally as a way of endorsing certain basic beliefs that are useful (i.e., species-preserving) errors but that eventually "knowledge and the striving for the true finally took their place as needs among the other needs" and "knowledge became a part of life, a continually growing power, until finally knowledge and the ancient basic errors struck against each other, both as life, both as power, both in the same person . . . after the drive to truth has *proven* itself to be life-preserving power, too" (*GS* 110). The problem with this argument is that it cannot account for the unconditional character of our will to truth, our conviction "that truth is more important than anything else, than every other conviction"(*GS* 344). Thus, Nietzsche argues, in book V of *The Gay Science* added five years later:

> Precisely this conviction could never have originated if truth *and* untruth had constantly made it clear that they were both useful, as they are. So, the faith in science, which after all undeniably exists, cannot owe its origin to such a calculus of utility; rather it must have originated *in spite of* the fact that the disutility and dangerousness of "the will to truth" or "truth at any price" is proved to it constantly. Consequently, "will to truth" does *not* mean "I do not want to let myself be deceived" but—there is no alternative— "I will not deceive, not even myself"; *and with that we stand on moral ground.* (*GS* 344)

So, if Nietzsche is to give a satisfying account of how we come to be characterized by our faith in the unconditional value of truth, this will have to be integrated into his account of the formation of Christian morality. Notice though that while it is our faith in science that is to compel us to abandon our religious and, more importantly, moral commitments and, hence, to recognize the necessity of a re-evaluation of values, appeal to our faith in science cannot do all the work necessary since this faith in science is itself an expression of the morality whose value Nietzsche is concerned to call into question. As Nietzsche acknowledges:

> But you will have gathered what I am getting at, namely, that it is still a *metaphysical faith* upon which our faith in science rests—that even we knowers of today, we godless anti-metaphysicians, still take *our* fire, too, from the thousand-year old faith, the Christian faith which was also Plato's faith, that God is truth; that truth is divine. (*GS* 344)[9]

With these remarks Nietzsche both situates his own philosophical activity within the terms of the death of God and acknowledges that if he is to demonstrate the necessity of a re-evaluation of our moral values, this must include a demonstration of the need for a re-evaluation of the value of truth that appeals to nothing more than our existing motivational set in its stripped down form, that is, our will to truth. If Nietzsche can provide such an account, he will have resolved one dimension of the problem of authority that confronts his project since he will have demonstrated that the necessity of the re-evaluation of Christian morality with respect to its claim concerning the unconditioned character of its highest values is derived from the central commitments of that morality itself. However, as Nietzsche acknowledges (see *GS* 346), accomplishing this task does itself raise a further potential threat, the threat of nihilism, which we can gloss in Dostoevsky's terms: God is dead, everything is permitted. To avoid this threat, Nietzsche needs to provide an account of how we can stand to ourselves as moral agents, as agents committed to, and bound by, moral values that does not require recourse to a metaphysical perspective. This issue is closely related to the third of the problems that Nietzsche identifies with *Daybreak*.

IV

In his responses to both of the preceding problems that Nietzsche identifies with his understanding of his project of re-evaluation in *Daybreak*, Nietzsche has been compelled to recognize that the requirements of this project involve providing a compelling account of how we have become subject to Christian morality as a morality that both involves a particular ranking of values and claims an unconditional authority. In approaching the third problem that he identifies with *D*, namely, the need for well-grounded naturalistic criteria for evaluating moral values, Nietzsche confronts the other dimension of the problem of authority that bedevils his project. We can put it this way: even if Nietzsche finds a way of demonstrating that we should disavow the unconditional status claimed by Christian morality and, hence, demonstrates that we cannot value Christian morality for the (metaphysical) reasons that we have hitherto, this would not suffice to provide a criterion in terms of which our valuing should be conducted. Moreover, Nietzsche comes to see that this problem is connected to another problem, namely, his inability to give an adequate account in *D* of the motivation for, and success of, the re-evaluation of the values of antiquity accomplished by Christianity. What connects this explanatory problem to Nietzsche's evaluative problem is that, *at a general and abstract level*, Nietzsche's concern to translate man back into nature (see *GS* 110 and *BGE* 230) entails that his account of the motivation for a re-evaluation of Christian morality must be continuous with his account of the motivation for the Christian re-evaluation of the morality of antiquity. Both the re-evaluation accomplished by Christianity and the re-evaluation proposed by Nietzsche need, in other words, to be explicable in terms of basic features of human beings as natural creatures in order to exhibit the right kind of continuity. To the extent that Nietzsche has a candidate for this role in *D* and the original edition of *The Gay Science*, it is self-preservation (see *GS* 116). However, there is a problem with this candidate in that it doesn't obviously fit well with forms of human activity that risk or, indeed, aim at self-destruction on the part of individuals and communities (or, to put the same point another way, it doesn't seem well poised to account for forms of growth or expansion on the part of individuals or communities that are not directed to developing resources for self-preservation).[10] While Nietzsche acknowledges that self-preservation can be a powerful motive for action, this limitation led him to propose another candidate: *will to power*.[11]

The doctrine of will to power is proposed by Nietzsche as an empirical hypothesis concerning life:

> Physiologists should think twice before positioning the drive for self-preservation as the cardinal drive of an organic being. Above all, a living thing wants to *discharge* its strength—life itself is will to power—: self-preservation is only one of the indirect and most frequent *consequences* of this. (*BGE* 13, cf. also *GS* 349)

However, while Nietzsche argues that human beings are continuous with other organic creatures in terms of being characterized by will to power, he also stresses that the fact that human beings are characterized by self-consciousness entails that they are distinct from other organic creatures in terms of the modality of will to power that they exhibit. The implication of the fact that human beings are self-consciousness animals is that the *feeling of power* that human beings enjoy as agents need have no necessary connection to the *degree of power* that they express in their agency. Nietzsche's point is this: because human beings are self-conscious creatures, the feeling of power to which their agency gives rise is necessarily mediated by the perspective in terms of which they understand themselves as agents and, crucially, the moral evaluation and ranking of types of action expressed within that perspective—but if this is the case, it follows that an expansion (or diminution) of the feeling of power can be an effect of the perspective rather than of an actual increase (or decrease) in the capacities of the agent. A clear illustration of this point is provided in *GS* 353.

> The true invention of the religion-founders is first to establish a certain way of life and everyday customs that work as a *disciplina voluntatis* while at the same time removing boredom; and then to give just this life an *interpretation* that makes it appear illuminated by the highest worth, so that henceforth it becomes a good for which one fights and under certain circumstances even gives one's life. Actually, the second invention is the more important: the first, the way of life, was usually in place, though alongside other ways of life and without any consciousness of its special worth.[12]

Under such conditions of perspective-change, Nietzsche makes plain, the feeling of power attendant on the exercise of one's capacities within a given way of life can be wholly transformed without any change in one's actual capacities or their exercise. Moreover, as Paul Patton points out: "If Nietzsche's conception of human being as governed by the drive to enhance its feeling of power breaks the link to actual increase of power, then it also dissolves any necessary connection between the human will to power and hostile forms of exercise of power over others" (Patton 2001: 108). The feeling of power can be acquired through the domination of others but it can equally be acquired through compassion toward others, through the disciplining of oneself, and the like, depending on the moral perspective in terms of which agents experience their activity. The central point is that this principle provides Nietzsche with a general hypothesis in terms of which to account for human agency as governed by an architectonic interest in the feeling of power.[13] The continuity between the motivation for the Christian re-evaluation of the values of antiquity and for Nietzsche's proposed re-evaluation of Christian values is, thus, that both are to be understood as expressions of will to power.

But what of criteria for evaluating moral perspectives? This issue also turns on Nietzsche's stress on the point that an increase in one's feeling of power need have no necessary connection to an increase in one's powers of agency. The point for Nietzsche is whether our moral perspective is such that the enhancement of our feeling of power expresses the development of our powers of agency. Thus, for example, Nietzsche's use of the concept of *degeneration* in *Beyond Good and Evil* (which foreshadows his discussion of *decadence* in the post-*Genealogy* works) suggests that the feeling of power enjoyed by human beings who understand themselves in terms of "*the morality of herd animals*" that Nietzsche takes to be characteristic of modern Europe expresses the diminution, rather than enhancement, of our powers of agency (*BGE* 202–3).[14] It is in this context that we can grasp Nietzsche's point when he comments:

> You want, if possible (and no "if possible" is crazier) *to abolish suffering*. And us?—it looks as though *we* would prefer it to be heightened and made even worse than it has ever been! Well-being as you understand it—that is no goal; it looks to us like an *end*!—a condition that immediately renders people ridiculous and despicable—that makes their decline into something *desirable*! The discipline of suffering, of *great* suffering—don't you know that *this* discipline has been the sole cause of every enhancement in humanity so far? (*BGE* 225, cf. *BGE* 202–3, *TI* "Skirmishes" 41)

Nietzsche's claim is that the desire to abolish suffering is insane just in virtue of the fact that the development of our intrinsic powers is conditional on being subject to the constraints of a discipline that necessarily involves suffering on our part.[15] The import of these remarks is to suggest that the criterion of evaluation is to be whether the feeling of power expresses actual powers of agency, where this criterion can be taken to be well-grounded just insofar as the principle of will to power provides a compelling explanation of human agency. This follows because *if* one accepts the principle of will to power as a principle of explanation, then one has accepted that human beings are characterized by an architectonic interest in the self-reflexive experience of agency, and since it is a necessary condition of the self-reflexive experience of agency that the feeling of power is taken to express actual powers of agency, then one must also accept that moral perspectives and the valuations of which they are composed can be evaluated in terms of the proposed criterion (cf. *BGE* 19 on willing). But the proposal of this criterion raises two further issues. The first concerns the conditions under which the feeling of power expresses actual powers of agency. The second relates to Nietzsche's perspectivism in respect of the conditional character of the preceding argument.

Nietzsche's argument with respect to the first of these topics is to argue that the feeling of power expresses actual powers of agency insofar as it is free, that is, characterized by a certain kind of self-relation that he often glosses as *becoming what you are* (e.g., *GS* 270) or, as he'll later put it in *Twilight of the Idols*, "Having the will to be responsible to oneself" (*TI* "Skirmishes" 38). This argument relates to his reasons for deploying the deliberatively provocative use of the notions of *herd* and *herd-morality* in his depictions of his modern human beings and the Christian moral inheritance that he takes to characterize them. The basic thought here is that there are two necessary conditions of freedom.

The first is that we are entitled to regard our agency (our intentions, values, beliefs, actions, etc.) as our *own*,[16] where a condition of being entitled to regard our agency as our own is that the intentions, beliefs, values, etc. that we express in acting are self-determined. Nietzsche, in common with other advocates of an expressivist understanding of agency for whom *"Das Thun ist alles"* (*GM* I:13),[17] takes the relationship of an artist to his work as exemplifying the appropriate kind of self-relation, that is, (a) one in which one's actions are expressive of one's intentions where this means that one's intention-in-acting is not prior to its expression but rather is realized as such only in being adequately expressed (the work is *his* to the degree that it adequately expresses his intentions and his intentions become choate as *his* intentions only through their adequate expression)[18] and (b) one's activity appeals to no authority independent of, or external to, the norms that govern the practice in which one is engaged. The case of the artist's relationship to his work is exemplary in virtue of the fact that the artist's feeling of power is a direct function of his actual powers of agency.[19] This is the background against which we can grasp the point of Nietzsche's recourse to stressing the first person pronoun in talk of *"my* truths" (*BGE* 232) and assertions such as "My judgment is *my* judgment, no one else is easily entitled to it" (*BGE* 43). The second necessary condition is that we engage in critically distanced reflection on our current self-understanding. Nietzsche's point is that freedom demands "the ability to take one's virtues and oneself as objects of reflection, assessment and possible transformation, so that one can determine who one is":

> As Nietzsche pointed out "whoever reaches his ideal in doing so transcends it." To take ourselves as potentially free requires that we are not merely bearers of good qualities but self-determining beings capable of distanced reflection. So to attain one's ideal is always that and also to attain a new standpoint, from which one can look beyond it to how to live one's life in the future." (Guay 2002: 315)

It is just such a process that Nietzsche sought to give expression in "Schopenhauer as Educator."[20] Notice that the thought expressed here is analogous to the thought that the artist in having completed a work that adequately expresses his intentions can take that work as an object of critical reflection and assessment—and so move on. In the light of this concept of freedom, we can see the point of Nietzsche's talk of the *herd* as referring to (and seeking to provoke a certain self-contempt in) those who fail to live up to the demands of freedom, and of his talk of *herd-morality* as a form of morality that obstructs the realization of freedom by, on the one hand, construing agency in nonexpressive terms such that the feeling of power has no necessary relationship to actual powers of agency—and, on the other hand, presenting moral rules as unconditional (in virtue of their source in an extra-human authority) and, hence, as beyond critical reflection and assessment. Herd-morality, to return to the artistic analogy, is characterized by a relationship to one's work in which (a) one treats "the medium through which its work is to be done as a mere vehicle for the thought or feeling it is attempting to clarify" (Ridley 1998b: 36), and (b) takes the standards according to which a work is to be judged as external to the artistic tradition.[21] The salience of this discussion for our consideration of Nietzsche's criterion of evaluation is that the feeling of power expresses our powers of agency just insofar as the moral values according to which we act are our *own*, are self-determined, that is, are constraints that we reflectively endorse as conditions of our agency.[22] We should note further that this account of freedom serves to provide Nietzsche with the account needed to address Dostoevsky's worry about moral agency *per se* following the death of God in that it makes the basis on which moral norms are constituted as binding.

Yet, and here we turn to the second issue, this may seem simply to move the problem of authority back one step. Will to power (and the account of freedom that goes along with it) is, it may be pointed out, simply part of Nietzsche's perspective; the fact that the doctrine of will to power provides Nietzsche with a way of accounting for perspectives (including his own) and, indeed, for perspectivism does not imply—incoherently—that it has a nonperspectival status, merely that it is an integral element in Nietzsche's efforts to develop a perspective that is maximally coherent.[23] But if will to power is part of Nietzsche's perspective, a perspective oriented to translating man back into nature, then what authority can it have for those who do not share this perspective? To see how Nietzsche addresses this issue, we need to sketch out his perspectivism in more detail than the hitherto rather fleeting references to perspectives have done.

In common with a number of other contemporary commentators on Nietzsche's perspectivism,[24] I take this doctrine to offer "a *deflationary* view of the nature of justification: there is no coherent notion of justification other than ratification in the terms provided by one's perspective" (Reginster 2000: 40). A perspective as a system of judgments denotes the space of reasons "which constitute an agent's *deliberative viewpoint*, i.e., the viewpoint from which he forms his all-things-considered judgments about what to do" (Reginster, 2000: 43).[25] In endorsing this stance,

Nietzsche thus confronts the very issue raised with respect to will to power in its most acute form, namely, how he can justify the authority of his perspective. What Nietzsche needs here is a way of showing those committed to holding another perspective that they should endorse his perspective in the light of reasons internal to their current perspective. Moreover, since (as we have seen) Nietzsche also holds that reasons motivate only insofar as they appeal to values that are part of the motivational set of those to whom the reasons are addressed, then for his argument to be effective, the reasons that he adduces must express values intrinsic to the perspective currently held by those he is concerned to persuade. What Nietzsche needs, it seems, is an argument with the following form: insofar as you are committed to perspective A, then reasons x and y provide you with grounds to acknowledge the superiority of perspective B in terms of value z, where z is an intrinsic (i.e., independently motivating) value in perspective A.[26] But although an argument of this type looks sufficient for the kind of internal criticism needed in that it provides independently motivating reasons to move from perspective A to perspective B, it is not sufficient for this move to be reflectively stable. The problem is this: if it is the case that we are motivated to move from perspective A to perspective B in terms that appeal to value z, then if value z is not an intrinsic value in perspective B, we find ourselves in the position of reflectively endorsing perspective B on the basis of a value that is not an intrinsic value within this perspective, that is, for reasons that do not count as the appropriate (i.e., independently motivating) kind of reasons (if, indeed, they count as reasons at all) within this perspective.[27] Consequently, if our reasons for endorsing perspective B are to stand in the right kind of motivational relationship to both perspective A and perspective B, the value to which these reasons appeal must be an intrinsic value not only in perspective A but also perspective B. The implication of these reflections is that Nietzsche's claims concerning perspectivism, will to power, and freedom have authority for us only insofar as we are provided with reasons that are authoritative for us, given our existing perspective, and stand in the right kind of motivational relationship to both our existing perspective and Nietzsche's perspective. If the project of re-evaluation is to be coherent, Nietzsche needs to supply an argument that does this work.

CONCLUSION

Nietzsche's reflections on the problems with his initial view of the character and requirements of the project of re-evaluation in *Daybreak* have led to very significant extensions, developments, and refinements of his understanding of this project and its demands. The principal demands that Nietzsche now takes this project to involve are three. First, consequent to his development of the view of Christianity as a perspective expressing a taste for the unconditional, Nietzsche needs an account of how we have become subject to this taste and held captive by this perspective. Second, consequent to his development of the view of our will to truth as internal to the

Christian perspective, Nietzsche needs an account of how the will to truth develops that explains how it is possible for us to free ourselves from the grip of the Christian perspective and the taste for the unconditional that it expresses and why we ought to disavow this taste. Third, consequent to his development of, and commitment to, the doctrines of will to power and of perspectivism, Nietzsche needs to develop the account demanded by the first and second requirements such that it secures the authority of Nietzsche's perspective in a reflectively stable manner. It is the necessity of meeting these demands that motivates Nietzsche's development of genealogy as a mode of enquiry.

If this argument is cogent, it has significant implications for the current debate concerning genealogy in that it provides a *prima facie* case for the claim that the philosophical function of genealogy is oriented to providing, contra Leiter, a form of internal criticism of our modern moral perspective that, contra Ridley, rests its authority on an appeal to a value (i.e., truthfulness) that is an intrinsic value in both our modern moral perspective and Nietzsche's perspective (rather than on flattery and seduction). At the same time, it suggests that Geuss's contention that Nietzsche's target audience is Christian as opposed to simply persons who are committed to Christian forms of valuing is mistaken, as is also Geuss's view that Nietzsche's perspective is simply an expression of his own substantive moral values. It may, of course, be the case, even if the reconstruction of Nietzsche's path to genealogy in this essay is compelling, that Nietzsche's view developed further in the *Genealogy* itself—but this reconstruction does at the very least shift the onus onto the defenders of views that are incompatible with the reasons reconstructed here to provide an explanation of this incompatibility that is both textually and philosophically satisfying.

REFERENCES

Anscombe, E. (1981). "Modern Moral Philosophy," in *Ethics, Religion, and Politics: Collected Philosophical Papers, Vol. 3*. Oxford: Basil Blackwell, 26–42.

Cavell, S. (1990). *Conditions Handsome and Unhandsome*. Chicago: Chicago University Press.

Clark, M. (1990). *Nietzsche on Truth and Philosophy*. Cambridge: Cambridge University Press.

Clark, M., and B. Leiter. (1997). "Introduction," in *Daybreak*, vii–xxxvii. Cambridge: Cambridge University Press.

Conant, J. (1995). "Nietzsche, Kierkegaard, and Anscombe on Moral Unintelligibility," in T. Tessin and M. von der Ruhr (eds.) *Morality and Religion*. New York: St. Martins Press, 250–99.

Conant, J. (2001). "Nietzsche's Perfectionism: A Reading of *Schopenhauer as Educator*," in R. Schacht (ed.) *Nietzsche's Postmoralism*. Cambridge: Cambridge University Press, 181–257.

Conway, D. (1997). *Nietzsche's Dangerous Game*. Cambridge: Cambridge University Press.

Danto, A. (1988). "Some Remarks on *The Genealogy of Morals*," in R. Solomon and K. Higgins (eds.) *Reading Nietzsche*. Oxford: Oxford University Press, 13–28.

Gemes, K. (1992). "Nietzsche's Critique of Truth," *Philosophy and Phenomenological Research* 52: 47–65.

Geuss, R. (1994). "Nietzsche and Genealogy," *European Journal of Philosophy* 2: 275–92.

Guay, R. (2002). "Nietzsche on Freedom," *European Journal of Philosophy* 10: 302–27.

Leiter, B. (1994). "Perspectivism in Nietzsche's *Genealogy of Morals*," in R. Schacht (ed.) *Nietzsche, Genealogy, Morality*. Berkeley: University of California Press, 334–57.

Leiter, B. (1998). "The Paradox of Fatalism and Self-Creation in Nietzsche," in C. Janaway (ed.) *Willing and Nothingness: Schopenhauer as Nietzsche's Educator*. Oxford: Oxford University Press.

Leiter, B. (2000). "Nietzsche's Metaethics: Against the Privilege Readings," *European Journal of Philosophy* 8: 277–97.

Leiter, B. (2002). *Nietzsche on Morality*. London: Routledge.

MacIntyre, A. (1977). "Dramatic Narratives, Epistemological Crises and the Philosophy of Science," *The Monist* 60: 453–72.

MacIntyre, A. (1990). *Three Rival Versions of Moral Inquiry*. Notre Dame: University of Notre Dame Press.

May, S. (1999). *Nietzsche's Ethics and His War on "Morality."* Oxford: Clarendon Press.

Owen, D. (1998). "Nietzsche, Enlightenment and the Problem of the Noble Ideal," in J. Lippitt (ed.) *Nietzsche's Futures*. Basingstoke: MacMillan, 3–29.

Owen, D., and A. Ridley. (2003). "On Fate," *International Studies in Philosophy* 35(3): 63–78.

Patton, P. (2001). "Nietzsche and Hobbes," *International Studies in Philosophy* 33(3): 99–116.

Reginster, B. (2000). "Perspectivism, Criticism and Freedom of Spirit," *European Journal of Philosophy* 8: 40–62.

Reginster, B. (2001). "The Paradox of Perspectivism," *Philosophy and Phenomenological Research* 62: 217–33.

Richardson, J. (1996). *Nietzsche's System*. Oxford: Oxford University Press.

Ridley, A. (1998a). *Nietzsche's Conscience*. Ithaca, NY: Cornell University Press.

———. (1998b). *Collingwood*. London: Phoenix.

———. (2005). "Nietzsche and the Re-evaluation of Values," *Proceedings of the Aristotelian Society* 105:171–91.

Schacht, R. (1983). *Nietzsche*. London: Routledge.

Tanner, Michael. (1994). *Nietzsche*. Oxford: Oxford University Press.

Wittgenstein, L. (1975). *On Certainty*. Oxford: Basil Blackwell.

NOTES

*I am grateful to Aaron Ridley and James Tully for their comments on earlier drafts of this essay and, in particular, to Aaron, whose article (reprinted in this volume), "Nietzsche and the Re-evaluation of Values," provided much of the spur to write this essay as well as some of the conceptual resources needed for it. I also received some seemingly small but actually very helpful suggestions from the anonymous referees that have (I hope) improved its clarity and made the conclusion punchier. I owe much thanks to my wife, Caroline Wintersgill, one of whose perfections is the ability to work on improving my prose style without ever (quite) succumbing to the condition of (rational) despair.

1. Ridley argues that Nietzsche's authority "is built on that most peculiar form of flattery, the kind that makes welcome even the most unpleasant revelations about ourselves provided that it also makes us feel more interesting (to us and to him)." However it should be noted that Ridley has since rejected this view and he (2005) offers a nuanced account of re-evaluation that informs the argument of this essay and also provides a devastating critique of the view of re-evaluation adopted in Leiter (2002).

2. For citations of Nietzsche's writings, I rely upon the following translations: Diethe's *GM*; Hollingdale's *A, D, HH,* and *UM*; Large's *TI*; Nauckhoff and Del Caro's *GS*; and Norman's *BGE*.

3. See *D* 14 and 98 for remarks on innovation in general and *D* 70–2 for comments on Christianity as a successful innovation, whose success is due, not least, to the ways in which it draws on and powerfully synthesizes a number of moral currents and beliefs already present within Jewish and Roman society.

4. The distinction between extensional and intensional forms of suffering is borrowed from Danto (1988) in which he characterizes intensional suffering as consisting in an interpretation of extensional suffering and goes on to point out—using the example of male impotence in our culture—that while one may be able to do relatively little about the extensional suffering to which those subject to impotence are exposed, it would undoubtedly reduce the overall suffering to which they are subject if sexual potency were not connected to powerful cultural images of masculinity. See in this context *D* 77–8.

5. By the shadows of God, Nietzsche is referring to the metaphysical analogues of God and, more generally, the deployment of our conceptual vocabulary as expressing metaphysical commitments, namely, to a particular conception of the will. See *GS* 127.

6. Cf. Wittgenstein, *On Certainty* 105. As James Conant (1995) and Michael Tanner (1994: 33–35) have independently observed, Nietzsche's argument here bears a striking resemblance to the argument advanced by Elizabeth Anscombe (1981) in her essay "Modern Moral Philosophy."

7. Hence, within the grip of this metaphysical perspective, as Nietzsche points out in *BGE* 186, philosophers have understood their task to be that of providing secure foundations for morality, a task that "even constitutes a type of denial that these morals *can* be regarded as a problem."

8. The meaning of the death of God will have become clear to us, on Nietzsche's account, once we recognize that "there are no viable external sources of authority," as Guay (2002: 311) points out. The same point is also made by Gemes (1992: 50).

9. It is a feature of the lengths to which Leiter is forced in maintaining his claim that genealogy does not involve internal criticism that Leiter (2002: 175n7) argues that the value of truth is not internal to Christian morality although produced by it. This strikes me as a very strained reading of the textual evidence here and in *GM* III. Leiter is motivated to maintain this view by his commitment to the claim that Nietzsche does not want the majority to change their views, only the exceptional individuals predisposed to the values that Leiter takes Nietzsche to be espousing.

10. The contrast between Nietzsche and Hobbes is an apposite one here that has been illuminatingly explored by Patton (2001).

11. It is worth noting that Nietzsche had been edging toward the idea of will to power even when his official line focused on self-preservation. See, for example, *D* 23, 112 and 254, and *GS* 13.

12. Note that this passage marks an important shift from *Daybreak* in that it allows Nietzsche to distinguish between the origin of a custom or way of life and its meaning; the importance of this point is stressed in *GM* II:12 with respect to his genealogical project.

13. See Warren (1998) for a clear exposition of this view. Notice that this doctrine does not imply that agents aim directly at the feeling of power but, rather, that engagement in action directed at such-and-such ends produces the feeling of power to the extent that in so acting the agent enjoys the self-reflexive experience of agency (i.e., efficacious willing) which, in turn, leads agents to value forms of activity that support and enhance, and devalue forms of activity that undermine and diminish, their self-reflexive experience of agency. This construal of the doctrine of will to power avoids, it seems to me, the worries expressed by Maudemarie Clark concerning this doctrine without requiring that we adopt the rather implausible view to which she comes, namely, that the doctrine of will to power should be read "as a generalization and glorification of *the* will to power, the psychological entity (the drive or desire for power)" through which Nietzsche expresses his own "moral" values. See Clark (1990: 224) and chapter 7 of her book more generally.

14. See Conway (1997) chapter 2 for a good discussion of decadence.

15. The centrality of discipline for Nietzsche is rightly stressed May (1999: 27–29). The issue of constraint with respect to giving style to one's character has been illuminatingly discussed by Ridley (1998: 136–42) while the relationship between freedom, constraint, and fate in Nietzsche is taken up in Owen and Ridley (2003); see particularly the critical discussion of Leiter (1998) and the defense of the position advocated by Schacht (1983, chapter 5).

16. This point is already stressed in "Schopenhauer as Educator," and it remains a prominent theme in *Daybreak*, esp. *D* 104.

17. One can think here of the early Romantics, Hegel (on some readings), Collingwood, Wittgenstein, and Charles Taylor. It should be noted that this aspect of Nietzsche's thought is closely related to his inheritance, via the Romantics and Emerson, of Kant's reflections on genius; for an illuminating discussion of this point, see Conant (2001: 191–96).

18. Notice that it is an implication of Nietzsche's commitment to this view that the judgment that such-and-such action adequately expresses my intention is only intelligible against the background of practices in which we give and exchange reasons. What is more, I do not stand in any privileged relation to the judgment that such-and-such action adequately expresses my intention.

19. In the light of the preceding footnote we should note that while an artist's feeling of power may be based on a mistaken view of his activity, the publicity of his judgment entails that such a mistaken feeling of his power cannot be reflectively sustained.

20. See Conant (2001) for a demonstration of this claim.

21. This view aligns Nietzsche's talk of herd-morality to his processual perfectionism. See Guay (2002) who calls this "meta-perfectionism" to stress the point that there is no end point or *telos* as such to Nietzsche's perfectionism and Conant (2001) who suggests that Nietzsche's stance is akin to the Emersonian perfectionism elucidated in Cavell (1990). A strongly contrasting view is forthrightly argued by Leiter (2002). However, it is worth noting that not only had Nietzsche already criticized the elitist understanding of human excellence proposed by Leiter in "Schopenhauer as Educator" but also that Leiter's failure to address Nietzsche's concept of freedom entails that he fails to recognize that Nietzsche's remarks on herd-morality are perfectly explicable in terms that do not require the elitist understanding of human excellence to which Leiter takes Nietzsche to be committed.

22. Note "self-determined" does not mean "self-imposed": the constraints may be there anyway. Rather self-determined means affirming these constraints as conditions of one's agency. In this respect, Nietzsche's concept of freedom is closely related to his concept of fate. For a fuller discussion of this issue, see Owen and Ridley (2003) and, in particular, the detailed critique of Leiter's (1998) argument concerning Nietzsche's understanding of human types (an argument that Leiter deploys to support his claims concerning Nietzsche's commitment to the elitist view of human excellence).

23. For a powerfully developed alternative view in which perspectivism with respect to the empirical world is seen as a product of a nonperspectival metaphysics of will to power, see Richardson (1996). For some skepticism—of the right kind—toward Richardson's view, see Reginster (2001).

24. Clark (1990) is the principal figure here but other noteworthy advocates of this view include Daniel Conway, David Hoy, Brian Leiter, Bernard Reginster, Aaron Ridley, and Richard Schacht among others.

25. Note that there are two ways in which we can take Nietzsche's assertion of perspectivism. On the one hand, we make take Nietzsche to be asserting a tautology. On the other hand, we may take him to be asserting a position that risks a dilemma in which this assertion is either a performative contradiction or a claim from Nietzsche's perspective. In contrast to Reginster, I incline to the former of these views.

26. This is the position that I take Reginster (2000: 49–51) to argue for.

27. They might still be reasons if value z is an instrumental value in perspective B but they would not be the right sort of reasons to play the reflectively stabilizing role that they are called to play. Compare MacIntyre (1977). It is one of the ironies of MacIntyre's reading of Nietzsche and, in particular, of genealogy (1990) that he fails to see how close Nietzsche's way of dealing with the issue of authority is to the account sketched out in his own 1977 essay.

3

The Genealogy of Genealogy

Interpretation in Nietzsche's Second *Untimely Meditation* and in *On the Genealogy of Morals**

Alexander Nehamas

In coming to terms with our past, Nietzsche writes, "The best we can do is to confront our inherited and hereditary nature . . . , combat our inborn heritage and implant in ourselves a new habit, a new instinct, a second nature, so that our first nature withers away. It is an attempt to give oneself, as it were *a posteriori*, a past in which one would like to originate in opposition to that in which one did originate."[1] But a contrary current in Nietzsche's thought is manifested by his going on to claim that "here and there a victory is nonetheless achieved, and for the combatants, for those who employ critical history for the sake of life, there is even a noteworthy consolation: that of knowing that this first nature was once a second nature and that every victorious second nature will become a first" (*HL* 3).

This intriguing passage seems to cast doubt on the solidity of the distinction between "first" and "second" nature. It suggests that there is no such thing as an absolutely first nature, that everything seemingly fixed has been at some point introduced into history and that the distinction between first and second nature is at best provisional—between a second nature that has been long accepted and one that is still new. And this of course casts doubt on the idea of a second nature as well. What Nietzsche here calls "critical" history begins to appear as the unearthing of an infinite chain of second natures with no necessary first link.

*Excerpted from *Literary Theory and Philosophy*, edited by Richard Freadman and Lloyd Reinhardt (London: Macmillan, 1991), 269–83. Reproduced with permission of Palgrave Macmillan.

Here, then, we have one of the elements out of which genealogy eventually emerges. For genealogy is a process of interpretation that reveals that what has been taken for granted is the product of specific historical conditions, an expression of a particular and partial attitude toward the world, history, or a text that has been taken as incontrovertible.

In *On the Use and Disadvantage of History for Life*, Nietzsche also prefigures another element of genealogy:

> To what end the "world" exists, to what end "mankind" exists, ought not to concern us at all for the moment except as objects of humour: for the presumptuousness of the little human worm is the funniest thing at present on the world's stage; on the other hand, do ask yourself why you, the individual, exist, and if you can get no other answer try for once to justify your existence as it were *a posteriori* by setting before you an aim, a goal, a "to this end," an exalted and noble "to this end." Perish in pursuit of this and only this—I know of no better aim in life than that of perishing, *animae magnae prodigus,* in pursuit of the great and the impossible. (*HL* 9)

Here as well two conflicting ideas are conjoined. If there is to be a purpose in life, Nietzsche claims, it will have to be a purpose *constructed* by each particular individual and capable of redeeming the life that was lived, and perhaps lost, for its sake. But such a purpose can never be fully achieved, insofar as it aims to effect a real change in the world—hence Nietzsche's description of it as "impossible."

It is out of these two sets of conflicts, I would now like to suggest, that Nietzsche eventually develops the view of interpretation and of our relationship to our past that characterizes *On the Genealogy of Morals*. The step most crucial to this development was his coming to give up the view that the causal description of objects and events in the world corresponds to their true nature. He therefore no longer had to believe that interpretation or reinterpretation, which cannot really affect such causal sequences, cannot possibly change the events in question and thus introduce something genuinely new into the universe. If the causal description of the world is not a description of its real nature, if in fact there is no such thing as the world's real nature, then reinterpretation need not be, as Nietzsche had believed when he composed his earlier works, falsification.

The *Genealogy* contains a sustained effort on Nietzsche's part to show that morality is a subject fit for interpretation, that we can ask of it, as we usually put the point, "What does it mean?" This is in fact the very question Nietzsche asks of the asceticism, the denial of the common pleasures, that has been traditionally associated with philosophy. Traditionally, the fact that philosophers have tended toward asceticism has been considered natural. Nietzsche, instead, sees it as a question. "What does that *mean?*" he asks, and continues: "For this fact has to be interpreted: *in itself* it just stands there, stuipid to all eternity, like every 'thing in itself'" (*GM* III:7).

The great accomplishment of *GM* is the demonstration that morality in general and asceticism in particular are indeed subjects of interpretation, that they can be added to our interpretative universe. Now, how is it, in general, that we can show that something can in fact be interpreted? In the first instance, we can only show it by actually offering an interpretation. That is, in order to establish a new subject of interpretation, we must produce an *actual* interpretation of that subject: we must in fact establish it *as* such a subject by means, moreover, of an interpretation that makes some sort of claim to the attention of others.

Nietzsche, I believe, offers such an interpretation of morality. The first and perhaps the most important feature of that interpretation is that, as Nietzsche emphasizes throughout this work, morality itself is an interpretation to begin with. And this establishes at least a partial connection between genealogy and the discussion of history in the second *Untimely Meditation*: morality, that is, something that we have considered so far as absolutely basic, solid, foundational, is shown to be a particular reaction to a preexisting set of phenomena; a first nature, as it were, is shown to be a second nature whose status has been concealed.

The notion that morality is an interpretation is absolutely central to Nietzsche. "There are altogether no moral facts," he writes, for example, in *Twilight of the Idols*; "morality is merely an interpretation of certain phenomena—more precisely, a misinterpretation" (*TI* "Improvers" 1). Where others had previously seen merely a natural development of natural human needs, desires, and relationships, where others had "taken the value of [moral] values as given, as factual, as beyond question" (*GM* P:6), Nietzsche saw instead what he described as a system of signs. Such a system, naturally, like all systems of signs, remains incomprehensible until we know what its signs are signs of and signs for. In order, then, to show that morality can be interpreted, Nietzsche actually interprets it; and his interpretation involves a demonstration that morality itself is an interpretation to begin with.

We have just seen that Nietzsche considers that morality is a misinterpretation. He is therefore obliged to offer an alternative account of the phenomena morality has misconstrued, or (as he would prefer to put it), has construed in a manner that suits it. This account depends crucially on his view that one of the most important features of the moral interpretation of phenomena is the fact that its status *as* an interpretation has been consistently concealed:

> Morality in Europe today is herd animal morality—in other words, as we understand it, merely *one* type of human morality beside which, before which, and after which many other types, above all higher moralities, are, or ought to be, possible. But this morality resists such a "possibility," such an "ought," with all its power: it says stubbornly and inexorably, "I am morality itself and nothing besides is morality." (*BGE* 202)

Let us then suppose (a considerable supposition!) that morality is an interpretation. What is it an interpretation of? Nietzsche's general answer is that it is an interpretation of the phenomenon to which he refers as "human suffering." His own attitude toward this phenomenon is very complex. In one mood, he debunks it. He attributes it not to a divine cause (as, we shall see, he claims that morality does), not even to anything serious but to the lowest and crudest physiological causes. Such a cause, he writes,

> may perhaps lie in some disease of the *nervus sympathicus*, or in an excessive secretion of bile, or in a deficiency in potassium sulfate and phosphate in the blood, or in an obstruction in the abdomen which impedes the blood circulation, or in degeneration of the ovaries and the like. (*GM* III:15)

For years, I have considered this as one of those horribly embarrassing passages that Nietzsche's readers inevitably have to put up with in defensive silence. Then I realized that Nietzsche was actually making a joke, that he was reducing one of the "highest" expressions of being human—our capacity for suffering—to one of the "lowest." And, having seen the passage as a joke, I realized that it was after all serious or, at least, that it was a complex joke with a point to make. For the list of ailments Nietzsche produces is not haphazard. A disease of the (nonexistent) *nervus sympathicus* could well be supposed to be the physiological analogue of the excess, even of the existence, of pity—the sentiment that is the central target of the *Genealogy*, which takes "the problem of the value of pity and the morality of pity" (*GM* P:6) to be its originating concern. "Excessive secretion of bile," of course, traditionally has been associated with malice and envy, which are precisely the feelings those to whom the *Genealogy* refers to as "the weak" have always had for those who are "strong," while weakness and, in general, lassitude and the inability to act are in fact a direct effect of potassium deficiency. Impediments to the circulation of the blood are correlated with the coldness, ill will, and lack of sexual potency Nietzsche associates with the ascetic priests, and such impotence, along with infertility whose spiritual analogue would be the absence of any creativity, may well be the physiological/moral correlate of ovarian degeneration (whatever that is).

In another mood, Nietzsche attributes the suffering to which we are all inescapably subject to necessary social arrangements:

> I regard the bad conscience [this is one of his terms for referring to suffering] as the serious illness that human beings were bound to contract under the stress of the most fundamental change they ever experienced—that change which occurred when they found themselves finally enclosed within the walls of society and of peace. . . . All instincts that do not discharge themselves outwardly *turn inward*—this is what I call the *internalization* of human beings: thus it was that we first developed what was later called our "soul." (*GM* II:16)

It is very important to note at this point that Nietzsche, though he offers in this work an interpretation of morality according to which morality is an interpretation of suffering, never characterizes his own accounts of suffering as themselves interpretations. Only the moral approach to suffering, but none of the explanations he offers, is an interpretation:

> Human beings, the bravest of animals and those most accustomed to suffering, do *not* repudiate suffering as such; they *desire* it, they even seek it out, provided they are shown a *meaning* for it, a *purpose* of suffering. The meaninglessness of suffering, *not* suffering itself, was the curse that lay over mankind so far—and the ascetic ideal offered them meaning. . . . In it, suffering was *interpreted*. (*GM* III:28)

What is it, then, that makes the moral account of suffering, but not Nietzsche's own, an interpretation? My own answer, in general terms, is the following. According to Nietzsche, the ascetic priests take the fact of suffering, the existence of the bad conscience which *he* considers as "a piece of animal psychology, no more," and claim that it is prompted by, perhaps equivalent to, a sense of guilt produced by sin. "Sin," Nietzsche writes, "is the priestly name for the animal's 'bad conscience' (cruelty directed backward)." Convinced by the priests to see their suffering in such terms, Nietzsche continues, human beings

> receive a hint, they receive from their sorcerer, the ascetic priest, the *first* hint as the "cause" of their suffering: they must seek it in themselves, in some *guilt*, in a piece of the past, they must understand their suffering as a *punishment*. (*GM* III:20)

Nietzsche's introduction of the idea of "a piece of the past" here is crucial for our purposes. For it is connected with the search for a meaning that is thought to inhere in history—in our own history in this case—and which is there to be discovered by us if we go about it in the right way. This piece of the past, according to Nietzsche, is nothing other than our inevitable engagement in acts and immersion in desires all of which—sensual, ambitious, self-serving, egoistic—are, as he believes, characteristically human and which, therefore, we cannot possibly avoid.

Yet morality, interpreting such desires and actions as sinful, enjoins us to distance ourselves from them as much as is humanly possible. Its effect is twofold. In the first instance, it offers suffering a meaning—it is God's punishment for the fact that we are (there is no other word for it) human. Morality therefore makes suffering, to the extent that it accounts for it, tolerable. In the second instance, however, and in the very same process, it "brings fresh suffering with it, deeper, more inward, more poisonous, more life-destructive suffering" (*GM* III:28).

This, in turn, is brought about in two ways. First, because the forbidden desires, impulses, and actions can be fought against only by the same sort of desires, impulses, and actions, we can curtail our cruelty toward ourselves only by acting cruelly toward ourselves. The effort to curtail them, therefore, secures their own perpetuation: it guarantees that suffering will continue. Second, because if this sort of behavior is, as Nietzsche believes, essentially human, then the effort to avoid it and not to give expression to the (equally essential) impulses on which it depends perpetuates the suffering caused by any obstacle to the tendency of instinct to be "directed outward." In a classic case of the double bind, the moral approach to suffering, in its interpretation of it as sin, creates more suffering the more successfully it fights it and the more tolerable it makes it.

Now the reason why morality is for Nietzsche an interpretation of suffering is that it gives suffering a meaning and a reason ("reasons relieve") and accounts for its persistence by means of attributing it to some *agent*. "Every sufferer," Nietzsche claims,

> instinctively seeks a cause for his suffering; more exactly, an agent, still more specifically, a guilty agent who is susceptible to suffering—in short, some living thing upon which one can, on some pretext or other, vent his affects, actually or in effigy.

Suffering is taken as the result of someone's actions. Whose actions? Here is the answer to this question:

"I suffer: someone must be to blame for it"—thus thinks every sickly sheep. But the shepherd, the ascetic priest, replies: "Quite so, my sheep! Someone must be to blame for it: but you yourself are this someone, you alone are to blame for it—*you alone are to blame for yourself*!" (*GM* III:15).

This moral account of suffering, in contrast to Nietzsche's explanations, is an interpretation, I now want to claim, because it appeals to intentional vocabulary, because it construes suffering as the product or result of someone's actions—in this case, of the actions of the sufferers themselves and of God's—because it says, in effect, "What you feel is as it is because of who you are and of what you have done."

In my opinion, what is essential to interpretation is to construe a particular phenomenon as an action and thus to attribute to it some agent whose features account for the features of that action.[2] And if I am right in claiming that the connection between interpretation and intention is essential, then Nietzsche's account of human suffering—at least what we have seen of it so far—is not interpretative. The reason is that Nietzsche is careful to avoid the description of suffering as a general phenomenon in intentional terms. We have seen that, in general, he attributes it to physiological or social causes and that he believes that, at least in one sense of that term, suffering is meaningless. There is no reason, no agent, no purpose, no "For the sake of what?" in it.

This allows me to return to my discussion of *HL*. For it may be tempting to suppose that just as in that earlier work Nietzsche believed that in reality history is meaningless, so in the *Genealogy* he believes that suffering is meaningless and that this is a brute fact with which we shall simply have to live from now on. This is actually the view of Arthur C. Danto, who has argued that the main point of the *GM* is the idea that "suffering really is meaningless, there is no point to it, and the amount of suffering caused by *giving* it a meaning chills the blood to contemplate." Danto continues:

> The final aphorism of the *Genealogy*, "man would rather will the nothing than not will," does not so much heroize mankind, after all: what it does is restate the instinct of *ressentiment*: man would rather his suffering be meaningful, hence would rather will meaning onto it, than acquiesce in the meaninglessness of it. It goes against this instinct to believe

what is essentially the most liberating thought imaginable, that life is without meaning. In a way, the deep affliction from which he seeks to relieve us is what today we think of as hermeneutics: the method of interpretation primarily of suffering.[3]

This is in many ways a wonderful interpretation. The meaning it attributes to the *Genealogy*, that exemplary book of interpretation, is that there is no meaning anywhere for anyone. Danto's interpretation of Nietzsche's interpretation of the moral interpretation of suffering says, in effect, "Stop interpreting immediately; don't even begin." But since, of course, Danto's view *is* an interpretation, it does just what it says we shouldn't do, and thus instantiates, in a manner Nietzsche would have been only too happy to acknowledge, the execution of the impossible task it proscribes. In addition, by attributing to Nietzsche the view that only the uninterpreted (or unexamined) life is worth living for a human being, it establishes him in yet another dimension as Socrates' antipodes. The trouble, however, is that ultimately this interpretation will not stand.

I agree with Danto that Nietzsche believes that suffering has no meaning—it has, after all, only causes, social or physiological. But this is a view to the effect that no one has already given suffering a meaning, a point (say, as punishment for sin) which is the same for everyone and there for us to discover and live with. *In itself*, suffering has no meaning—in itself, as we have seen in connection with every thing in itself, it just stands there, stupid to all eternity. But the consequence that follows from this is not necessarily the idea that since in reality there is no meaning, we should give up the goal of trying to create meaning altogether. This would be the view of *The Birth of Tragedy* and of the second *Untimely Meditation* minus Nietzsche's insistence that we should still try to accomplish something with our lives despite the knowledge that nothing is thereby accomplished. It would be to hold the metaphysics of those works without the aesthetic justification of life they demand.

But what separates these works from the *Genealogy* is Nietzsche's realization that the fact that suffering or history is meaningless in itself does not force the conclusion that any attempt to give it a meaning would necessarily falsify it. Instead, it implies that *in themselves* both suffering and history are irrelevant to us. And this is precisely what allows the conclusion that if one were to succeed in making something out of one's own suffering or one's own history (and, on my reading, Nietzsche offers himself as his favorite example[4]), then the suffering that that individual life, like every life, is bound to have contained will also thereby have acquired a meaning.

This meaning will be its contribution to the whole of which it will have then become a part—and this is true, in my opinion, not only of life but of all meaning, particularly of the meaning of texts. In this way, if a life has had a point, if it has made a difference, if it has changed something, then everything in it, everything that happens or has happened to the person whose life it is becomes significant. It becomes part of a work whose author is the person in question and, as we should have expected, it becomes something we can describe in intentional terms. It becomes something for which one is willing, "*a posteriori*," to accept responsibility, something that one in a very serious sense of the term *is*. This idea, that even events in our past can in this manner become things we did and therefore things we are, becomes explicit in *Thus Spoke Zarathustra*, where it is applied specifically to suffering and punishment:

> "No deed can be annihilated: how could it be undone by punishment? This, this is what is eternal in the punishment called existence, that existence must eternally become deed and guilt again. Unless the will should at last redeem itself and willing should become not willing." [This is the aim of asceticism.] But my brothers, you know this fable of madness.
>
> I led you away from this madness when I taught you, "The will is a creator." All "It was" is a fragment, a riddle, a dreadful accident [it is meaningless]—until the creative will says to it: "But thus I willed it." Until the creative will says to it, "But thus I will it; thus I shall will it." (*Z*:II "On Redemption")

This passage shows that Nietzsche cannot possibly be the enemy of hermeneutics Danto describes. He is, however, a relentless enemy of the view that the significance of the events in a life, of the components of history, of the parts of a text, is given to them antecedently, that it inheres in them, and that it is therefore the same for everyone. If, indeed, we want to find out what anything means to everyone, the answer is bound to be "nothing," and the inference we may be tempted to draw from it will be that nothing is meaningful in itself, or in reality, and that all meaning is therefore illusory. This is not unlike Nietzsche's early view. In the late works, when he no longer believes in anything in itself, when history is all there is, he comes to believe that what the events in each life mean differs according to what, if anything, one makes of one's life. This, in turn, can be seen to be connected with his turn away from the effort directly to influence the culture of his time.[5] Whereas the second *Untimely Meditation* seems to envisage that all the "young" have the ability to accomplish something great and different, the later works start from the observation that most people are not at all capable of anything remotely like this. Since, then, most people do not succeed in making a difference, the events in most people's lives turn out not to mean very much at all—in which case, people might as well believe that they are a punishment: Christianity is not to be abolished, and a new culture is no longer called for. It is difficult enough to organize "the chaos one is" for oneself.

The crucial difference, then, between Nietzsche's early and late works on the question of our relationship to our past and of its interpretation is that in the *Genealogy* Nietzsche does not believe that the establishment of meaning must falsify history or the text. There is no order of events in themselves which do, or do not, have a significance of their own. Only what is incorporated into a specific whole has a meaning, and its meaning is nothing other than its contribution to that whole. How the value of that whole is to be in turn established is a question as difficult to answer as it is independent of the view of interpretation put forward here.

NOTES

1. *Ed. note*—Translations of Nietzsche are drawn from Hollingdale's *HL*; Kaufmann and Hollingdale's *GM*; and Kaufmann's *BGE* and *Z*.

2. I have made an argument for this claim in my essay, "Writer, Text, Work, Author," in *Literature and the Question of Philosophy*, ed. Anthony J. Cascardi (Baltimore: Johns Hopkins University Press, 1987), 267–91.

3. Arthur C. Danto, "Some Remarks on *The Genealogy of Morals*," *International Studies in Philosophy* 18 (1986): 13.

4. This is the central thesis of my *Nietzsche: Life as Literature* (Cambridge, MA: Harvard University Press, 1985).

5. An interesting connection between Nietzsche's and Franz Overbeck's attitude toward this issue is established in Lionel Gossman's "Antimodernism in Nineteenth-Century Basle," *Interpretation* 16 (1989): 359–89.

4

Nietzsche's Style of Affirmation
The Metaphors of Genealogy*

Eric Blondel

Nietzsche strives at turning language out of itself, so to speak, at making it point and return to its origin or source: the *reality* of life and particularly the *body*. This double movement or trend accounts for his strategy of an indirect, metaphorical affirmation of the body, in opposition to its denial (e.g., as in Christian morality) and to its direct, intuitive extralinguistic affirmation (which can be no philosophical affirmation, but a mere extradiscursive, activist position or disposition). Why does Nietzsche take this impossible dilemmatic course?

Contrary to most of his great predecessors in philosophy, such as Descartes, Spinoza, or Kant, Nietzsche is extremely sensible of, not to say sensitive to polysemia, to the interpretative profundity, to the rich and creative enigma of reality, and especially of life and existence. In that sense (and this distinguishes him from Kierkegaard's insistence on the irreducibility of existence to the general concept), Nietzsche's philosophy is that of a *philologist*, that is, of someone who tends to consider reality as a text (that is to say *not* as a thing which can be intuitively or conceptually seen as it is, but as a set of rich, ambiguous, and even mysterious signs that can only be interpreted, deciphered, and construed, almost as an enigma), and who therefore never ceases to read more and more in texts. Reality, for him, means always more (and sometimes less), and otherwise than it seems: in this respect, Prince Hamlet is one of the symbolic names to which Nietzsche appeals. *But* at the same time, Nietzsche's philosophy is the philosophy of a *"misologist"* (to use Plato's famous

*Excerpted from *Nietzsche as Affirmative Thinker*, edited by Y. Yovel (The Hague: Martinus Nijhoff Publishers, 1986), 136–46. Excerpt reprinted with permission of Springer.

phrase in its original and derived sense: opposition to reason and to philology), of someone who tries to let appear the depth and profundity of what exists *outside* the texts, and thence to relate text and language to their hidden origin, to their repressed *alter* ego, to their outside, in short: who strives to relate and refer language to its body as its deeply hidden reality.[1] Here we can find the sense together with the specific dilemma of genealogy as an effort to manifest, through the language, in the language, *that* which the language, being as such metaphysical, tends to hide and deny, and to let the body appear or loom out, whereas the body (taken as an origin of meaning, and of course not as the plain physical, material object) manifests itself *only by signs*.[2] This is what Nietzsche has in mind when he says that we ought not to take morality at its face value, "word for word," for what it expressly says (*wörtlich*), and describes it on the contrary as a "*Semiotik*," a "*Zeichenrede*," a "*Symptomatologie*" that "reveals the most valuable realities of cultures and inner beings who *knew* too little about themselves."[3]

Here it should be pointed out that, in saying this, Nietzsche cuts himself off from two opposite assertions, from which two types of possible affirmation could have been derived: (1) that language can *be* or express directly and fully the reality (e.g., of the body): it is only a set of *signs* (*against idealism* of language and of philologists, who tend to see language and texts as realities in themselves); and (2) that the body, or ultimately reality, can be *intuitively* seen, directly looked into, known as it is, without the medium of signs and language (*against dogmatic realism*).[4]

In order to illustrate the double and self-contradictory task of genealogy as a kind of philology and physiology, Nietzsche uses three series or sets of very coherent and self-sufficient metaphors:[5] (1) reading (philology); (2) hearing; and (3) smelling. They aim at showing how an *immaterial* set of signs (words, texts, sounds, smells) brings out and betrays the hidden, indirect, or distant presence of a *material* origin. That is the way in which Nietzsche's metaphorics of genealogy tend toward what I would call an *indirect referential insistence*.

SOME MAIN ASPECTS OF
THESE METAPHORICAL SETS

Reading (Philology)[6]

Nietzsche presents himself very often as a philologist (from *WPh* to *BGE* 22, for instance) and it is as such that he describes himself as a genealogist or, to use another term commonly used by him as an equivalent, as a psychologist and *Rattenfänger* (*TI* P; *BGE* 295). This self-description must be taken literally. It first means that Nietzsche, as a philologist, turns his genealogical object, culture (morality, metaphysics, Christianity, science) into a *text*, or sees it as a text that he has to read, decipher, construe, and handle critically. Second, the text of decadent culture appears to him in this respect as a defective one, as a text full of absurdities, contradictions, misunderstandings, and wrong construings (*Widersinn, Missverständnis*), a text that interprets reality falsely or denies it by inventing a host of fictitious notions (*falsche Übersetzung, Mangel an Philologie*, etc.). Thus Christianity invents (*erfindet*) beings that do not exist (*A* 15); translates reality into a false, incorrect, religious language (*A* 26); is a false *interpretation* of reality and texts, even of the Bible itself (*D* 84, *A* 52). This is not only obvious from the philological terms that Nietzsche uses to discard these interpretations and denials of reality through a false language, but also in his *constant* use of quotation marks (*Gänsefüsschen*) whenever he quotes critically or has to make use himself (in another meaning) of any piece of the moral, metaphysical, or religious vocabulary: "soul," "self," "spirit," "God," "Christian," "remorse," "free will," "sin," "nature," "world," "eternal life," "Last Judgment," and so on, and even, what is still more interesting, "truth," "being," "cause and effect," "will," and so on (see for instance *A* 15, 16, 52, and everywhere in the posthumous papers and *WP*). On the contrary, Nietzsche claims that one should distinguish the real text from its interpretations and respect the rules of "philology," that is, of "honesty" (*Rechtschaffenheit*). He therefore presents himself as a good reader and philologist of texts and of reality (as text), and, what is more, as a good translator, not only of reality but of the incorrect moral texts into their right terms (cf. *BGE* 230 and the very common phrases such as "As *I* would say," "in my own language," "*auf Deutsch*," and the like).[7] It is along this line that Nietzsche practices or reformulates genealogy as an etymologist (see *GM* I, and especially his explicit linguistic and etymological question in the final remark at the end of the first Essay) and refers it to interpretation and grand style.

Now it appears that, if Nietzsche's philology implies a *formal* aspect as regards his criticism of the "moral" language, it also, and perhaps primarily, has a *referential* intention, insofar as it tries to display, *in* the language and the text, precisely that which refers to their *physiological* origin (style: see *BGE* 246, 247; *EH* "Books," esp. 4; *TI* "Ancients") or to their *history* (etymology, history of language, translation: *GM* I), that is to say, generally speaking, to their "outside." Thus it is literally true that "in my writings a psychologist speaks" (*EH* "Books" 5). In that respect, genealogy should be in the first place a kind of stylistics, according to the following principles of style: "The important thing is *life*: style ought to *live*. Style must prove that one *believes* in one's thoughts, and not merely *thinks* his thoughts but *feels* them" (*KSA* 10:1[109].1 and 7).

Reading-Listening[8]

That the style of a text reveals something of the body and instincts appears more clearly from the metaphors that Nietzsche links with philology. Reading, according to Nietzsche, should not be understood as simply understanding thoughts and meanings, but also as *hearing* the physical and physiological conditions in which a number of sentences are written, articulated, and spoken out (see again *BGE* 246, 247). In the preface of *Twilight of the Idols*, Nietzsche refers to his philosophy as an auscultation and sounding (*Aushorchen*), and talks about his "wicked ear" (*böses*

Ohr). I want to stress in the first place that this substitution of the sense of hearing for the sense of sight is perfectly consistent with the image of twilight in the title, which suggests the fading out of Truth and Being as light in the philosophical tradition (Plato's Cave, the light of the world in the Gospel, Descartes's description of God at the end of the Third Meditation) and the correlative disparagement of knowledge described as vision (*eidos, évidence, theoria*, intuition are all terms that relate to the sense of sight and imply light [God] as their cause). What does Nietzsche do instead? Since night has come, his genealogical method cannot rely on the sense of sight, but must have recourse to the sense of hearing.

But what is the result of this new type of method? Provided one "has a second pair of ears,"[9] one can guess the nature or the condition of the body that resounds, and "hear that famous hollow sound which betrays something of flatulent bowels" (*TI* P). In that case, the philologist is therefore an acoustician, a musicologist as well as a physiologist. Whereas most metaphysicians are deaf (*TI* "Skirmishes" 26), the genealogist, like Nietzsche, is musical, for he perceives what is unheard (*Unerhörtes*) or almost inaudible for common ears, even "events which creep on with dove feet" (*Z*; see also *GM* I:14 and *BGE* 10), even the meaning of "silent events" and the imperceptible difference between the affirmative "*Ja*" and the donkey's submissive "*I-A*," between "*gerecht*" (just) and "*gerächt*" (avenged) (*Z*).

This also implies that the philologist-genealogist is a phonologist and physicist: a sound is a sensation produced in the ears by the vibrations of air caused by the movements of a *living* or inanimate body; it is uttered by a chest, a tongue, a throat, lips, or sent out by any object that is hit or set in movement. Any sound therefore reveals the quality, nature, and physical condition of that which sends it out: what we call its *tempo* (a frequent word in Nietzsche's texts) and its ring (*Klangfarbe*) betrays the physical state of its origin: bronze, wood, steel, stone, and the like; hollow or full, ill or sound, solid or cracked, and so on.

Last, this set of metaphors accounts for the real function of the "philosophizing with the hammer": the latter is but seldom and secondarily a sledge-hammer or any such instrument used to destroy or break (and sculpt), but a "music" instrument, a *Stimmhammer* (tuning hammer), compared with a *Stimmgabel* (tuning-fork), a piano hammer, a medical sounding-hammer (for percussion of the body), or a metallurgic instrument (test hammer or jeweller's hammer). It should help the genealogist to "oblige to talk out that which precisely wishes to remain quiet" (*TI* P).[10]

Through sound, the body as a *physical* being is affirmed by Nietzsche.

Smelling[11]

But if we now turn to the set of metaphors of smelling, which Nietzsche frequently uses to describe the method of genealogy, we find that they not only intend to insist on the relation of the symptom to a hidden or distant body (as can be the case for both sound and smell, but remarkably *not* for sight, which is again instructive), but this time also point out the *physiological* nature of the *living* body (*Leib* as opposed to the general *Körper*). *"Ich höre und rieche es,"* I hear and smell it (*Z* III "On Apostates" 2): hearing and smelling means to guess something of the living body, although it is not exposed to the sight, although it is hidden, distant, obscure, and deep—unconscious. The genealogist, like the psychoanalyst (as Freud explicitly says) should have a fine sense of smell (or nosing out: *Witterung*): "What fine instruments of observation we have with our senses! The nose, for instance, which no philosopher ever spoke of with respect and gratitude, is even, in the meantime, the most delicate instrument we dispose of: it is able to ascertain infinitesimal differences of movement which the spectroscope itself is not even sensitive to" (*TI* "Reason" 3).

Just a few examples here: we may call to mind Nietzsche's insistence on the bad smell of churches and of the New Testament (*GM* III:22; *TI* "Improvers" 3), on the *Stubenrauch* of Christian life (*A* 52), on the confined, sickly, and stinking atmosphere of the idealistic "den" (*GM* I:14)—and, on the contrary, Nietzsche's desire and longing for fresh air, windy places (the mistral), pure air of the high icy mountains where ideals are "deep-frozen" (*EH* P 3 and *EH* "Books" HH 1).

This valuation of the sense of smell should remind us that genealogy is in the final account anti-idealistic, medical, and "medicynical," that even in the "pure" would-be disincarnate ideal, we can smell out the carefully hidden traces of a diseased body, or traces simply of blood, breath, bowels, and matter of a living and sensible body.[12]

The otorhinological, so to speak, genealogy in Nietzsche is thus a derivation from philology to physiology and indicates a referential insistence, an indirect affirmation of the body. Hence the question asked by Nietzsche in *Ecce Homo*: "Why philologist and not rather medical doctor?"[13] takes its real and full meaning. Since the body cannot be a simply somatic, mechanical, physical thing, distinct from the "soul" (*psyche*), as in the dualistic view, but a "psychosomatic" whole (*grosse Vernunft*), *what* is indeed that body that Nietzsche thus affirms indirectly, negatively, when he genealogically points at its transcriptions in the text of ideals?

THE METAPHORICAL AFFIRMATION OF THE BODY

Unexpectedly, though in fact explicably, Nietzsche gives no positive and conceptual physiological doctrine of the body as a counterpart to his genealogical criticism of idealism and as a foundation for his genealogy leading indirectly to an ontological affirmation. Nietzsche affirms the body, he holds that the body *is* the reality of ideals: but *how* is it so, and *what* is it, *what* is thus *affirmed*, which could play the role, either of Being (*eidos*, substance, *hypokeimenon*, subject, self, will, God, and so forth), or at least of a transcendental constitutive point of will to power, and thus replace, in Nietzsche's thought, the dead "God" (whether it were essential or substantial Being or any kind of *ego cogito, ich denke*, and the like)?

To put it briefly: it looks as if Nietzsche left us at a loss in this respect, for he eventually leads us not to a definition and description of the body, but to the ultimate notion of interpretation, in the sense that (1) the body in the end is an interpretative constellation (naturally as far as meaning and knowledge of "being" is concerned, the body as an "object" to which genealogy refers, as its "*Leitfaden*"); and (2) interpretation itself is not otherwise described than through metaphors of the body.

I will just sketch here how Nietzsche has recourse to another set of metaphors in order to describe the body (*Leib*).

Digestion

What is the body? Since Nietzsche views it as an inseparably psychic *and* somatic whole, he describes it in terms of drives (*Triebe*), which unceasingly try to increase their own power and to absorb or digest each other. This first range of digestive metaphors is very common and constant in Nietzsche's texts, from, namely, *Daybreak* 109 and 119 down to *On the Genealogy of Morals* II:1[14] and the posthumous papers until 1888: *Assimilation, Einverleibung, Ernährung, hineinnehmen, Verdauen, fertig werden, Durchfallen, Appetit, hinunterschlucken* (*EH* "Books"; *CW* 1). There are hundreds of passages in the texts where Nietzsche describes the mutual relations of the *Triebe* in the "body" (as *Selbst*, as a *grosse Vernunft*) in terms of nutrition, swallowing, digestion, elimination, rejection—a set of metaphors that is extended to the whole kingdom of life and to culture as a struggle for domination between forces. The sense of this is that power tends to reduce plurality and diversity to sameness and unity (*assimilation* as *ad simile reductio*).

Politics

But how does this assimilation proceed? As before, we can see that another set of metaphors relays the former in order to interpret it (what I call a process of concatenation-transference). We ought to pay attention to this mode of interpretative explanation of the description, since it warns us that Nietzsche is quite conscious of giving no descriptively explanatory definition, but seems to imply that the body can *only* be described in terms of interpretative metaphors, that is, only interpreted "Auslegung, *nicht* Erklärung," interpretation, *not* explanation.[15] In the present case, the relaying set of metaphors is politics, which tends to show how and according to which rules the drives fight, absorb, and reject each other. One of the most typical texts in this respect is to be found in 599 of volume 13 in the Kröner edition (*KSA* 11: 37[4]), in which Nietzsche compares the conscious self with the stomach and describes the "body" as a plurality of "*Bewusstein*" (consciousness) to be compared with a political society: a reigning collectivity, an aristocracy, where the conscious selves in turn obey and command, elect a dictator, constitute a regency council, and so on. The "body" is a stomach, which could be in its turn compared with a political collectivity: how is the self to make *one* will from a *plurality* of voices, in a body that Nietzsche elsewhere describes as "a herd and shepherd"?

Philology

But this metaphorical description needs again to be interpreted. How do the selves choose, elect, command over each other? "Every one of these voluntary actions implies, so to speak, the election of a dictator. But that which offers this choice to our intellect, which has previously simplified, equalized, interpreted (*ausgelegt*) these experiences, is not that very intellect [. . .]. This choice [is] a way of abstracting and grouping, a *translation* (*Zurückübersetzung*) of a will" (ibid.).[16] We have therefore but signs of the body as a kind of text that we see on the *conscious* level as arranged, simplified, falsified, translated, abbreviated: in short, interpreted. The body "is" a world of signs—or at least we can only see it as such, because commanding is "a way to take possession of facts by signs," to "abbreviate," to "master by means of signs" (ibid.). Commanding (and what else do the wills to power inside the body do?) is interpreting: therefore, the body, as will to power, a stomach, a fighting-place "is" that which interprets signs.

Here we find ourselves eventually brought back to our initial philology metaphor. This means first that the body cannot be strictly defined in terms of explanation, of mechanism, or as any sort of substance (and we have seen that Freud has to deal with the same problem when he tries to define and describe the unconscious—a notion very closely akin to Nietzsche's conception of the body as mostly unconscious and instinctive "great reason").

In the second place, it should be emphasized that this antisubstantialist description precludes any temptation to biologize Nietzsche, as was often done in early interpretations of his thought.

Now, without entering further into the difficult questions implied by my second remark ([2] above), saying that interpretation is never explicitly defined by Nietzsche, but only "described" again by metaphors (and so, in a circular way, interpreting is like digesting—the famous "ruminating"—like fighting, choosing, simplifying, multiplying, and so on), I would just like to state a few points about the initial question of affirmation.[17]

(1) Nietzsche *affirms indirectly* insofar as he reveals the will to power of the body as the hidden principle of the ideals (genealogy) and refuses its denial in idealistic culture (morality, religion, metaphysics).

(2) But, first, *what* does Nietzsche affirm? Not the body as an assignable and definable essence, or being, but as the central (?), fundamental (?), and anyway *plural* location of interpretation. No *ego cogito*–rather a *cogitatur*, as Nietzsche suggests in a fragment (Kröner, XIV, 7, see *WP* 484)—no originally synthetic unity of apperception, but a multiple center of interpretation of reality, a reality that, however, cannot be taken hold of and apprehended as a substance, but only through it, and perhaps is partly made up by the body. Nietzsche thus is *displacing* the affirmation.

Second, *how* does he affirm? Since the body is, as a multiple center, essentially hidden, distant (hearing and smell), this "great reason," this interpretative reality cannot be explained but by signs, that is, metaphorically, in a displaced way. In that sense, Nietzsche is a *displaced* (and displacing) thinker, a thinker of signs, and not of a real "Being" that could be in the end unified, totalized, and equalized. Now, at this point, the question may be asked whether this is not a failure on his part: to which it might be also answered that this kind of failure is the condition *sine qua non* of his nonmetaphysical affirmation and taking into account of the body and, through it, of a richer affirmation of Being, of the metaphorical power of life than had ever been the case in the rationalist tradition of metaphysicians, "those albinos of concept," as he calls them. Or, in other words, Nietzsche's final lesson might be that thought *has* to fail, in a certain way, when confronting life and the body (which is also, though differently, Kierkegaard's and Freud's lesson, if one takes their mistrust toward philosophy and metaphysics into account).

But Nietzsche's own original metaphoric way is also instructive as such, philosophically speaking—for he never gives up philosophy. Between the *negation* of the real body in idealism and the realistic *affirmation* of Being (Will, Body . . .)[18] leading to an eventually entropic activism, Nietzsche seems to affirm that, for us, what should be *affirmed* can be neither a substantial Being (to be ultimately known), nor sheer nothingness, but, taking the word in its literal sense, "*Selbstüberwindung*," an overcoming of identity and sameness (*selbst*), an interpretative meta-phor (transference), a dis-placement (*Übertragung*) of Being opening on into a world of signs. Nietzsche writes: "'Truth' is therefore not something there, that might be found or discovered—but something that must be created and that gives a name to a process, or rather to a will to overcome that has in itself no end—Introducing truth as a *processus in infinitum*, an active determining—not a becoming-conscious of something that is in itself firm and determined. It is a word for the 'will to power.'"[19] "Truth" (and "Being") therefore differ from themselves: whereas, in Hegel, Time was that which made Being and Truth unequal to their own substance, I would suggest that, in Nietzsche's conception, it is the sign, that is, signification, interpretation. Reality, for Nietzsche, *is* not, it signifies (itself). So, God is dead, but Nietzsche believes in signification: only it is lost and even wasted in the empty space, since God is missing: "There are far more languages than one thinks; and man betrays himself far more often than he would wish to. Everything speaks [*Alles redet*]! But very few are those who can listen, so that man, as it were, pours his confessions out into the empty space; he lavishes his own 'truths' as the sun lavishes its light. Isn't it a pity that the empty space has no ears?"[20] Ambiguity, obscurity, but also richness and infinite plurality of signs therefore replace the stability and transparent unity of Being. Hence: "Interpretation, *not* explanation. There is no state of things, everything is fluent, incomprehensible, receding. What is most durable in the end: our opinions. To project sense into things (*Sinn-hineinlegen*)—in most cases a new interpretation thrown over an old one that has become unintelligible, that is itself now only a sign" (*KSA* 12:2[82]).

Such a kind of "Truth" and of "Being," as we suspected from the beginning, cannot properly be *affirmed*, that is to say "solidified," "made firm," considered as a "firm" object (*ad-firmare*), that is, seen, handled, and finally grabbed. To a "text," to an interpretation, to a world of signs that is continually "in the making," one can only, as Nietzsche puts it quite precisely and coherently, "*say* 'yes' ": "*Ja sagen.*"

NOTES

Editor's Note: Blondel's references have been modified to follow the style of the volume, and his references to *KGW* have been converted to *KSA*.

1. The same problem occurs in psychoanalysis as an attempt to fill in the gap between the unconscious *Trieb* (originating in the body, properly the *libido* in its Latin psychophysiological meaning) and the conscious language of the patient talking out his psychic representations. To put it in a short formula: how should one relate the conscious *Liebe* to the unconscious *libido*? Similarly, to use a fashionable phrase (which designates but does not explain), Nietzsche's genealogy (or "psychology") originates in a "psychosomatic" philosophy—or how to know something of the Unknown.

2. As a philosopher, Nietzsche seems to consider that there is nothing to *say* about the "real" existence of the body in itself, apart from language. It apparently can only be felt or lived, and manifests itself in the blank spaces separating Nietzsche's aphorisms.

3. *TI* "Improvers" 1. *Ed.*—All the quotations of Nietzsche in English are Blondel's translation, unless otherwise stated.

4. I tried to develop this at more length in my Thèse de doctorat: *Nietzsche, le corps et la culture*, and suggested that this double opposition could be described analogically as a kind of Copernican philological revolution (the body *is* in itself, but can be only *known* as speech—*Erscheinung*), which relates Nietzsche both to Schopenhauer's realism (will to life as body) and to Kant's transcendentalism (philologically reinterpreted).

5. Since I cannot give here a sufficient number of examples, I must insist that this coherence should rest on a number of samples from Nietzsche's texts, and not only, as is often the case, on the extrapolation from such and such an isolated passage by the unbridled phantasies of the reader himself, or on the misconstruing of German idiomatic phrases into specific and original Nietzschean metaphors. See Richard Roos, "Régles pour une lecture philologique de Nietzsche," in *Nietzsche aujord' hui?* (Paris: Union générale d'édition "10/18," 1973), vol. II.

6. For further detail, see my "Les guillemets de Nietzsche," in *Nietzsche aujourd' hui?*

7. See also: "My task is to translate the apparently emancipated and denatured moral values back into their nature—i.e., into their natural 'immorality' " (*WP* 229; Kaufmann trans.).

8. I dealt with these themes more at length in my "Götzen aushorchen," in *Perspektiven der Philosophie* 7 (1981) (repr. in *Nietzsche Kontrovers*, I, Würzburg: Königshausen & Neumann, 1981), which is mainly a detailed commentary upon the metaphors to be found in the preface of *TI*. See also my translation and commentary of the same book, *Crépuscule des idoles* (Paris: Hatier, 1983).

9. "*Ohren hinter den Ohren*," or "a third ear," as Nietzsche writes in *BGE* 246, and as psychoanalyst Theodor Reik not surprisingly entitled his book: *Listening with the Third Ear* (New York: Grove Press, 1948).

10. This conception of the idols is reminiscent of the biblical description of the idols as "dumb." It has been remarked that Luther's translation of the Bible insists more particularly

upon the acoustic and olfactive images than on the visual ones (L. Febvre). The same applies to Nietzsche, a regular Bible reader.

11. More about this range of images is in my Thése de doctorat, *Nietzsche, le corps et la culture* (Paris: PUF, 1986). [*Ed.*—Published in English as *Nietzsche: The Body and Culture*, translated by Sean Hand (Berkeley, CA: Stanford University Press, 1991.]

12. Gaston Bachelard, who beautifully analyzed these metaphors of air in Nietzsche's works, does *not* relate them to their genealogical, bodily origin (*L'Air et les Songes* [Paris: Librarie José Corti, 1943], chap. V). Nonetheless, he rightly stresses the metaphorical unity of Nietzsche's thought "*as a poet*," in a true antidualistic insight.

13. *EH* "Clever" 2. See particularly the details Nietzsche gives in this latter book, chap. 2, about his regime and his numerous "medicynical" remarks: most of them refer to a smelling body: "All prejudices arise from the bowels," "German spirit arises from disturbed bowels, and the like. Incidentally, he writes there that all places fit for geniuses have a remarkably dry *air*, and quotes some famous towns: he is right about Jerusalem, *not* about Paris!

14. Many of these images are in fact borrowed from Schopenhauer, *World as Will and Representation*, Supplements to Book I, chap. 14, *in fine*.

15. *KSA* 12: 2[82], 2[78], 2[86]; see also *WP* 492. This should be compared with the similar problem of the "description" of the unconscious by Freud: we eventually *can* have nothing more than a metaphorical insight, that is, an interpretation of it (or else, would it be unconscious?). Freud has recourse to the metaphors of hydraulics, of war, of a boiler and, once, of the . . . stomach (*New Introductory Lectures on Psychoanalysis*, chap. IV). [*Ed.*—In Blondel's second reference (2[78]), the text reads "Ausdeutung, nicht Erklärung." "Ausleg-ung, nicht Erklärung" also appears in a list of prospective chapter titles at 12:5[50].]

16. We can find the same interpretative concatenation of metaphors in *WP* 492 (*KSA* 11:40[21]).

17. *Ed.*—This essay was originally published in a collection of conference proceedings on "Nietzsche and the Affirmative."

18. As for instance in Schopenhauer's thought.

19. *WP* 552, Kaufmann trans. (*KSA* 12:9[91].65) Notice here the quotation marks!

20. Kröner *Grossoktavausgabe, XIII*, 363. *Ed.*—Cf. *KSA* 10:18[34].

5

Nietzsche and the Re-evaluation of Values*

Aaron Ridley

Toward the end of his effective life, Nietzsche repeatedly claimed that what was really needed was a "re-evaluation of values."[1] In the preface to the *Genealogy*, he describes this as a "*new demand*: we need a *critique* of [existing] values": "*the value of these values must . . . be called into question*";[2] and in the foreword to *Twilight of the Idols*, he identifies *The Anti-Christ* as the first of a projected four-volume set to be called "The Re-evaluation of All Values"—a project that he never completed, and may indeed have abandoned, given that *The Anti-Christ*, itself originally to have been subtitled "The Re-evaluation of All Values," was published in the event with the more succinct byline "A Curse on Christianity." But it would be a mistake to think that Nietzsche never got round to his re-evaluation project, since, in one way or another, and as many commentators have observed, all of his published works are plausibly to be understood as contributions to it. So what *is* it to re-evaluate values? And what might Nietzsche's practice of re-evaluation have to tell us about the value of our existing values?

THE AUTHORITY PROBLEM

The second of these questions has often been answered in the following way. The re-evaluation of values, it is said, can only be undertaken from some evaluative standpoint or other; in order to be authoritative, that standpoint itself must be

*This chapter was edited by the author after its original publication in *Proceedings of the Aristotelian Society* 105 (2005), 171–91. Reprinted by courtesy of the Editor of the Aristotelian Society, copyright 2005.

somehow immune to re-evaluation (or at any rate to devaluation); Nietzsche, however, gives us no reason to think that his own evaluative standpoint is immune to
re-evaluation in the relevant way; therefore the only thing that Nietzsche's re-evaluation can tell us about the value of our existing values is how they look from the
perspective of his own preferred values, values whose superiority he merely asserts,
rather than defends or demonstrates. Therefore, if we are comfortable with our existing values, and with our existing evaluations of them, there can be nothing in what
Nietzsche says to cause us much anxiety; for at bottom, the answer concludes, we
might just disagree with him about which evaluative standpoint is best. Nietzsche's
evaluative standpoint, and the re-evaluation that he undertakes from it, need have
no authority for us. This response, or objection, deserves to be treated seriously, I
think; and, in trying to say what I take Nietzsche's re-evaluation of values to be, I
shall be trying, inter alia, to assess the strength of that objection, and to assess Nietzsche's resources for dealing with it.

TYPES OF VALUE

First, though, some preliminary remarks about Nietzsche's conception of value. He
rejects as incoherent the notion of unconditional value, a notion to which he thinks
philosophers have been unduly attached (e.g., *DGL* 2). A value, V, is unconditional,
in Nietzsche's sense, if (1) the value of V is not conditional upon any other value;
(2) the value of V is not conditional upon any contingent matter of fact; (3) the
value of V is not relational—its value is, as it is sometimes put, "absolute"; (4) V
has the value it has necessarily: it is valuable "in itself"; and (5) V cannot be defeated
by any other value. To describe something as unconditionally valuable, then, is to
say that it is valuable no matter what; that its value in this world is wholly independent of any other values or of any fact or facts that are or might be peculiar to this
world; that it is valuable, and valuable absolutely, *whatever else is or might be the case.*
It is this conception of value that Nietzsche rejects as incoherent—and with some
reason. I won't review his arguments here, but will simply note that, according to
the conception of value that he rejects, any V that is unconditionally valuable would
be valuable even in a world in which all valuing beings were united in their denial
of, or in their obliviousness to, the value of V, and indeed in a world in which there
were no valuing beings at all. I take it that the claim that such a conception is incoherent is at least plausible. Two further points should be made. First, if no values are
unconditionally valuable, no values are immune to re-evaluation—and that includes
Nietzsche's own values, from the standpoint of which his own efforts at re-evaluation are undertaken. This sharpens the question about the authority of Nietzsche's
project that I mentioned a moment ago. And second, the fact that all values are in
some sense only conditionally valuable doesn't by itself mean that no values are or
can be objectively valuable, in a perfectly straightforward sense of "objectively."[3]

The notion of objectivity does not depend for its sense, that is, on the notion of unconditionality. Nietzsche accepts, and indeed emphasizes, both of these points.

How, then, does Nietzsche understand the (conditional) value of values? The answer is that he understands it in either of two ways: as instrumentally valuable or as intrinsically valuable.[4] Something has *direct instrumental value*, I shall say, if its value resides chiefly in its being a means toward some kind of (valuable) end. So, for example, from an act utilitarian perspective, my keeping some particular promise is instrumentally valuable if, and only if, it directly increases utility. Something has *indirect instrumental value*, by contrast, if its value resides chiefly in its promoting or making more likely the realization of some kind of (valuable) end, even though it does not function directly as a means to that end. So, for instance, from a rule utilitarian perspective, the keeping of promises in general may be instrumentally valuable if it tends to promote utility, even if some particular instances of promise-keeping do not promote it, and even if no instance of promise-keeping is undertaken with the end of utility in mind. Instrumental value, whether direct or indirect, is thus conditional upon the fact of ends that are themselves valuable. Such ends are treated by Nietzsche as intrinsically valuable, where something has *intrinsic value* if, given what else is the case, its value does not reside chiefly in its being a means or an enabling factor toward some further kind of (valuable) end. Intrinsic value is thus conditional upon facts—natural, social, practical, or cultural—that are or might be peculiar to particular ways of living, as well as (often) upon the relations of the value in question to the other values having a place in some particular way of life.[5] The point can also be put like this. A value is intrinsically valuable with respect to a given way of living if, other things being equal, it can, by itself, *motivate*: so, for example, if the fact that such and such a course of action is an instance of promise-keeping is reason enough by itself for someone to perform it, that shows that promise-keeping is intrinsically valuable with respect to that person's way of life.[6] It should be noted that nothing in this conception of intrinsic value entails that an intrinsic value can never, under any circumstances, be trumped by another value: in principle, any intrinsic value is capable of being trumped (depending on what other things are, and aren't, equal). It is, however, this conception of the intrinsically valuable that, from a perspective deep within some particular way of living, may be, and often is, according to Nietzsche, mistaken for the unconditionally valuable (e.g., *BGE* 186). The facts and other values upon which an intrinsic value is conditional are so familiar, so taken for granted, as to have become invisible, and as they fade from sight so the conditionality of the intrinsic becomes invisible too.

A DEVELOPMENT IN NIETZSCHE'S THOUGHT

The earlier Nietzsche reassigns the value of morality as a whole from the intrinsic to the instrumental, and construes the end that it promotes in terms of survival (e.g., *HH* 40). When he deals with the individual values constitutive of morality, moreover, he tends to side explicitly with thinkers such as La Rochefoucauld, whose claim that the "virtues" are just nice-sounding names that we give to the effects of our passions, so that we can "do what we wish with impunity," he cites approvingly (*HAH* 36). At this stage in his thinking, then, Nietzsche's re-evaluations essentially consist in unmasking a value said to be intrinsic as really directly instrumental and in characterizing the end to which it is a means in some highly unflattering, and usually reductively egoistic, way. The earlier Nietzsche was thus committed to the view that there are no genuinely moral motivations at all, and that the apparently intrinsic values upon which people say that they act, or believe themselves to act, are in fact only instrumentally valuable for bringing about certain kinds of self-centered ends, those ends being the only real candidates for intrinsic value in play.

By the time of writing *Daybreak*, however, he had arrived at a considerably subtler and more interesting position. He now accepts that "moral judgments" may be "motives for action," but claims that, where they *are* the motives, "it is *errors* which, as the basis of all moral judgment, impel men to their moral actions" (*D* 103).[7] This is a subtler and more interesting position for several reasons; but the chief one for present purposes is that, in allowing for the reality of moral motivations, it also allows that, with respect to a given way of living, moral values may, genuinely, be intrinsic values, and not merely instrumental ones in disguise. And this means that the project of re-evaluation itself becomes subtler and more interesting, as the emphasis shifts from attempts to re-evaluate, as instrumental, values masquerading as intrinsic, to attempts to re-evaluate intrinsic values as, indeed, intrinsic. And the upshot of *that* process, as the same section from *D* makes clear, may not be any sort of debunking at all. Nietzsche puts it like this:

> It goes without saying that I do not deny—unless I am a fool—that many actions called immoral ought to be avoided and resisted, or that many called moral ought to be done and encouraged—but I think that one should be encouraged and the other avoided *for other reasons than hitherto*. We have to *learn to think differently*—in order at last, perhaps very late on, to attain even more: *to feel differently*. (*D* 108)

Here, then, Nietzsche presents the project of re-evaluation as a critique of the structure of reasons immanent to a given way of living, a structure that the values intrinsic with respect to that way of living hold in place. And that, evidently enough, is a very different project from La Rochefoucauld's.

THE RE-EVALUATION OF INTRINSIC VALUES

So what might a re-evaluation of intrinsic values (as intrinsic) involve? One essential prerequisite, clearly enough, is the adoption of a degree of distance from the way of living whose values are under scrutiny. And the degree at issue may vary between cases. So, for instance, for certain kinds of re-evaluation, the values drawn upon in the re-evaluation may be internal to the same way of living as the value under scrutiny: in which case, while it is certainly true that a degree of reflective distance is essential, there is no need to treat the value under scrutiny as anything other than intrinsic, purely and simply. In other cases, where the values drawn upon in the re-evaluation are not, or may not be, internal to the same way of living as the value under scrutiny, a longer reflective step back may be required, perhaps to a perspective from which the value under scrutiny can be acknowledged as intrinsically valuable to a given way of living, but can at the same time be evaluated for its *effects*, for its indirectly instrumental tendencies, in terms that may or may not be internal to the way of living in question. With this in mind, I think that there are at least five ways in which one might attempt to pursue the project of re-evaluating intrinsic values (as intrinsic); and of these, at least four can be discerned in Nietzsche's writings. The five ways can be summarized as follows:

1. Showing that V, although an intrinsic value, is indirectly instrumental in realizing ends said to be bad, although not ends that could be acknowledged as "bad" from the standpoint of the relevant way of living.
2. Showing that V, although an intrinsic value, is indirectly instrumental in realizing a good end from the standpoint of the relevant way of living.
3. Showing that V is indeed an intrinsic value for a given way of living, but not one held in place by the reasons or other values that are usually supposed.
4. Showing that V is indeed an intrinsic value, but is held in place by reasons or other values that, from the standpoint of the relevant way of living, are bad.
5. Showing that V, although an intrinsic value, or a set of intrinsic values, is indirectly instrumental in realizing ends that can, in principle, be grasped as bad from the standpoint of the relevant way of living.

It may seem as if a sixth permutation is missing, namely, showing that V is indeed an intrinsic value, but is held in place by reasons and other values that are bad, although not by reasons and values that could be acknowledged as "bad" from the standpoint of the relevant way of living. This permutation, however, although formally distinct from the first kind of re-evaluation, is always likely in practice to collapse into it, since the badness of the reasons and other values holding V in place is largely going to show up via a critique of the *effects* of those reasons and values playing the role that they do in the context of some particular way of living. Given which, therefore, this form of re-evaluation slides into the re-evaluation of an intrinsic value as indirectly instrumental in realizing ends that, from a perspective excluded by the way of living in question, are said to be bad, that is, into 1.[8]

THE FIRST FORM OF RE-EVALUATION

The first form of re-evaluation is rather radical in intent, and is also the one with which Nietzsche is, I think, most usually identified. Brian Leiter, for example, regards re-evaluation of this form as the "core" of Nietzsche's critique of traditional morality: "What unifies Nietzsche's seemingly disparate critical remarks," he says, "—about altruism, happiness, pity, equality, Kantian respect for persons, utilitarianism, etc.—is that he thinks a culture in which such norms prevail as morality will be a culture which eliminates the conditions for the realization of human excellence," where "human excellence or human greatness" is what has "*intrinsic* value for Nietzsche."[9] From this point of view, Nietzsche's style of re-evaluation consists in showing that a value such as, for instance, altruism, although perhaps an intrinsic value from the standpoint of traditional morality, is indirectly instrumental in suppressing higher types of human being (or of suppressing "ascending" or "healthier" types of life), and is therefore, from Nietzsche's own evaluative standpoint, a bad thing; whereas from the standpoint of traditional morality, on the other hand, with its emphasis on values such as equality, such an outcome can only be regarded as welcome. (Leiter sometimes speaks as if traditional morality in fact *aims* at the suppression of higher types—as if, in other words, its values were *directly* instrumental in bringing about that end, a claim that he describes as Nietzsche's "Callicleanism."[10] But this claim, if it reflects Nietzsche's view at all, does so—at most—only when he is describing the inception of the values of traditional morality (e.g., *GM* I:14); it altogether bypasses his recognition in *Daybreak*, noted above, of the reality of moral motivations once those values have become culturally established.[11]

To attribute this form of re-evaluation to Nietzsche is to raise, in a very acute way, the authority problem that I mentioned at the outset. From the perspective of traditional morality itself, after all, it is hardly much of an objection to a given value that it indirectly inhibits the emergence of types who, from that perspective, are a bad thing, however much *Nietzsche* might insist that the types so inhibited are higher and healthier. Indeed, from the traditional perspective, this form of re-evaluation—if it isn't just discounted outright—is altogether more likely to look like an inadvertent demonstration that a certain kind of fringe benefit attends the intrinsic values apparently under attack—to look, in other words, like an accidental version of 2. There is no common ground here, and, without it, the whole re-evaluation project threatens to collapse into a mere series of disagreements about preferences. Leiter recognizes this problem, and seeks to address it by limiting Nietzsche's proper audience "to those who share Nietzsche's evaluative taste, those for whom no justification would be required: those who are simply 'made for it,' who are 'predisposed and predestined' for Nietzsche's insights."[12] The point of Nietzsche's re-evaluation, then, is simply to "alert 'higher' types to the fact that" traditional morality "is not, in fact, conducive to their flourishing," so that they can wean themselves away from its values and realize their potential for human excellence.[13] The authority problem is thus removed by restricting Nietzsche's audience to those for whom his re-evaluations *do* have authority.

This strikes me as a somewhat desperate tactic. It is also a tactic that collapses, at once, in the light of what Leiter goes on to say next, about the temperature of some of Nietzsche's rhetoric: "Given, then, that Nietzsche's target is a certain sort of misunderstanding on the part of higher men, and given the difficulty of supplanting the norms that figure in this misunderstanding (the norms of morality [in the pejorative sense]), it should be unsurprising that Nietzsche writes with passion and force: he must shake higher types out of their intuitive commitment to the moral traditions of two millennia!"[14]—which rather indicates that the members of Nietzsche's "proper" audience are not "predisposed" to accept the authority of his evaluative standpoint after all. The fact is that, even on Leiter's reading, Nietzsche needs somehow to reach inside traditional morality, and to address those who, whether through some sort of misunderstanding or not, are intuitively committed to its values; and this is hardly likely to be achieved by merely insisting, against those intuitions, that the values in question are indirectly instrumental in realizing ends said (by Nietzsche) to be bad, however heatedly he says it. The authority problem is thus reinstated, with all of its original force.

If it were true, as Leiter claims, that this form of re-evaluation is the "core" of Nietzsche's critique of traditional morality, then the outlook for that critique would be rather gloomy, it seems to me. But Leiter's claim is false: whether or not Nietzsche ever does engage in the first form of re-evaluation, it is certainly not the main plank of his approach, and it is certainly not the key to understanding Nietzsche's critical project as a whole. The re-evaluation of intrinsic values, as Nietzsche practices it, is a considerably subtler affair than Leiter acknowledges, and it revolves chiefly around the remaining four forms of re-evaluation (items 2–5 in the list above), deployed in a continually shifting range of combinations. The fact that Nietzsche hardly ever engages in only one form of re-evaluation at a time does make illustration tricky; but the following examples should be enough to indicate the kinds of distinctions that I have tried to sketch out.

THE SECOND FORM OF RE-EVALUATION

The second form of re-evaluation is, in one way, the mildest and least critique-like of them all, since its main point is, in effect, to bolster the value of a value that is intrinsic anyway. But the results of such a re-evaluation can still be surprising. The clearest instance of it, perhaps, is from the *Genealogy*, where Nietzsche argues that the ideal of the ascetic priest—which "treats life as a wrong road, . . . as a mistake" and produces "creatures filled with a profound disgust at themselves, at the earth, at all life"—is nonetheless a great preserver of life itself: indeed, as he puts it, "it must be . . . in the *interest of life itself* that such a self-contradictory type does not die out" (*GM* III:11). Nietzsche's diagnosis of this apparent contradiction is, briefly, that the ascetic ideal, in making sense of all suffering as punishment for guilt, thereby prevents the meaninglessness of suffering from functioning "as the principal argument *against* existence" (*GM* II:7). In effect, that is, existence is rendered tolerable—meaningful—precisely on the condition of the sort of self-loathing (as guilty, sinful, and the like) that the ideal produces. From the perspective of this morality, then, self-loathing is intrinsically valuable; but it is also indirectly instrumental in preserving the way of living for which it *is* intrinsically valuable; and since, from the perspective of that way of living, a life of self-loathing is the only kind of life of any value at all, that indirect effect is itself of value from that perspective. This form of re-evaluation, then, reinforces the value of an intrinsic value for a particular way of living by drawing attention to the fringe benefits that having that value has—benefits that are graspable as such from the perspective of that way of life. A contemporary example of this kind of re-evaluation might be found in a nonreductive version of evolutionary ethics—in an account that held that the regarding of such-and-such as an intrinsic value (by us, say) has, or has had, the indirectly instrumental effect of making the survival of the species more likely, a result, or fringe benefit, that we ourselves might welcome or think was a good thing.

THE THIRD FORM OF RE-EVALUATION

Nietzsche's comments about justice, in the second essay of the *Genealogy*, can be seen as an instance of the third form of re-evaluation. It is common, he thinks, to regard justice—by which he means, among other things, a legal system empowered to set and exact certain penalties—as, essentially, a formalized system of vengeance, "as if justice," he says, "were at bottom merely the further development of the feeling of being aggrieved." From this point of view, which he attributes to "anarchists," "antisemites," and the philosopher Eugen Dühring,[15] the value of justice is held in place as intrinsic by the "reactive sentiments" of those to whom an injury has been done. But this, according to Nietzsche, is the opposite of the truth: "[T]he *last* sphere to be conquered by the spirit of justice," he says, "is the sphere of the reactive feelings!" Justice, he continues, represents

> the struggle *against* the reactive feelings, the war conducted against them . . . to impose measure and bounds upon the excess of the reactive pathos and to compel it to come to terms. . . . [Indeed,] in the long run, [it] attains the reverse of that which is desired by all revenge that is fastened exclusively to the viewpoint of the person injured: from now on the eye is trained to an ever more *impersonal* evaluation of the deed, and this applies even to the eye of the injured person himself. (*GM* II:11)

On Nietzsche's view, then, justice is held in place as a value within a given "system of purposes" (*GM* II:12) precisely by the need to limit and to redirect the reactive sentiments, rather than by the need to give expression to them. And construed in this way, the value of justice, although differently grounded, remains thoroughly intrinsic, as Nietzsche makes clear: true justice, he says, constitutes "a piece of perfection and supreme mastery on earth" (*GM* II;11). In this case, then, the effect of the re-evaluation is to resituate an intrinsic value within a given structure of reasons and other values, so that, although still intrinsically valuable, it comes to be understood *as* a value in that structure "for other reasons than hitherto."

THE FOURTH FORM OF RE-EVALAUTION

The fourth form of re-evaluation can be illustrated equally quickly. Nietzsche is famously opposed to what he calls the "morality of pity," and his critique of it is complex. But one (important) aspect of his opposition emerges fairly clearly from the following two remarks from *The Gay Science*: "Pity is the most agreeable feeling," he says: it promises "easy prey—and that is what all who suffer are . . . ; [it] is enchanting" (*GS* 13); or, again, "Pity is essentially . . . an agreeable impulse of the instinct for appropriation at the sight of what is weaker" (*GS* 118). In these and other passages—examples could be given from any of his mature works—Nietzsche is drawing attention, not only to a certain opportunism in the experience of pity, but to a moment of disrespect in (many) of its instances; and he aligns that moment with another value, in this case the negative one, from the perspective of the "morality of pity," of suffering. Suffering may be useful for one, he insists; but this is

> of no concern to our dear pitying friends: they wish to *help* and have no thought of the personal necessity of distress, although terrors, deprivations, impoverishments . . . are as necessary for me and for you as are their opposites. It never occurs to them that, to put it mystically, the path to one's own heaven always leads through the voluptuousness of one's own hell. . . . [F]or happiness and unhappiness are sisters and even twins that either grow up together or, as in [their] case, *remain small* together. (*GS* 338)

Nietzsche's point, clearly enough, is that from the perspective of a way of life in which "respect," "heaven," and "happiness" are intrinsic values, and Nietzsche nowhere suggests that the "morality of pity" does not share such a perspective, "pity"—understood as the (disrespectful) obligation to alleviate suffering wherever possible—can only be held in place as an intrinsic value for bad reasons, for reasons that are bad from the perspective of that way of living itself. In this case, then, the effect of the re-evaluation is to suggest that pity, although an intrinsic value for certain ways of living, ought not to be, and ought not to be in light of other values that are themselves immanent to those ways of living.[16]

THE FIFTH FORM OF RE-EVALUATION

The fifth form of re-evaluation is a crucial and constant presence in Nietzsche's later work, although it can be difficult in practice to distinguish from the fourth form, since it is, in the end, really only a deeper version of it.[17] It differs from the fourth, however, in this much: while the fourth form of re-evaluation seeks to bring to light an internal inconsistency among values that are already, with respect to a given way of living, explicitly embraced as intrinsic, the fifth form of re-evaluation, in showing that a value or set of values is indirectly instrumental in realizing ends that could *in principle* be grasped as bad from the standpoint of the relevant way of living, seeks to bring to light an inconsistency between values that are already explicitly embraced as intrinsic and a further value that has not so far, or that has only implicitly, been so embraced, but which could or should be embraced explicitly. To the extent, then, that this latter value is already implicitly acknowledged as intrinsic with respect to the way of living in question, the fifth form of re-evaluation will tend to shade into the fourth.

When Nietzsche engages in the fifth form of re-evaluation, its basic outline shape is this. Commitment to such-and-such a value, or to such-and-such a set of values, intrinsically valuable with respect to a certain way of living, has the effect of making us obscure to ourselves, or—which is a different way of saying the same thing—has the effect of inhibiting our capacity to experience ourselves, fully, as agents; this is bad for us, and the fact that it is bad for us should, in principle, be graspable from the perspective of the way of living in question; therefore we (or they) should no longer be committed to that value, or to those values, at least as it or they have so far been understood.[18] Nietzsche's clearest employment of this form of re-evaluation is, again, to be found in the *GM*,[19] where the re-evaluation is directed, in effect, at a system of values—"slave," or traditional, morality—which is itself, according to Nietzsche, the product of a radical re-evaluation of an earlier, "noble" system of values.[20] Indeed, it is partly in proposing that, and in attempting to explain how, traditional morality *is* the product of such a re-evaluation that Nietzsche's own re-evaluation consists.

His idea is this. Prior to the "slave revolt in morality," the slave was constrained to understand and value himself exclusively through the terms set by the noble style of valuation, since that was the only style of valuation available. The nobles—seizing "the lordly right of giving names" (*GM* I:2)—had, in effect, determined the shape of the evaluative landscape, leaving the slaves, as inhabitants of it, with no option but to think of themselves as the nobles thought of them—that is, as "low, low-minded, common and plebeian," as, in a word, "bad" (*GM* I:2). Or, as Nietzsche puts it in *Beyond Good and Evil*: "the common man *was* only what he was *considered*: not at all used to positing values himself, he also attached no other value to himself than his masters attached to him (it is the characteristic *right of masters* to create values)" (*BGE* 261). In this sense, therefore, the slaves were "committed" to the values of noble morality, however much this fact might have compounded the misery attaching to their situation in any case. Specifically, their (necessary) captivity within the noble style of valuation not only provided them with no obvious resources for understanding themselves or their lives as valuable, or for understanding themselves as efficacious with respect to their own lives, it positively conspired to render any such resources invisible. Noble morality, Nietzsche claims, "acts and grows spontaneously, it seeks its opposite only so as to affirm itself more gratefully and triumphantly . . . —'we noble ones, we good, beautiful, happy ones!'" (*GM* I:10); and from the perspective of that system of values, which was also the slaves' perspective, there simply weren't the means for the slaves to attach those positive terms, and the self-understanding that went with them, to themselves.

Hence the revolt. Consumed with *ressentiment* at their position, that *ressentiment*, as Nietzsche puts it, finally turned "creative," and gave birth to a style of valuation from the perspective of which the slaves could, for the first time, affirm themselves as valuable, as effective agents, in their own right.[21] "[P]rompted by an instinct for . . . self-affirmation," the "oppressed"

> exhort one another with the vengeful cunning of impotence: "let us be different from the evil, namely good! And he is good who does not outrage, who harms nobody, who does not attack, who does not requite . . . , like us, the patient, humble, and just"—this . . . has, thanks to the counterfeit and self-deception of impotence, clad itself in the ostentatious garb of the virtue of quiet, calm resignation, just as if the weakness of the weak—that is to say, their *essence*, their effects, their sole ineluctable, irremovable reality—were a voluntary achievement, willed, chosen, a *deed*, a *meritorious* act. (*GM* I:13)

The slaves thus came to see, or to judge, that a set of values—noble values—intrinsic to a certain way of living (their own) was in fact instrumental in realizing ends that could be grasped as bad—as "evil"—from that very same standpoint, namely, the ends of denying the newly "good" ones a sense of their own efficacy and worth. Where before they had been obscure to themselves, seeing themselves only through the nobles' eyes, they now had a style of valuation that allowed them to understand themselves as their "instinct" for "self-affirmation" required them to. The values that this style of valuation answered to—the senses of efficacy and self-worth—were encoded in the noble style of valuation against which the slaves revolted, but were values to which that same style of morality denied them first-personal access. From the standpoint of that way of living, therefore, these values were, for the slaves, implicit at best.

In the first essay of the *Genealogy*, therefore, Nietzsche suggests that traditional morality arose not only from a re-evaluation of preexisting values, but from a re-evaluation of such values that depended upon those (or a subset of those) for whom the values in question were authoritative, coming to recognize that such values were, in fact, indirectly instrumental in rendering other, dimly glimpsed, values unrealizable in their own lives. The slave revolt in morality is thus offered by Nietzsche as an exercise in the fifth form of the re-evaluation of values.

In the remainder of the *Genealogy*, it is a large part of Nietzsche's concern to show that, in the wake of the death of God, the values of slave, or traditional, morality—once crucial in enabling us to understand ourselves as efficacious, as agents in our own right—now have the effect of making us obscure to ourselves, of undermining our sense of our own agency and, hence, of occluding our sense of the (potential) value of our lives. Nietzsche is insistent on these points. The "good man" of traditional morality, he says, "is neither upright nor naïve nor honest and straightforward with himself. His soul *squints*" (*GM* I:10); "one *may* not demand of [good people] that they should open their eyes to themselves, that they should know how to distinguish 'true' and 'false' in themselves. . . . [W]hoever today accounts himself a 'good man' is utterly incapable of confronting any matter except with *dishonest menda-ciousness*—a mendaciousness that is abysmal but innocent, truehearted, blue-eyed, and virtuous" (*GM* III:19). And Nietzsche contrasts the "good man" of traditional morality with the "noble man," who "lives in trust and openness with himself" (*GM* I:10) and, above all, with the *"sovereign individual"*—one

> liberated again from the morality of custom, autonomous and supramoral (for "autono-mous" and "moral" are mutually exclusive). . . . The proud awareness of the extraordi-nary privilege of *responsibility*, the consciousness of this rare freedom, this power over oneself . . . , has in his case penetrated to the profoundest depths and become instinct, the dominating instinct. (*GM* II:2)

Autonomy—which is to say, agency, the having of "power over oneself"—is thus, on this view, predicated on escaping from the self-misunderstandings engendered by traditional morality once God is dead;[22] and these self-misunderstandings, because they are "innocent" and "truehearted"—because they are based, that is, on a certain set of intrinsic values taken *as* intrinsic—may be very hard to shake free of; and this, in turn, requires that the re-evaluation of the relevant values reach *inside* traditional morality, and attempt to show from there, as it were, that those values do indeed have the effect of making us obscure to ourselves, of compromising our power over ourselves. It requires, that is, a further exercise of the fifth form of re-evaluation.[23]

If Nietzsche is right in making these claims, the current *effect* of the values of traditional morality is unquestionably an indirect one. It is also unquestionably a bad effect—not just from Nietzsche's perspective, but from the perspective, one is tempted to say, of any recognizably human way of living at all (as his account of the slave revolt in morality indicates). Self-understanding, the sense of having "power over oneself," is plausibly a value that sufficiently transcends the kinds of parochial consideration that I have concentrated upon, under the label "way of living," as to have a claim to be an intrinsic value for human beings in general. And, if so, and if it is violated—even if only instrumentally and indirectly—by some particular set of values intrinsic to some particular way of living, then that fact constitutes an effec-tive critique of those values, indeed a re-evaluation of them.

NIETZSCHE'S AUTHORITY

The fifth form of re-evaluation is probably the most important, and it is relatively easy to see how, if its critique is to be accessible to those for whom traditional moral-ity is (currently) authoritative, it is more or less bound to go together with, and to some extent to depend upon, versions of the third and fourth. It is also not very hard to see how, taken together with the second form of re-evaluation, the fifth might appear to be really a version of the first, as Brian Leiter in effect concludes—especially given that Nietzsche's "sovereign individual" is without question an exemplar of the "higher type" of human being whose interests, we can all agree, Nietzsche has at heart. But the sovereign individual has been "liberated" from morality; he has won back his autonomy from the self-misunderstandings that traditional morality engenders; and that, as I have already argued, is not a result that the first form of re-evaluation has the right kind of authority to achieve. The fifth form of re-evaluation, by contrast, does have the right kind of authority, at least in principle, as do the second, third, and fourth. The third and fourth forms, being internal to the way of life whose values are under scrutiny, pose no difficulties: whether Nietzsche's re-evaluations succeed or persuade will be a function, quite routinely, of whether his arguments and the considerations he offers are any good. Nor is the second form problematic, even though it is conducted from an external perspective: for it appeals, in the end, only to values that are internal to the way of living in question. And the fifth form brings no special problems with it either: its power is conditional only upon the quality of the arguments it contains, and upon the plausibility of its claim to speak, as it were, from the perspective of, or on the behalf of, values that ought to be, and perhaps implicitly are, intrinsic for any human way of living at all.

The account that I have offered of the fifth form of the re-evaluation of values is a relative of those offered by Richard Schacht and Philippa Foot. Schacht proposes that Nietzsche's re-evaluation proceeds from a "privileged" perspective, "which an understanding of the fundamental character of life and the world serves to define and establish";[24] and the "availability of this standard," he suggests, "places evaluation on a footing that is as firm [i.e., as authoritative] as that on which the comprehension of life and the world stands."[25] Foot suggests that the evaluative standpoint from which Nietzsche conducts his re-evaluation is essentially an "aesthetic" one, rooted in "the interest and admiration which is the common attitude to remarkable men of exceptional independence of mind and strength of will"—in "our tendency to *admire* certain individuals whom we see as powerful and splendid."[26] Again, then, there is nothing in Foot's position that would render the kind of re-evaluation that she envisages altogether inaccessible to the adherents of traditional morality (indeed, if anything, quite the reverse[27]), and this is, with respect to the authority problem at least, a point in its favor.[28]

So the account proposed here has in common with Schacht's and Foot's the highlighting of an evaluative standpoint that is in principle accessible to those who are committed to the values whose value is under scrutiny, and who might therefore come to regard the re-evaluation of those values as authoritative. It differs from Schacht's and Foot's, however, in highlighting a standpoint structured by the values of self-understanding and autonomy; and it differs, too, in distinguishing the re-evaluation conducted from that standpoint from at least three other forms of re-evaluation in which Nietzsche also engages (often at the same time), and in indicating how the various forms of re-evaluation might be thought to operate together. Collectively, I suggest, these features of the present account give it an explanatory advantage over any of its obvious competitors, and does so in at least two respects: first, the present account gives a much more nuanced analysis of what a (pointful) re-evaluation of the values of traditional morality might (pointfully) involve; and second, it shows that Nietzsche might indeed have been engaged in such an enterprise—that his tactics are at least of the right general *sort* to deliver the results that he was after. Whether or not he in fact does deliver those results, however, is a question that lies beyond the scope of this essay, and I have not tried to address it here.

NOTES

My thanks to Maria Alvarez, Alex Neill, David Owen, and Genia Schönbaumsfeld for discussion and for comments on earlier versions of this essay. My thanks, too, to the organizers of and participants in a workshop on Nietzsche and value held at the University of Sussex in December 2002, at which an ancestral version of this essay was read: many of the things said there were very helpful.

1. I prefer "re-evaluation" to "revaluation," incidentally, on the perhaps slender grounds that the latter seems to suggest that the result of the process in question will always be the assignation of a new or different value to the value under scrutiny, while the former feels (to me, at least) as if it leaves open the possibility that the value of a given value might emerge from the process unchanged, or perhaps vindicated; and to leave that possibility open is, I think, truer to the spirit of Nietzsche's project.

2. *GM* P:6. For translations I utilize the following: Kaufmann and Hollingdale's *GM*; Kaufmann's *BGE*; Hollingdale's *HH*; Hollingdale's *D*; Kaufmann's *GS*.

3. This is a point rightly emphasised by Richard Schacht: see his "Nietzschean Normativity," in R. Schacht, ed., *Nietzsche's Postmoralism* (Cambridge: Cambridge University Press, 2001), 160.

4. I overlook Christine M. Korsgaard's insistence that one should keep the distinction between the intrinsic and the extrinsic separate from the distinction between ends and means. Her point is an interesting one, but it does not affect the reading of Nietzsche offered in the present essay: see Korsgaard, "Two Distinctions in Goodness," in her *Creating the Kingdom of Ends* (Cambridge: Cambridge University Press, 1996), 249–74.

5. Or, as Bernard Williams puts it, if a value is intrinsic for someone, then "he can understand this value in relation to the other values that he holds, and this implies . . . that the intrinsic good . . . , or rather the agent's relation to it, has an inner structure in terms of which it can be related to other goods," *Truth and Truthfulness* (Princeton: Princeton University Press, 2002), 92.

6. This conception of (intrinsic) value is consistent with that proposed by Joseph Raz; see his *Practical Reason and Norms* (London: Hutchinson, 1975), 34. See also Raz, *The Practice of Value* (Oxford: Oxford University Press, 2003), 143–45.

7. Nietzsche continues: "Thus I deny morality as I deny alchemy, that is, I deny their premises: but I do *not* deny that there have been alchemists who believed in these premises and acted in accordance with them."

8. Given that the relation between this putative sixth form of re-evaluation and the first precisely mirrors that between the fourth and fifth, it might seem as if these two should be collapsed together as well. I choose not to do this, however. While the first form of re-evaluation, as I argue in the next section, is bound to be ineffective, the fifth need not be; and since

part of my interest is to give a nuanced account of the (potential) power of Nietzsche's project, it makes sense to distinguish more finely between the latter pair (the fourth and fifth) than between the former.

9. Brian Leiter, *Nietzsche on Morality* (London: Routledge, 2002),128–29.

10. Ibid., 53.

11. Something that is emphasized, incidentally, in the introduction to Hollingdale's *Daybreak* coauthored by Leiter and Maudemarie Clark.

12. Leiter, op. cit., 150.

13. Ibid., 155.

14. Ibid. For a rather subtler account of the role of Nietzsche's rhetoric in his attempt to re-evaluate values, see Christopher Janaway, "Nietzsche's Artistic Revaluation," in J. Bermúdez and S. Gardner, eds., *Art and Morality* (London: Routledge, 2003), 260–76.

15. —and should also have attributed to his earlier self: the position he attacks is precisely the one that he had espoused in *HH*; see, namely, sections 92 and 629.

16. The re-evaluation also seeks to have another effect, of course—namely, to show that the structure of values within which pity has been held in place as an intrinsic value actually accommodates suffering as an instrumental value more convincingly; and certainly that it will not accommodate suffering as an intrinsic disvalue.

17. See footnote 8, above.

18. For an illuminating discussion of this point, see David Owen, "Nietzsche, Re-evaluation, and the turn to Genealogy," *European Journal of Philosophy* 11:3 (2003), section 4. [*Ed.*—Owen's essay is reprinted in this volume.]

19. —which is no coincidence; again, see Owen, ibid., 249–72.

20. In *BGE* 46, Nietzsche expressly refers to slave or Christian morality as the product of a "re-evaluation of antique values."

21. For an account of the conceptual innovations required for the slave revolt, and of the resources implicit in noble morality that made those innovations possible, see Aaron Ridley, *Nietzsche's Conscience: Six Character Studies from the "Genealogy"* (Ithaca, NY: Cornell University Press, 1998), chapters 1 and 2.

22. I here sidestep the interesting question of where, in Nietzsche's chronology, the sovereign individual is supposed to be situated. Some considerations would appear to place him prior to traditional morality; others suggest a distinctively post-traditional achievement. Either way, though, and I prefer the latter, the sovereign individual's place in the scheme of things is emphatically not *within* traditional morality, and that is all that the point I make here requires.

23. It is this exercise that has, in effect, been taken over and given contemporary expression by Bernard Williams in his various critiques of the "morality system": see, namely, *Ethics and the Limits of Philosophy* (London: Fontana, 1985) and *Shame and Necessity* (Berkeley: University of California Press, 1993), chapter 3. For an excellent discussion of the affinities between Nietzsche and Williams, see Maudemarie Clark, "On the Rejection of Morality: Bernard Williams's Debt to Nietzsche," in R. Schacht, ed., *Nietzsche's Postmoralism* (Cambridge: Cambridge University Press, 2001), 100–22.

24. Richard Schacht, *Nietzsche* (London: Routledge, 1983), 349.

25. Ibid., 398.

26. Philippa Foot, "Nietzsche: the Revaluation of Values," in R. Solomon, ed., *Nietzsche: A Collection of Critical Essays* (Notre Dame: University of Notre Dame Press, 1973), 163.

27. As Leiter also notes, op. cit., 145. Leiter goes on to suggest—plausibly, I think—that this is a flaw in Foot's position: it makes the business of securing an audience for Nietzsche's re-evaluation too easy.

28. Actually, Foot seems to have changed her mind about Nietzsche's re-evaluations: she now appears to espouse a position that is more like an extreme version of Leiter's. See her *Natural Goodness* (Oxford: Oxford University Press, 2001), chapter 7. For the reasons given earlier, however, I regard any move in this direction as a mistake.

6

Genealogy, the Will to Power, and the Problem of a Past*

Tracy B. Strong

All beings that have existence in the world have pasts. To have a past means to embody for oneself and for others some quality that was and shapes the way one's being is in the world. Only God does not have a past and that is because God exists only in the present, which is what the meaning of eternity is.[1] For a range of thinkers in the nineteenth and early twentieth centuries, having a past was seen as a form of coercion. Marx, in the first page of *The Eighteenth Brumaire of Louis Napoleon*, found that the past "lay like a nightmare on the brain of the living." For James Joyce's Stephen Daedalus, the past "was a nightmare" from which he was trying to awake. For Freud, the cumulated weight of childhood experiences distorted present agency into neurotic behavior. Marx theorized revolution, which he saw as necessarily sundering the integument that held the new world in the ashes of the old. Joyce tried to make that past available in the odyssey of Leopold Bloom and in Molly's ecstatic affirmation. Freud held that psychoanalysis is to reform the past, so as to keep it from distorting the present. The sense that what drives humans is what they have been, that they have been driven willy-nilly into behavior that they neither intend nor want, is a major concern of philosophical thought after the French Revolution. Indeed, the Revolution had shown a stunned Europe that what had started as a minor *jacquerie* over the price of bread led to the imposition of the metric sys-

---

*Portions of what follows draw upon material of mine that is appearing in a book edited by Tobias Hoffman on weakness of the will to appear with Catholic University Press, and from an article in *New Nietzsche Studies* 6, no. 3/4 (Winter 2005) and 7 no. 1/2 (forthcoming, Fall 2006): 198–211).

tem on continental Europe. The past seemed to have an ineluctable stranglehold over the unfolding of human affairs.

These concerns, common to all those for whom history became the principle muse, were unavoidable to serious thinkers in the nineteenth century. It is thus no surprise that from early in his career, Nietzsche was concerned with the possibility of transforming the present by changing its past. Thus he can write in the *Use and Misuse of History for Life*:

> For since we are the outcome of earlier generations, we are also the outcome of their aberrations, passions and errors, and indeed of their crimes; it is not possible to free oneself wholly from this chain. If we condemn these aberrations, and regard ourselves free of them, this does not alter the fact that we originate in them. The best we can do is to confront our inherited and hereditary nature with our knowledge of it, and through a new, stern discipline combat our inborn heritage and implant in ourselves a new habit, a new instinct, a second nature, so that our first nature withers away. It is an attempt to give oneself, as it were a posteriori, a past in which one would like to originate in opposition to that in which one did originate:—always a dangerous attempt because it is so hard to know the limit to denial of the past and because second natures are usually weaker than first. What happens all too often is that we know the good but do not do it, because we also know the better but cannot do it. But here and there a victory is nonetheless achieved, and for the combatants, for those who employ critical history for the sake of life, there is even a noteworthy consolation: that of knowing that this first nature was once a second nature and the every victorious second nature will become a first. (*HL* 3)

This is not simply a "theoretical" problem. Nietzsche was centrally concerned with the issue in his own existence. In *Ecce Homo*, he claims to be a throwback to ancient Polish nobility; later in the passage he will claim paternity from Caesar or Alexander (*EH* "Wise" 3). What is important here is that Nietzsche is claiming that his relation with his father is so attenuated that he now exists as himself as if Caesar had been his father. Indeed, he will go so far as to claim that he is "all names in history," as if all surnames were his.[2] He associates his lowest point (1880) with the same age at which his father died. This is also the period of his life when his eyes give him the most trouble and he finds himself but a "shadow" of himself. But it is precisely the experience of this going under that permits his new birth: *The Wanderer and his Shadow* will be followed by *Break of Day*. Nietzsche, one might say, is concerned to give himself a new genealogy. As he remarks in *Human, All Too Human* I:381, "If one does not have a good father one must give oneself one."

Yet how might one do this? To ask this question is to investigate the nature of genealogy, for *genealogy is the actuality of the past in the present*. How does genealogy, however, manifest itself in present action? One might think, as do many of the standard interpretations, as a matter of will. It is thus essential to ask if it is possible by human volition to shape one's present so that it is not subject to a past. In the chapter "On Redemption" in *Thus Spoke Zarathustra*, Nietzsche raises the question of the relation of temporality and the will. He is concerned with the way that what we have been in the past shapes what we do in the present to make a future. If the will is the human faculty to construct the future and is both structured and held prisoner by its past, then the possibility of human freedom seems greatly diminished or eradicated. Nietzsche examines a number of proposed understandings of will (he includes—without naming them—Hegel, Kant, Schopenhauer, Wagner, and, I believe, his own work in *The Birth of Tragedy*) and concludes that they are all deficient in that they either simply ignore the weight of the past or too easily assert the possibility of escaping from it.[3]

Why so? The problem, he avers, is that they have all misunderstood will: "My idea," he writes in a later note, "is that the will of earlier psychology is an unjustified generalization, that this will does not exist at all, that instead of grasping the formulation of a single given will in many forms, one has eliminated the character of the will, in that one has subtracted the content, the 'whither' (*Wohin*)" (*KSA* 13:14[121]). Nietzsche's first point is that an understanding of the will as a single entity or faculty is mistaken.[4]

I shall come back to what might constitute such redemption toward the end of this chapter but, for now, note that for Nietzsche, none of these previous writers provides access to a realm that would escape or transfigure a human past. The past remains a problem. At the end of the chapter, he drops a hint that the "will that is the will to power" might possibly be able to will "backwards."

The will to power cannot be grasped as something that can be satisfied: it requires a "*Wohin*," and whatever we call will is to be understood in terms of its *Wohin* (whither). Will is thus a *bringing about* rather than something that is bought about. The will, he says, "wants to go forward and always again become master of that which stands in its way." The will to power is constant motion and finds expression as the overcoming of borders and obstacles. It does not in itself seek a *particular* state of affairs—in the English version of Freud's terminology it has "motility of cathexis"[5]—just that there *be* a state of affairs. Importantly it does not seek pleasure, nor to avoid pain: it is simply the "attempt to overcome, to bring to oneself, to incorporate" (*KSA* 13:14[174]). In fact, from the standpoint of the will to power "there are no things at all, but only dynamic quanta." Nietzsche continues, "[T]he will to power, not being, not becoming, but a *pathos* is the most elementary fact from which a becoming, a working first arises" (*KSA* 13:14[79]).

An important clue is offered by this designation of the will to power as a *pathos*. In the *Gay Science*, Nietzsche made a distinction between *pathos* and *ethos* and suggested that as long as humans continue to think of a particular form of life they tend to think of it as an *ethos*, that is, as "the only possible and reasonable thing." A true understanding, however, is that life is "pathos," as it is "not one's lot to have certain particular sensations for years." (*GS* 317). *Pathos* means "that which happens to a person or a thing," "what one has experienced, good or bad"; it refers sometimes to the "incidents of things."[6] In no case does it imply a notion of growth or development, but only the different states a person or a thing may assume.[7] Will to power thus "cannot have become" (*KSA* 13:11[29]). It is movement itself and thus has neither being nor becoming. The most basic quality of all organisms is their attempt to incorporate into and as themselves all that they encounter; thus they will define all that they meet. All the forms that any organism acquires it assumes, and taken as a whole they constitute its will to power. The various *Wohins* are the instances of the will to power of a particular organism. These *Wohins* can assume different qualities: among the categories Nietzsche identifies are optimism or pessimism, activity or passivity, superfluidity or lack—much of his later years are spent sorting out these differences. It is thus quite sensible from this understanding to proclaim, as he does in one of his most famous remarks, that life is "will to power." The full remark is this: "What are our valuations and tables of the good worth? What comes from their control? For whom? In relation to what?—Answer: for life. But what is life? Here is needed a new more definite formulation of the concept 'life.' My formula for that goes: *Leben* ['Life' or 'to live'] is will to power. . . . What does evaluation mean? . . . Answer: moral evaluation is an exegesis, a *way of interpreting*" (*KSA* 12:2[190].47; my italics).

The will to power is a "way of interpreting." Indeed, elsewhere, Nietzsche is explicit: "The will to power interprets: it is a question of interpreting during the building of an organ; it sets limits, defines degrees, differences of power. . . . In truth, interpretation is a means to become master of something. The organic process presupposes continuing interpretation" (*KSA* 12:2[148]). To interpret is to place oneself as the lens through which the observed is seen. The important thing then about the will to power is that it refers to the quality that living beings have to make or understand the world in their own image. Etymologically, *Macht* (as in *Wille zur Macht*) is archaically related to the same root from which we get our word "might," which in turn has a meaning of the ability to make or do something.[8] The will to power is thus the quality that all life has *of giving form*, that is, of giving rise to the *pathoi* that are (a) life.—But *what* form?—The form that is given must be the form of the giver. Thus "cognition" itself is said to be will to power (*KSA* 11:34[185]). In the *Genealogy* the will to power is a "form giving . . . force" (*GM* II:18); elsewhere the will to power is held to interpret the "new in the forms of the old."[9]

This, however, means that the particular past of a willing agent so shapes that will that it simply repeats a particular pattern; changing that pattern would require changing the past of a will or determining a way not to be caught by it. This is why the question of temporality is central to Nietzsche's discussion of the will.[10]

GENEALOGY AND WILL

A point that emerges from the above consideration is that everyone, perhaps even every*thing*—all life—has or rather *is* will to power. We see immediately a problem relevant to slave morality: if whatever will one exercises is one's *own* or rather is what one means by one's self, what is the nature of the self that exercises such and such a will? So a question raised by this investigation of "the" will must be: "what kind of beings are we?" And here it is noteworthy that Nietzsche associates a particular weakness of will with our present moral world in general. Thus: "Today the tastes and virtues of the time diminish and debilitate the will. Nothing is so timely as will-weakness (*Nichts ist so sehr zeitgemäss als Willensschwäche*)" (*BGE* 212). This is immediately referred to as quality of character: "Turned around: the need for belief, for some unconditional yes and no, is a need for weakness, all weakness is of the will (*alle Schwäche ist Willensschwäche*): all weakness of will stems from the fact that no passion, no categorical imperative, commands" (*KSA* 13:11[48].318; cf. *BGE* 207). I shall return to the importance of the reference to Kant at the end of the chapter. For this condition, Nietzsche coins a term: *Entselbstung*—"de-selfing," we might translate it. The preliminary sense is that a weak will is associated with not being a self, thus unable to own, to be one's own self, to have a right to what is one's own. Such a weak will is not weak at a particular moment: weakness is its nature.

Given what I have said, there must be wills to power of different qualities of character (that is, of different *Wohins*), a will to power, for instance, that is masterly or nobly moral as well as another will to power that is slavely moral. And this is precisely what the *Genealogy* is (among other things): a story of how it came to be that one form of life replaced another and how it might happen that yet a new second nature might replace that which has become our first nature. What is absolutely essential here is to recognize that both noble and slave morality are wills to power.

The matter is of considerable complexity. One might suppose that slaves are simply less than the noble, ineffective in relation to the masters, and are thus to be held in opprobrium. This, however, is not Nietzsche's position or is rather a vast oversimplification of it. Let us look at these two wills to power.

The terms master (or noble) and slave are often given negative resonance by those who read Nietzsche—memories of Nazi and racial contexts lead easily to the conclusion that Nietzsche is, as one always half suspected, whether or not a bad thinker, certainly a bad man. Yet the idea of master and slave has an obvious apparent ancestry in Rousseau ("He who believes himself to be the master of others is all the more a slave than they" [*Social Contract* I, 1]) and in Hegel (*Herrschaft* and *Knechtschaft* in the *Phenomenology*). At the time that Nietzsche was writing, Marx was developing an entire theory of history based on the interaction of the oppressor and the oppressed. Nietzsche had read the left-Hegelians and explicitly found resonances between his work and Bruno Bauer's;[11] he may have read of Marx in other texts.[12] Nietzsche's main exploration of different kinds of will to power appears in the *Genealogy*.

In a number of passages, Nietzsche delineates and distinguishes the quality of the will in nobles and in slaves. The nobles, he says, "do not know guilt, responsibility, or consideration." They are "born organizers" (*GM* II:17–18). In *Beyond Good and Evil*, he writes that "when the ruling group determines what is 'good,' the exalted proud states of the soul are experienced as conferring distinction and order of rank. . . . The noble type of man experiences itself as determining values; . . . it knows itself to be value creating" (*BGE* 260).

The noble moral type says—to paraphrase Al Lingis's paraphrase of Bataille— "My God, am I good! How beautiful, strong, and powerful I am! You offer no possible contest for me and would be a waste of my time. You are no match for me and are bad." "Good" here means something like "worthy of being dealt with." Think of the exchange between Glaukos and Diomedes in book 6 of the *Iliad* (lines 80ff) where the two warriors, having met on the field of battle must first determine whether or not the other is a worthy opponent (one is much younger), that is, "good" in noble moral terms, for without this there would be no reason to fight someone who is not as you are (i.e., is "bad"). They thus run through their respective genealogies to establish their worth to the other. (As it turns out their grandparents were guest-friends and the bond is such that they do not fight but exchange battle gear.)[13] More contemporarily, any of us who were chosen last to a team because of our lack of skill, or put out to play right field, have some idea of what it means to live in a masterly moral world (and remember the sense of self derived from the time where we were chosen first, or, better yet, got to do the choosing). Thus also does the concept, still surviving, of a "worthy opponent" remind us of master morality. I do not here wish to develop further the credibility of master morality as a moral form:[14] precisely its strangeness (and the fact that I move most easily to sports examples), is testimony to the fact that we now think of morality in and only in its "good and evil" form.

Yet what happens? Here it is important to understand that "good/evil slave morality" is quite different from "good/bad noble morality," not simply the inverse. The slave says in effect, "My goodness, do I suffer! You make me suffer, you are evil and I am the opposite of you and therefore am good. Why do you make me suffer?" The definition of self of the slavely moral is thus the conclusion of a dialectical argument. Several things are worth noting: First, this situation is not all that different from what Hegel described in the *Phenomenology* where the self is attained by a progressive differentiation first from nature and then from others. Second, this form of attaining identity—this form of moral agency—*requires* oppression. That is, unless I suffer, I will have nothing to negate. Hence it is important for the continuity of my self that I maintain a source of suffering, and nothing that I do should or may put an end to the possibility of suffering. Over time, Nietzsche argues, humans incorporate the source of suffering into themselves; they become their own oppressor (this is how he interprets the idea of original sin): he will trace this dynamic through various stages in the second and third books of the *Genealogy*.

Slave morality is thus *not* just the noble morality stood on its head—a reversal of the structures of domination. It is structured in a different manner and thus is a different way of being in the world. Nietzsche works this out in a parable of the eagle and the lamb.

It is, in fact, not surprising that the lamb dislikes the eagle. After all, for no apparent reason every so often a bird of prey swoops down and carries off one of the flock.

Since it is not clear that this is in response to something one has done wrong, it is also quite possible that one day this might happen to anyone. The lamb clearly would like to put an end to this situation. The eagle is evil; the lamb is the opposite of the eagle, thus it must be "good."[15] But the bird keeps swooping down.

What the lamb must want is for the eagle not to behave as an eagle, to be ashamed of its desires, of itself—to acquire another, new character such that it would live under the domination of time past. On the face of it this is silly. As Nietzsche continues, "[T]o demand of strength that it *not* express itself as strength, that it *not* be a will to overpower, to cast down, to become master, a thirst after enemies, oppositions and triumphs, is just as absurd as to require weakness to express itself as strength" (*GM* I:13). *The lamb wants, however, precisely this "absurdity."* He wants the eagle not to act as an eagle; that is, he wants the eagle not to act in accord with what he, the eagle, considering all things, knows to be his eagle's desire.

But there is a problem: the eagle has no other will than the will of an eagle. So what we learn here from Nietzsche is that the eagle must require the *acquisition* of *specific* qualities of character, ones that are not, as it were, natural to a particular being. What does the lamb require of the eagle? He requires, first, that the eagle need a *reason* for doing what it does; second, he requires that the eagle have a *choice* in doing what he does (this follows from and requires the first); this requires, third, that there be an *independent common framework* in terms of which both the eagle and the lamb can make judgments; and this requires, finally, that the eagle be *reflective.* The lamb wants the eagle to be rational.

RATIONALITY AND THE GENEALOGY
OF SLAVE MORALITY

These considerations lead us to a third element. They correspond to the acquisition by the eagle of reflective rationality ("why am I doing this?"), that is, to the acquisition of those qualities for which Nietzsche attacked Socrates. In Nietzsche's reading, Socrates sought to get people to give reasons for their beliefs. The Greek found that *das Unbewusste* (the "unconscious" but note that this is a dangerous translation) could not account for itself. So Socrates, in the *agora* as in the theater, Nietzsche avers, wanted reasons for why individuals or characters act or think as they do, and this made it impossible for him to accept tragedy *as* tragedy. "Whereas," Nietzsche writes in *BT*, "in all productive men the instinct is precisely the creative-affirmative power and consciousness (*Bewusstsein*) operates in a critical and dissuasive way, in Socrates the instinct becomes a critic and consciousness the creator. . . . Here the logical nature is, by a hypertrophy, developed . . . excessively." (*BT* 13). As Nietzsche remarks in an early public lecture, a remark that shocked his audience: "*Wenn Tugend Wissen ist, so muß der tugendhafte Held Dialektiker sein.*—If virtue is knowledge, then the virtuous hero must be a dialectician" ("Sokrates und die Tragödie," *KSA* 1, 547).

If we take these thoughts back to the problem of the will of slave morality, it appears that slave morality is something that *one can learn* to have. The eagle will continue to want to carry off the lamb, but having been subject to dialectical frustration, he will change his mind and not do what he desires but rather what is "good"—in the "good/evil" sense of good. Most considerations of weak willedness hold that one's will is weak when one does not do what one thinks is in one's best interest, all things considered.[16] Here, however, the transformed eagle becomes weak precisely in taking account of all things. In this case, though, he has had to learn to take these things into account. The noble qua noble cannot have a weak will because for him *character is in fact destiny*.

It is thus the case that the lamb requires that the eagle exhibit what one writer has in a different context approvingly identified as "a normal amount of self-control,"[17] self-control defined in terms *external* to what the eagle is as eagle. In Nietzsche's reversal, slave morality consists in controlling oneself in terms of an external and given framework; nonslave morality is thus to do *what is one's own*, no matter what the expectations.

The matter does not stop here. The weakness of the will of the slave is in fact the source of its victory over the noble or the strong. For what happens is that the *Unbewusstheit* of the noble is unable to resist the dialectics of the slave: *the victor is always the weak*.[18] Nietzsche is quite clear on this: the ability to induce the knowledge that one could have done otherwise is a decisive weapon. For Nietzsche the weak person—that is, the person who from his or her own viewpoint "could have" acted otherwise—is actually the victor because of the fact that he or she can blame someone else. Eventually, for Nietzsche, the genius of Christianity will be to find in oneself the source of oppression: hence the problem of maintaining the constant source of oppression necessary to slave morality is permanently and irretrievably solved in this world. The only way out will be a redemption from oneself. The point of Nietzsche's analysis here is the recognition that *the victory is always to the weak*— that the quality of character that allows one to be weak of will is the source of strength. And the source of the triumph of slave morality over the noble morality will always derive from the fact that the slave is *rational*. Nietzsche thus has stood the standard analysis of the "weak" will on its head or back on its feet: rationality, which was to counter weakness of will, is for him the central and defining quality of those who *have* weak wills, and this, seemingly paradoxically, is the source of their domination over those whose will is strong.

The slavely moral type responds to the presence of a generalizable, hence reasoned, external or internalized threat of oppression. The slavely moral type can thus not stand for him- or herself because that self depends on a dialectical relationship to someone or something other, to a fixed and general framework. This is the reason that Nietzsche refers to this condition as one of *Entselbstung*, as if slavely persons had nothing that was theirs, as if they did not have selves of their own. Such beings do not in fact have, one might say, the right to their actions, those actions are not really their own.[19]

It is in this sense that the will of the slavely moral is powerful and triumphs over the master precisely because it is weak. By "powerful" Nietzsche means something like "having on one's terms, be those terms authentic or not." By "weak" he means here "not authentically one's own." This, however, does not get us very far. What does it mean for an act not to be authentically one's own? Where contemporary philosophers of weakness of will see the *akrates* as acting "surd"[20]—without voice or reason—Nietzsche sees him as acting from a being that is not his own. Nietzsche's analysis thus calls into question the notion that rationality can provide a counter to the dangers of slave morality—in fact, for Nietzsche, rationality makes slave morality possible.

The politics of the slave are thus epistemological: they consist in altering the moral grammar of the erstwhile noble. Here one might ask if there is anything to be done. The genealogy of slave morality leads, as we saw above, to a situation where persons would rather "will the void than be void of will," the condition of nihilism.

Against this Nietzsche sets a number of possibilities. They include the "sovereign individual" (his reworking of Kantian autonomy), the "Overman," and, of important focus in the *Genealogy*, the person with the "right to make promises."[21] I shall focus on the first and last here.

Why and how should an individual ever want to acquire the "right to make promises"? After all, why should one want to bind oneself to a future that one might well regret? How can one? As Nietzsche poses it, the question of not living in slave morality can be brought back to the question of why and how it is that one should ever *be able* to so bind oneself, or to find oneself bound.

The movement of the text in the first three sections of the *GM* II is a first key.[22] In each of them Nietzsche describes the possibility of a particular kind of being-in-the-world (the right to make promises, the sovereign individual, the acquisition of conscience) and then circles back to give an account for the genealogy of that quality. Thus the right to make promises requires first the development of calculability, regularity, and necessity (*GM* II:1). The sovereign individual requires the development of a memory. This is the acquisition of a temporal dimension to the self. Each of these qualities is what Nietzsche calls a "late" or "ripest" fruit, the coming into being of which therefore has required ripening.

Nietzsche is quite clear that these earlier developments are the *means to making possible* a "sovereign individual" (for instance). Nietzsche refers to this as "a preparatory task" and includes in it what he calls human "prehistory." What is key here is the understanding of history: the past has made possible the present, but it has not necessarily monotonically determined it. The resources for a variety of different presents are all in the past, if we can deconstruct the past we have received and reassembled it.

What quality does the sovereign individual—whom I take here to be an individual who has earned the right and capacity to say what s/he is, something that slave-moral individuals do not have and noble-moral individuals neither need nor have? Nietzsche details a number of qualities in *GM* II:2, all of which sound like or are intended to sound like the *megalopsuchos* of Aristotle.[23] Yet there is a difference between Nietzsche's sovereign individual and the great soul in Aristotle, for the sovereign individual is the result of an achievement, a process by which a consciousness has become instinct (cf. *HL*, cited above). What is important here is the insistence that Nietzsche places on the "*right* to make promises."[24]

What then would/could keep me from not keeping my promises (being weak of will) if, as we have established, rationality is for Nietzsche of no actual avail? Nietzsche is, I think, correct to say that one does not keep one's promise because one has a reason to do so—I do not need a reason to keep my promise. Nietzsche says that promising requires that I have "mastery over circumstances, over nature, and over all more short-willed and unreliable creatures" (*GM* II:2). Those who have the right to promise are like "sovereigns," because they can maintain their promise in the face of accidents, even in the "face of fate." To have the right to a promise is to have taken upon oneself, as oneself, all the circumstances present and future in which the promise may occur. It is to maintain that promise—the requirement that the present extend into the future—no matter what befalls. Thus when Kaufmann translates the key passage—*für sich als Zukunft gut sagen zu können* as "able to stand security for his *own* future," one may pass by Nietzsche's point, which is that one should be able "to be able to vouch for oneself *as a* future." One must earn entitlement to one's "own."

What this means is that a person who has the right to make promises does not regard his actions as choices. (What counts as a choice varies from person to person and responds to who they are). A promise is thus a declaration of what I am, of that for which I am responsible: as it is not a choice among other choices, there is no possibility of slave morality. It is a way of being. As Stanley Cavell says: "You choose your life. This is the way an action Categorically Imperative feels. And though there is not The Categorical Imperative, there are actions that are for us categorically imperative so far as we have a will." [25]

In this, and despite obvious echoes, Nietzsche's position is not Kant's. In the *Grundwerk* and elsewhere Kant argues that one cannot break a promise because to do so would in effect deny the point of the entire institution of promising. Kant took this position with its very strong denial of the relevance of intention because, as he argued, any breaking of a promise or uttering of a lie for contingent reasons (say, as with Sartre, you were being asked by the Gestapo the location of the partisan they were seeking) would mean that you claimed to know precisely what the consequences of your action would be. Since such a claim was epistemologically impossible, it followed that one must be bound by the only certainty one might have, that of one's nontemporally limited reason.

Kant's reason for keeping a promise or not telling a lie was consequent to the interplay of a fixed and actually rational self and an incompletely graspable world. The difference in Nietzsche's analysis of the right to keep promises comes in his insistence that neither the external world nor the self is knowable. The self is, for him, what it has the power to be responsible for. Hence the binding of the self to a promise can only be rightfully accomplished by a power "over oneself and over fate" and must penetrate below the level of assessment—where it remained with Kant—to become part of the assessing itself, what Nietzsche calls "instinct" or the "*unbe-wusst*." This means that promising must become part of what I am, for me to have the right to it.

Nietzsche is also clear—now contra Kant, and post-Kantians from Rawls to Habermas—that the self that is so committed is committed also to all the pain and all the reversals that will and may occur—pains that can be seen in his exploration of what he calls mnemotechnics. In this, the sovereign individual in Nietzsche will find an instantiation in Weber's person who has the vocation for politics and who can remain true to his vocation, "in spite of all." (One might note here that the insistence on the necessity of the pain and cruelty of existence was already central to the argument in *BT*). Pain and cruelty are endemic to the possibility of life—they are part of what make the sovereign individual possible.

In a note from 1885 he writes: "Basic idea: new values must first be created—we must not be spared that! The philosopher must be a lawgiver to us. New types. (As earlier the highest types (e.g., Greeks) were bred: this type of 'accident' to be willed consciously.)" (*KSA* 11:35 [47]). So the question that Nietzsche raises for us in relation to the overcoming of slave morality is that of the qualities that are necessary to have in order to have a different nonslavely will and of the politics by which those qualities are acquired. If rationality produces or is a quality of slave morality it cannot be the solution. A question remains: if rationality cannot be the basis of keeping one's promise (which is what Nietzsche tells us), what can possibly be the case that ensures that someone will keep his or her promise? What does it mean to be a person with the "right to make a promise"? If rationality is not the question—hence his praise of the body against Plato—what qualities does such an individual have? If the problem with slave morality is *Entselbstung*, what is the basis of *Verselbstung*?

Verselbstung is to be actually the person you know you are: it is as such that the claim of time past and thus the possibility of slave morality is abolished. From his youth on, one of Nietzsche's touchstone passages was from Pindar's Second Pythian: *génoi oíos éssi mathón*, rendered by Barbara Fowler as "Be what you know you are,"[26] and by Alexander Nehamas as "Having learned, become who you are."[27] As the voice of his "Gewissen," his knowing conscience, Nietzsche tells us: "*du sollst der werden wer* (or *was*) *du bist*—You should become the one you are" (*GS* 270).[28] We learn from Nietzsche that the slavely moral are those who cannot become what they are, nor can they ever know what that is: there is no self that can become their own (*KSA* 13:14 [102]). They "bob around like corks" in the image he uses in *Zarathustra* and takes from Pindar. Slave morality for Nietzsche is not having a self that is one's own.

So the question of how to escape or change the genealogy of slave morality is for Nietzsche the question of how to be able authentically to use the first person singular, to say "I" and use the word correctly. As it turns out—and this should be no surprise—this is the other problem confronting those who found Clio to have become the principle muse. Kant, at the beginning of What is Enlightenment?" insists that the problem is finding one's own way and each of the questions that set up the three critiques is framed in terms of the first person singular (What can *I* know? What ought *I* to do? For what may *I* hope?). Likewise, John Stuart Mill sought in *On Liberty* to establish the conditions by which one might freely be one's own person rather than someone whose actions and desires were shaped by and respondent to the conformities in society. Nietzsche continues this enterprise—but as we have seen he understood the problem as far more difficult than did even Kant and Mill.

NOTES

My thanks to Christa Davis Acampora for her insightful work editing this manuscript.

1. In John 8:58, Jesus says, "Before Abraham was, I am."
2. Here, as in performativity theory, contests over naming are contests over Being. See Austin, Butler, Derrida, Wittig, and others.
3. See the complete discussion in my *Friedrich Nietzsche and the Politics of Transfigura-tion*, 3rd ed. (Champaign: University of Illinois Press, 2000), ch. 8.
4. This is not yet what Nietzsche means when he says there is "no will," see below. See also chapter eight in my *Friedrich Nietzsche and the Politics and Transfiguration*, and Wolfgang Müller-Lauter, *Nietzsche: His Philosophy of Contradictions and the Contradictions of His Philos-ophy* (Urbana: University of Illinois Press, 1999). [*Ed. Note*: Müller-Lauter's chapter that includes discussion of the "whither" of the will is reprinted in full in this volume.]
5. What Freud called *Besetzung*—taking a place, or being cast as a character.
6. Such as *Phaedo* 96a: "Now I will tell you my own experience in the matter, if you wish." It also refers to emotion and, in rhetoric, to the appeal to emotion.
7. I am helped by Liddell and Scott. It is thus not at all what is meant by *physis* and, while I cannot deal with the matter here, insofar as Heidegger wants to tie the idea of will to power to *physis*, it seems to me he is mistaken. *Physis* has a number of meanings but it is centrally the natural constitution of a thing as the result of growth. Nietzsche tends to use it to refer to an achieved culture. See, namely, *KSA* 7:30 [15]; *HL* 10; *SE* 3. *Physis* has, in other words, a temporal or teleological dimension that pathos does not have.
8. A *Macher* is a maker, an active leader, in both Middle High German and Yiddish.
9. Nietzsche, *Die Unschuld des Werdens: Der Nachlaß*, ed. Alfred Bäumler, 2nd ed. (Stutt-gart: Kröner, 1978), vol. 2, 78 (not in the *KGW*).
10. I leave unexamined here the complex relation of Nietzsche to the Kantian architec-tonic. On Nietzsche as a radical Kantian see, inter alia, the fruitful discussion in B. Babich, *Nietzsche's Philosophy of Science* (Albany, NY: SUNY Press, 1994).
11. *KSAB* 6, 242; 7, 270, 275; 8, 106, 205, 247, 370.
12. See Thomas H. Brobjer, "Nietzsche's Knowledge of Marx and Marxism," *Nietzsche-Studien* 31 (2002): 298–313, and especially Howard Caygill, "The Return of Nietzsche and Marx," in *Habermas, Nietzsche, and Critical Theory*, ed. Babette E. Babich, (New York: Humanity Books, 2004), 195–209. I leave aside here the differences and similarities between

the Rousseau/Hegel/Marx dialectical view of the relation of master and slave and Nietzsche's genealogical one to look at what Nietzsche has to say about the master-slave relation.

13. I should note that Glaukos apparently gets cheated ("Zeus had stolen [his] wits away")—Homer presents the whole scene in such a manner that one must read it as a doubly ironic commentary on the war itself.

14. It has been done by Alasdair MacIntyre in his consideration of Homer in *After Virtue* (Notre Dame: The University of Notre Dame Press, 1984), chs. 10 and 11.

15. Note that in the passages explicating these terms Nietzsche puts "good," "evil," and "bad" in scare quotes.

16. One might argue that it is not a matter of best interest but rather of what is right. Thus strength of will would have to do with the strength to do what is right. The Nazi guard claims that he was simply carrying out his duty, claiming strength of will. Hannah Arendt's rebuke, which for many readers is insufficient, consists in pointing out how little strength of any kind is involved in the ordinariness of doing what is expected of one and which everyone else does as well. Thanks to Professor Babette E. Babich for a discussion on these matters.

17. Gary Watson, "Skepticism about Weakness of Will," *Philosophical Review* 86 (1977): 316–39. The question here is as to the status of "normal."

18. Thus Marx foresaw the victory of the proletariat. Neither Nietzsche nor Marx was a Social Darwinian.

19. We have an entry here into what Kant was after when he began his essay "What is Enlightenment?" by asserting the importance of attaining one's *own way*.

20. See, namely, Donald Davidson, "How is Weakness of Will Possible?" in D. Davidson, *Essays on Actions and Events*. (Oxford: Clarendon Press, 1980), 40.

21. For an interesting if, to my mind, somewhat overly Kantian, discussion of possibilities, see Aaron Ridley, *Nietzsche's Conscience: Six Character Studies from the Genealogy* (Ithaca, NY: Cornell University Press, 1998).

22. It is worth noting that most readings of the second essay of *GM* II pass over the first two sections and go immediately to section 3 on conscience. See, namely, Werner Stegmaier, *Nietzsches Genealogie der Moral* (Darmstadt: Wissenschaftliches Buchgesellschaft, 1994), 131ff. He gets to the question of the sovereign individual on p. 136 without, however, the sense of the genealogical development that Nietzsche sees. See also Mathias Risse, "The Second Treatise in *On the Genealogy of Morality*: Nietzsche on the Origin of the Bad Conscience," in *European Journal of Philosophy* 9:1 (2001): 55–81, who does not begin until after the first two sections.

23. See *Magna Moralia* I 25–26.

24. One of the very few commentators to focus on this is Randall Havas, *Nietzsche's Genealogy* (Ithaca, NY: Cornell University Press), 193ff, who does so with an eye to the move from "animality" to "humanity," which I think misleading. He is on sounder ground on p. 196 where he relates the idea of "right" to that of the responsibility for intelligibility. See also, importantly, David Owen, "The Contest of Enlightenment: An Essay on Critique and Genealogy" in *Journal of Nietzsche Studies* 25 (Spring 2003): 35–57 and David Owen, "Equality, Democracy, and Self-Respect: Reflections on Nietzsche's Agonal Perfectionism" in *The Journal of Nietzsche Studies* 24 (Fall 2002): 113–31. Further discussion appears in Randall Haras, "Nietzsche's Idealism" and Aaron Ridley, "Ancillary Thoughts on an Ancillary Text," both in *The Journal of Nietzsche Studies* 20 (2000): 90–99 and 100–108, respectively. See in this volume Christa Davis Acampora, "On Sovereignty and Overhumanity: Why It Matters How We Read Nietzsche's *Genealogy* II:2."

25. See the discussion in Stanley Cavell, *The Claim of Reason* (Oxford: Clarendon Press, 1979), 309.

26. *Archaic Greek Poetry: An Anthology*, selected and trans. Barbara Fowler (Madison: University of Wisconsin Press, 1992), 279.

27. Alexander Nehamas, *The Art of Living: Socratic Reflections from Plato to Foucault* (Berkeley: University of California Press, 1998), 128. I am indebted for these two citations to Babette E. Babich, "Nietzsche's Imperative as a Friend's Encomium: On Becoming the One You Are, Ethics, and Blessing," *Nietzsche-Studien* 33 (2003): 29–58.

28. There is a considerable literature about what in Nietzsche's renderings happens to the *mathón*. Babich's paper (2003) deals with this very effectively. One can point out also that by placing the imperative as that which the conscience says, Nietzsche has incorporated it also.

II

READING NIETZSCHE'S *GENEALOGY*—FOCUSED ANALYSES OF PARTS AND PASSAGES

7

Slave Morality, Socrates, and the Bushmen

A Critical Introduction to *On the Genealogy of Morality, Essay I**

Mark Migotti

The first tract of *On the Genealogy of Morality* tells the story of a "slave revolt in morality" (*GM* I:10),[1] In the present essay, I inquire first into the internal coherence of this story, the slave revolt hypothesis, and second into its agreement with historical fact. I conclude that Nietzsche's hypothesis is coherent, plausible, and illuminating.

BARBARIAN MASTERS, CREATIVE SLAVES

In the beginning were knightly-aristocratic "masters" who determined for themselves that they were "good," and everybody else "bad." Not surprisingly, the numerous and miserable bad resented their lot. Somehow, sometime, their *ressentiment* became creative, and bore fruit in the form of an unheard of new morality, according to which those who had previously been regarded as wretched and bad in fact are in fact pure and good. The masters, meanwhile, are deemed not good but "evil." Shockingly, this idea caught on in a very big way; so much so that modern Europeans tend to assume without further thought that certain values specific to slave morality—altruism, for example—are in fact constitutive of any morality wor-

---

*This chapter has been revised and excerpted by the author after its publication in *Philosophy & Phenomenological Research* 58:4 (December 1998): 745–80.

thy of the name. Hence, according to Nietzsche, the need for a genealogy of morality—and for the uncommon patience, erudition, acumen, and daring needed to
carry it out well.

Noble morality is self-established. Developing "from a triumphant affirmation of
itself" (*GM* I:10), it is the morality of "self-glorification" (*BGE* 260). Against the
"bungled" genealogy of morals of unnamed "English psychologists," Nietzsche
insists that

> the judgment "good" did *not* originate with those to whom "goodness" was shown!
> Rather it was "the good" themselves, that is to say, the noble, powerful, high-stationed
> and high-minded, who felt and established themselves and their actions as good, that
> is, of the first rank, in contradistinction to all that is low, low-minded, common and
> plebeian. It was out of this pathos of distance that they first seized the right to create
> values and to coin names for things. (*GM* I:2)

When the English moral historians maintain that "originally, . . . one approved of
unegoistic actions and called them good from the point of view of those to whom
they were done, that is to say, those to whom they were *useful*" (*GM* I:2), they are,
Nietzsche thinks, twice mistaken. Not only does morality not originate in a favorable assessment of self-sacrifice and unegoistic behavior, it is also not by nature
beholden to the value of utility. Noble morality, in fact, is constituted by an exuberant *transcendence* of the standpoint of utility, a lofty disregard for the importance of
mere comfort and survival:

> What had [nobles] to do with utility! The viewpoint of utility is as remote and inappro-
> priate as it possibly could be in relation to such a burning eruption of the highest rank-
> ordering, rank-defining judgments: for here feeling has attained the antithesis of that
> low degree of warmth which any calculating prudence, any calculus of utility, presup-
> poses—and not for once only, not for an exceptional hour, but for good. (*GM* I:2)

A crucial part of what nobles affirm about themselves is their very ability to raise
themselves above the common crowd and its vulgar needs. This ability, however,
would be unintelligible if it were not supported by other "first order" excellences.
Without such support, we would have no idea *why* nobles should be spontaneously
self-affirming. The founders of noble morality are able to think well of themselves
because they have "received bountifully from the enormously diverse and splendid
mass of happy and desirable attributes" (Frithjof Bergmann, "Nietzsche and Analytic Ethics," in Schacht, ed., *Nietzsche, Genealogy, and Morality* [Berkeley: University of California Press, 1994], 78). Initially and typically, their superiority is made
manifest in activities that involve strenuous physical effort and large and dramatic
risks; "knightly-aristocratic value judgments presuppose a powerful physicality, a

flourishing, abundant, even overflowing health, together with that which serves to preserve it: war, adventure, hunting, dancing, competitive sports [*Kampfspiele*], and in general all that involves vigorous, free, joyful activity" (*GM* I:7). In deigning to engage in them, nobles take themselves to honor these activities (cf. *BGE* 260), when they excel at them, they can therefore honor themselves all the more. Nietzsche's nobles set exigent standards of achievement and think well of themselves when they meet these standards with aplomb.

Because the criteria of nobility are self-appointed, noble values are *ultimately* self-generated and self-grounded. But because measuring up to these self-appointed criteria is often a matter of fact, not opinion, because superiority in respect of strength, daring, or prowess, for example, is generally an ascertainable rather than a debatable matter, noble values are also grounded in the world. Nobles are nobles because they set themselves certain targets and successfully hit them; and they set the targets and strive to hit them, . . . just because; not, that is, because they are constrained to, but because they freely choose to. A noble zest for life is manifested in activities engaged in for their own sakes, not demanded by material circumstance or external authority.[2] So noble morality is a morality of *intrinsic value*, a morality of lives lived for the sake of the happiness inseparable from engaging in actions and activities deemed worthwhile in and of themselves, together with the honor consequent upon excelling at them in the eyes of one's peers.[3] In Thorstein Veblen's terms, the defining feature of a Nietzschean nobility is its legislation of an "invidious" contrast between the routine activity needed to sustain the material conditions of life—valued only instrumentally, as a necessary precondition for something better—and the pursuit of "exploit," which is valued for itself and constitutes that for the sake of which it is worth seeing to mundane matters.[4]

The powerful physicality and hearty ferocity of Nietzsche's early nobles is of a piece with their "crude, coarse, external, narrow, and altogether *unsymbolical*" (*GM* I:6) habits of mind. Although the masters value distinguishable qualities and activities, they experience each element in the "aristocratic value-equation," "good = noble = powerful = beautiful = happy = God-beloved" (*GM* I:7), as part of an indivisible whole, so many facets of the single "*Urwert*" of "being and doing as we are and do." Readers of *GM* cannot, in consequence, experience life as Nietzsche imagines the originators of noble morality to have experienced it; their form of life is *practically inaccessible* to modern men and women. It does not follow from this, though, that the perspective of master morality[5] is *epistemically unavailable* to inhabitants of the modern world. Noble values are not so bizarre as to render it doubtful that we can understand what it might have been like to live in accordance with them.

Nietzsche's nobles live according to a crude "unity of the virtues" thesis. Since their self-exaltation and commitment to their aristocratic value equation is instinctive, the thesis will not appear to them to stand in need of articulation or defense; but since excellence in running, jumping, hunting, dancing, fighting or commanding are objective matters, the virtues of the nobles are rooted in something better than sheer mystification or groundless prejudice. It is not that anyone, then or now, need think that the noble identification of "superior in certain respects"—running, hunting, commanding, and the like—with "just plain superior," "intrinsically better overall," is intellectually defensible; it is simply that the relevant achievements of the nobles are genuine achievements. And it is because of this basis in fact that the pejorative view of the slavish "other" entailed by noble morality can be something of a logically necessary afterthought; to the nobles, "the bad" are simply those who lack the ensemble of desirable qualities that they have. The distinction introduced by the slave revolt in morality, between good and evil, is a radically different sort of contrast.

When slave moralists deny that the masters are good, the term "good" means something different from what it means for masters. In order to think of the masters as evil, slave moralists must first "dye [them] in another color, interpret [them] in another fashion, see [them] in another way, through the venomous eye of *ressentiment*" (*GM* I:11). When the eye of *ressentiment* looks at the nobles, it does not see the tightly wound skein of power, wealth, courage, truthfulness and the like that the nobles themselves had perceived; it sees instead only cruelty, tyranny, lustfulness, insatiability, and godlessness (*GM* I:7). Once the *ressentiment* of the weak becomes creative and gives birth to a new kind of morality, slaves are able to look at themselves and see not unrelenting, unredeemed misery, but a new kind of goodness, constituted by the voluntary cultivation of submission, humility, and a sense of equality.

The most important accomplishment of slave morality, though, is not its turning the tables on the masters and deeming the erstwhile bad to be good and the erstwhile good to be evil; what is most important is that slave morality does this by introducing a new type of value, *impartial* value. Slave morality is the morality of impartial value in that it is the morality of value chosen by an (allegedly) impartial subject, one who is in himself neither master nor slave but can *freely choose* to behave and to evaluate either as the one or as the other. Slave moralists, says Nietzsche, "maintain no belief more ardently than the belief that *the strong man is free* to be weak and the bird of prey to be a lamb—for thus they gain the right to make the bird of prey *accountable* for being a bird of prey" (*GM* I:13).[6]

In light of the "pathos of distance" separating nobles from their inferiors, it needs to be asked how slave morality could ever have made its astonishing incursion into noble morality, how this sublimely subtle slave revolt succeeded in a way unparalleled by any political or economic revolt of the poor and the weak against the strong and the wealthy. According to Rüdiger Bittner ("*Ressentiment*," in Schacht, ed), slave morality *cannot* have originated in the slave revolt posited by Nietzsche. On the Nietzschean hypothesis, slave morality was invented as a means of compensating slaves for their wretched lives, but nobody can compensate himself by means of a revenge that he himself recognizes to be imaginary (133). *Pace* Bittner, however, the revenge of the slaves as Nietzsche portrays it resembles not the sour grapes of Aesop's fox, but a kind of collective *Schadenfreude*: the slaves make themselves happy by making the masters unhappy. What matters is that the slaves *actually* be motivated by their desire to exact revenge on the masters, not that they be clearly *aware* of this.[7]

Slave morality makes masters unhappy by making them feel guilty. Masters lose their grip on their own morality by being made to feel anxious for being who they are and doing what they do. "Men of *ressentiment*," we read in *GM* II:14, "could achieve "the ultimate, subtlest, sublimest triumph of revenge . . . if they succeeded in forcing their own misery, forcing all misery, *into the consciences* of the fortunate so that one day the fortunate began to be ashamed of their good fortune and perhaps said to one another: 'it is disgraceful to be fortunate; *there is too much misery.*'" But how could masters be persuaded of anything by slaves, given that they rarely speak to them at all and tend, when they do, to remain in the imperative mood? No satisfactory answer will be possible if we follow Richard Rorty in thinking of the bellicose nobles as "narcissistic and inarticulate hunks of Bronze Age beefcake."[8] Nietzsche's nobles are not *inarticulate* but rather *dialectically incompetent*. Only because they are articulate can they be *argued* into granting that they are free to choose whether and how to allow expression to their deepest urges to act; only because they are dialectically incompetent can they be argued into *granting* the point, which Nietzsche himself believes to be false and pernicious.

A precondition of masters being coaxed into examining the Trojan Horse of slave morality is their having already developed among themselves the practice of settling certain issues by persuasion rather than by force. Not only are Nietzsche's nobles articulate, they are also, in their relations with one another, wonderfully "resourceful in consideration, self-control, delicacy, loyalty, pride, and friendship" (*GM* I:11). By frightful contrast, in their relations with the bad or the alien they could (and often apparently did) behave "not much better than uncaged beasts of prey" (ibid.). Master morality thus operates (without a second thought) according to a double standard; conduct that would not become a noble in his dealings with peers is not regarded as similarly disgraceful vis-à-vis those beyond the pale.[9] Before the advent of slave morality, this double standard is held not to have given the nobles any pause; they practiced it with a good conscience.

Nobles become infected with bad conscience when they begin to worry about whether they are responsible, not simply for conducting themselves as befits a noble, but for *being* noble. These seeds of doubt in place, they are half way to being half convinced that they are *not* justified in thinking of themselves in the way that they had done. The inability of masters to justify themselves before the bar of impartial value is the result principally of their inability intellectually to defend two features of their outlook: the double standard that allows the bad or the alien to be treated ignobly, and the powerful physicality that infuses the activities that nobles value intrinsically.

SOCRATES

In addition to recognizing among themselves the difference between persuasion and force and to acknowledging a peer-relative sense of responsibility, Nietzsche's master class typically contained within it a priestly caste, a species of nobility that pays special attention to the value of purity. Initially, this element in the value-equation is, like all the others, construed in gross, tangible terms. "'The pure one,'" Nietzsche writes, "is from the beginning merely a person who washes himself, who forbids himself certain foods that produce skin ailments, who does not sleep with the dirty women of the lower strata, who has an aversion to blood—no more, not much more" (*GM* I:6). Nevertheless, he goes on to say, "there is from the first something *unhealthy* in . . . priestly aristocracies and in the habits ruling in them which turn them away from action and alternate between brooding and emotional explosions" (ibid.). Because they become used to turning away from action, priests begin to *spiritualize* the notion of purity to the point at which it demands as much abstention as possible from the physical and the sensual altogether; and the more thoroughgoing this spiritualization, the more likely it is that "the priestly mode of valuation [will] branch off from the knightly aristocratic and then develop into its opposite," slave morality and the ascetic ideal (*GM* I:7).

It is thus in the very idea of a priestly form of life that we find the beginnings of a Nietzschean explanation of how slave moralists get the attention of nobles. But how could brawny, marauding warlords have come to harbor brooding, neurasthenic priests in their midst?

According to *GM* II:19, prehistoric tribes "recognized a juridical duty towards earlier generations." The members of such tribes believed that "it is only through the sacrifices and accomplishments of the ancestors that the tribe *exists*—and that one has to pay them back with sacrifices and accomplishments: one thus recognizes a debt that constantly grows greater, since these forebears never cease, in their continued existence as powerful spirits, to accord the tribe new advantage and new strength" (*GM* II:19). As the tribe prospers, so waxes the debt that the living owe to the dead, especially the longest dead, the founders, until "in the end the ancestor must necessarily be transfigured into a *god*" (*GM* II:19). Initially, in other words, ancestors and gods may be propitiated by sacrifices and accomplishments of a familiarly predatory and aggressive sort; with time, though, there grows a sense that the metaphysical "otherness" of these specially powerful beings demands that they be treated with commensurately refined and mysterious forms of respect, with, for example, buildings, sights, sounds, and smells dedicated to them alone. The priesthood thus becomes that department of the nobility that takes charge of commerce with gods and spirits, leaving the knightly aristocrats to deal with mortal humans and animals.

Nietzsche says that slave morality entered world history via the cult and culture of ancient Judaism (cf. *GM* I:7 and *BGE* 195) and that its success is epitomized by the triumph of Christianity (cf. *GM* I:8). But the origination of slave morality in the world of the Hebrew Bible cannot account for its insinuation into masterly circles, for it was not through widespread conversion to Judaism that slave morality achieved its conquests. And although Christians eventually succeeded in spreading the slavish word on a heretofore unprecedented scale, conversions to Christianity cannot count as examples of slave morality's reaching knightly-aristocrats in the very first place. The late Hellenistic and early Roman world within which Christianity emerged and grew was already familiar with the crucial notions of impartial value and antisensual purity, it was a culture within which master morality had already been contaminated by slave morality's characteristic mode of evaluation. In fact, the key to Nietzsche's solution to his problem is found not in the *Genealogy* but in his interpretation of Socrates.

Nietzsche's Socrates confronted the nobility of Athens with a fateful puzzle. An ugly, irritating plebeian, whose characteristic mode of inquiry by cross-examination was impertinent by noble standards, he nevertheless *commanded* attention; he was "the buffoon that *got himself taken seriously*" (*TI* "Socrates" 5). Socrates got himself taken seriously by "discovering a new kind of *agon*" (*TI* "Socrates" 8), a dialectical *agon*; he "fascinated in that he touched the agonistic drive of the ancient Hellene,—he introduced a variant form of wrestling between young men and youths. Socrates was also a great *erotic* (*Erotiker*)" (ibid.). In virtue of their inability to understand him or to defeat him in the game of question and answer, Socrates' noble contemporaries were forced to admit that where he was concerned, they were no longer *in charge of the situation*. Since being a noble, being "one of us excellent specimens of humanity," was supposed to guarantee the wherewithal always to be in charge insofar as that was humanly possible, this admission brings with it an uncomfortable cognitive dissonance.

So when, to give a signal example, Alcibiades declares in the *Symposium* that Socrates is the only man capable of making him feel ashamed of himself, the slave revolt hypothesis would have us understand this on two levels. First, Alcibiades is ashamed of himself by the standards of master morality. When Alcibiades realizes that, since he cannot "prove Socrates wrong," he must agree that he is living his life according to priorities that he cannot defend,[10] he faces the following trilemma by his own lights: either (1) he is not as noble as he had thought; or (2) the practice of justifying his choices with reason and argument is not something worth his noble attention; or (3) he need not care whether or not he is able intellectually to defend himself against the plebeian Socrates. The second option is foreclosed because Alcibiades must recognize that it is frequently incumbent upon nobles to justify actions and decisions to other nobles, for example in councils of war or on other matters of public policy. And the third is foreclosed because Alcibiades has already been seduced into caring very much how he fares in the eyes of Socrates; he has been smitten by Socrates' strange new brand of eroticism. Hence a first spate of shame, brought on by his failure to live up to his own standards of achievement.

Nietzsche holds that the inability of an Alcibiades to close his mind to the demands of Socratic dialectic is already symptomatic of decay on the part of the noble morality of fifth-century Athens. Socrates, he writes, "understood . . . [that] the old Athens was coming to an end, . . . [that] the instincts were everywhere in anarchy," and that as a result "all the world had *need* of him" (*TI* "Socrates" 9). The robust appearance of noble morality turns out to have been deceptive, its naive exuberance and unexamined self-confidence inherently fragile and subject to endogenous disintegration. Because of this undiagnosed and only inchoately felt degeneration of fifth-century Athenian noble instincts and values, Socrates was able to radicalize the practice of defending oneself with reasons in two ways: he demanded that his interlocutors justify themselves to Socrates, a plebeian, and he demanded that they justify the *fundamental* principles according to which they lived, rather than simply justifying particular, local matters against the background of an unquestioned code of noble conduct.

Once ashamed *as* a noble in virtue of not being able to defeat Socrates in his novel *agon* of the *elenchus*, a figure like Alcibiades is ripe for experiencing further shame—bordering on guilt—for not adopting the standards of evaluation Socrates is proposing. When Alcibiades bemoans his "personal shortcomings," he is speaking as one already infected by Socratic values, one who has been forced intellectually to agree that "reason = virtue = happiness" (*TI* "Socrates" 9), that one should never voluntarily harm another, even if one has been wronged, and that the established exemplars of wisdom, courage, piety, and justice are sadly ignorant of what wisdom, courage, piety, and justice truly are. Practically speaking, though, Alcibiades has not been *really* convinced:

> [T]he moment I leave [Socrates'] side, I go back to my old ways: I cave in to my desire to please the crowd. My whole life has become one constant effort to escape from him and keep away, but when I see him, I feel deeply ashamed, because I'm doing nothing about my way of life, though I have already agreed with him that I should. (*Symposium* 216c)

Alcibiades thus bears witness, not only to the loosening grip of noble values on their adherents, but also to the emerging confusion of master and slave morality, for he himself does not separate the two distinct sources of shame that a Nietzschean analysis reveals, but speaks rather of a single disconcerting experience of inadequacy in the face of Socrates.

In the second half of the chapter, I bring empirical evidence to bear on the slave revolt hypothesis. This is necessary on the assumption that *GM* I is meant to include a historically serious reconstruction of the roots of modern Western ethical consciousness. And this assumption had better be true. For the philosophical heart of *GM* I's moral critique is the claim that the idea of impartial value originated in self-estranged *ressentiment*, while the phenomenon of intrinsic value originated in a self-affirming "active force" (*GM* II:18), and this means that the soundness of the critique depends in large part upon the truth of the claim. I argue first that the slave revolt hypothesis receives initial support from certain enduring facts of language use in English and other European languages;[11] and second that it is not impugned by the existence of foraging societies with a strikingly egalitarian mode of life but no history of nobles and slaves. If Nietzsche thought that egalitarianism required a slave revolt, such societies would falsify it outright. But an examination of the erstwhile "Bushmen," or San, of southern Africa[12] in the context of a charitable reading of his work will show that Nietzsche thought no such thing. If anything certain Bushmen/ San practices provide positive evidence for his account of the role of *ressentiment* in human psychology.

MORAL VOCABULARY

According to Peirce, a hypothesis is an attempt to account for something that would otherwise be surprising. In an 1878 paper, he offers the following as an example of the sort of thing he has in mind: "fossils are found; say, remains like those of fishes, but far in the interior of the country. To explain the phenomenon, we suppose the sea once washed over this land. This is [a] hypothesis."[13] Consider now the continued presence in English of a number of ambiguous words and phrases that fit the following two descriptions:

(1) The central ambiguity in question is that between an evaluative and a descriptive sense.
(2) From the perspective of a wholeheartedly egalitarian morality, the evaluative content runs directly contrary what would have been expected on the basis of the descriptive sense.

The words "noble" and "common" can serve as examples. *The Oxford English Dictionary* (OED) has as the second entry under "noble": "illustrious by rank, title, or birth; belonging to that class of the community which has a titular pre-eminence over the others," and as the fourth: "having high moral qualities or ideals; of great or lofty character." The potential for discrepancy between the two senses is nicely exploited in an 1829 citation, from Kenelm Digby. "The soldiers of Pavia were far more noble than their Emperor, Friedrich II, when they remonstrated against his barbarous execution of the Parmesan prisoners." Under "common," the OED has twenty-three entries, divided into three main groups. The first group of (nine) entries rings changes on the general sense "belonging equally to more than one,"[14] the second group (of six) is introduced with the phrase "of ordinary occurrence and quality, hence mean, cheap," while the final grouping contains various technical senses, from mathematics and the law among other areas. The homonymy covering the first two groups evidently conforms to the following logic: nothing that is too common, in the sense of shared equally by many, can be very distinguished(!) or desirable. The most revealing entry in the second group is sense fourteen, according to which, "common" when predicated of "ordinary persons, life, language, etc." means "lower class, vulgar, unrefined."[15]

These ambiguities of "noble" and "common" cannot be explained away as a theoretically unpromising peculiarity of the English language, as the ambiguity of "poor" between "indigent" and "substandard" can perhaps be; for the same ambiguity occurs in other European languages; in, for example, the German *"vornehm"* and *"gemein"*[16] and the French *"noble"* and *"commun."* Why should single words yoke together, on the one hand a politico-genealogical conception of superiority with a meritocratic, characterological one, and on the other hand, an innocuous concept of being shared with a pejorative term of opprobrium? According to the slave revolt hypothesis, these ambiguities are what the English anthropologist E. B. Tylor called "survivals": remnants of a time *before* good and evil, linguistic analogues of Peirce's inland fish fossils. What today might seem a tendentious *yoking* of disparate senses was once, according to Nietzsche, a perfectly natural conceptual mixture.

In *GM* I:5, Nietzsche supports the slave revolt hypothesis by appealing to the not easily translatable meanings of the ancient Greek *"agathos," "esthlos," "deilos,"* and *"kakos."* The Liddell and Scott Greek-English Lexicon (L&S) gives four primary meanings for *agathos*: (1) well-born, gentle, (2) brave, valiant, (3) good, serviceable, and (4) good in a moral sense; two for *esthlos*: (1) brave, stout, noble, and (2) morally good, faithful; three for *deilos*: (1) cowardly, hence vile, worthless, (2) low-born, mean, (3) miserable, wretched, with a compassionate sense;[17] and five for *kakos*: (1) ugly, (2) ill-born, (3) craven, base, (4) worthless, sorry, unskilled, (5) morally evil, pernicious. On Nietzsche's view, the distinctions made by L&S are useful and intelligible only to *us,* inheritors of the slave revolt trying to understand the language and culture of ancient Greece. What is notable about the way the words were used in their natural habitat is that they unproblematically blended together aesthetic, ethical, and socioeconomic qualities.[18] If Nietzsche is right, the very possibility of sharply distinguishing the descriptive from the evaluative senses of terms of this sort does not become a live option until slave morality has developed to a suitably sophisticated level.[19]

Etymology and usage cannot on their own establish the crucial Nietzschean connection between the emergence of impartial value and the expression of *ressentiment.* The systematic ambiguities I have looked at show that our (still) current moral language is not monolithic, but stratified, and that the older semantic stratum embodies an aristocratic scheme of value, while the younger one shows an accelerating tendency to identify the truly moral with a distinctively impartial, egalitarian mode of evaluation. On their own, the ambiguities cannot show that it was *ressentiment* that sparked the formation and spread of the egalitarian scheme of value.[20] Nietzschean attention to the enduring stratification of our moral vocabulary does, however, bring into relief a need for explanation on two fronts: that of the unexpected emergence of the egalitarian stratum and that of the surprising vestigial persistence of the aristocratic stratum.

And once aware of the subterranean presence of the older scheme of value within a culture ever more committed both to purifying the moral realm of contamination from considerations of brute force, or wealth, or beauty, or mental or physical dexterity, . . . or anything else that does not belong properly to morality, and to championing the moral equality of persons, reflective souls in the modern world face a consequential choice between the project of expunging the anomalous evaluative usages in an effort to carry on ethical life in the exclusive terms of an austerely impartial, rigorously purified conception of moral value and that of rethinking the nature and foundations of moral value. According to Nietzsche, the former choice is nihilistic, the latter bold and hopeful.[21]

THE BUSHMEN

To identify the historical subject of *GM* I, to say what the historical story it tells is supposed to be a story of, we can do no better than reach back for the term "Christendom": *GM* I attempts to lay bare the ethical significance of Christendom by laying bare its true origins. As Homer provides Nietzsche with his *terminus a quo*, the knightly-aristocratic mode of living and valuing, so is his *terminus ad quem* the "modern moral milk-sop," provided by that familiar nineteenth-century figure, the tender-hearted intellectual who responds to a waning conviction in the truth of Christian metaphysics with an ever more rationalized and spiritualized "cling[ing] . . . to Christian morality" (*TI* "Skirmishes" 5).

Certain of *GM* I's central claims, however, seem to transcend this culturally specific ambit. When we read that it is *certain* that "*sub hoc signo* [the slave revolt] Israel, with its revenge and revaluation of *all* values, has thus far again and again triumphed over *all* other ideals, over all more noble ideals" (I: 9, emphases added, emphasis deleted), we might take Nietzsche to hold that slavish, egalitarian values are inherently reactionary, and can originate *only* in *ressentiment* and revenge. But if this is his view, the existence of egalitarian peoples such as the San of southern Africa poses a problem. For it is widely agreed that such peoples have never developed the sort of hierarchically organized form of life that is supposed to be necessary for the existence of noble values, and that they demonstrate in their most firmly entrenched customs a strikingly high regard for peaceable and equitable group relations; they appear not simply to have *happened* not to develop distinctions of rank among themselves, they actively see to it that "there are no distinct haves and have-nots,"[22] that physical hostilities are rare, and that actions or attitudes likely to increase the risk of hostility in any form are assiduously discouraged by "unspoken social laws."[23] Richard Lee goes so far as to say that the egalitarianism of the San "is not simply the *absence* of a headman and other authority figures, but a positive insistence on the essential equality of all people and a refusal to bow to the authority of others."[24] So the San seem to abide by something very like an impartial respect for each other, even though this outlook cannot have originated in a slave revolt in morality.[25]

To make matters worse, there are elements of San culture more reminiscent of Nietzschean nobles than his slaves. The San take an intense and vital delight in music and dance,[26] are skilled, enthusiastic hunters, are known for their elaborate and beautiful paintings on the walls of caves and on rockfaces, and are inveterate storytellers. Their world, in other words, despite the absence of political hierarchy and economic complexity, suffers from no lack of "vigorous, free, joyful activity" of just the variety Nietzsche prizes when it is engaged in by Homeric Greeks and their like.[27] And it is hard to imagine that they do not value these self-expressive sorts of activity intrinsically by contrast with the (presumably instrumental) value accorded to the "menial tasks" devoted to "elaborating the material means of life." But if the *Sittlichkeit* of the San is to qualify as a form of master morality, it is a master morality without masters, since there is no evidence that San contrast themselves and their excellences with anything perceived as "low, low-minded, or plebeian."

If a commitment to peaceable egalitarianism entails a commitment to the impartial value characteristic of slave morality, then San culture falsifies the slave revolt hypothesis. But the conditional that grounds this inference is foreign to Nietzsche's moral anthropology, which explicitly recognizes an epoch of peaceable egalitarianism that precedes the emergence of master morality. In *GM* I:5 Nietzsche refers to "the commune" as "the most primitive form of society"; in *Beyond Good and Evil*, he distinguishes the "pre-moral" phase of human history, during which "the value or disvalue of an action was derived from its consequences," from the genuinely moral phase, governed by the aristocratic habit of determining the value of an action by reference to its "ancestry" or "origin" (*Herkunft*) (*BGE* 231); and in *Human, All Too Human* he characterizes the first stage of human morality, "the first sign that an animal has become human," as that in which "behavior is no longer directed to . . . momentary comfort, but rather to . . . enduring comfort," and contrasts it with a "higher stage" in which "man acts according to the principle of *honor*" (*HH* 94). For Nietzsche, in other words, we find in the *very* beginning of moral history groups of early humans struggling to survive and reproduce, and doing so in conformity with "The First Principle of Civilization," that "any custom is better than no custom" (*D* 16). Though different particular groups developed different particular customs, all of them agreed on two fundamental ideas: "that the community is more important than the individual and that a lasting advantage is preferable to a transient one" (AOM 89). Only after the human species had maintained itself in groups of this kind for some time did the knightly-aristocratic inventors of master morality emerge onto the scene. Nietzsche's description of this earliest form of ethical life as that of "the commune" strongly suggests that he takes it to be egalitarian in nature.

Nietzsche's willingness to allow that a morality of, as they might be called, *ur*-communities constitutes a form of ethical life distinct from both the master morality that breaks from it, and the slave morality that in turn breaks from master morality, means that he need not be troubled by the discovery of groups such as the San whose attitudes and behavior cannot be smoothly assimilated either to the ethos of the masters, nor to that of the slave revolt. In fact, adding the hypothesis of a morality of *ur*-communities to Nietzsche's theoretical framework enables two interesting features of San culture to turn up on the credit rather than the debit side of Nietzsche's theoretical ledger.

The role of *ressentiment* according to the slave revolt hypothesis together with the brief account of the origins of the state found in *GM* II:17 should lead us to expect *ur*-communities to be marked by the relative absence both of the pent-up *ressentiment* alleged to have engineered the slave revolt in morality, and of government by a state. According to *GM* II:17, the function of the oldest "state" (the scare quotation marks are Nietzsche's) was to "weld . . . a hitherto unimpeded and unshaped populace into a fixed form." The scare quotation marks are there, Nietzsche explains, because he takes himself to be talking about nothing more than "some pack of blond beasts of prey, a conqueror and master race which, organized for war and with the ability to organize, unhesitatingly lays its terrible claws upon a population perhaps vastly superior in numbers but still formless and nomad" (ibid.). What we know as the state, in other words, is descended from something invented by barbarian nobles, and so cannot be supposed to figure in the lives of communities that have experienced no admixture of master morality.[28]

If conformity to custom is not enforced by a superordinate authority such as the state, it must presumably be enforced by all against each and each against all. It follows from this, I think, that the bonds that bind egalitarian *ur*-communities together could not long survive any significant growth in *ressentiment* on the part of its members. Not that Nietzsche would portray *ur*-communities as free of *ressentiment* as such; that would run counter to his view that the experience of *ressentiment* is strictly coeval with the emergence of a distinctively *human* animal.[29] What is variable across time and type according to Nietzsche is the *manner* in which *ressentiment* is experienced and handled. In a noble, Nietzsche tells us, "*ressentiment* consummates and exhausts itself in an immediate reaction, and therefore does not *poison*" (*GM* I:10). And in an *ur*-community, no significant admixture of this latter, venomous form of *ressentiment* would be tolerable. For supposing it to crop up in an individual or subgroup, it would be directed either against other individuals or subgroups, or in some generalized way, against the community as a whole. In either case, the persistence of "undischarged" *ressentiment* would severely handicap the mechanisms of consensual decision making and behavior enforcement demanded by a morality of *ur*-communities. We should, consequently, expect the members of *ur*-communities to share with nobles the habit of dealing with immediately experienced *ressentiment*—that is, the immediate response to perceived encroachments, humiliations, inequities, and the like—by means of similarly immediate, outwardly directed action.

When we test these consequences of the slave revolt-*ressentiment* hypothesis against ethnographic evidence, it is confirmed on both counts. That the San have no indigenous counterparts to state power and authority as these are understood in the West is evident. As George Silberbauer observes, the regular dispersal of a Bushman/San band into smaller household-like groups during seasons of scarcity would render "a centralized, hierarchical structure, with specialized personnel and roles . . .

unable to function [during these periods]."[30] And that they refuse to tolerate just the sorts of festering grievance that feed the poisonous *ressentiment* ascribed by Nietzsche to the originators of slave morality is attested to by the variety of "venting" practices they have developed, which serve to sustain cooperative harmony and inhibit divisive hostility.

Silberbauer, for example, divides the relationships that an individual G/wi has with his or her kin (which will typically include the entire band to which the individual belongs) into "joking relationships" and "avoidance/respect relationships." Avoidance/respect holds between an individual and his or her parents, opposite sex siblings, and children past the age of seven or eight; while joking relatives include the individual's grandparents, same sex siblings, opposite sex siblings-in-law, and cousins.

> An avoidance/respect relationship [writes Silberbauer] . . . requires that those so related should ≠ao (v.t., to be reserved or respectful toward, to be scared of) one another. Their proper behavior is characterized by:
>
> - Not sitting close together and generally avoiding bodily contact if not of the same sex.
> - Being careful not to swear or make bawdy remarks in the obvious hearing of those in an avoidance relationship.
> - Not touching their possessions without permission; if an object is to be passed between avoidance relatives, an intermediary should, properly, be used and a direct transfer avoided.[31]

These restrictions on acceptable interaction virtually preclude direct conflict between avoidance relatives.[32]

Many G/wi conflicts will thus be articulated and resolved within joking relationships, and it is of the essence of the joking relationship, Silberbauer argues, to allow disputes to be conducted in such a way as to minimize the dangers of escalation and lasting resentment. "The behavior appropriate to the joking relationship," he explains, "permits free and trenchant public criticism of the actions of a joking partner and imposes an obligation to accept the criticism without the kind of resentment that might exacerbate the conflict."[33] Writing twenty years earlier than Silberbauer about the Nyae Nyae !Kung, Lorna Marshall had come to the same conclusion, observing that the !Kung's vigilant attention to "getting things into words" is something that "keeps everyone in touch with what others are thinking and feeling, releases tensions, and prevents pressures from building up until they burst out in aggressive acts."[34] Richard Lee, meanwhile, remarks of the Dobe !Kung, that

> they have evolved elaborate devices for puncturing the bubble of conceit and enforcing humility. These leveling devices are in constant daily use—minimizing the size of others' kills, downplaying the value of others' gifts, and treating one's own efforts in a self-deprecating way. *Please* and *thank you* are hardly ever found in their vocabulary; in their

stead is a vocabulary of rough humor, backhanded compliments, put-downs, and damn-
ing with faint praise.[35]

Egalitarian cultures such as that of the San are not, therefore, counterexamples to
the slave revolt hypothesis.

But, I ask in conclusion, if a sustained commitment to treating everyone alike
together with a pronounced aversion to arrogance and a tendency to shun competi-
tion do not add up to a commitment to impartial value, what does? Impartial value
in my quasi-technical sense, I answer, can be found only in moral outlooks similar
enough to that which has emerged in the course of Western civilization; its vague
identity condition is simply a sufficient conceptual resemblance to our, Western
sense of the concept. The slave revolt hypothesis presupposes that the diverse, inter-
related paradigms of slave morality—the Hebrew Bible, the New Testament, the
canonical moral philosophers from Socrates to Schopenhauer—exhibit enough
unity among them to make the proposed identity condition for commitment to
impartial value theoretically useful. So if it were to turn out that what divided, say,
Aquinas from Kant from Mill was more philosophically significant than anything
that united them, the hypothesis would be commensurately weakened. By the same
token, though, to identify a network of concepts or commitments that, there is reason to think, are common to the canonical slave moralists and that are of genuine
philosophical interest, is to have the materials for a satisfying answer to the question:
What does it take to be committed to impartial value? The answer would be that it
takes familiarity with these concepts and commitment to these views, the ones integral to the Hebrew Bible, and the New Testament, and Socrates, and the others on
the list.

When introduced in the first section of this chapter, the concept of impartial
value was characterized as "value chosen by an [. . .] impartial subject," one "who
is in himself neither master nor slave, but can *freely choose* to behave and to evaluate
either as the one or as the other" (cf. above, p. 112). This account implies that a
commitment to impartial value is bound up with a commitment to a certain conception of agency. Of a piece with impartial value is the conception of a distinctively
moral sense or locus of agency. What are the conditions of moral agency? What are
the legitimate grounds of appraisal of a distinctively moral—as opposed to aesthetic,
athletic, epistemic, prudential, . . .—sort? These are questions that will occupy
thinkers within the culture labeled by Nietzsche, with malice aforethought, the culture of slave morality; impartial value is an umbrella concept comprising the nest of
ideas and assumptions about value that generate the kind of question just listed.

Examining and rejecting the idea that the egalitarian culture of the San might
pose a counterexample to the slave revolt hypothesis has led us in conclusion to
recognize a deeper and more precise sense in which the history of *GM* I is a history
of *Western* morality. For Nietzsche's most interesting and defensible historical claim
is that it is distinctive of *our* culture, the culture that has roots in both the Hebrew
Bible and the Homeric epics, that self-affirmation and intrinsic value entered it by

way of a knightly-aristocratic leisure class, whose moral scheme was overthrown by a slave revolt that introduced a novel morality of impartial value. Whether having this history is our fortune or our misfortune is as maybe; more to the Nietzschean point, it is our *fate*.

NOTES

I would like to thank audiences at Bishop's University, The University of Miami, The Canadian and American Philosophical Associations, and Hamilton College for questions that helped me improve earlier drafts of this chapter. I would like most especially to thank Rüdiger Bittner, Ken Gemes, Jean Grondin, Susan Haack, Aimee MacDonald, Eric Saidel, James Stayer, Allen Wood, and an anonymous referee for detailed criticisms and helpful suggestions; and Christa Davis Acampora for help in trimming the originally published paper to its present size.

1. For translations of Nietzsche's works, I have relied upon Kaufmann and Hollingdale's *GM* and *WP*; Hollingdale's *HH*, *D*, *Z*, and *TI*; and Kaufmann's *GS* and *BGE*, I have often altered the translation of particular words and phrases.

2. The inclusion of war on Nietzsche's list of characteristic noble activities might seem to count against the suggestion that these activities are all engaged in for their own sakes. With Aristotle, it might be thought that "nobody chooses to make war or provoke it for the sake of making war; a man would be regarded as a bloodthirsty monster if he made his friends into enemies in order to bring about battles and slaughter" (Aristotle, *Nicomachean Ethics*. J. A. K. Thompson, trans., Hugh Tredennick, revised trans. [New York: Penguin Books, 1979], X 1177b10). To think this, though, is to fail to understand the scheme of value that governed the lives of barbarian nobles. If Aristotle's remark is an ethical truism, then Nietzsche's heroic warriors are indeed "bloodthirsty monsters." As Nietzsche says, the nobles' "indifference to and contempt for security, body, life, comfort, their appalling cheerfulness (*entsetzliche Heiterkeit*) and profound joy in all destruction, in all the voluptuousness of victory and cruelty—all this came together in the minds of those who suffered from it, in the image of the 'barbarian,' the 'evil enemy,' perhaps as the 'Goths,' the 'Vandals'" (*GM* I:11, 275/42). Now there is nothing in the thesis that, as Arthur Danto puts it, Nietzschean nobles take warmaking to be "not so much what [they] do but what [they] are, so that it is not a matter of warring for, but as, an end" ("Some Remarks on *On the Genealogy of Morals*," in Richard Schacht, ed., *Nietzsche, Genealogy, Morality: Essays on* On the Genealogy of Morals, 35), that precludes acknowledgment that nobles might *also* have valued war for the sake of extrinsic goods such as territory, plunder, and honor that can be obtained by waging it successfully. The case is entirely akin to, for example, valuing athletic ability both for its intrinsic rewards *and* for its conduciveness to good health. Cf. on the intrinsic value of war, Zarathustra, "Of War and Warriors": "You say it is the good cause that hallows even war? I tell you: it is the good war that hallows every cause" (*Z*:1).

3. My characterization of master morality as a morality of intrinsic value has evident affinities with Danto's description of it as a morality of "absolute and unconditioned value" and the "categorical good" (*Nietzsche as Philosopher* [New York: Columbia University Press, 1980], 159). But I think that Danto is mistaken to add that the contrast between master and

slave morality "reduce[s] to a fairly simple and, since Kant, routine distinction between an absolute and unconditional value, and a hypothetical or contingent value" (ibid.). For Kant, the unconditioned good must be independent of circumstance or restriction of any kind, including restrictions having to do with contingent features of us. So for Kant a truly uncon-ditioned good could not possibly be good for some but not for others, while the goods valued intrinsically by Nietzsche's nobles fit just this description; they are thought to be good for nobles, but not for commoners. Just as the former view menial employments as unworthy of them, so they view slaves as unworthy of honorable activity. For a Nietzschean noble, the fact that he takes, for example, leading the troops into battle to be an intrinsically valuable thing to do does not entail that it would be good for one of the troops to attempt the same feat. At root, the difference between Kantian unconditioned value and the intrinsic value I am attrib-uting to Nietzsche's nobles is the difference between: a "value in itself" identified by *contrast* to mere "value for us," and a "value in itself" identified by *reference to* "us nobles"; as Nietz-sche puts it in *BGE*: "the noble type of man . . . judges, 'what is harmful to me is harmful in itself.'" [*Ed. note*: Extensive discussion of intrinsic value in Nietzsche is found in Ridley, included in this volume.]

4. Thorstein Veblen, *The Theory of the Leisure Class* (New York: Random House, 1934).

5. As Alexander Nehamas (*Nietzsche: Life as Literature* [Cambridge, MA: Harvard University Press, 1985], 254) points out, Nietzsche only uses the phrase "master morality" once in his published works (in *BGE* 260). Nevertheless, he speaks often enough of "noble morality" (*GM* I:10 and *A* 24), "aristocratic values and value judgments" (*GM* I:2, 7, 16) and "nobler ideals" (*GM* II:9), and he identifies nobles with masters unambiguously enough to warrant the use of the term as a natural and convenient contrast to "slave morality." I shall, in any case, use "master morality" interchangeably with "noble morality."

6. Nietzsche's model for the ethos of primeval man is the ethos of Homeric man. The casual noble (mis)treatment of inferiors is vividly illustrated by Odysseus's rebuking of Ther-sites in Book Two of the *Iliad*. See *The Iliad*, translated by Richmond Lattimore (Chicago: University of Chicago Press, 1961), Book II, lines 246–64.

7. Bittner thinks that if we are to speak of creative *ressentiment* and a slave revolt, we must imagine the earliest slave moralists to be in a situation analogous to La Fontaine's fox; they must look at the lives of nobles, "know" that such lives are healthier and happier than their own, and yet convince themselves (and others) that the masters are in fact worse off than themselves. I think it more charitable to interpret Nietzsche as holding, with Bittner himself, that the evolution of slave morality was a long, slow process. Why could Nietzsche not agree that slave morality "may have dawned on the slaves and grown on them, without ever having been set up expressly" (Bittner, 133)? Because, Bittner says, his "pathos of creativ-ity" demands that a slave revolt spring from a creative act and something's being the result of a creative act is incompatible with its "just growing on us." In effect, Bittner assumes that a creative slave revolt requires fully-fledged Sartrean self-deception, and I disagree.

8. Richard Rorty, "Against Belatedness," *London Review of Books*, 16 June–6 July 1983: 3.

9. In *GM* I's most incendiary passage concerning the propensity of nobles periodically to exempt themselves from their own standards of civilized behavior and return to the innocence of a "predator conscience" (*GM* I:11), Nietzsche speaks of the nobles' releasing their pent-up aggression on "*das Fremde*" (the foreign or alien), rather than on their inferiors. Furthermore, the fact that the marauding warriors are depicted as "returning from a disgusting procession

of murder, arson, molestation, and torture, exhilarated and undisturbed of soul, as if it were no more than a student prank, convinced that the poets will have much to sing about for a long time to come" (ibid.), suggests that Nietzsche has in mind an expedition such as that of the Greeks to Troy rather than a day-to-day diet of less dramatic brutalities inflicted upon the weak by the strong. I do not, therefore, think it obvious that master morality's double standard entailed that dealings between nobles and their subordinates were governed by no remotely humane standards at all.

10. Plato, *Symposium*, Alexander Nehamas and Paul Woodruff, trans. (Indianapolis, IN: Hackett, 1989), 216b–c.

11. In so doing, I will be expanding upon suggestions found in *GM* I:4 and 5, as well as in a modest way responding to Nietzsche's proposed prize question: "What light does linguistics, and especially the study of etymology, throw on the history of the evolution of moral concepts?" (*GM* I:17).

12. The term "Bushman" derives from the Dutch "Bojesman," and was used by the Dutch settlers of southern Africa to refer to one of the two quite different native groups that they had found upon arrival. I have retained the word in my titles because, as Richard Lee observes, it is the name by which these people "became known to the world" (*The !Kung San* [Cambridge: Cambridge University Press, 1979], 29). But I have chosen to refer to them as the San in the text, since there seems to be a consensus amongst those who work on and with the people in question, that the term "Bushman" has acquired an unpleasantly derogatory connotation (see Lee op cit., 29–31 and Edwin Wilmsen, *Land Filled with Flies* [Chicago: University of Chicago Press, 1989] 26–33) but note that George Silberbauer in *Hunter and Habitat in the Central Kalahari Desert* [Cambridge: Cambridge University Press, 1981] chooses Bushman over San to refer to the larger group to which the G/wi, who are the focus of his study, belong). As it happens, even San is not, as Lee remarks, "an entirely satisfactory term," since it has a connotation signifying "rascal" in Khoi-Khoi, the language spoken by the *other* native people found by the Dutch in the seventeenth century, and it is not used by any of the people referred to by it to refer to themselves. But in the absence of any single term that does cover just the people under discussion and is used by those people themselves, it seems to me that "San" is, at the risk of sounding mealy-mouthed, the "safest" term there is for my purposes.

13. Charles Sanders Peirce, "Deduction, Induction, Hypothesis," in *Collected Papers*, Vol. 2. (Cambridge, MA: Harvard University Press, 1932), paragraph 625.

14. The definition is Dr. Johnson's.

15. "Vulgar" is itself a word that exhibits the ambiguity under discussion, and it is not therefore surprising to find that "common" appears regularly in the OED's entries for it. Many of these senses are evaluatively neutral, for example, "common or usual language, vernacular," "in common or general use," "of common or general kind," while others are strongly disparaging, for example entry thirteen: "having a common and offensively mean character; coarsely commonplace; lacking in refinement or good taste; uncultured, ill-bred." While we're at it, "mean" (as an adjective) offers yet another instance of the phenomenon. It has a large number of senses clustering around "intermediate," "moderate," "of average value, as in 'mean pressure, temperature' etc.," and it can also be predicated of things to mean "poor in quality, of little value, inferior, petty, unimportant, inconsiderable" and of persons, their characters and actions to mean "destitute of moral dignity or elevation, ignoble, small-minded."

16. According to the etymological conjectures favored by the OED and others, *"gemein"* is cognate both with "common" ("ge-mein," like "co-mon") and with "mean."

17. Note in passing the support that this third sense gives to Nietzsche's contention, canvassed above, that "almost all the [ancient Greek] words referring to the common man have remained as expressions signifying 'unhappy', 'pitiable'" (*GM* I:10).

18. The modern lexicographer's need to provide, for *agathos, esthlos,* and *kakos,* a separate entry stressing that the words can mean "morally" good or bad as the case may be, is a good example of the lack of philosophico-historical depth that *GM* attempts to combat. When Liddell and Scott illustrate the fourth listed sense of *agathos* with passages from Theognis and Plato, as if in the same breath, they are, according to Nietzsche, eliding exactly the gulf to which attention needs to be drawn. According to Nietzsche, Theognis is a spokesman for noble values, while Plato is involved in a campaign to undermine them.

19. As to the question whether Nietzsche *is* right on this point, he appears to be so. Walter Kaufmann's translation of *GM* includes, at I §5, an editorial footnote that cites Gerald Else in support of Nietzsche's view. Else writes, inter alia, that "Greek thinking begins with and for a long time holds to the proposition that mankind is divided into 'good' and 'bad,' and these terms are quite as much social, political, and economic as they are moral" (*Aristotle's Poetics: The Argument* [Cambridge, MA: Harvard University Press, 1957], 75). To Else could be added Moses Finley, *The World of Odysseus,* revised ed., (New York: Viking Press, 1978), and William Prior, *Virtue and Knowledge: An Introduction to Ancient Greek Ethics* (New York: Routledge, 1991). The former notes that in the world of the Homeric poems, "'warrior' and 'hero' are synonyms, and the main theme of a warrior culture is constructed on two notes—prowess and honour. The one is the hero's essential attribute, the other his essential aim. Every value, every judgment, every action, all skills and talents have the function of either defining honour or realizing it" (113), and maintains as well that "it is self-evident that the gods of the *Iliad* were the gods of heroes, or, plainly spoken, of the princes and the heads of the great households" (ibid., 139). The latter characterizes the Homeric hero as "a person of noble rank who functions in a highly stratified society according to a strict code of conduct. He lives for glory, which he achieves by the display of virtue or excellence, particularly excellence in combat, and which is accorded to him by his fellow heroes in the form of gifts and renown" (9).

It is perhaps worth anticipating an objection to the effect that the Nietzschean view for which I am claiming scholarly confirmation is in fact so well known and accepted as to be insignificant rather than striking. It seems to me sufficient in reply to point out that Nietzsche expounded these ideas at a time in which no less an aficionado than Gladstone was able to find in Homer, not only "the 'essential germ' of the form of constitution enjoyed in Britain and America" (Richard Jenkyns, *The Victorians and Ancient Greece* [Cambridge, MA: Harvard University Press, 1980), 202), but also a remarkable degree of convergence with Christian theology. Richard Jenkyns reports that Gladstone thought it "evident that Jupiter, Neptune and Pluto (he used the Roman names) were a memory [*sic*!] of the Trinity, Apollo was a relic of belief in a Messiah, as can be seen from his double character as Saviour and Destroyer (a page is allotted to demonstrating that Apollo's rape of Marpessa was 'not of a sensual character'). Was Minerva the Logos or the Holy Spirit? Did Latona represent Eve or the Virgin Mary? How curious that the poems contained no mention of the Sabbath!" (ibid., 203).

20. I am grateful to Allen Wood for showing me the force of this point.

21. A defense of these claims is, of course, beyond the scope of this chapter.

22. Lorna Marshall, "Sharing, Talking, and Giving: Relief of Social Tensions among the

!Kung," in Richard B. Lee and Irven DeVore, eds., *Kalahari Hunter Gatherers* (Cambridge, MA: Harvard University Press, 1976), 357.

23. Ibid., 351, 370–71.

24. Lee, op cit., 457.

25. The view of San life that I am taking as canonical is not universally shared. Edwin Wilmsen, for example, thinks that the image of the San that I accept here for the sake of argument is scarcely more solidly grounded in the actual lives and history of the people in question than was the eighteenth- and nineteenth-century image of the noble savage. If this is so, the San do not pose nearly as direct a threat to the slave revolt hypothesis as I am assuming they do. So I do not think that I need take a stand as between Wilmsen on the one hand and Lee and Marshall on the other.

26. Van der Post writes that "music was as vital as water, food, and fire to [the Bushmen]. . . . We never found a group so poor or desperate that they did not have some musical instrument with them. And all their music, song, sense of rhythm, and movement achieved its greatest expression in their dancing (Laurens van der Post, *The Lost World of the Kalahari* [Hammondsworth: Penguin Books, 1958], 225–26).

27. In addition to all this, Laurens van der Post provides evidence that, while they may not have developed a barbarian fondness for conquest on their own, the San can respond to attacks from others in the manner of masters rather than slaves.

> What, indeed, [writes van der Post] could be prouder than the Bushman's reply to the young Martin du Plessis, a boy of fourteen who was sent into a great cave . . . where the Bushman was surrounded in his last stronghold by a powerful commando? The boy   besought him to surrender, promising to walk out in front of him as a live shield against any treacherous bullets. At last, impatient that his refusal was not accepted, the Bushman scornfully said: "Go! Be gone! Tell your chief I have a strong heart! Go! Be gone! Tell him my last words are that not only is my quiver full of arrows but that I shall resist and defend myself as long as I have life left. Go! Go! Be gone!" (van der Post, op. cit. 46)

The preference for death before cowardice and dishonor exhibited here, it seems, is entirely of a piece with that of an Achilles, a Hector, or the heroes of the Norse or Irish sagas. Note, though, Elizabeth Marshall Thomas's contrary conclusion that "it is not in [the] nature of [Bushmen] to fight" and that "they would much rather run, hide, and wait until a menace has passed than to defend themselves forcefully" (Elizabeth Marshall Thomas, *The Harmless People* [New York: Alfred A. Knopf, 1970] 21). Marshall Thomas goes so far as to say that "Bushmen deplore and misunderstand bravery. The heroes of their legends are always little jackals who trick, lie, and narrowly escape, rather than larger animals such as lions (who in the Kalahari are something of a master race)" (ibid., 22). Wilmsen would take Marshall Thomas's evidence to be indicative, not of anything intrinsic to San culture as such, but rather of the subjugated position into which the San have been forced over the past several hundred years by other native Africans and by Europeans.

28. It might be thought that Nietzsche's references to prenoble *ur*-communities are inconsistent with his account of the origin of the state in *GM* I:17. For that account is developed in the course of articulating "a first, provisional statement of [an] hypothesis concerning the origin of 'bad conscience,'" and according to that hypothesis bad conscience was "a serious illness that man was bound to contract under the stress of the most fundamental change he ever experienced—that change which occurred when he found himself finally (*endgültig*) enclosed within the walls (*in den Bann*) of society and peace" (ibid.). Does this mention of

"society and peace" not imply that Nietzsche here identifies the origin of the state with the origin of socialization *überhaupt*, that he sees no substantial difference between hierarchically structured human society and human society as such? In a word, no.

Translated more literally than he is by Kaufmann, Nietzsche (1) speaks of man finding himself "*conclusively under the spell* of society and peace," (2) refers twice in the opening sentences of *GM* II:17 to identifiable "populations" (*Bevölkerungen*) that are conquered, subjugated, and reformed by more powerful and hierarchically minded invaders, and (3) maintains that punishments figure prominently among the "fearful bulwarks with which the political (*staatliche*) organization protected itself against the old instincts of freedom" (ibid.). In light of all this, Nietzsche's argument in *GM* II:16–17 positively requires the assumption that life in hierarchically structured state-governed communities is preceded by something simpler, more amorphous, and more egalitarian. It is the cataclysmic advent of the state that demands the instinctual repression responsible for the growth of bad conscience. Life in a prehierarchical state is *comparatively* unformed, not yet fully "under the spell of society and peace," which is to say that such communities lack the sort of sharply defined political identity made possible by the institutionalized authority of law and the state. Chief among the "bulwarks" of social order we can expect to be missing from *ur*-communities will be publicly enforced and codified practices of punishment. Kaufmann's free translation of "*in den Bann der Gesellschaft und Frieden*" as "within the walls of society and peace" makes the interpretation I wish to defend rather hard to bring into view, for it would seem that groups must be located either inside or outside such walls, with no third location possible. On my view Nietzsche's language draws attention, not only to *the fact of being in a condition of society and peace*, but also to *the means by which this condition is achieved*; namely by a kind of mental captivation reminiscent of a magical spell. This subtlety, allows one to hold that egalitarian *ur-communities* are peaceful societies (rather more peaceful in fact than the militaristic societies that succeed them) without yet being "conclusively under the *spell* of society and peace" (or "under the sway of" them, as Clark and Swensen put it), that is, without regarding society and peace as conditions that have to be enforced—*le mot juste* for once—*hegemonically*. I would like to thank the anonymous reviewer for *Philosophy and Phenomenological Research* for bringing this point to my attention.

29. I am assuming here that *ressentiment* in its most generic form can be identified with the turning inward of an instinct denied outward discharge spoken of in *GM* II:16.

30. Silberbauer, op cit., 168.

31. Ibid., 143.

32. Ibid., 175.

33. Ibid., 172.

34. Marshall, op cit., 355.

35. Lee, op cit., 458.

8

Lightning and Flash, Agent and Deed (*GM* I:6–17)*

Robert B. Pippin

THE STRONG AND THE WEAK

In his *On the Genealogy of Morals*, Nietzsche expressed great skepticism about the moral psychology presupposed by the proponents of "slave morality," the institution that we know as antiegoistic, universalist, and egalitarian morality *simpliciter*.[1] He claimed to identify the foundational claim in such a moral psychology—belief in "the submerged changeling, the 'subject'" (*GM* I:13)—and he then offered a historical and psychological narrative about the origin of the notion. His story purported to show why a certain type ("the weak," the "slavish") would try to justify its position relative to the stronger type by portraying the stronger's "expression of strength" as evil, and the situation of the defeated slave (powerlessness, humility) as good. This, in turn, if it was to be an effective condemnation (rather than a mere report of the facts), had to go one step farther than characterizing those who end up by nature as such overpowering types, one step farther than just characterizing the weak type, those who happen in empirical fact to be meek, humble, sympathetic to the suffering of others, and so forth. The real genius of the slave rebellion, according to Nietzsche, lies in its going beyond a simple inversion of value types, and in the creation of a new way of thinking about human beings: the creation of a subject "behind" the actual deed, one who could have acted to express his strength (or virtu-

*This chapter originally appeared in *Friedrich Nietzsche, Genealogie der Moral*, edited by Otfried Höffe (Berlin: Akademie Verlag, 2004), 47–63. Reprinted with permission of the author.

ous weakness) *or not*, and who thus can be condemned and held individually and completely responsible for his voluntary oppression of others, even as the slave can be praised for his supposedly voluntary withdrawal from the struggle. Nietzsche's psychological narrative points to a distinct motive that explains this ideological warfare and invention—his phrase is, "thanks to the counterfeit and self-deception of impotence"—and he draws a conclusion about the realization of this motive, such that the slave can act, "just as if the weakness of the weak—that is to say, their essence, their effects, their sole ineluctable, irremovable reality—were a voluntary achievement, willed, chosen, a deed, a meritorious act. This type of man, prompted by instinct for self-preservation and for self-affirmation, needs to believe in a neutral, independent 'subject'" (*GM* I:13).

The experience of the two differing motivations cited in these two passages is obviously supposed to be linked. Nietzsche appears to assume that the experience of such impotence itself is, if confronted unadorned, unbearable in some way, threatens one's very "self-preservation"; requires a "self-affirmation" if one is to continue to lead a life. Hence the "self-deceit," the compensatory belief that one's "impotence" is actually an achievement to be admired. In sum, this invention of a subject (or soul) independent of and "behind" its deeds is what "the sublime self-deception that interprets weakness as freedom, and their being thus-and-thus as a merit, makes possible" (*GM* I:13).

However, as in many other cases, Nietzsche is not content merely to ascribe these psychological motivations to the originators of some moral code. Even if the slaves had such a "need," establishing that would not of itself establish the further claim that this slavishly motivated commitment is actually false, *necessarily* deceived. Nietzsche clearly realizes this, and certainly wants to establish that further point. He suggests how he intends to demonstrate that in a famous simile proposed in *GM* I:13, just before the passages cited above. The simile appears to assert an ambitious, sweeping metaphysical claim (despite Nietzsche's frequent demurrals about the possibility of metaphysics). His main claim is stated right after he notes that there is nothing surprising or even objectionable in the fact that "little lambs" insist that the greatest evil is "bird of prey" behavior, and that the highest good is little lamb behavior. Nietzsche goes on, "To demand of strength that it should not express itself as strength, that it should not be a desire to overcome, a desire to throw down, a desire to become master, a thirst for enemies and resistances and triumphs, is just as absurd as to demand of weakness that it should express itself as strength. . . . For just as the popular mind separates the lightning from its flash and takes the latter for an action, for the operation of a subject called lightning, so popular morality also separates strength from expressions of strength, as if there were a neutral substratum behind the strong man, which was free to express strength, or not do so. But there is no such substratum; there is no 'being' behind doing, effecting, becoming; the doer is merely a fiction added to the deed—the deed is everything" (*GM* I:13; see also *BGE* 17).

This denial of a subject behind the deed and responsible for it is so sweeping that it immediately raises a problem for Nietzsche. It is the same question that would arise for anyone attacking the commonsense psychological view that holds that a subject's intention (normally understood as a desire for an end, accompanied by a belief about means or a subject's deciding or "willing" to act for some purpose or end) must stand both "behind" and "before" some activity in order for the event to be distinguished *as a doing (Thun) at all*, as something *done* by someone. We must be able to appeal to such a subject's "intending" for us to be able to distinguish, say, someone volunteering for a risky mission, as an ontological type, from steel rusting or water running downhill or a bird singing. (The identification of such a prior condition is, in Wittgenstein's famous words, what would distinguish my arm going up from me raising my arm.) It is "behind" the deed in the sense that other observers see only the movements of bodies—say, someone stepping out from a line of men—and must infer some intending subject in order to understand and explain both what happened and why the action occurred. (If there "is just the deed," we tend to think, stepping out of line *is* just body movement, metaphysically like the wind blowing over a lamp.) A subject's intention is "before" the deed because that commonsense psychological explanation typically points to such a prior intention as the *cause* of the act; what best answers the question, "why did that occur."

NATURALISM?

Now Nietzsche is often described as a "naturalist," perhaps a psychological naturalist in his account of moral institutions. Nowadays, naturalism is understood as the position that holds that there are only material objects in space and time (perhaps just the entities and properties referred to by the most advanced modern sciences), and that all explanation is scientific explanation, essentially subsumption under a scientific law. However, even with such a general, vague definition, it is unlikely that Nietzsche accepts this sort of naturalism, especially the latter condition. In *GM* II:12, he rails against the "mechanistic senselessness" of modern science, and he contrasts what he here and elsewhere calls this democratic prejudice with "the theory that in all events a will to power is operating" (*GM* II:12). But many people think he accepts at least the former condition, and that such acceptance may partly explain what is going on in the denial of any separate soul in *GM* I:13; that is, that Nietzsche mostly means to deny "free will."

And Nietzsche's descriptions of the strong and the weak in *GM* I:13 have indeed already expressed the antivoluntarist view that the strong can "do nothing else but" express their strength. He seems to treat the commonsense psychology just sketched as essentially and wholly derivative from the slave or ultimately Christian compensatory fantasy of self-determining subjects and a "could have done otherwise" sense of freedom. This all does make it tempting to regard him as indifferent to the distinction between ordinary natural events and actions, and as perfectly content to consider the "reactive force" most responsible for the slave rebellion—*ressentiment*—as one of the many natural forces in the (psychological) world that we will need to appeal to in order to account for various social and political appearances. All this by contrast with a separate subject which could act or not, depending on what it "decides." We could interpret *GM* I:13 as only denying the possibility of this metaphysically free or spontaneous, self-determining subject behind the deed and attribute to Nietzsche a broadly consistent naturalism. Nietzsche certainly believes that the free will picture *is* a fantasy (*BGE* 19, 21; *TI* "Errors" 7). And in *GM* I:13 he obviously thinks that the classic picture of a commanding will and the resultant action give us, paradoxically and unacceptably, *two* actions, not one (cf. Williams 1994, 243), and that it pushes the basic question of origin back yet again.

The trouble with proceeding very far in this direction is that Nietzsche does not seem interested in merely naturalizing all talk of motives, goals, intentions, and aversions; he denies that whole model of behavior. The passages just quoted do not appear to leave room for *corporeal* states causing various body movements, as if, for example, a subject's socially habituated fear for his reputation (where fear is understood as some sort of corporeal brain-state or materially embodied disposition) were "behind" his stepping out of line and acting in a way he knew would count for others as volunteering. If that model were adopted, we would still be pointing to some determinate causal factor "behind" and "before" the deed. The perplexing lightning simile is unequivocal, though and we would not be following its suggestion if we merely substituted a material *substance* (like the brain or brain states or corporeally embodied desire) for an immaterial soul. Moreover, such a naturalist account relies on the material continuity through time of some identical substance in order to attribute to it various manifestations and expressions as interconnected properties. If there were no substance or subject of any kind behind or underlying various different events, it is hard to see how we might individuate these expressions of force, and even if we could, how we might distinguish a universe of episodic, atomistic force-events from the world that Nietzsche himself refers to, a world with some clear substantial continuities: slaves, masters, institutions, priests, and so on. He nowhere seems inclined to treat such a world as arbitrarily grouped collections of force-events (grouped together by whom or what, on what basis?), as if there were either "becoming-master" events or "becoming subdued by" events, and so forth. We thus still need a credible interpretation of: "But there is no such substratum; there is no 'being' behind doing, effecting, becoming; the doer is merely a fiction added to the deed—the deed is everything" (*GM* I:13). Materialist or naturalist bloody-mindedness is not going to help.

SUBJECTS AND PSYCHOLOGY

In order to understand what such an extreme claim could mean ("there is no lightning behind the flash and responsible for it," "no subject behind the deed"; there is just the deed), we might turn to Nietzsche's own psychological explanations of the slave revolt, and what appears to be his own general theory about the psychological origins of normative distinctions. One would certainly expect consistency between his own account and *GM* I:13. In some places, there is certainly language consistent with the antiagent language of *GM* I:13, but at the same time and more frequently, language immediately in tension with it. In *GM* I:10, Nietzsche appears to attribute explanatory power to forces themselves, as if causally efficacious force-events: "The slave revolt in morality begins when *ressentiment* itself becomes creative and gives birth to values" (*GM* I:10). It is odd to say that resentment itself could become creative and could *do* something, and not that a subject, motivated by such resentment, acted, but perhaps Nietzsche is deliberately looking ahead to his own denial of any causal agent. Nietzsche also speaks of "the noble mode of valuation" as if it were an independent explicans (although both these expressions still seem to "substantialize" force and a dispositional mode and to distinguish them from the manifestations they cause). And in his most important statement in *On the Genealogy of Morals* of what appears to be his will to power "doctrine," Nietzsche seems to be trying to deliberately avoid *any* commitment to an agent-cum-intention causing-the-deed model. "[A]ll events in the organic world are a subduing, a becoming master, and all subduing and becoming master involves a fresh interpretation, an adaptation through which any previous 'meaning' and 'purpose' are necessarily obscured or even obliterated. . . . But purposes and utilities are only signs that a will to power has become master of something less powerful and imposed upon it the character of a function" (*GM* II:12). And likewise: in the Second Essay, he talks freely of such things as a "struggle between power complexes" (*GM* II:11).

On the other hand, Nietzsche would seem to be right in *GM* I:13 about the *inevitably* substantializing tendencies of language itself, even throughout his own account. Immediately after his claim using *ressentiment* as the subject of a sentence, he cannot himself resist parsing *this* as "the ressentiment of *natures* that are denied the true reaction, that of deeds, and compensate themselves with an imaginary revenge" (*GM* I:10, my emphasis). This reintroduction of the substantive bearer of the property, "natures," who express *ressentiment*, rather than any claim about *ressentiment*-events occurring, is also more consistent with the overall psychological manner of explaining morality. It is hard enough to imagine appealing to something like forces without substrates in which they inhere, of which they are properties, but the core idea of Nietzsche's account is a picture of a social struggle, lasting over some time, among human beings, not forces, which results in a situation of relative stability, a successful subduing and a being subdued, wherein, finally, the reaction of the subdued finds another outlet of response than a direct counterforce. This last is caused by an apparently unbearable feeling, impotence, responsible then for a reaction motivated by an attempt to revalue such impotence. So, as he must, Nietzsche refers both to "the noble mode of valuation" as explicans and directly to "the noble man" as someone with motives, intentions, a self-understanding, a certain relation to the slavish, and so forth. I say that Nietzsche "must" so refer because, as several others have pointed out (Rüdiger Bittner with regard to Nietzsche, Bittner 2001,

34–46; Axel Honneth with regard to Foucault, Honneth 1991), there cannot just "be" *subduing* and *subdued* events. *Someone* must be subdued and be *held* in subjection, be prevented from doing what he might otherwise do, by the activities of someone else who is not so restricted, or by some internalization of such originally external constraint (cf. Nietzsche's account of "internalization" [*Verinnerlichung*] in *GM* II:16). (Otherwise, we don't have a becoming-*master*, just an episodic, quantitative more or less.) Even the "will to power" passages cannot end by pointing to a mere "becoming-master" *event*. If such a striving is successful, what we are left with is *a Master*, not the residue of an event, and thereby correspondingly a slave.[2]

Finally, throughout *On the Genealogy of Morals* Nietzsche treats his own explanation of the slave revolt in morality as something not acknowledged by, something that would be actively disputed by, the proponents of such a revolt, and for such an account to make sense, there must be such proponents, now quite complex proponents it turns out. That is, while he might invoke the language of psychological naturalism, the language of instincts, to account for this moralizing reaction, he also notes that this instinctual force is not "for itself" what it is "in itself," to adopt a non-Nietzschean form of expression. It is not just experienced as a desire pushing for satisfaction. The "moral reaction" is not experienced by such a subject as what it really is, even though the reaction could not be satisfying unless *also* "experienced," somehow, as some sort of revenge.[3] Morality is a "counterfeit" and "self-deceit," and its effectiveness as a weapon against the Master would disappear if it were correctly understood by its proponents as a psychological ploy or strategy in the search for an indirect route to power over one's oppressors.

But then, it would seem, it cannot be that "the deed is *all* there is (*das Thun ist Alles*)." Nietzsche himself, it would appear, is only able to account for the deed being what it is (a reactive, revenge-inspired rebellion, motivated by the frustrations of impotence) by appeal to the standard psychological language of a subject's "true intentions," the struggle to realize that intention, the conflict with other subjects that this produces, and, as we have just seen, he must also be able to refer even to the possibility of a *self*-deceived commitment to an intention, acting for the sake of an end one consciously and sincerely would disavow. Nietzsche's claim is that the deed in question *is not* a discovery, or even the attempt at a discovery, of the true nature of good and evil, but a revolt, *because* it is motivated by a vengeful reaction. But if there were "only the deed, not a doer," the question—*what* deed?—would, it appears, be unanswerable, or at least it could not be answered in the "divided subject" way Nietzsche appears committed to. Indeed, in pursuing that question, we are not only back with a "subject" and a subject's intentions behind the deed, but involved in a hunt for true, genuine intentions, lying "back there" somewhere, but hidden and unacknowledged, even though causally effective.

And finally the whole direction of Nietzsche's narrative seems to depend on what *GM* I:13 denies. Since the revolt is something the slaves *did*, is a deed, and not something that happened to them, or merely "grew" in them, it is something that can be *undone*, that, in the right situation, can be countered by a new "legislation of values," once the "crisis of Christian honesty" occurs. (Oddly, this alternative *deed*, or "revaluation" seems to be an idea that Nietzsche both accuses the slave of fabricating in order to focus absolute blame on the master, and a possibility Nietzsche himself seems to want to preserve, the possibility of an eventual "self-overcoming.") And all of this requires not only subjects of deeds, but even possibilities inhering yet unrealized in such subjects. Again, the denial of a causally autonomous soul, the free will, and freely undertaken commitments does not get us very far in understanding Nietzsche's own enterprise in a way that is consistent with *GM* I:13. And so we need to think again about what "the deed is all there is" might amount to.

NIETZSCHE'S PROBLEM

Now it may be that Nietzsche is such an unsystematic thinker that at some point in any philosophical reconstruction, one will simply have to pick and choose, follow one of the paths Nietzsche opened up and ignore another, inconsistent path that he also pointed to.[4] But if we reject the substantializing of the will to power, or any substantializing, the social account that results from its application would look like so many heterogeneous episodes of conflicting and discontinuous fields of contingent forces and it would resemble not at all the typology that Nietzsche so clearly relies on. Accordingly, Rüdiger Bittner has encouraged us to discard the "will to power" explanation as a dead end, one ultimately wedded to a "creationist" and projective theory of value and concentrate on what Bittner thinks is closer to Nietzsche's interest: an adequate account of life and living beings, and therewith the instability and provisionality of any substance claim. To understand the domain of "life," we have to rid ourselves of substance presumptions and concentrate on subject-less "activity" itself. (Bittner also wants us to take *GM* I:13 as the heart of Nietzsche's project, and abandon completely the language of subjects' "creating value.")

But, as we have seen, if we accept *GM* I:13 at face value, and insist that there is *no* doer behind the deed, we have to give up much more than the metaphysics of the will to power, and its assumptions about exclusively created value. We will make it very difficult to understand the whole of Nietzsche's own attack on the moral psychology of Christian morality, since he appears to rely on a traditional understanding of act descriptions (that the act is individuated as an act mainly by reference to the agent's intentions), and he invokes a complex picture of unconscious motives, operative and motivating, but inaccessible as such to the agents involved. Without Nietzsche's *own*, prima facie inconsistent Doer-Deed language, the question of *what* is supposedly happening in the slave revolt, which in his account clearly relies on notions of subjection to the will of others, resentment, and even "madness" (*GM* II:22), will be difficult to understand. Values cannot be said to simply "grow" organically, given some sort of context. For one thing, as Nietzsche famously remarked, we must *make* ourselves into creatures capable of keeping promises, and this requires many "centuries" of commitment, perseverance, and so the unmistakable exercise of subjectivity. It seems a question-begging evasion to gloss all such appeals as really about "what happens *to* us," what madness befalls us, in situations of subjection. There would be little reason to take Nietzsche seriously if he were out to make what Bernard Williams has called the "uninviting" claim that "we never really do anything, that no events are actions" (Williams 1994, 241).

THE INSEPARABILITY OF SUBJECT AND DEED

We might do better, I want to suggest, to appreciate first that the surface meaning of the claims made in *GM* I:13 remains quite elusive. As *GM* II:12 pointed out, the notion of an "activity" functions as a "fundamental concept" in what Nietzsche himself claims, and he insists in that passage on a contrast between such an activity and the "mechanistic senselessness" of the ordinary modern scientific world view. We thus need to return to *GM* I:13 and appreciate that Nietzsche is not denying that *there is* a subject of the deed; he is just asserting that it is not *separate*, distinct from the activity itself; it is "in" the deed. He is not denying that strength "*expresses* itself" in acts of strength. He is in fact asserting just that, that there is such an *expression*, and so appears to be relying on a notion of expression, rather than intentional causality to understand how the does is in the deed. ("To demand of strength that it should not express itself as strength" is the expression he uses. He does not say, "there are just strength-events.") That—the appeal to expression—is quite an important clue. He is not denying, in other words, that there is a genuine deed, and that it must be distinguishable from any mere event. He maintains that distinction. He has only introduced the category of deed or activity so quickly and metaphorically that it is difficult to flesh out what he means. (Put in terms of his image, in other words, the "flash" (*Leuchte*) is not *just* an electrical discharge in the air. A certain sort of meteorological event is "expressed," and so a phenomenally identical "flash" might not be lightning, but could be artificially produced. It would be a phenomenally identical event, but not lightning.)

In order to understand this claim about a doer "in" the deed, I want to suggest a comparison with another philosopher that will seem at first glance quite inappropriate. Assume for a moment that there is a brotherhood of modern anti-Cartesians, philosophers united in their opposition to metaphysical dualism, to a picture of mind shut up in itself and its own ideas and so in an unsolvable skeptical dilemma about the real world, and opposed as well to the notion of autonomous, identifiable subjects, whose intentions and finally "acts of willing" best identify and explain distinct sorts of events in the world, actions. There is a range in such a group, including Nietzsche and Wittgenstein and Heidegger, but surely a charter member is also Hegel. And in his Jena *Phänomenologie*, Hegel formulated this issue of how to "find" the agent "in" the deed in a way that suggests something of what Nietzsche may have been thinking. Consider: "The true being of a man is rather his deed; in this the individual is actual, and it is the deed that does away with both aspects of what is [merely] 'meant' [intended] to be: in the one aspect where what is 'meant' has the form of a corporeal passive being, the individuality, in the deed, exhibits itself rather as the negative essence, which only is in so far as it supercedes mere being. . . . It [the deed] is this, and its being is not merely a sign, but the fact itself. It is this and the individual human being is what the deed is . . . even if he deceives himself on the point, and, turning away from the action into himself, fancies that in this inner self he is something else than what he is in the deed" (Hegel 1979, 178–79; Engl. 194). And even more clearly, in §404: "Whatever it is that the individual does, and whatever happens to him, that he has done himself, and he is that himself. He can have only the consciousness of the simple transference of himself from the night of possibility into the daylight of the present, from the abstract in-itself into the significance of actual being, and can have only the certainty that what happens to him in the latter is nothing else but what lay dormant in the former. . . . The individual, therefore, knowing that in his actual world he can find nothing else but its unity with himself, or only the certainty of himself in the truth of that world, can experience only joy in himself" (ibid., 220; Engl. 242).

Modern Hegel scholarship owes a great debt to Charles Taylor for having focused so much of our attention on this "expressivist" notion of action, as opposed to an intentionalist or causal account, and it is quite relevant here for understanding how Nietzsche could appear to deny any standard picture of agency and of normal volitional responsibility, and yet still speak of *actions*, and of the expression of a subject in a deed, indeed *wholly* in the deed.[5] The main similarity turns on what might be called a *nonseparability* thesis about intention and action, and a corresponding *nonisolatability* claim about a subject's intention (that the determinate meaning of such an intention cannot be made out if isolated from a much larger complex of social and historical factors).

According to the first or nonseparability thesis, intention-formation and articulation are always temporally fluid, altering and being transformed "on the go," as it were, as events in a project unfold. I may start out engaged in a project, understanding my intention as X, and, over time, come to understand that this was not really what I intended; it must have been Y, or later perhaps Z. And there is no way to confirm the certainty of one's "real" purpose except *in* the deed actually performed. My subjective construal at any time before or during the deed has no privileged authority. The deed *alone* can "show" one who one is. This means that the act description cannot be separated from this mutable intention, since as the intention comes into a kind of focus, what it is I take myself to be doing can also alter. This is partly what Nietzsche has in mind, I think, when he objects to the way other genealogists search for the origin of punishment by looking for a fixed purpose that subjects struggle to realize with various means. "[A]nd the entire history of a 'thing,' an organ, a custom can in this way be a continuous sign-chain of ever new interpretations and adaptations whose causes do not even have to be related to each other, but, on the contrary, in some cases succeed and alternate with one another in a purely chance fashion" (*GM* II:12). This is why, in the next section, Nietzsche writes that "only that which has no history is definable" and that we must appreciate "how accidental the 'meaning' of punishment is" (*GM* II:13).

Likewise there is a common "nonisolatability" thesis between Hegel and Nietzsche: attending only to a specific intention as both accounting for why the act occurred and what is actually undertaken, distorts what is necessary for a full explanation of an action. In the first place, the conditions under which one would regard an intention as *justifying* an action (or not, or connectable at all with it) have to be part of the picture too, and this shifts our attention to the person's character and then to his life-history and even to a community as a whole or to a tradition. We have to have all that in view before the adoption of a specific intention can itself make sense. Indeed this assumption is already on view from the start in Nietzsche's genealogy, since he treats the unequal distribution of social power as an essential element in understanding "what the slavish type was attempting." The psychology that Nietzsche announces as "the queen of the sciences" is also a social and historical psychology.

And while, on the standard model, the criterion for success of an action amounts to whether the originally held purpose was in fact achieved, on this different model "success" is much more complicated. I must also be able to "see myself" in the deed, see it as an expression of me (in a sense not restricted to my singular intention), but also such that what I understand is being attempted and realized is what *others* understand also. I haven't *performed the action*, haven't volunteered for the mission, say, if nothing I do is so understood by others as such an act.

Now Hegel and Nietzsche are going to part company radically very soon in this exposition, but it is important to have in view this way of understanding action as "mine" without our needing to say that some prior "I" caused it by deciding it should happen. On this model, as Hegel notes, we should understand successful action as a continuous and temporally extended, an everywhere mutable translation or expression of inner into outer, but not as an isolated and separated determinate inner struggling for expression in imperfect material. Our "original" intentions are just provisional starting points, formulated with incomplete knowledge of circumstances and consequences. We have to understand the end and the reason for pursuing it as both constantly transformed, such that what I end up with, what I actually did, counts fully as my intention realized or expressed.

Thus, if I start out to write a poem, I might find that it does not go as I expected, and think that this is because the material resists my execution, my inner poem, and so what I get is a "poorly expressed poem." This is a very misleading picture on this account, as misleading as "the commanding will" of *BGE* 19. The poem is a perfect expression of what your intention *turned out to be*. To ask for a better poem is to ask for another one, for the formation and execution of another intention. If the poem failed; everything has failed. It (the expression of what has turned out to be the intended poem) *just turned out to be a bad poem; not a bad expression of a good poem.*

As Nietzsche keeps insisting, our egos are wedded to the latter account; but the former correctly expresses what happened.

Now, philosophically, a great deal more needs to be said before this understanding of "the doer in the deed" could be defended. The anti-Cartesian and broadly anti-Christian account asks for something quite unusual. These passages in Hegel and Nietzsche seem to be asking us to relocate our attention when trying to understand an action, render a deed intelligible, from attention to a prior event or mental state (the formation of and commitment to an intention, whether a maxim, or desire-plus-belief, and the like) to "what lies *deeper* in the deed itself" and is expressed in it. (Where "deeper" does not mean already there, hidden in the depths, but not yet fully formed and revealed.) Rather, the interpretive task focuses on a continuing expression or translation of the subject into the actuality of the deed, and conversely our translation back into "who the person is." As Hegel put it in his clearest expression of this anti-intentionalist position: "Ethical self-consciousness now learns from its deed the developed nature of what it actually did" (Hegel 1979, 255; Engl. 283).

This can all sound counterintuitive because it seems obvious that the final deed may not express the agent simply because some contingency intervened and prevented the full realization (thus reinstituting a "separation" between the subject in itself and the deed that actually resulted, shaped as it so often is by external circumstances and events). Or we easily accept that if someone did something unknowingly and innocently, he cannot be said to be properly "in" the deed, even though the deed came about because of him and no one else, as when someone genuinely does not know that he is revealing a secret, and *does* so, but "guiltlessly," we want to say.

The issues are quite complicated and cannot be pursued here. The central question is: should not Nietzsche be aware that, by eliminating as nonsensical the idea that appears to be a necessary condition for a deed being a deed—a subject's individual causal responsibility for the deed occurring—he has eliminated any way of properly understanding the notion of *responsibility*, or that he has eliminated even a place for criticism of an agent. If the strong is not at all free to be weak, is not free to express that strength in any way other than by "a desire to overcome, a desire to throw down, a desire to become master, a thirst for enemies and resistances and triumphs," in *what* "responsibility sense" *is* the agent *in* the deed if not "causally"? A plant's life-cycle or nature might be said to be "expressed" in its various stages, but, as we have seen, Nietzsche rejects such a reductionist reading, he shows no indication of wanting to eliminate his "fundamental concept," activity.

Now it is true that sometimes Nietzsche seems content with a kind of typological determinism. People just *belong* to some type or other (whether biological or socially formed) and some just *are* weak, base, vengeful, and ugly; others are strong, noble, generous, and beautiful (cf. *BGE* 265). There is no way to justify these distinctions; that is the ("Socratic") trick the former group tries to play on the latter. The whole point is that you have to *be* a member of the latter group to appreciate the distinction. But on the one hand, Nietzsche's own evaluations are not so tied to this fixed typology. About the weak he also says: "Human history would be altogether too stupid a thing without the spirit that the impotent have introduced into it" (*GM* I:7). Likewise, he certainly seems to be criticizing the nobility by contrast when he says: "[I]t was on the soil of this essentially dangerous form of human existence, the priestly form, that man first became an interesting animal, that only here did the human soul in a higher sense acquire depth and become evil—and these are the two basic respects in which man has hitherto been superior to other beasts" (*GM* I:6). Such passages suggest a radical flexibility and indeterminateness in the normative value of such distinctions, an unpredictability in what they "turn out" to mean, as if Nietzsche thinks that such oppositions look one way in one context and another in another context. That raises the question of how this variation works, how this interpretive struggle is to be understood and what its relation might be to the psychological struggle.

Nietzsche has a great many things to say about this hermeneutical warfare, but we should note that his remarks confirm attributing the "nonisolatability" thesis to him, as noted above, and the second "success" condition for actions, as understood on this alternate model. Not only is the determinate meaning of a subject's intention not a matter of inner perception and sincerity, but a function in some way of a certain social context, but also "what is going on" in such a context is itself constantly contested among the participants. As he put it in a famous passage, "all events in the organic world are a subduing, a becoming master, and all subduing and becoming master involves a fresh interpretation, an adaptation through which any previous 'meaning' and 'purpose' are necessarily obscured or even obliterated" (*GM* II:12).

He makes the same sort of point about the variability and contestability of the various understandings of punishment (*GM* II:14) and notes that even the noble man *needs* the appropriate enemies if his actions are to have the meaning he sees expressed in them (*GM* I:10). In such cases, "the subject" is not absent; he is "out there" in his deeds, but *the deeds are "out there" too*, multiply interpretable by others (and that means, in Nietzsche's understanding, in multiple ways can be "appropriated" by others). These interpretations are themselves already expressions of various types that cannot be isolated from historical time and from the contestations of their own age. They are not existential "projections," motivated by some sort of self-interest or self-aggrandizement (cf. Geuss 1999, 16). And we have already good reason to be cautious of interpreters who think that there must be something appealed to, underlying Nietzsche's account, as a kind of criterion: "life," and/or "the will to power," to cite the most frequent candidates. If life must also *turn against itself* to be life, and if we don't know what really counts as *having established power*, or even *what power is*, we have only returned again to a social struggle about the meaning of deeds. In other words, if the most important deed is *the legislation of values*, what *actually* is legislated cannot be fixed by the noble man's strength of resolve *alone*, or guaranteed by his "pathos of distance." There is a difference between "actually" legislating values, that is, *succeeding* in doing so, and, on the other hand, engaging in a fantasy of self and value creation.

It is at this point that the similarities between Nietzsche and Hegel end. In a sense one can read Nietzsche's infrequent, published references to the "will to power" as attempts to dramatize the simple claim that there is no best, appropriate, finally reconciling resolution to these sorts of conflicts. "There is" *only the conflict*, at once potentially tragic and ennobling, and potentially dispiriting, a source of nihilistic despair. Hegel of course claims that such conflicts have an inherent "logic," that a developmental story can be told, say, in the *Phenomenology*, from the conflict between Antigone and Creon, to the partial overcoming of morality in "Forgiveness," and that the heart of that story is the ever more successful realization of freedom as a kind of rational agency. There is no corresponding logic or teleology in Nietzsche; just the opposite.

GUILT AND RESPONSIBILITY

I want to conclude by returning to the intuitive difficulties created by *GM* I:13, especially about responsibility. We should note, that is, Nietzsche's own response to the responsibility question—how, on his picture of how an agent is wholly in the deed, not separate from it—such reactions as regret, sorrow about what one did, and the like, might be understood.

Not surprisingly (given their similarities on so many issues) Nietzsche turns to Spinoza to make his point, and his remarks in *GM* II:15 are perfectly consistent with, and I think, confirm the position attributed to him above. He muses that Spinoza might have "one afternoon" asked himself, given that there is no "free will" or separate subject underlying the deed in Spinoza's own system, what could remain in that system of the *morsus conscientiae*, the sting of conscience. This is the very intuitive or commonsense question we have posed above. Nietzsche first appeals to Spinoza by making his own attempt at a "becoming master" as a "new interpretation" of Spinoza, invoking essentially Nietzschean language (especially the concept of "innocence"), and announcing: "The world for Spinoza had returned to that state of innocence in which it had lain before the invention of the bad conscience" (*GM* II:15). But then he notes that Spinoza reinvented this *morsus conscientiae* in the *Ethics*. "'The opposite of gaudium,' he finally said to himself—'A sadness accompanied by the recollection of a past event that flouted all of our expectations.' *Eth. III, propos. XVII, schol. I.II* Mischief-makers overtaken by punishments have for thousands of years felt in respect of their transgressions just as Spinoza did: 'here something has unexpectedly gone wrong,' not: 'I ought not to have done that'" (*GM* II:15). So, disappointment that I was not who I thought I was, sadness at what was expressed "in" the deed, replaces guilt, or the sort of guilt that depends on the claim that I could have done otherwise. Indeed, it is a kind of regret that depends on my *not* really having had the option to do otherwise; or at least that counterfactual option, on this view, is like considering the possibility that *I might not have been me*, a fanciful and largely irrelevant speculation, a mere thought experiment.

None of this settles the many other questions raised by Nietzsche's position: What are the conditions necessary for rightly identifying what it *was* that I did? What role do the judgments of others properly play in that assessment? Deeds, even understood as expressions, rather than caused results, conflict, express incompatible if also provisional and changing, purposes. How do we, as nonparticipants, understand and even evaluate such conflicts? Are not our interpretations the expressions of *current* contestations, and if so what would count as success, as prevailing now? How much of "who I am" can be said to be expressed in the deed? How might I distinguish important "discoveries" about myself that I had not known and would have denied, from trivial or irrelevant revelations? If whatever it is that is expressed in such deeds is not a stable core or substantial self, neither as an individual soul nor as a substantial type, what could form the basis of the temporal story that would link these manifestations and transformations?

These are difficult questions, but, I have tried to show, they are the right sort of questions raised by Nietzsche's remarks in *GM* I:13, and they are very different from questions about metaphysical forces, naturalized psychologies, instinct theories, or existential, groundless choices, leaps into the abyss. Whether Nietzsche has good answers to such important questions is another story.

REFERENCES

Bittner, R. 1994. "Ressentiment," in *Nietzsche, Genealogy, Morality*, ed. R. Schacht, University of California Press, 127–38.

Bittner, R. 2001. "Masters without Substance," in *Nietzsche's Postmoralism: Essays on Nietzsche's Prelude to Philosophy's Future*, ed. R. Schacht, Cambridge University Press, 34–46.

Geuss, R. 1999. *Morality, Culture and History: Essays on German Philosophy*, Cambridge University Press.

Hegel, G. W. F. 1979. *Phenomenology of Spirit*, transl. A. V. Miller, Oxford University Press. German text: *Phänomenologie des Gesites*, Bd. 2, Hauptwerke in sechs Bänden, Hamburg 1999.

Honneth, A. 1991. *The Critique of Power: Reflective Stages in a Critical Social Theory*, transl. by Kenneth Baynes, MIT Press.

Taylor, C. 1975. *Hegel*. Cambridge University Press.

Taylor, C. 1985. *Human Agency and Language. Philosophical Papers*. Vol. 1. Cambridge University Press.

Williams, B. 1994. "Nietzsche's Minimalist Moral Psychology," in *Nietzsche, Genealogy, Morality*, ed. R. Schacht, University of California Press, 237–47.

NOTES

1. Nietzsche does not treat "morality" as univocal and certainly not as a phenomenon with a single necessary essence. But it is clear that he has a standard form of nineteenth-century

Christian morality often in his sights. For a summary of its characteristics, see Geuss 1999, 171. For my citations of Nietzsche's writings, I have used Kaufmann's translations of *BGE*, *GS*, and *Z*; Kaufmann and Hollingdale's *GM*; and Hollingdale's translations of *TI* and *A*.

2. There are of course, several other genealogical origins of morality sketched in *On the Genealogy of Morals*: suffering itself seems to require a compensatory mechanism; there is the feeling of guilt traced back to debt; the "Verinnerlichung" of aggression, turning it toward oneself, and so forth. But all of these raise the same problem, the compatibility of their psychological accounts with *GM* I:13.

3. Bittner claims in "Ressentiment," that this makes no sense; that there can be no such thing as self-deception (1994, 127–38). That's one way to solve the problem.

4. Cf. also Bernard Williams's remark, "With Nietzsche . . . the resistance to the continuation of philosophy by ordinary means is built into the text, which is booby-trapped, not only against recovering theory from it, but in many cases, against any systematic exegesis that assimilates it to theory" (1994, 238).

5. Cf. "Aims of a New Epoch" in Taylor 1975, 3–50; "What is Human Agency" and "Hegel's Philosophy of Mind," in Taylor 1985, 15–44, 77–96.

9

On Sovereignty and Overhumanity

Why It Matters How We Read Nietzsche's
*Genealogy II:2**

Christa Davis Acampora

There is *nearly* unanimous agreement, among those who bother to pay attention to Nietzsche's anomalous claim about the "sovereign individual" in the second essay of *On the Genealogy of Morals* that the "sovereign" is Nietzsche's ideal, and many more still take sovereignty as the signature feature of the overman Nietzsche heralds in his *Thus Spoke Zarathustra* and other writings. I describe the reception among Nietzsche scholars as "*nearly* unanimous" because there has been at least one cry of dissent: that issued by Lawrence Hatab.[1] Curiously, his brief but incisive comments about the problematic nature of several readings along these lines continue to be ignored. With this chapter, I add my voice to his and call for a rally. Emphases on Nietzsche's sovereign individuality encourage what I shall argue is a *misreading* of the passage in question. Moreover, this mistake has far-reaching consequences insofar as it supports a mischaracterization of Nietzsche's philosophy generally and results in a failure to consider significant ways in which Nietzsche's conception of the subject might be relevant for contemporary moral philosophy.

Nietzsche most certainly is not upholding what he calls "the sovereign individual" as an ideal for which we should strive, and there is plenty of evidence to support the assertion. Few matters in Nietzsche interpretation are clearly and decisively settled, but I intend to add this one to that meager stock. In what follows, I scrutinize the context of the passage in question and its resonance with the overarching theme of

*Revised by the author from its original publication in *International Studies in Philosophy* 36:3 (Fall 2004): 127–45.

the work in which it appears (my section I). I then consider what would be necessary to further support the majority view and show why such projects are untenable (section II). Finally, I briefly discuss why I think it matters very much that we get this one right (section III). The "sovereign individual" has animated numerous discussions of Nietzsche's politics and ethics. How we read *GM* II:2 strikes at the heart of what we take to be the most significant features of Nietzsche's *constructive* philosophical projects.

I. "THE SOVEREIGN INDIVIDUAL": WHAT IT IS

The passage in question is familiar:

> If we place ourselves at the end of this tremendous process, where the tree at last brings forth fruit, where society and the morality of custom at last reveal *what* they have simply been the means to: then we discover that the ripest fruit is the *sovereign individual*, like only to himself, liberated again from morality of custom, autonomous and supramoral (for 'autonomous' and 'moral' are mutually exclusive), in short, the man who has his own independent, protracted will and the *right to make promises*—and in him a proud consciousness, quivering in every muscle, of *what* has at length been achieved and become flesh in him, a consciousness of his own power and freedom, a sensation of mankind come to completion.[2]

A good place to begin is to consider what is the nature of "this tremendous process" so that we can better appreciate how it is that the sovereign individual is its *fruit*. The second essay of the *Genealogy* explicitly treats the development of concepts associated with moral responsibility and culpability. There, Nietzsche considers the fundamental basis of "'guilt,' 'the bad conscience,' and the like," beginning with promise-making. Nietzsche is essentially asking: What sort of being, *what sort of animal*, must one become in order to be able to make promises?[3]

On our way toward considering how Nietzsche addresses this question, which orients the rest of the essay, we might note a consideration to which we will return in the next section: Kaufmann and Hollingdale's translation of the very first sentence of the second essay has led many astray. It is often cited precisely as it appears in their English translation: "To breed an animal *with the right to make promises*—is not this the paradoxical task that nature has set itself in the case of man? is it not the real problem regarding man?" ["Ein Thier heranzüchten, das *versprechen darf*— ist das nicht gerade jene paradoxe Aufgabe selbst, welche sich die Natur in Hinsicht auf den Menschen gestellt hat? ist es nicht das eigentliche Problem vom Menschen?" (*KSA* 5, 291)] Rendering "das *versprechen darf*" as "with the right to make promises" has encouraged those who rely on the translation to think that Nietzsche sees promise-making as an entitlement that one must earn or which one is granted, and which presumably stands in contrast with something to which one might be inherently obliged. As I shall discuss at greater length below, it has been associated with a certain kind of freedom. Moreover, since Nietzsche seems to emphasize orders of rank and entitlement throughout his writings, some compound their first error with a second in suggesting that it is Nietzsche's position that this sort of entitlement is something that might actually be desirable, that our seizure of it would represent some sort of completion of ourselves, the full realization of humanity. The more literal translation "who is permitted to promise" or "who is capable of promising" clearly better captures the sense of Nietzsche's phrase, since the very next sentence contrasts promising with its counteracting *Kraft*—the power or force of forgetting.[4] Thus read, we better appreciate Nietzsche's suggestion that promising relies upon some kind of power (we soon learn that it is *remembering*) that has been cultivated to the point that it outstrips forgetting. Promising depends upon a *Kraft*—it is not an entitlement or right—and its enhancement emerged through a developmental process in which a counteracting *Kraft* was diminished.

The second account of the genealogy of morality that constitutes *GM* II charts the struggle of the two opposing forces of remembering and forgetting, thereby casting morality in terms similar to how Nietzsche describes tragic art as resting upon the contest of the artistic forces of creation and destruction in *The Birth of Tragedy*. The task of *GM* II is to offer an account of how the *Kraft* of remembering accomplished its victory, and to chart the deleterious effects of the atrophy of forgetting in the course of human development. The message is: the acquisition of the kind of willing that is had in promise-making came with a price—the diminution of forgetting, and we allow it to wither only at our peril. This interpretation is reinforced in Nietzsche's insistence that forgetting is not merely an absence or failure of remembering, but is rather something that *is positively active in its own right*. Nietzsche couches the matter in organic, biological terms of nutrition and digestion: "it [forgetting] is . . . responsible for the fact that what we experience and absorb enters our consciousness as little while we are digesting it (one might call the process 'inpsychation')—as does the thousandfold process, involved in physical nourishment—so-called 'incorporation'" (*GM* II:1). Were it not for forgetting, it is suggested here, we would not have a soul, a *psyche*, much as we would not have a body, *a corpus*, were we not able to eat. The themes of forgetting as an *active force* and Nietzsche's use of metaphors for digestion have not gone unnoticed. But what seems to have been overlooked is what this has to do with what Nietzsche says in the very next section of essay two in which the reference to the sovereign individual occurs. How is the sovereign individual the product of a process in which the active forces of remembering and forgetting struggle, with the result that remembering surmounts and suppresses its opponent? More precisely, what in the course of this struggle does the sovereign individual trump?

Answering the latter question leads us back to a deeper investigation of forgetting. Briefly, we can recall that the good of forgetting, as Nietzsche writes in *GM* II:1, issues from its effects of *inpsychating* consciousness; another way of putting it is that forgetting plays a role in the regulatory process that permits us to appropriate our experience such that we take from it what is necessary and rid ourselves of what is not.[5] Nietzsche does not think that an individual is simply a monadic unitary entity.

Instead, we are composed of a multiplicity of forces such that "our organism is oligarchically arranged." Nietzsche's claim about the organization of the kind of organism we are warrants underscoring here, because it is both *consistent* with what Nietzsche *does* write about the "fiction" of the concept of individuals (e.g., *BGE* 16–20 and *GM* I:13), and *inconsistent* with (what he *doesn't* write about) an individual who *actually* is sovereign and self-legislating. We shall have occasion to address this issue in greater detail in the second section of this chapter.

Returning to the matter with which Nietzsche's second essay begins, we can now reformulate its inaugural question thus: What must have happened—from an organic developmental standpoint—in order for us to be able (*for nature to have granted us the ability*) to make promises? Clearly, this is a question that is raised about humankind generally. It applies to the kind of being that makes us human beings. It is not asked about individual humans. Indeed, each of the essays of the *Genealogy* endeavor, from a variety of perspectives, to offer a creation story of how the human animal, generally, came to be what it is, entwined with an etiology of moral concepts. The second essay is about the development of humankind as the animal with a conscience. What characterizes our species, at least as it is cast in this second essay, is the fact that some forces were strengthened over others in the course of our development. This process was *completed* (hence, it is not some tantalizing possibility for future philosophers to achieve) in pursuit of a particular "consciousness of . . . power and freedom," a "sensation" stemming from having and exercising the kind of power realized in promise-making. Hooked on that feeling, so to speak, human beings have (perversely) embraced their characteristic deformity (i.e., the atrophy of forgetting that occurs through the hyper-development of remembering). Indeed, the aesthesis of power that courses throughout the entire economy of promise-making—making promises, breaking them, and punishing others who are unable or unwilling to keep promises—is so great that humans have even instigated their own further deformity (i.e., more sophisticated mnemonics and the extirpation of forgetfulness).

Nietzsche's preoccupation with this process in *On the Genealogy of Morals* and elsewhere is tied to his concern for figuring out whether autonomy really is the *telos* of humanity that modern philosophy and the emerging social sciences claim it to be. What development might take us beyond ourselves, Nietzsche asks, and what would we be like if we overcame humanity as such? Would such *overhumanity* entail sovereign individuality? I believe Nietzsche thinks not, at least not as it is described in *GM* II:2.

II. "THE SOVEREIGN INDIVIDUAL": WHAT IT IS *NOT*

In the course of sorting through this particular issue it is necessary to consider how the idea of the sovereign individual has been pressed into service in various interpretations in the scholarly literature, to consider what general image of Nietzsche those interpretations support, and to see whether such readings become difficult to sustain once the support lent by the concept of the sovereign individual is withdrawn. It is quite difficult to select which readings of *GM* II:2 should serve as the basis of this discussion. Once I committed myself to this topic, I was surprised to discover just how rampant the problem is, and how frequently the "sovereign individual" creeps into all manner of discussions of Nietzsche's works.[6] Those who point to the sovereign individual as Nietzsche's ideal generally associate it with "the higher men," and sovereign individuality is often discussed in the context of clarifying what it means to "become what one is." In this section, I shall recount Hatab's points against the prevailing readings of the sovereign individual, supplement his claims, and critique several recent exemplary discussions that affirm the sovereign as Nietzsche's ideal.

In his *A Nietzschean Defense of Democracy*, Hatab asserts that the "sovereign individual" names "the modernist ideal of subjective autonomy," and that "Nietzsche *displaces*" rather than embraces such ideals.[7] This becomes clear when one notices, as virtually no one else does, that Nietzsche thinks that modern conceptions of the individual as autonomous have been crafted in order to press them into the service of moral accountability and retribution: "'Autonomy,'" Hatab writes, "is something that Nietzsche traces to the inversion of master morality; freedom in this sense means 'responsible,' 'accountable,' and therefore 'reformable'—all in the service of convincing the strong to 'choose' a different kind of behavior (*GM* I:13)."[8] Thus, the distinguishing characteristic of the sovereign individual as it is described in *GM* II:2—namely, that it autonomous—is precisely what Nietzsche identifies as the legacy of moralization, which has produced the decadence that he associates with humanity in its modern form.[9] I have addressed above how Nietzsche advances a quasi-physiological hypothesis about this process in terms of the development of powers of forgetting and remembering, and I shall return to this matter below.

Related to the issue of autonomy is Nietzsche's conception of freedom, which ambiguous as it may be, Hatab advises, is nevertheless clearly in tension with the kind of freedom associated with the sovereign individual who would be "master of *free* will." Hatab asks his readers to recall *BGE* 21 in which Nietzsche rejects idea of the completely free will: "the desire to bear the entire and ultimate responsibility for one's actions oneself, and to absolve God, the world, ancestors, chance, and society involves nothing less than to be precisely [a] *causa sui*," which Nietzsche describes as "the best self-contradiction that has been conceived so far, it is a sort of rape and perversion of logic." But Nietzsche's rejection of free will does not signal his supposition of a completely *unfree* will instead: "Suppose someone were thus to see through the boorish simplicity of this celebrated concept of 'free will' and put it out of his head altogether, I beg of him to carry his 'enlightenment' a step further, and also put out of his head the contrary of this monstrous conception of 'free will': I mean 'unfree will,' which amounts to a misuse of cause and effect." Nietzsche advances ideas about the concept of causality in numerous works. In the passage under consideration from *BGE*, Nietzsche advises holding "cause" and "effect" as "pure concepts," fictions that are useful for communication but which do not have *explanatory* power.[10]

Finally, Hatab notes that, "the sovereign individual is described as claiming power over fate, which does not square with one of Nietzsche's central recommendations, *amor fati* (*EH* II, 10)."[11] About the so-called sovereign individual, Nietzsche writes, "The proud awareness of the extraordinary privilege of *responsibility*, the conscious-ness of this rare freedom, this power over oneself and over fate, has in his case pene-trated to the profoundest depths and become instinct, the dominating instinct. What will he call this dominating instinct, supposing he feels the need to give it a name? The answer is beyond doubt: this sovereign man calls it his *conscience*" (*GM* II:2). Committing oneself to conquering fate, which the sovereign individual of *GM* II:2 does as part of taking responsibility for the promises he makes, would seem to stand in the way of, would specifically bind one to an idea that would prevent one from, loving one's fate. *Replacing* the ideal that prevents one from loving one's fate is precisely what Nietzsche envisions at the end of *GM* II, and Zarathustra is sup-posed to make such overcoming possible.[12] As I shall discuss below, it is overcoming the ideal of humanity as ultimately and fundamentally *sovereign* in the sense pro-vided in *GM* II:2 that "overhumanity" is supposed to represent.

But, the fact that the "sovereign individual," as described in *GM* II:2, is at odds with how Nietzsche thinks about the composite nature of the self, his critique of the concept of free will, and his emphasis on *amor fati*, does not hinder those keen on locating sovereign individuality at the heart of Nietzsche's philosophy. A representa-tive view of the sovereign as Nietzsche's ideal is advanced in David Owen's "Equality, Democracy, and Self-Respect: Reflections on Nietzsche's Agonal Perfectionism,"[13] and Richard White devotes an entire book to the concept of sovereignty in Nietz-sche's philosophy, *Nietzsche and the Problem of Sovereignty*,[14] both of which I con-sider here. Without doubt, others could be added, and the meager review of the literature that I am able to elaborate here by no means represents every approach to the topic.[15] Although I do think I engage some of the most significant and promi-nent themes, the literature would repay yet more specific consideration. There are two general points I wish to make about the use of the sovereign individual in vari-ous interpretations: (1) there is little in the way of support for the majority view that the sovereign individual is one of the core ideas of Nietzsche's positive project given that reference to such a being is limited to the one section under discussion here; and (2) any interpretation that places sovereign individuality at the heart of Nietzsche's philosophy requires committing him to affirming other ideas, particularly about the nature of human subjectivity, which he clearly finds problematic.

The first point is very easily addressed. There is no mention of sovereignty per se in *Z*, preoccupations with the *Übermensch* withstanding. One finds not a peep about the *souveraine Individuum* in *BGE* (where one might expect to encounter it in its political context, especially if such individuals are supposed to have earned special rights) or the works that follow the *GM*. There are just a smattering of references to things "souverain" in the notebooks between 1882 and 1889, and these scant references support the reading of that I have offered in the first section of this chapter. Simply put, there is not enough textual evidence to support the general and oft-repeated claim that the sovereign individual of *GM* II:2 is Nietzsche's ideal type.

The more interesting issues emerge when we consider what one must take Nietzsche to be saying when one considers the sovereign individual to be the ideal. A prominent feature of such discussions revolves around the matter of "having the right to make promises." I take it that those who are wont to emphasize this phrase wish to draw a distinction between promising as an obligation that "the herd" imposes upon others in order to protect itself, and those who have risen above simply meeting that imposed obligation and who are willing to accept the responsibility to secure their word for themselves.[16] Put another way, the distinction drawn appears to be: (1) relying upon the institution of promise-keeping (and the desire people have to avoid the harm that might come from the breaking of promises *given* to them) as the basis upon which a promise is made versus (2) agreeing to serve as the guarantor of one's word for oneself. I can see how such an interpretation can be rendered consistent with Nietzsche's preoccupation with drawing distinctions between the herd and those who somehow escape it, but how could it be that the Nietzsche who so emphasizes *becoming*, and who is suspicious of the concept of the subject (as the "doer behind the deed"), could think that is desirable—let alone *possible*—that a person could *ensure* his or her word in the future? How could one promise to do something, to stand security for something, that cannot be predicted and for which one is, in a sense, no longer the one who *could* be responsible for it? Either Nietzsche in *GM* II:2 temporarily sets aside the concerns that preoccupy not only his earlier thinking but also the very same book in which the passage in question appears (cf. *GM* I:13), or there is something wrong with attributing such views to Nietzsche. I am inclined to think the latter is the case, because this is not the only inconsistency at the heart of such interpretations.

Not only does Nietzsche think of the human subject, and all other entities for that matter, as having their being as a kind of becoming, but there is plenty of evidence that Nietzsche also thinks that our very conception of individuals is suspect. Nietzsche conceives of human beings, like all other organisms, as pluralities, as complexes of forces, not as discrete individual entities. This is not to say that there are no individuals; the particularity of the relations among (or arrangement of) the forces we are accounts for our individuality.[17] The very interesting recent work on Nietzsche's knowledge of and conception of science bears out this matter and traces the relevant literature.[18] Nietzsche thinks that a well-functioning plurality, as noted above, is one that is governed as an oligarchy (and this stands in contrast with the view of Plato's Socrates in the *Republic*, who characterizes the best soul as modeling an aristocracy).

It is at this point that the earlier discussion of forgetting, which sets the theme of the second essay, becomes significant again, because forgetting makes the oligarchic

arrangement possible. A pretense to sovereignty is achieved with the substitution of
monarchic aspirations.[19] The process of strengthening the force of remembering for
the purposes of achieving moral accountability bears the fruit (i.e., yields the result
upon its completion) of an entity that undermines the very purposes for which its
direction was set: in the course of producing a morally responsible agent, the hyper-
cultivation of remembering and the withering of forgetting yields a so-called sovereign individual who, as sovereign, no longer recognizes the claims of moral law.
Thus the process of moralization that produces such an individual overcomes or
undermines its very end. Like Christianity, discussed in *GM* III, a morality that
endeavors to ground itself in radical autonomy is *self-overcoming*. The question that
the *Genealogy* raises, without conclusively answering it, is—*What comes next?*—and
we cannot begin to try to answer that question if we misread (or ignore) the beginning of *GM* II. Given that Christian morality and its secular alternatives have turned
out to undermine their very own foundations, what, if anything, can serve as the
basis for how we should cultivate ourselves and our relations to others? How can
any action at all become meaningful or significant?

To consider how the problem plays out in a specific interpretation, I wish to
return to the troublesome issue of promising. If it is really such a crucial feature of
the ideal Nietzsche envisions, then why is it that one finds nowhere else such great
emphasis placed upon promise-making and promise-keeping? Those who wish to
proffer this idea must undertake some serious contortions in order to have it appear
as though Nietzsche really does say as much himself. David Owen does this well.
He reconciles Nietzsche's sovereign-individual-as-promise-maker with the egoistic
strands in Nietzsche's philosophy by claiming that the sovereign individual realizes
his sovereignty first and foremost in relation to himself. And that such is a condition
for the possibility of meeting others on these terms. Autonomous individuality is
cast as the pinnacle of Nietzsche's aspirations, and Owen endeavors to ascribe to
Nietzsche the view that one has *a duty* (first to oneself, and then presumably to
others) to "own" one's humanity, which fundamentally lies in recognition of oneself
as a sovereign individual. Thus, servility, or herd mentality, is a *failure* to undertake
one's duties. And failure to recognize sovereign individuality in others, Owen claims,
"undermine[s] the grounds of my own recognition self-respect, that is, that I am,
qua human being, a being who can stand to myself as a *sovereign individual*."[20] Perhaps so, if those lupine beasts of prey from *GM* I can be donned in Kant's civil
sheepish clothing. But Owen's specification of the defining characteristic of humanity is telling: "I am, <u>*qua* human being</u>, a being who can stand to myself as a *sovereign
individual*" (underlined emphasis mine). Nietzsche's discussion begins with consideration of what the human animal is, the "breeding" or developmental process
required in order to make it capable of promising (i.e., chiefly by hypertrophic development of the power of memory and the withering of forgetting). What Nietzsche
anticipates as the future for humanity in *GM* III and in *Z* is precisely the overcoming
of the human such that even if we don't become a different species altogether, we
might at least develop different capacities or different relations among the order of

forces that characterizes human existence generally. Nietzsche does not call us to realize the height of our humanity in becoming sovereign individuals (a capability already characteristic of the human animal, a "fruit" already borne)[21] rather, he anticipates overcoming the concept of autonomy that buoys the contradictory ideal of the sovereign individual, and *that* requires the cultivation and heightening of *different* powers, which are not alien to us but which are nonetheless latent.

Owen does the best job of finessing how the sovereign individual stands in relation to Nietzsche's emphasis on becoming. It is worth considering his account at some length. The confines of this chapter do not afford the opportunity to give Owen's paper the full consideration it deserves, so I shall focus only on a passage that constitutes Owen's most explicit definition of the sovereign individual, which as Owen describes it, is "not a *telos*" but rather a dramatization of

> an attitude, a will to self-responsibility (in Emerson's language: self-reliance), which is manifest in the perpetual striving to increase, to expand, one's powers of self-government such that one can bear, incorporate and, even, love one's fate—one's exposure to chance and necessity. (In other words, the *sovereign individual* represents the attitude of *amor fati*, that is, the affirmation of the fact of our exposure to *fortuna*.) The noble soul reveres itself because it is engaged in overcoming itself. To stand to oneself as a *sovereign individual* is, thus, to stand to oneself as one who seeks to extend oneself beyond one's current powers. In holding this view, Nietzsche is committed to a processual (i.e., non-teleological) perfectionism.[22]

If the sovereign individual can be conceived as realizing or manifesting its sovereignty as an on-going process, then we can resolve a number of the issues that I have identified as problematic, most notably the conception of subjectivity and its faculties that *seem* to be required for the kind of activity that is characteristic of the animal who has the capacity to make promises—namely, regularity, completeness, and identity. This reading wriggles out of conflict with Nietzsche's other more prominent theme of hostility toward teleological thinking, suggests how it can be reconciled with *amor fati*, and somehow ties it to self-overcoming and an extension of powers as a kind of self-enhancement. But notice what is *not* emphasized in this part of Owen's interpretation, indeed what completely disappears, namely the idea of sovereignty as tied to promising. This is no accident. Rather than an exercise of self-legislating freedom, the autonomy of sovereign individuality instead becomes an *attitude* toward necessity and change. Promise-making completely recedes as it must, because what is required for promising—successfully distinguishing between chance and necessity, thinking causally, correctly predicting the future, being mindful of the future in the present, even at the expense of the present, being able to decide with certainty about what it would be right to do and how to go about doing it, being calculable, etc. (*GM* II:1)—cannot be garnered while emphasizing the "processual" and perpetual striving that the self becomes when we are attentive to most of the rest of Nietzsche's philosophy.[23] This leads me to wonder what good it does to tie the model of self-reliance as "processual perfectionism" with the obscure refer-ence to the *souveraine Individuum* in *GM* II:2. Deriving a basis for democratic respect (and perhaps respectability for Nietzsche among those with Kantian and lib-eral philosophical inclinations) seems to be Owen's goal, but I do not think it would be Nietzsche's. Moreover, I am unsure that Nietzsche's work is the best place to look for the richest notion of what democratic respect might be, and I do not think it advisable to distort Nietzsche's texts in order to make it such.

III. READING *GM* II:2—WHY IT MATTERS

At the root of the notion of the sovereign individual is the ideal of radical autonomy and, along with it, a kind of power over oneself and freedom or distance from oth-ers.[24] Once ascribed to Nietzsche, the idea seems to easily fit with the general reading of Nietzsche's critique of morality, which would presumably constrain radical autonomy, and, more curiously, with his appeals to a new nobility (given the talk of special "rights" and entitlements that the sovereign individual has "earned"). Thus, even when the sovereign individual is not called by name, its core idea stands—namely, that Nietzsche envisions the emergence of an ideal type whose sig-nature characteristic is a form of autonomy so highly developed that it can success-fully exercise its will tyrannically not only in matters political but also in those epistemic and axiological. But if, as I have argued above, the sovereign individual is not Nietzsche's ideal—on the grounds that both terms are problematic for Nietz-sche—then the core idea of the power and freedom of autonomy, of which the "sov-ereign individual" is supposedly emblematic, is similarly undermined. And with that, the interpretations that radiate from that fault line are also thrown in doubt. Thus, it matters very much how we read *GM* II:2.

By the dramatic conclusion of the section in question, the process of producing a conscience is summarized in its entirety. With that, Nietzsche suggests the process of our development that is contained in our current concept of human beings is completed. The question remains whether this is truly the pinnacle of human exis-tence. The sensation of power we get from the mnemonics of responsibility leads us to *believe* it is, but Nietzsche entertains the thought that there are some possibili-ties—beyond continuing relishing and relentlessly endeavoring to manifest sover-eign individuality—that remain open to us. If we mistake the sovereign individual as Nietzsche's ideal for that which we ought (or might want) to strive, then we over-look what Nietzsche envisions beyond the overcoming of humanity anticipated in third and final essay of the *Genealogy*.

Most associate the sovereign individual with "higher humanity,"[25] claiming that they are the same or at least quite similar. But I have sought to make the case for the claim that Nietzsche sees the sovereign individual as standing at the end of a process of becoming the kind of animals that human beings are. In other words, the sovereign individual is the pinnacle of the current state of existence of *humankind*.[26]

If it is the case that Nietzsche envisions a kind of overcoming of humanity, some sort of development toward what we might call *over-humanity*, and the sovereign individual stands at the end of the process that produced human animals, then *overcoming* the sovereign individual is what Nietzsche envisions. If the sovereign individual continues to stand as our end, even if the character of "the end" is construed so as to reconcile it with becoming, then we will fail both in understanding the task of pursuing that something higher that Nietzsche anticipates, and, consequently, in reaching it.[27]

Still, the ideal of sovereignty is certainly not alien to Nietzsche, and clearly the exercise of will that is cultivated in the strengthening of memory that promise-making requires is compatible with Nietzsche's emphasis on willing and its role in the creation of meaning and significance. If the sovereignty of the sovereign individual named in *GM* II:2 is not precisely that for which Nietzsche is striving, then what is the other sense of sovereignty that Nietzsche can be said to affirm? How does it differ from the sovereign of *GM*? In brief, I think much of this work has been done already by Richard White, whose interpretation of what he describes as Nietzsche's problem of sovereignty deserves greater attention and careful examination. White argues that Nietzsche presages the problem of sovereignty in which we find ourselves caught since modern, humanist conceptions of the subject have been undermined by the likes of philosophers as diverse as Derrida and Dennett. Our contemporary philosophical labors seems to leave us with something of a false dilemma regarding how we conceive the self: either the self is determined by nature and "sovereignty" is merely a product of history so that the sovereign individual is something that can be appreciated from an *aesthetic* point of view as the "creation" of necessity, *or* sovereignty is found in the freedom *of* necessity in which case "the sovereign individual represents the transfiguration and salvation of nature from itself."[28] White proposes a third alternative that casts Nietzsche as holding the view that sovereignty is something that is a "*strategic* possibility," something Nietzsche advances from a "*performative* perspective" and that his writings aim to "*provoke*" in his readers. This allows White to take seriously Nietzsche's writings about eternal recurrence, fate, and necessity, while considering their tension with Nietzsche's appeals to creativity, willing, and a new sense of freedom. White does this without much reference to the sovereign individual of *GM* II:2,[29] and I think the direction of further study should follow White's lead.

The misreading of *GM* II:2 and its overemphasis on Nietzsche's interest in power *potentially* mischaracterizes his explorations (and exhortations) of mastery. It encourages associating Nietzsche's views with certain strands of existentialism that are actually quite at odds with many things Nietzsche has to say about fate, his interest in naturalism, and his complex views on freedom and necessity. Finally, such readings overlook and even obscure significant ways in which Nietzsche works through several problems in contemporary philosophy, particularly regarding the issue of conceiving the subject as contingent and relational while at the same time "natural," and articulating the bases upon which we might model our relations to other subjects in light of contemporary critiques of the ideals of rationality and autonomy.

The *real* problem of sovereignty draws us toward more deeply exploring how we might reconcile Nietzsche's appeals to creative willful activity with his critiques of subjectivity and the key ideas about identity and causality that are crucial for the conception of sovereign individuality that serve as the basis of Kantian moral philosophy and contemporary theories of justice and moral psychology. This is a problem for Nietzsche scholars, and its pursuit just might point toward promising further contributions Nietzsche's philosophy could make to contemporary moral philosophy. But if we continue to misread *GM* II:2, I think we will miss those opportunities, and, both within and outside the community of those who endeavor to practice reading well, Nietzsche will continue to be read as one obsessed with romantic existential fantasies about radical self-creation or self-transcendence and whose ideal type is nearly thoroughly unsuited for social life and unable to achieve the bonds of meaningful community.

NOTES

1. See his *A Nietzschean Defense of Democracy: An Experiment in Postmodern Politics* (Chicago: Open Court, 1995), 37–38.

2. Here, I cite Kaufmann and Hollingdale's translation, which I amend below. *KSA* 5, 293: "Stellen wir uns dagegen an's Ende des ungeheuren Prozesses, dorthin, wo der Baum endlich seine Früchte zeitigt, wo die Societät und ihre Sittlichkeit der Sitte endlich zu Tage bringt, wozu sie nur das Mittel war: so finden wir als reifste Frucht an ihrem Baum das *souveraine Individuum*, das nur sich selbst gleiche, das von der Sittlichkeit der Sitte wieder losgekommene, das autonome übersittliche Individuum (denn 'autonom' und 'sittlich' schliesst sich aus), kurz den Menschen des eignen unabhängigen langen Willens, der *versprechen darf*—und in ihm ein stolzes, in allen Muskeln zuckendes Bewusstsein davon, was da endlich errungen und in ihm leibhaft geworden ist, ein eigentliches Macht- und Freiheits-Bewusstsein, ein Vollendungs-Gefühl des Menschen überhaupt."

3. Subsequent to the original publication of this chapter, Paul S. Loeb published an article endorsing my view that Nietzsche's ideal is not the "sovereign individual" but arguing for a different reading of Nietzsche's claims about forgetting ("Finding the *Übermensch* in Nietzsche's *Genealogy of Morality*," *Journal of Nietzsche Studies* 30 [Autumn 2005]: 70–101; revised excerpt included in this volume). Loeb further develops what comes after the "overcoming of humanity." In this slightly revised version, I add a few minor clarifications in light of Loeb's comments. Rather than argue point by point, I simply note here that Loeb and I apparently disagree considerably on Nietzsche's conception of nature and the status of the human in relation to nonhuman animals in Nietzsche's texts. This bears quite significantly on whether Nietzsche has a view of human beings (and further, the *overhuman*) as somehow transcending nature. Although I do not think Loeb would explicitly endorse the latter, it is implied in his argument. I do not find Nietzsche distinguishing between the "mere animal" and the "human." As they are characterized in *GM*, humans are the animals who make promises—they have not transcended their animality on account of their being able to make promises,

despite the common view to the contrary in the history of Western philosophy; the *overhuman* does not constitute a transcendence of this nature either.

4. Thus, for translation of this section, the best we have is the one rendered by Maude-marie Clark and Alan J. Swensen (Hackett, 1998), but that will change with the new edition of the Cambridge translation by Carol Diethe, edited by Keith Ansell Pearson (*On the Geneal-ogy of Morality* [Cambridge: Cambridge University Press, forthcoming 2006]). In their notes on the phrase in question, Clark and Swensen take notice of my first point about the absence of any language associated with rights and entitlements, but they do not follow me in my second point about the context of making a comparison between powers and capabilities.

5. Forgetting, it seems, is an important condition for experience—important for giving the shape, form, rhythm, texture, and depth that make the seemingly endless stream of possi-ble objects of concern and attention *an* experience, to recall Dewey's famous distinction, not simply by piling experiences up or onto one another, but by taking some away, by encourag-ing some to fade, recede, fall away. Forgetting in this sense *grants* rather than evacuates or eliminates; too much remembering leaves us with experience without pause and strips from us possibilities for action. Nietzsche engages in more elaborate discussion of this idea in his earlier writings, particularly *BT* (in the association of the Dionysian with forgetting) and *HL* (where differentiation of the "stream of becoming" is described as necessary).

6. The best defense of the case for the sovereign individual is found in Keith Ansell Pear-son's "Nietzsche on Autonomy and Morality: The Challenge to Political Theory," *Political Studies* 39 (1991): 276–301.

7. Hatab, *A Nietzschean Defense of Democracy*, 37.

8. Hatab notes that *HH* 618 refers to "Individuum" in a similar vein.

9. I provide further textual evidence drawn from Nietzsche in support of this claim as I interpret his analysis of the mnemonics of punishment in my "Forgetting the Subject," in *Reading Nietzsche at the Margins*, edited by Steven Hicks and Alan Rosenberg (West Lafayette, IN: Purdue University Press, forthcoming 2007).

10. I discuss this idea at greater length in my "Nietzsche's Moral Psychology," *Blackwell Companion to Nietzsche*, edited by Keith Ansell Pearson (Malden, MA: Blackwell Publishers, Inc., 2006), 314–33.

11. Hatab, *A Nietzschean Defense of Democracy*, 38.

12. Interestingly, Kaufmann and Hollingdale inappropriately insert the notion of rights in their translation of the passage with which the second essay concludes. They render the last sentence as follows: "At this point it behooves me only to be silent; or I shall usurp that to which only one younger, 'heavier with future,' and stronger than I has a right—that to which only *Zarathustra* has a right, *Zarathustra the godless*.—" But there is nothing in the German original that implies that Nietzsche is talking about *rights*. Instead, he is clearly indicating a kind of *freedom*, not entitlement, when he writes, "—was allein Zarathustra freisteht, Zara-thustra dem Gottlosen" (*KSA* 5, p. 337).

13. David Owen, "Equality, Democracy, and Self-Respect: Reflections on Nietzsche's Agonal Perfectionism," in *The Journal of Nietzsche Studies* 24 (Fall 2002): 113–31.

14. Richard White in his *Nietzsche and the Problem of Sovereignty* (Chicago: University of Illinois Press, 1997).

15. Subsequent to the original publication of this article are Loeb's article noted above; and Thomas Miles, "On Nietzsche's Ideal of the Sovereign Individual" (unpublished paper presented to the North American Nietzsche Society, 28 April 2005).

16. Randall Havas makes this point. See his *Nietzsche's Genealogy: Nihilism and the Will to Knowledge* (Ithaca, NY: Cornell University Press, 1995), esp. 193ff. I briefly discuss the views of Havas and Aaron Ridley in a note below.

17. On this idea, see Steven D. Hales and Rex Welshon, *Nietzsche's Perspectivism* (Urbana: University of Illinois Press, 2000).

18. Numerous commentators have developed these ideas at greater length, particularly along the lines of Nietzsche's conception of language and grammar and his relation to Boscovich and Spir. For a concise review on the relevant issues, see Wolfgang Müller-Lauter, "On Judging in a World of Becoming: A Reflection on the 'Great Change' in Nietzsche's Philosophy," in *Nietzsche, Theories of Knowledge, and Critical Theory*, edited by Babette E. Babich and Robert S. Cohen (Boston: Kluwer Academic Publishers, 1999), 168–71. Compare Nietzsche's own discussion in "On the Prejudices of Philosophers" in *BGE*. See further Greg Whitlock's "Roger J. Boscovich and Friedrich Nietzsche: A Re-Examination" in *Nietzsche, Epistemology, and Philosophy of Science*, edited by Babette E. Babich and Robert S. Cohen (Boston: Kluwer Academic Publishers, 1999); Robin Small, "Boscovich Contra Nietzsche," in *Philosophy and Phenomenological Research* 1984 (46): 419–35; Robin Small, *Nietzsche in Context* (Aldershot, England: Ashgate, 2002); Gregory Moore, *Nietzsche, Biology, and Metaphor* (Cambridge: Cambridge University Press, 2002); and Michael Steven Green's *Nietzsche and the Transcendental Tradition* (Chicago: University of Illinois Press, 2002).

19. This is not at all to suggest that Nietzsche claims we should aim to return to our prehuman history—it should be quite obvious that such is not possible in the same way that it is not possible for anyone to selectively return to some prior stage of human evolutionary development. The history of Western philosophy exhibits a severe allergy to forgetting and an association with knowledge, or enlightenment, strictly with remembrance. I find the same in Loeb's conception of the "second forgetting" associated with Zarathustra's "enlightenment," which curiously involves a forgetting (in the sense of foregoing) forgetting (in the sense of not remembering); see pp. 166, 170–71.

20. Owen, "Equality, Democracy, and Self-Respect," 116.

21. Owen is one of the few who at least recognize that the sovereign individual is not Nietzsche's ideal in the sense of a *future* possibility (although Owen appears to think it is a worthy ideal for the present). Owen rightly points out that Nietzsche associates the sovereign individual with the "morality of custom," a stage, in Nietzsche's historical account of the development of morality that he considers "premoral" (with Kant, *Sittlichkeit* precedes *Moralität*). However, I consider the sovereign individual to be the ideal that serves as the inaugural transition between the premoral and moral stages. Since the *Genealogy* appears to be oriented toward envisioning a "postmoral" stage of development, it is curious that Owen would endeavor to sketch Nietzsche's view about that stage by drawing on the type produced by the process of premoral customs.

22. Owen, "Equality, Democracy, and Self-Respect," 118. Compare with David Owen and Aaron Ridley, "On Fate," *International Studies in Philosophy* 35:3 (2003): 63–78.

23. Instead, Owen seems to emphasize "self-responsibility" and upholding one's commitments. For some concise accounts of the sovereign individual that do keep promise-making front and center, see Randall Havas, "Nietzsche's Idealism" and Aaron Ridley, "Ancillary Thoughts on an Ancillary Text," both in *The Journal of Nietzsche Studies* 20 (2000): 90–99 and 100–8, respectively. For Havas, the sovereign individual is the paradigmatic willing subject: he offers us instruction on what it means to will something: "giving our word" is

how this happens, and it is in this that we realize our "shared humanity" with others. Ridley apparently attributes to Nietzsche the idea that taking responsibility is a achievement or an accomplishment for which we might aim. I have endeavored to argue that Nietzsche is challenging the idea that sovereign individuality and all that it entails is the pinnacle of human progress. I am not suggesting that Nietzsche does not see anything at all that is valuable in the process of moralization and the working of the bad conscience that produces the sovereign individual as an ideal type. Indeed, I think a very interesting and persuasive case could be made that Nietzsche considers the practice of willing that the (vain) pursuit of sovereign individuality allows us to exercise has significant advantages, much as the slave revolt in morality (discussed in *GM* I) makes human beings interesting and creative in ways they had not been previously, and much as the ascetic ideal is shown to have been a highly effective (yet also destructive) mechanism for producing value (in *GM* III). But the ideal of the sovereign individual like slave morality (and, perhaps, the ascetic ideal) is something that Nietzsche envisions *overcoming*.

24. It is precisely this reading that leads many to claim that Nietzsche's politics are decidedly aristocratic and antidemocratic. Owen and Havas endeavor to associate Nietzsche's views with perfectionism and liberalism, thereby making Nietzsche's philosophy compatible with democratic theory. But if we grant that Nietzsche is *not* embracing the sovereign individual, but rather is calling for its overcoming, the need to discuss how sovereign individuality can be rendered compatible with democratic political theory disappears. Lawrence Hatab accomplishes the same without recourse to the sovereign individual.

25. As an example, see Richard Schacht, *Nietzsche* (New York: Routledge, 1983), 294.

26. This is not to say that we are all *already* sovereign individuals but rather that the concept of humanity that we presently hold is one that takes sovereign individuality as a real and desirable possibility for us to endeavor to achieve.

27. I maintain that whatever is involved in *overhumanity*, and I have not endeavored to describe it here, the beings who attain it or are involved in the process of pursuing it remain nonetheless *animals*. Nietzsche thinks the human is animal *through and through*. Of course, the human animal has its distinctive features, just as other animals do, but there's no reason to think that *these particular features* somehow make the human animal *more than merely an animal*, they merely make the human an animal of a particular sort. The focus upon some possible flight from or transcendence of animality is precisely what Nietzsche aims to overcome in his philosophical anthropology, and it plays a significant role in his critique of morality (e.g., *GM* II:7). Further discussion of this can be found in the numerous essays included in *A Nietzschean Bestiary: Becoming Animal Beyond Docile and Brutal*, edited by Christa Davis Acampora and Ralph R. Acampora (Lanham, MD: Rowman & Littlefield Publishers, Inc., 2004).

28. Richard White, *Nietzsche and the Problem of Sovereignty*, 86.

29. White reads Nietzsche as affirming the sovereign individual, but his discussion of the relevant passage is rather limited (see his *Nietzsche and the Problem of Sovereignty*, 144ff). Still, his account of sovereignty and Nietzsche's conception of the individual is richer than those that *begin* from the sovereign individual as Nietzsche's paradigm. Sovereignty is a decidedly problematic issue for Nietzsche, on White's account; it is not a specific ideal that we ought to pursue.

10

Finding the *Übermensch* in Nietzsche's *Genealogy of Morality**

Paul S. Loeb

Although scholars quite reasonably tend to assume that Nietzsche's later thinking supersedes his earlier thinking (see, e.g., Clark 1990), he himself instructs his readers to think of his analysis in the *Genealogy* as preemptively superseded by the philosophy of his earlier *Zarathustra*. *GM*, he writes, is a "fish hook" meant to attract and prepare readers for the superior insights of his earlier *Z*. *GM*, he tells us is a No-saying, destructive book focused on the contemporaneous; while his earlier *Z* is a Yes-saying, constructive book focused on the future (*EH* "BGE"). In this chapter, I will show more specifically how Nietzsche's supposedly immature and discarded *Z* concept of the *Übermensch* does indeed supersede his supposedly mature and final ideas in *GM* II.[1]

The most obvious candidate for the *Übermensch* in the *Genealogy* is Nietzsche's famous "sovereign individual." In *GM* II:2 and 3 Nietzsche praises this sovereign individual as the completion of humankind, as emancipated from morality, and as the master of a free will with power over himself and over fate. This is why Simon May, for example, writes that the sovereign individual is "none other than the *Übermensch*: for in mastering every obstacle to promising himself, he, like the *Übermensch*, has nothing left to overcome" (May 1999, 117).[2] However, as Christa Davis Acampora has recently argued, there are several good reasons for rejecting this suggestion (Acampora 2004). First, the sovereign individual is not mentioned or cele-

*Excerpted and revised by the author from its original publication in *Journal of Nietzsche Studies* 30 (Autumn 2005): 70–101. Reprinted with permission of the Pennsylvania State University Press.

brated anywhere else in Nietzsche's published writings, nor is he explicitly linked anywhere to the *Übermensch*. Second, the introductory section to *GM* II celebrates the instinctive, regulative, and active force of forgetting and warns about the costs of countering it. In the mnemonic sovereignty, by contrast, no room is left in consciousness for the proper oligarchic functioning of our instincts. Third, the kind of freedom and autonomy Nietzsche associates with the sovereign individual—responsibility, promise-keeping, accountability—are traced by him in the first essay to slave morality, and so cannot be regarded as his ideal. Finally, although Nietzsche says that the sovereign individual represents the already-attained completion of humankind, Zarathustra insists that humankind must be overcome in the future *Übermensch*.

I do not agree completely with Acampora's reasons, however. First, although Nietzsche does praise animal forgetting, it is clear that he does not atavistically think that humankind can somehow go back to this state (*TI* "Skirmishes" 43, 48–49). Yet Acampora valorizes the *pre*-human forgetting of *GM* II:1 and does not say anything about what Nietzsche thinks forgetting might look like *after* our millennia-long history of mnemonic breeding. I will do so. Second, Nietzsche claims at the end of *GM* II that Zarathustra will employ the resources of bad conscience, rather than abolish it. This suggests that Acampora is too quick to dismiss the sovereign individual's perfection of bad conscience. Although she rightly notes Nietzsche's depreciation of the *sovereign individual*'s talent for responsibility and autonomy, she assumes without much argument that these qualities are *in themselves* depreciated by Nietzsche.[3] But this assumption is contradicted by Zarathustra's extravagant praise and exemplification of these qualities: as obtaining, for example, in the self-legislator who must obey his own laws and commands (*Z*:II "On Self-Overcoming"); or, more radically, in the spirit-become-child and self-propelled wheel that wills its own will (*Z*:I "On the Three Metamorphoses"). So perhaps Nietzsche depreciates the sovereign individual because he is not responsible and autonomous *enough*—compared, that is, to Zarathustra or the *Übermensch*. I shall argue that this is indeed the case. Finally, although I think Acampora is right to cite Zarathustra's claim that the already-completed human must be overcome in the future *Übermensch*, this citation assumes precisely what Nietzsche scholars usually deny (see, e.g., Leiter 2002, p. 115n2) and what I aim to show here: namely, that the *Z* concept of the *Übermensch* continues to play a crucial role in the later *Genealogy*.

A key to understanding this role is Nietzsche's claim that the sovereign individual is the ripest fruit of bad conscience. But bad conscience, he argues further, is an illness, in fact the worst illness ever contracted by the human animal, one from which it has not yet recovered, one that makes the human animal the sickest animal on earth (*GM* II:13, 16, 19; see also *GM* III:20). As Nietzsche vividly describes the terms of this illness, it involves above all a kind of social incarceration or imprisonment in which the will to power cannot be externally discharged and therefore must be turned inward so as to inflict self-torture, self-punishment, and self-cruelty. According to Nietzsche, the conquered, imprisoned, and tamed human animal invented bad conscience in order to hurt itself. Worse yet, it then seized upon the presupposition of religion so as to drive its self-torture to its most gruesome pitch of severity and rigor. Whereas previously the human animal felt itself able to repay its debts to its ancestors and gods (for example, through sacrifice and achievements), the aim now was to invent a holy God so as to preclude pessimistically, once and for all, the prospect of a definitive repayment. In this new psychic cruelty, where the human will now infected the fundamental ground of things with the problem of eternal guilt and punishment, Nietzsche finds an unexampled madness and insanity of the will, an earth that has become a madhouse (*GM* II:21; see also *GM* III:20).

Now, as far as I know, no one has yet pointed out that these famous remarks contain clear allusions back to Nietzsche's earlier *Thus Spoke Zarathustra* chapter, "On Redemption" (*Z*:II). For Zarathustra speaks there of the human will as a prisoner in chains or fetters, as being powerless and impotent, as foolishly trying to escape its dungeon by seeking a revenge that it calls "punishment," and finally as becoming insanely obsessed with finding this punishment in the very nature of existence. Even more specifically, Nietzsche's analysis of bad conscience and guilt in *GM* II alludes back to Zarathustra's further claim in that same speech that the prison of the human will is *the past*.[4] For although Nietzsche emphasizes the role that social confinement plays in the inhibition and suppression of the human animal's instincts (so that they are eventually internalized), his deeper point is that the socially-bred *memory faculty* is the true inhibitor and suppressor of these instincts.[5] This is because the memory faculty suspends or disconnects (*ausgehängt*) active forgetting and represents an active will not to let go, to keep willing, that which it once willed *in the past* (*GM* II:1–3). But this means that the remembering human animal is forced to recognize for the first time an entire arena of possible willing—much more extensive than the sphere outside society—that is completely and forever outside of its reach: namely, that which was willed and can now never be unwilled, deeds that can never be undone, in short, the past, the "it was." Before socially bred memory, the prehuman will actively forgot anything outside the present moment that could confine its activity. But with the advent of society and its mnemo-techniques, some things were impressed upon the moment-centered animal affects so that they remained there—inextinguishable, omnipresent, fixed—*just as they once were*. The human will therefore now perceived itself as confronted with a new stone, a new barrier, "that which was," which it could not move and in relation to which it felt impotent and inhibited.

It is ironic, then, that the start of *GM* II emphasizes the power and freedom of the sovereign individual. For insofar as this power and freedom depend upon the sovereign individual's highly developed faculty of memory, they are in fact sharply curtailed. Unlike the mere animal, the sovereign individual that is the completion of the human animal is at each and every point confined and burdened, not only by his own immovable "it was," but also by the "it was" of the whole human prehistory of custom and tradition that has led up to him. The sovereign individual may seem to have power and mastery over circumstances, nature, accidents, fate, himself, and others less reliable than himself. But since he has no power over any of the "it was" that determined all of these, he ultimately has no power over these either. Indeed, because the sovereign individual's mnemonic will has itself been determined by a past that is fixed and gone forever, it cannot be said to ordain the future in advance after all. So the sovereign individual's power over time turns out to be illusory. This is why Nietzsche describes the sovereign individual in terms that he has already *criticized* in *Z* as being linked to the spirit of the camel and the spirit of gravity: namely, as bearing on his strong shoulders a tremendous responsibility and weight that makes him proud, self-conscious, measured, controlled, serious, solemn, and grave.

So what is required for the human will to free itself from the prison of the past imposed by its socially bred millennia-old capacity of memory? Nietzsche suggests at the end of *GM* II that Zarathustra—the man of future who makes the will free again—must turn bad conscience against the unnatural inclinations. But bad conscience is fundamentally memory, and the unnatural inclinations are all traceable to bad conscience. Further, the law of life, the law of necessary self-overcoming, dictates that all great things are the cause of their own destruction (*GM* III:27). Hence, in an act of self-cancellation, memory must be turned against memory itself so as to bring about the kind of *forgetting* that Zarathustra equates with freedom and the absence of guilt (*Unschuld*, usually translated as "innocence"): "Innocence is the child and forgetting, a new beginning, a play, a self-propelling wheel, a first movement, a holy Yes-saying" (*Z*:I "On the Three Metamorphoses").[6] However, this cannot be a going back to the forgetting of our animal ancestry, to the "partly obtuse, partly flighty understanding of the moment (*Augenblicks-Verstande*)," or to "the moment-enslaved (*Augenblicks-Sklaven*) affects and desire" (*GM* II:3). Nor should we hope for such a return (*TI* "Skirmishes" 43).[7] Instead, Nietzsche suggests, we must go forward and exploit to its fullest the very illness that is also a pregnancy in order to attain a new and *übermenschlich* forgetting.

What Nietzsche means by this is that memory—or the suspension of mere animal forgetting—is what forces the human will to hold on to the past, to fix the past, and thereby to recognize an immovable "it was" in relation to which it feels impotent and inhibited. Memory is what teaches the human animal that it cannot will backward. In order to liberate itself, therefore, the human animal must employ this same memory to recover the past so deeply and so completely that it is led to *forget* the past in a new and *übermenschlich* sense—that is, to let go of the past, to unfix the past, and thereby to recognize that the "it was" is not immovable after all. But what causes the human will to perceive the "it was" as immovable is its limited perspective on time that shows it running forward in a straight line for eternity. From the perspective of the human animal's present willing, the "it was" always appears behind and gone forever out of reach. As Zarathustra says in his redemption speech, the will sees that everything passes away and that time devours her children. The human animal must therefore use its memory to recover the past so thoroughly that it recognizes that time actually circles back upon itself and that the "it was" always returns. Hence Zarathustra's new teaching: "Do not be afraid of the flux of things: this flux turns back into itself: it flees itself not only twice. All 'it was' becomes again an 'it is.' All that is future bites the past in the tail" (*KSA* 10:4[85]). With such a mnemonic self-overcoming, the human animal learns how to will backward, how to break time and its desire, and how to gain a true power over time (something higher than mere *reconciliation* with time).

These ideas refer us of course to Zarathustra's doctrine of the eternal recurrence of the same.[8] As Nietzsche describes it in *Ecce Homo*, this is a cosmological theory of the unconditional and endlessly repeated circular course of all things (*EH* "BT" 3).[9] Because he rejects any conception of universal and absolute time wherein time exists independently of these things, it follows for him that time itself has an endlessly repeated circular course.[10] And from this there follows the unconditional and endlessly repeated circular course of every human life (*KSA* 9:11[148]).[11] Thus, from his proof of the circular course of all things, Zarathustra deduces that he and his dwarf-archenemy must have already encountered each other before eternally and must return to encounter each other again eternally (*Z*:III "On the Vision and the Riddle" 2). And Zarathustra's animals know that he teaches "that all things recur eternally and we ourselves with them, and that we have already existed an infinite number of times before and all things with us." Similarly, from the revolving great year of becoming, these animals know Zarathustra's deduction that "we ourselves resemble ourselves in each great year, in the greatest things and in the smallest." And they know as well what he would say to himself if he were about to die: "But the complex of causes in which I am entangled will recur—it will create me again! [. . .] I shall return eternally to this identical and self-same life, in the greatest things and in the smallest" (*Z*:III "The Convalescent" 2).[12]

According to Zarathustra, therefore, every human animal has lived its qualitatively identical life innumerable times before. And since every human animal possesses a faculty of memory, it must be possible for it to remember these innumerable identical previous lives. More precisely, as we have seen, Nietzsche defines human memory as a counterfaculty by means of which animal forgetting is suspended or disconnected. And animal forgetting, he writes, is

> an active and in the strictest sense positive faculty of repression that is responsible for the fact that what is only absorbed, experienced by us, taken in by us, enters just as little into our consciousness during the condition of digestion (one might call it "inpsychation") as does the entire thousandfold process through which the nourishing of our body (so-called "incorporation") runs its course. (*GM* II:1)

Thus, every human animal subconsciously absorbs and experiences the reality of its innumerable identical previous lives, but this reality is actively forgotten and suppressed for the sake of psychic room and order. Still, this forgetting and suppression can be suspended, in which case the cosmic reality of eternal recurrence will enter into human consciousness and thought.[13]

Now, it might seem impossible that any human animal could ever remember the recurrence of its life. For any such memory would add something new to that life and thereby violate Nietzsche's insistence on the qualitative identity of that life.[14] However, this objection presupposes some initial or original life in which there was not yet a recollection of its eternal recurrence. On Nietzsche's view, there is no such original life, and as long every recurring life contains the qualitatively identical recollection of this recurrence, there is no inconsistency in supposing that there could be such a recollection. Indeed, quite the reverse: given Nietzsche's anthropological account of the human animal as the remembering animal, and given Zarathustra's cosmological teaching of the eternal recurrence of the human animal's qualitatively identical life, it *must* be the case that every human animal has the potential to recall this recurrence.

So why did Nietzsche emphasize Zarathustra's doctrine of eternal recurrence if he thought that this was something every human animal could remember on its own? The reason is that he did not think that anyone belonging to his age was strong or healthy enough to affirm the thought of an eternally recurring life. In fact, he admits this even of himself: "I do not want life *again*. How have I borne it? Creating. What has made me endure the sight? the vision of the *Übermensch* who *affirms* life. I have tried to affirm it *myself*—alas!" (*KSA* 10:4[81]). Due to their base-line life-impoverishment, he and his contemporaries were far from being well-enough disposed toward themselves and their lives to desire their identical return. In *GS* 341, Nietzsche imagines that he and his contemporaries would feel the thought of eternal recurrence as a crushing one: the question in each and every thing, "do you want this once more and innumerable times more?" would lie upon their actions as the greatest heavy weight. He even imagines that he and his contemporaries, upon hearing the news of eternal recurrence, would throw themselves down, gnash their teeth, and curse the bearer of this news as a demon.

But, according to the doctrine, this messenger, this news-bearer, must be memory itself. And according to Nietzsche's proto-Freudian psychology, the human animal will repress any memory that is too painful to bear: "'I have done that,' says my memory. 'I cannot have done that,' says my pride, and remains unyielding. Eventually—memory yields" (*BGE* 68). Extrapolating from *GS* 341, Nietzsche directs us to suppose a similar sequence of psychological events with respect to our memory of eternal recurrence: "I have lived this identical life innumerable times before," says my memory. "I cannot have done that," say my life-hatred and my self-hatred, and remain unyielding. Eventually—memory yields.[15] In terms of Nietzsche's definition of memory, although we may at some point be led to suspend our forgetting of the recurrence-reality that we have subconsciously experienced, we will certainly return to this forgetting if the recurrence-reality is too painful to bear. On Nietzsche's epistemic account of eternal recurrence, there is thus no important distinction to be drawn between the question whether we are able to *know* eternal recurrence and the question whether we are able to *affirm* it.[16]

In *GS* 342, Nietzsche presents us with his contrasting vision of a far stronger and healthier future age (enabled by Nietzsche himself) in which there will arise an individual, Zarathustra, so overflowing with energy and vitality that he is completely well-disposed toward himself and toward his life. Such an individual, he proclaims, will long for nothing more fervently than for the eternal recurrence of his identical life. For this reason, he will bless the news of such recurrence as an eternal confirmation and seal, and he will regard the bearer of such news as a god. This affirmation, Nietzsche predicts, will be the start of the "great noon" [*Grosse Mittag*] hour for humankind, that is, the hour in which the shadows of God cease to darken the human mind and the sun of human knowledge stands at its peak: "And in every ring of human existence as such there is always an hour in which the mightiest thought emerges, at first for one, then for many, then for all—the thought of the eternal recurrence of all things" (*KSA* 9:11[148]).[17] This is why Nietzsche ends *GM* II by proclaiming Zarathustra as "this bell-stroke of noon" [*dieser Glockenschlag des Mittags*] and why he begins *GM* by alluding to Zarathustra as "one divinely preoccupied and immersed in himself into whose ear the bell has just boomed with all its strength the twelve strokes of noon [and who] awakens all at once and asks himself: 'what really was that which just struck?'" (*GM* P:1).

By way of preparing Zarathustra's great-noon affirmation, Nietzsche spends some time showing that he carries within him a *latent* knowledge of his life's eternal recurrence.[18] For example, after his terrifying prevision of the serpent biting itself fast in the throat of the shepherd, Zarathustra speaks of having been bitten himself by the silent, burrowing and blind worm of his most abysmal thought (*Z*:III "On Involuntary Bliss," "The Convalescent"). This poetic image, with its allusion to death (worms burrowing in corpses), and to the ancient *ouroboros* symbol (a worm that bites its own tail), captures Nietzsche's idea that Zarathustra's eternally recurring life is a closed circle in which the end always returns to the beginning. Zarathustra's knowledge of eternal recurrence is most abysmal (*abgründlicher*) and blind because it lies burrowing in the darkest depths of his subconscious. And it is silent and sleeping because Zarathustra has so far repressed and buried it in subconscious depths where it is then carried as a fearfully heavy weight. This is why Nietzsche is especially interested in depicting Zarathustra's experience of falling asleep, when his conscious intellect drops away and "no time" passes for him until he awakens. In this blink of an eye (*Augen-blick*) between falling asleep and waking, Zarathustra paradoxically feels himself falling into "the well of eternity" (*den Brunnen der Ewigkeit*) and sleeping "half an eternity," in which he perceives the world as a perfect "golden round ring" (*Z*:IV "At Noon"). With these metaphors, Nietzsche indicates the descent of Zarathustra's sleeping mind into its subconscious awareness of his eternally recurring life. This awareness, Nietzsche suggests, necessarily has an infinite depth that is beyond the scope of Zarathustra's waking consciousness's comprehension (*Z*:III "Before Sunrise," "On the Three Evils").

At the right time, however, Zarathustra must choose to deliberately awaken and summon up his dormant knowledge so that it may speak to him directly (*Z*:III "On Involuntary Bliss"). Since the rest of humankind will still be concerned to keep this reality suppressed, Zarathustra will have to escape collective thought and choose the most solitary solitude (*einsamste Einsamkeit*) as a means of diving, burrowing and sinking into reality (*GS* 341; *Z*:III "On the Vision and the Riddle" 1; *GM* II:24). So in *Z* Nietzsche poetically imagines the strong and solitary Zarathustra summoning and awakening his knowledge of eternal recurrence out the darkness of his deepest depths (*Z*:III "On the Vision and the Riddle" 2; "The Convalescent" 1). This invocation leads to an awakening or enlightenment in which Zarathustra's long-hidden knowledge is finally revealed in the full light of day and rationally understood at a surface conscious level.[19] In the concluding chapters of the published ending of *Z*—and in keeping with the prevision in which Zarathustra sees himself springing up, no longer human, a transformed being, radiant, laughing a laughter that is no human laughter (*Z*:III "On the Vision and the Riddle" 2)—Nietzsche depicts the soul of this enlightened, laughing *Übermensch* as affirming and blessing the seal of eternal recurrence in just the manner he had anticipated in *GS* 341–42 (*Z*:III "The Seven Seals").

According to Nietzsche, then, the experience of the reality of the eternally repeating cosmos cannot be incorporated by mere animals (not even Zarathustra's) because they have no faculty of memory. Nor, however, can it be incorporated by most human animals, because their ill-disposition toward themselves and their lives keeps them from suspending their forgetting of this experience. Only an exceptionally strong and self-loving individual like Zarathustra, who fervently longs for nothing more than his own eternal recurrence, is able finally to recover and incorporate his deeply buried subconscious experience that this is actually the case. As a result, however, his relation to time is completely transformed. Since it is a cosmological truth that Zarathustra will eternally relive the qualitatively identical life he has already lived, his faculty of memory is no longer confined just to the "it was" of his life. Whereas mere animals can live only in their present moment, and whereas human animals can also mnemonically live in their past, Zarathustra's recovered memory of his eternal recurrence allows him to live even in his future. This is why Zarathustra calls himself a prophet (*Wahrsager*) throughout the narrative of *Z*, and this is why Nietzsche calls attention to Zarathustra's prophetic ability by constructing crucial narrative episodes in which Zarathustra has previsions that are later fulfilled. Although these previsions are usually interpreted as literary devices meant to convey Zarathustra's psychological states, Nietzsche's claim that eternal recurrence is the basic conception (*Grundconception*) of *Z* (*EH* "*Z*" 1) suggests instead that they are devices meant to convey the manifestations of Zarathustra's eternally recurring life.[20]

In *Thus Spoke Zarathustra*, then, Nietzsche imagines a future Zarathustra who employs his memory against itself so as to attain a kind of *second* forgetting of the remembered past that previously seemed fixed and gone forever. Unlike the mere animal, he still has a memory-faculty that allows him to transcend the present moment. But also, unlike the *merely human* animal, he is able to employ this faculty so as to transcend the past as well. Because he has a recovered memory of the entire circular course of his life, Zarathustra no longer shares the limited human perception that there is an asymmetry between the past and the future such that the past is always fixed and gone forever compared to the future. Instead, his recurrence-memory shows him that his eternally returning past also lies *ahead* of his present and is therefore just as open to his will's influence as is his future. Of course, this does not mean that Zarathustra can change or alter the past, or that he can undo what is already done. Nowhere does Zarathustra claim to have stopped the flow of time or reversed the direction of this flow.[21] In fact, he goes out of his way to trace the origins of such "stomach-turning" ideas to the thought of God (*Z*:II "Blessed Isles"). Instead, Zarathustra's recurrence-memory shows him only that what he has already done may be such precisely because of the influence of his willing in the present or even the future. Speaking to his "it was," he may therefore say: "But thus I will it! Thus I shall will it!" (*Z*:II "On Redemption").

Indeed, considered more closely, it is precisely Zarathustra's faculty of memory that makes his "backward-willing" influence possible. For by impressing or storing mnemonic messages, commands, or reminders to himself at an "earlier" stage in his life, the fully developed and perfected Zarathustra can transmit this very same development and perfection throughout his entire life so as to guarantee it meaning, necessity, and wholeness.[22] Alluding to Socrates' *daimonion* (*BT* 13–14; *TI* "Socrates"), as well as to the Christian conception of conscience as a kind of divine "voice" that conveys warnings or instructions (*GS* 335; *EH* "GM"), Nietzsche imagines that Zarathustra will hear disembodied whispers calling to him, admonishing him, and commanding him at critical times in his life when he is tempted away from himself or does not feel adequate to his destiny (see especially *Z*:II "The Stillest Hour"). Because this voice is easily identified as that of his own self at a "later" point in the narrative, Nietzsche imagines that Zarathustra will possess a kind of *second* conscience, a *recurrence-conscience*, that enables him to keep promises to his future self and to become who he is in the future (*GS* 270, 335). In fact, Nietzsche suggests, it is this very backward-willing that allows Zarathustra to affirm his life in such a way that he is led to long for its eternal recurrence and thereby becomes able to recover the experience of recurrence that teaches him backward-willing.[23] Zarathustra's self-liberated will is thus a truly sovereign "self-propelled wheel" (*ein aus sich rollendes Rad*) or *circulus vitiosus* (*BGE* 56) that wills its own will and that enables Zarathustra to become a fully self-actualized poet-artist-creator of his own life and self (*GS* 290, 299).[24]

To return to Nietzsche's famous formulation, human memory is an illness as pregnancy is an illness. By increasing its power and sophistication to a horrific and deforming extent, the human animal is at the very limit finally able to recover its deeply forgotten experience of life's eternal recurrence. Because this new knowledge releases and opens up an arena of possible willing that had seemed forever blocked, the self-overcoming human animal is once again free to fully externalize and express its instincts. This time, however, its will to power extends vastly further, and is directed in a vastly more focused manner, than that of his merely animal ancestor tethered to the present moment. Since the past is now just as open and malleable as the future, there is no longer any deterministic influence of the past to chain, imprison, haunt and burden its present willing. And because the "it was" is also the "it shall be," its memory (a suspension of its first forgetting) is now precisely the means whereby the self-overcoming human animal is able to attain a new kind of forgetting of the "it was" and to influence its own development in a way that truly grants it freedom, autonomy, and self-mastery. This new forgetting will extend to the past millennia of breeding and custom that produced its faculty of memory in the first place. Hence, the crushingly heavy debt of millennia that once seemed irredeemable will finally be lifted and redeemed.[25] From the womb of bad conscience, a new child will be born: self-propelled, free, weightless, innocent, affirming, joyful, and at play with novelty and creation.[26]

REFERENCES

Abel, Günter. *Nietzsche: Die Dynamik der Willen zur Macht und die ewige Wiederkehr, 2. Auflage.* Berlin: Walter de Gruyter, 1998.

Acampora, Christa Davis. "On Sovereignty and Overhumanity: Why It Matters How We Read Nietzsche's *Genealogy* II:2." In *International Studies in Philosophy* 36:3 (2004): 127–45.

Allison, David B. *Reading the New Nietzsche.* Lanham, MD: Rowman & Littlefield, 2001.

Clark, Maudemarie. *Nietzsche on Truth and Philosophy.* New York: Cambridge University Press, 1990.

Gooding-Williams, Robert. *Zarathustra's Dionysian Modernism.* Stanford: Stanford University Press, 2001.

Gödel, Kurt. "A Remark about the Relationship between Relativity Theory and Idealistic Philosophy." Pp. 557–62 in *Albert Einstein: Philosopher-Scientist. The Library of Living Philosophers, Vol. VII,* ed. Paul Arthur Schilpp. Evanston, IL: Open Court, 1949.

Gott, J. Richard. *Time Travel in Einstein's Universe.* Boston: Houghton Mifflin, 2001.

Klossowski, Pierre. *Nietzsche and the Vicious Circle.* Trans. Daniel W. Smith. Chicago: University of Chicago Press, 1997.

Leiter, Brian. "The Paradox of Fatalism and Self-Creation in Nietzsche." In *Nietzsche,* ed. John Richardson and Brian Leiter. New York: Oxford University Press, 2001: 218–321.

———. *Nietzsche on Morality.* New York: Routledge, 2002.

Loeb, Paul S. "The Moment of Tragic Death in Nietzsche's Dionysian Doctrine of Eternal Recurrence: An Exegesis of Aphorism 341 in *The Gay Science.*" In *International Studies in Philosophy* 30:3 (1998): 131–43.

———. "The Conclusion of Nietzsche's *Zarathustra.*" In *International Studies in Philosophy* 32:3 (2000): 137–52.

———. "Time, Power, and Superhumanity." In *Journal of Nietzsche Studies* 21 (2001): 27–47.

———. "Identity and Eternal Recurrence." Pp. 171–88 in *A Companion to Nietzsche,* ed. Keith Ansell Pearson. London: Basil Blackwell, 2006.

May, Simon. *Nietzsche's Ethics and His "War on Morality."* Oxford: Clarendon Press, 1999.

Moles, Alistair. "Nietzsche's Eternal Recurrence as Riemannian Cosmology." In *International Studies in Philosophy* 21 (1989): 21–35.

———. *Nietzsche's Philosophy of Nature and Cosmology.* New York: Peter Lang, 1990.

Richardson, John. "Nietzsche on Time and Becoming." Pp. 208–29 in *A Companion to Nietzsche*, ed. Keith Ansell-Pearson. London: Basil Blackwell, 2006.

Ridley, Aaron. *Nietzsche's Conscience: Six Character Studies from the Genealogy*. Ithaca, NY: Cornell University Press, 1998.

Savitt, Steven F. *Time's Arrows Today: Recent Physical and Philosophical Work on the Direction of Time*. Cambridge: Cambridge University Press, 1995.

Soll, Ivan, "Reflections on Recurrence: A Re-examination of Nietzsche's Doctrine, *Die Ewige Wiederkehr des Gleichen*." Pp. 322–42 in *Nietzsche: A Collection of Critical Essays*, ed. Robert C. Solomon. Garden City, NY: Doubleday, 1973.

Stambaugh, Joan. *The Other Nietzsche*. Albany: State University of New York Press, 1994.

Staten, Henry. *Nietzsche's Voice*. Ithaca, NY: Cornell University Press, 1990.

Yourgrau, Palle. *Gödel Meets Einstein: Time Travel in the Gödel Universe*. Chicago: Open Court, 1999.

NOTES

1. In the original complete publication of this chapter, I provide further evidence for my claim that Nietzsche instructs us in this fashion about the relation between *GM* and *Z*. I also provide an explanation as to why he does so.

2. See also Ridley 1998, 18, 143–45. However, May argues that Nietzsche does not actually endorse this figure as an attainable or desirable ideal but rather as an ironic depiction of the human "urge to be insulated from contingency" that he "so powerfully decries in its metaphysical or religious manifestation." By contrast, I argue below that the reason Nietzsche does not endorse the *GM* II sovereign individual as his *übermenschlich* ideal is that he is not sovereign *enough*.

3. The closest Acampora comes to making such an argument is her suggestion that the ideal of a reliable promise-keeper is at odds with Nietzsche's philosophy of becoming, especially as applied to the subject: "how could it be that the Nietzsche who so emphasizes *becoming*, and who is suspicious of the concept of the subject (as the 'doer behind the deed'), could think that it is desirable—let alone *possible*—that a person could *ensure* his or her word in the future? How could one promise to do something, to stand security for something, that cannot be predicted and for which one is, in a sense, no longer the one who *could* be responsible for it?" (Ibid., 134–35; see also p.138). I think that Acampora is right to raise the question whether promise-keeping is really *possible* for the sovereign individual and I argue below that, because of the "it was" problem, Nietzsche himself ultimately *denies* that it is. But this does not mean that he denies this capacity to the *Übermensch* who has solved the "it was" problem through Zarathustra's teachings of eternal recurrence and backward-willing.

4. Nietzsche also anticipates his later *GM* II analysis of guilt when he has Zarathustra teach that it is not a deed, but rather the pastness of a deed, its undoability, that leads to self-lacerating guilt: "No deed can be annihilated: how could it be undone through punishment! This, this is what is eternal in the punishment 'existence,' that existence too must be an eternally-recurring deed and guilt (*Schuld*)!" (*Z*:II "On Redemption"). Here and throughout this chapter I have consulted the translations of Nietzsche's writings by Kaufmann, and the translations of *GM* by Kaufmann and Hollingdale.

5. See, by contrast, Henry Staten's claim (1990, 51, 61, 65ff.) that for Nietzsche the

imprisonment in society is an *empirical* condition of *humankind,* while the imprisonment in the "it was" is a *transcendental* condition of *life.* But Nietzsche's emphasis on the mere animal's ignorance of the past, and on the human animal's socially inculcated and memory-enabled awareness of the past, shows that he considers the "it was" to be equally an empirical condition of humankind.

6. Most *Z* commentators (see Gooding-Williams 2001, 43–44) fail to notice this important link between Zarathustra's "Three Metamorphoses" speech on forgetting and *Unschuld,* on the one hand, and Nietzsche's *GM* II analysis of memory and *Schuld,* on the other.

7. See, by contrast, Joan Stambaugh's suggestion (1994, 105ff.) that Nietzsche aims for us to regain the state (as described by him at the beginning of *HL*) in which we live "totally in the moment, in the present."

8. Nietzsche first proposes this theory when, in *GS* 341, he has the demon make a categorical assertion as to the cosmological truth of eternal recurrence: "The eternal hourglass of being is turned over again and again." He returns to this same description in *Z* when he has Zarathustra's animals proclaim what they know his teaching must be: "You teach that there is a great year of becoming, a colossus of a year: this year must, like an hourglass, turn itself over again and again, so that it may run down and run out anew: so that all these years resemble one another, in the greatest things and in the smallest" (*Z*:III "The Convalescent" 2). And he expands upon this theory in *Z* when he has Zarathustra present a dialectical proof in support of cosmological eternal recurrence that is drawn from his own notebook proofs in support of what he called the most scientific of all possible hypotheses (*Z*:III "On the Vision and the Riddle" 2; *KSA* 12:5[71]).

9. As Günter Abel (1988) and Alistair Moles (1989, 1990) have shown, most of the ostensibly rigorous objections to the scientific status of Nietzsche's cosmological doctrine presuppose an outdated Newtonian physics of absolute universal time that was rejected by Nietzsche himself when formulating his premises for eternal recurrence. Most of these objections are also quite uninformed about the diversity and peculiarity of recent cosmological theories. In particular, Gödel's 1949 valid solutions to Einstein's GRT field equations, widely discussed today, certainly allow the kind of global closed time-like curve that seems described in *EH.* For a philosophical examination of Gödelian spacetime structure and its implications, see Yourgrau (1999) and the essays by Paul Horwich and John Earman in Savitt (1995). For a physics-based examination of other possible global time-like curves, see Gott (2001).

10. In Loeb 2001, I argue that Zarathustra's dismissal of *the dwarf's assertion* that time itself is a circle (*Z*:III "On the Vision and the Riddle") is not a dismissal of circular time. This is because the dwarf's Platonic answer assumes a background of atemporal reality compared to which time itself is an illusion.

11. Since Nietzsche holds a perspectival view of time, and since one's perspective does not exist in the time observed by others between one's death and one's recreation, one's last conscious moment is immediately followed by one's first conscious moment (*KSA* 9:11[318]). See Loeb 2006 for a further explanation of this argument that an individual's eternally recurring life has a self-enclosed circular course.

12. Commentators since Heidegger have pointed to the convalescent Zarathustra's ambivalence toward his animals' speeches, but have failed to note Nietzsche's careful narrative distinction between what Zarathustra's animals say that eternal recurrence is for those who think as they do, on the one hand, and what they say that eternal recurrence is according to Zarathustra's teaching, on the other (*Z*:III "The Convalescent" 2). Also, in his preparatory notes

for *Z*, Nietzsche has Zarathustra himself teach all of what the animals in *Z* say they know Zarathustra teaches (*KSA* 11:25[7]). Nietzsche's point, therefore, is not that Zarathustra's animals do not know what he teaches, but rather that they are not able to understand why this new teaching should cause him such pain, nausea and sickness. This point derives from Nietzsche's claim that mere animals have no memory, and therefore cannot be nauseated or burdened as Zarathustra is.

13. There are of course strong affinities between this epistemology of eternal recurrence and Plato's theory of *anamnesis*, and Nietzsche himself points to this influence when he alludes to Plato's *Phaedo* in *GS* 340–41 (see Loeb 1998) and when he depicts Zarathustra's dialectical contest with the Socratic dwarf (*Z*:III "On the Vision and the Riddle" 1). Although Pierre Klossowski is famously concerned to show that *"[a]namnesis* coincides with the revelation of the [Eternal] Return" (1997, 57), his point is quite different from mine. Whereas I am arguing that for Nietzsche forgetting eternal recurrence is a *suspendable* condition of *psychic efficiency,* Klossowski argues (see also Allison 2001, 122) that forgetting eternal recurrence is an *unsuspendable* condition of *the truth of eternal recurrence* (59).

14. See, for example, Ivan Soll's claim that "[a] person can have no direct memories of earlier recurrences." For if he did, "the increment of his mental life would make him different from his predecessors and hence not an identical recurrence of them" (Soll 1973, 340). I discuss this objection at length in Loeb 2006.

15. In Loeb 1998, I argue that *GS* 340–41 convey Nietzsche's conjecture that Socrates' hatred of life led him to conceal from himself his subconscious knowledge of his life's eternal recurrence until his deathbed *daemonic* reminder loosened his tongue and led him to take revenge on life. In Loeb 2006, I show how Nietzsche leads us to interpret the demon's message in *GS* 341 as a recollection of life's eternal recurrence.

16. Hence Zarathustra's challenge to the dwarf who is a symbol of the weak human: "I, however, am the stronger of us both—: you do not know my most abysmal thought! *That*— you could not bear!" (*Z*:III "On the Vision and the Riddle").

17. See *KSA* 9:11[196]; *GS* 108–109; *Z*:I, "On the Gift-Giving Virtue"; and *TI* "World." Although Zarathustra announces the dawn of his great-noon day at the ending of *Z*:IV, I argue in Loeb 2000 and 2004 that Nietzsche intended us to read this ending as leading *chronologically* into the start of the "Convalescent" chapter where the fully ripened and lion-voiced Zarathustra awakens his thought of eternal recurrence during the high-noon moment of this same great-noon day.

18. Although Nietzsche most often characterizes Zarathustra's doctrine of eternal recurrence as his "most abysmal thought" [*abgründlicher Gedanke*], he also has Zarathustra agree with his stillest hour that he "knows" [*weiss*] his teaching but will not speak it (*Z*:II "The Stillest Hour"). And Zarathustra's animals ask him if perhaps a new, bitter and oppressive "knowledge" [*Erkenntnis*] has come to him once he has awakened his most abysmal thought (*Z*:III "The Convalescent" 2).

19. See *TI* "Socrates," for Nietzsche's equation of surface and daylight with consciousness and reason, and of depth and darkness with the unconscious and instinct.

20. In particular, and most important, the convalescent Zarathustra tells his animals that his confrontation with his most abysmal thought was a horrific torture and crucifixion (*Z*:III "The Convalescent" 2). Since Nietzsche argues that pain is the most powerful aid to memory, it should be the case that he depicts this experience as the one Zarathustra remembers the best. And, indeed, in the "Prophet" and "Vision and Riddle" chapters, we see the younger

Zarathustra having an accurate prevision—that is, recurrence-memory—of this later experience. In Loeb 2001, I offer a further analysis of this scene that shows more precisely how Zarathustra's psychic pain is an aid to his recurrence-memory.

21. See, by contrast, Joan Stambaugh's interpretation of literally willing backward in time as "reversing the direction of time" so as to "change what has already occurred" (85–86). Given this extreme interpretation of literal backward-willing, Stambaugh (along with most other commentators), sees herself as forced to choose instead a merely *metaphorical* interpretation of backward-willing that "at least makes more sense"—namely, "to will things and events back, to will them to come again, to return." But Zarathustra's whole point in his redemption speech is that we *already do* will things and events to return, and that it is precisely this willing that *founders* against the immovable stone "it was." We will things and events in the past to return, but our willing seems impotent. Stambaugh's interpretation thus merely poses the terms of Zarathustra's problem without offering a reading of his solution.

22. See Loeb 2001 for an exegesis of *Z* that explains, supports, and illustrates this claim.

23. This interpretation should be sharply distinguished from the usual one according to which backward-willing is *merely metaphorical* and Zarathustra retrospectively reinterprets his past in such a way that he finds it all worthy of affirmation (see, for example, Richardson 2006, 224–25). In *GS* 277 Nietzsche argues that such metaphorical backward-willing must at some point involve some kind of self-deception and therefore never actually succeeds.

24. On my interpretation, then, Nietzsche's claim that Zarathustra *succeeds* in giving aesthetic style to his life and self depends on his assumption of the literal truth of cosmological eternal recurrence. As such, my interpretation helps to explain Nietzsche's famous but puzzling praise of physics (*Physik*) as the means whereby certain unique and incomparable individuals may become those they are, give laws to themselves, and create themselves (*GS* 335). By contrast with Walter Kaufmann's dissatisfying explanation of Nietzsche's term "*Physik*" (in his footnote to his translation of *GS* 335, also adopted by Leiter 2001, 315–16), my account explains Nietzsche's characterization of physics—"the study of everything that is lawful and necessary in the world"—as naturally pointing forward toward his unveiling, six aphorisms later, of the cosmological doctrine that "the eternal hourglass of being is turned over again and again" (*GS* 341). In addition, my interpretation shows how Nietzsche's doctrines of eternal recurrence and backward-willing allow him to conceive of a truly radical self-creation that does not depend upon the *causa sui* theory of free will that he criticizes in *BGE* 21 and that does not conflict with his teaching of *amor fati* (Leiter 2001, 292–93 and 286–89; see also Acampora 2004, 132–33, 140). By contrast, Leiter writes that we need to acknowledge "that by 'creation,' Nietzsche really doesn't mean 'creation' in its ordinary sense" (2001, 317) and that "his talk of 'creating' the self is merely the employment of a familiar term in an unfamiliar sense, one that actually presupposes the truth of fatalism" (2001, 319).

25. Nietzsche thus depicts Zarathustra's *übermenschlich* forgetting as lifting the weight of the past from his soul and as rendering him weightless so that his body dances and his spirit flies like a bird (*Z*:III "The Seven Seals" 6–7). Also, in contrast to the regular, calculable, and predictable sovereign individual of *GM* II, Zarathustra's *übermenschlich* soul is sudden like lightning and earthquakes, stormy like the wind, chance-governed like the dancing stars, playful like the gambling gods, and adventuring like the seafarer (*Z*:III "The Seven Seals" 1–3, 5).

26. At the published end of *Z*, Zarathustra describes his own redeemed soul as a newborn child that is just washed, naked, innocent, yes-saying, free, tied to time's umbilical cord, baptized with new names, and playing with colorful toys (*Z*:III "On the Great Longing").

11

The Genealogy of Morals and Right Reading
On the Nietzschean Aphorism and the Art of the Polemic

Babette E. Babich

> Dionysus is, as is known, also the god of darkness.
>
> —Nietzsche, *Ecce Homo* "GM"

Like René Descartes, an excerpt from whose *Discourse on Method* had served "in lieu of a preface" to the first edition of Nietzsche's *Human, All Too Human*, a book that was prototypical for both *Beyond Good and Evil* and *On the Genealogy of Morals*, Nietzsche was fond of betraying his intentions while nonetheless masking them: *larvatus prodeo*. Accordingly, Nietzsche attaches the warning subtitle, *A Polemic* to his *On the Genealogy of Morals*. Yet the title-page hint concerning the challenging dimension of the book has not prevented scholars from reading *On the Genealogy of Morals* as a *Tractatus* or straightforward account of Nietzsche's thinking on moral philosophy, and it is a commonplace to claim that *GM* is Nietzsche's most systematic and coherent book.[1]

Nietzsche himself was anxious about the likelihood of being misunderstood, above all: of being misread. Hence the anxiety of *noninfluence*, as we might call it, characterizes his most repeated tropes. The problem of misreading (a stylistic and rhetorical issue) is compounded by the subject matter of *GM* itself. In what follows, I question the rhetorical allusiveness of the book, an allusive indirection Nietzsche emphasizes in his bio-bibliographical reflections on the *Genealogy* in *Ecce Homo*:

"Every time a beginning calculated to mislead: cool, scientific, even ironic, deliberately foreground, deliberately holding back" (*EH* "GM").

At the conclusion of the preface of *GM*, Nietzsche details what he regards as an essential prerequisite for an adequate reading.[2] Not a matter of authorial responsibility, "the fault," Nietzsche writes, will rest with any reader who has not read his previous writings with unsparing attention. With this presupposition, Nietzsche demands more than that his readers be open to his writings—able, as he says referring to his *Zarathustra*, to be both "profoundly wounded and at the same time profoundly delighted by every word" (*GM* P:8). Beyond such readerly sensitivity, Nietzsche also supposes a writerly competence in the rhetorical form per se, a demand he placed on his readers following the failure of *The Birth of Tragedy* to find "right readers," even among (especially among) philologists supposedly trained in rhetoric. The "difficulty some people have with the aphoristic form" was thus for Nietzsche a limitation stemming from a lack of training, that is, "from the fact that today this form is *not taken seriously enough*" (*GM* P:8).

In an earlier text, Nietzsche had already underlined the therapeutic efficacy of "psychological observations" or "reflection on what is human, all-too-human" (*HH* 35). This salutary benefit was the function of the aphorism or maxim with respect to the subject matter of his friend Paul Rée's *On the History of Moral Sensations*[3] (a title Nietzsche uses in *HH*, and which could well have served as an alternate title for *GM*). True to its classical origins, in the psychological researches required for such a history (or genealogy) of morality, as Nietzsche recalls, the aphorism is a literary therapeutic form, a reference to both Hippocrates and the Stoic tradition in its Greek and its Roman instaurations. But Nietzsche would warn, and Pierre Hadot's *Philosophy as a Way of Life* recalls this caveat for contemporary thought,[4] a veritable art (or practice) of reading but also the craft of writing (as Nietzsche emphasizes) is required in order to understand the aphorism: "even the subtlest mind is not capable of properly appreciating the art of polishing maxims if he has not himself been educated for it and competed at it" (*HH* 35). Unless one has practiced the aphoristic art in the service of life—such reflections constitute the "*art* of living" as Marcus Aurelius articulates this technical spiritual practice in his *Meditations*—one will be inclined, in Nietzsche's words, to imagine the forming of maxims a trivial art, to think it "easier than it is" (*HH* 35).

In this way, Nietzsche's claims regarding the understanding of his work assume a complex interplay between *readerly* and *writerly* approaches to his text. There are a number of issues at stake, but to begin to consider these approaches here, I return to the question (and it should be regarded as a genuine question) of the role of the aphorism in Nietzsche's writings.

THE APHORISM IN NIETZSCHE—AND PHILOSOPHY

The aphorism seems to cut philosophy down to size—bite size. Armed with teeth, as Nietzsche might have said, the cutting edge or, even, the *violence* of the aphorism is manifest in the case of Nietzsche, nor is this less in evidence with respect to Heraclitus, his antique antecedent, nor indeed, though Nietzsche would have known nothing of this parallel, in the case of Wittgenstein.

The aphorism begins historically in the αφορισμοι of Hippocrates, that is, maxims in place of a handbook or physician's manual for the physician who would have no time to consult one in the field. Particularly apposite, we can recall the first and most famous of these: "Life is short, art long, opportunity fleeting."[5] Said otherwise, for the physician in the field, the life of the wounded soldier hangs in the balance, the conventions of the *art* of healing are protracted and cumbersome, the *chance* to act quickly lost, and so on.

On the battlefield, and this locus was shared by Nietzsche's favorite laconic poet-mercenary Archilochus, the healer had to carry his maxims in mind. Their brevity (and this is the ingeniousness of the structured design) is the reason the aphorism can be remembered. Above all, this same brevity is why it can be understood, at least in part. Short, one is able to *get* some bit of the point, even if one finds, in retrospect, that one has missed the half or more.

This is the beauty of the quick take. Quickly read, like the cold baths Nietzsche suggested as the best way to sidestep the announced visitation of nothing so seemingly unobtrusive as a letter (and today's experience of the urgency of e-mail offers a contemporary illustration of Nietzsche's sense of violation): the same tactical concision corresponds to the author's vanity, to offer and, at the same time, to conceal his offering (thereby an offering for everyone and no one).

Nietzsche expresses this ambitious presumption in *Zarathustra*, as he speaks of writing in blood: "Anyone who writes in blood and sayings does not want to be read but learnt by heart" (*Z*:I "On Reading and Writing"). More emphatically still, Nietzsche later affirms his "ambition" to say in the aphorism what others say—interrupting himself with a thought-slash (*Gedankenstrich*) to sharpen his point: "—what everyone else *does not say* in a book" (*TI* "Skirmishes" 51).

Unlike Hume, unlike Kant, unlike Heidegger (in spite of Heidegger's best efforts to imitate Nietzsche),[6] Nietzsche writes—or, as he says: he *composes* or *casts*—his aphorisms. And if Wittgenstein also wrote in aphorisms, Nietzsche is more readable by half and then some, (which is not to say that he is understood).

For the sake of a review of the complexity of the aphorism as a self-elaborating form of self-deconstruction and, simultaneously, of self-protection, we consider Nietzsche's own prefatory comment on the way an aphorism functions just because it reflects his prescription for reading his aphorisms, and thereby, his writings. Like the essay, treatise, or indeed, like the epigraph (with which, in the case of *On the Genealogy of Morals*, it is peculiarly liable to be mistaken), the aphorism is a particular literary form.[7] Beyond the rhetorical and poeticological, the aphorism has a singularly philosophical or reflective dimension.[8] In Nietzsche's hands, I argue, the aphorism implicates the reader in the reading and at the same time, formulaically and all too comfortably (we will return to this point later), the aphorism seems to absolve Nietzsche as author. It is also worth noting that, at least for some contemporary scholars, part of the difficulty in reading Nietzsche's aphorisms has been the problem of their identification.

Obviously enough, not everything Nietzsche wrote was an aphorism, what is more: the aphoristic form was one that he developed and perfected throughout his writings. But the first problem of identifying and distinguishing Nietzsche's aphorisms has called forth an instructively *nonhermeneutic* engagement on the part of traditionally analytically trained philosophers.[9] These scholars undertook the task of identifying the particular aphorism Nietzsche "fitted" or "pre-fixed" or, perhaps better, "set at the beginning (*vorangestellt*) of the third essay of *On the Genealogy of Morals*, the aphorism for which, in his words, "the entirety" of the third essay "is a commentary" (*sie selbst ist dessen Commentator*) (*GM* P:8). For many commentators, and this reading continues, a likely candidate for the contested aphorism has tended to be the epigraph to the third essay, but John Wilcox and Maudemarie Clark observe, and I agree, that is is rather the first section of third essay, titled "What is the meaning of ascetic ideals?" It is key to my reading that this identification that the second section (*GM* III:2) likewise begins with the same title question, the title question to be sure of the third essay as a whole.[10]

The first section of the third essay thus begins with a review of the meaning of ascetic ideals in the case of artists, philosophers and scholars, women, the "physiologically deformed,"—who constitute (as Nietzsche parenthetically tells us) "the *majority of mortals*"—as well as ascetic ideals in the case of priests and saints. This roster recalls the emphases advanced in the first and second essays, but the point here is that the overdetermination of ascetic ideals, that one would "rather will *nothingness* than *not* will" at all (cf., the final section of the third essay, *GM* III:28), requires the "art of exegesis" first invoked in Nietzsche's preface. Thus the first section of the third essay concludes with a resumé of the conclusion to the preface itself (and it could not be clearer that the whole of the third essay will thus serve as a commentary or explication): "—Am I understood? . . . Have I been understood? . . . *Not at all my dear sir*!—Well then, let us start again, from the beginning."[11]

It is as readers or scholars that we remain "unknown to ourselves" (*GM* P:1), an inevitable ignorance, Nietzsche reminds us at the start of his preface, because, "we have never sought ourselves" (ibid.). Thus we recall that at the end of the preface, the reader will be upbraided on the same terms. In an aggressive swipe at Aristotle and the straightforward ideal of authorial clarity, as we recall, Nietzsche challenges the reader who finds his writing "difficult to understand,"[12] declaring his texts "clear enough, presuming what I presume: that one has first read my early writing and without sparing oneself a few pains in the process" (*GM* P:8).

For Nietzsche, we recall further, the aphorism is not taken seriously enough. Note the compound complexity of Nietzsche's complaint as we have analyzed its function above. If the allure of the aphorism lies in its brevity and if the beauty of brief things is that one take them fast and light, like a witticism or a clever saying (and here we see why the epigraph could have been taken for the aphorism in question), Nietzsche's prescription to us is, by contrast, to take his aphorisms more slowly, *seriously*, as good medicine: and that is also to say, as philosophy, that is, again, the art of living.

This dissonant dimension echoes in Nietzsche's concluding word in his prefatory reflection on reading in his *GM*, where he also adds, for the art of reading his texts, a metaphor usually reserved for religious writings: sweet as honey, such texts are to be eaten.[13] Thus we are told that the way to understand Nietzsche's words will be to chew them over and over, to turn them over in ourselves, in our mouths, again and again, rumination, *das Wiederkäuen* (*GM* P:8).

But such rumination fails us, and we hastily pass over passage after passage, spurred on as often as not by well-meaning introductory works by noted scholars or the encouraging advice of helpful translators. One is advised to read Nietzsche until one finds a passage one likes, then look for another, and so on, just as one might surf the Internet, moving from link to link, until one finds something vaguely worthy of being "bookmarked" as a "favorite," or else, as one might take a tour through a vacation spot or shopping mall. By contrast with such "searching and finding," to use metaphors borrowed from the scholarly disaster that is an electronic or search-able text, Nietzsche instructs us that "an aphorism consummately coined and mol-ded, is not yet 'deciphered' in that it is read out; much rather has the interpretation first to begin" (*GM* P:8). Nor is it enough simply to begin to interpret. The herme-neutic *work* of reading is required here: we need an "art of interpretation" (ibid.).

The task of so interpreting Nietzsche's aphorism thus requires a commentary—indeed, a commentary that would otherwise be matched to what others say (or fail to say) "in a book." Nor do we lack an illustration of what such a commentary would look like. Nietzsche offers us an example of such a reading illuminated on the musical model of a coda. Note again that this is not simply prescribed or recom-mended on Nietzsche's part as a task for the reader to accomplish as he or she will. Instead, and this is the point, an example is provided in an elaborate form, going so far as to position a resumé (the scholar's nutshell) at the beginning of the third essay of the book, just where the author tells us to find it at the conclusion of his preface: "In the third essay of the book, I offer an exemplar of that which I name 'interpreta-tion' in such a case" (ibid.).

The Nietzschean aphorism can be as short as a sentence set on its own. Alter-nately, it can be a fragment of a longer sentence in a longer paragraph: "Assuming as a given, that truth is a woman"(*BGE* P), famously followed with an elaborate reflection on philosophers, on dogma, and dogmatists.[14] And the Nietzschean apho-rism can be very long indeed, as can be seen especially in the case of *HH* but also elsewhere, particularly in *Z*, if we do not read this book as a veritable novel of apho-risms but if we take it as a single aphorism, varied and tuned: Zarathustra as music. If brevity is the prime characteristic of the aphorism, it is not the only characteristic in Nietzsche's case.

The differential point above would suggest that the aphorism elaborated in *GM* III:1 resumes itself in its own recapitulation, an elaboration of which extends to the author's own commentary on it in the third part of the book as a whole. We have to do with an aphorism within an aphorism (indeed, and, of course, in a book of such aphorisms). This recapitulation is the effective point at the end of the aphorism, confirming the working power of Nietzsche's aphoristic style, where he poses the question, "What is the meaning of ascetic ideals?" This question appears three times in succession, two-thirds of the way into a book on the generation of those same ideals: one doesn't get it? is it still unclear? (The question, of course, replays an earlier question as we recall: *GM* I, especially I:8 and I:9.) The answer given is not coincidentally adapted from the dancing master or conductor: Shall we take it from the top! *da capo!* (*GM* III:1, cf. *BGE* 56).

Beginning in this way with the question, "What is the meaning of ascetic ideals?" the aphorism answers its own question by emphasizing both the problem of understanding and the need to *begin* a reflection. The task of reading, like writing, but also thinking or loving, is the kind of thing that needs, as Nietzsche always repeated, first to be learnt. In this sense, the aphoristic structure of *GM* III:1 announces itself as problematic, bearing out the need for commentary and although we cannot pursue this question further here, the aphoristic structure per se calls for an adequate hermeneutic. But the art of reading, the hermeneutic art, according to Nietzsche, is "something that has been unlearned most thoroughly nowadays" (*GM* P:8).

ON READING THE APHORISM

The aphorism as self-contained, as self-referring, as something that can and should be chewed over but also as something that can be carried beyond the text itself, has to be read both in itself and against itself. As a word, aphorism has the roots, as Liddell and Scott remind us, αφ-/απ- from, off, away; 'ορίζω: to divide, set apart, separate as a boundary. Hence and substantively, the essence of aphorism is almost preternaturally phenomenological. Nor has this gone without remark. One author observes that the word itself means "formal 'de-limination' and simultaneously substantively something 'manifestly removed from its usual horizon.'"[15] In this way, the aphorism presupposes or better said, and this is why Nietzsche favored it as a stylistic form, it *accomplishes*, achieves, or effects an *epoché* or bracketing of the phenomenon.

Nietzsche's aphorisms thus read themselves into the reader and what is intriguing about his stylization of this form is that they do this in spite of the reader's prejudices and more often than not *because* of these: playing with such readerly convictions and turning them inside out. An example of this reader-involved efficacy is Nietzsche's discussion of Jewish morality in the first part of the *Genealogy* (*GM* I:7).

Reading the working of the aphorism in this way, we note that its tactical tempo only increases in its intensity—a plainly seductive appeal playing to the prejudices of the anti-Semite. This play is at work from the start in *On the Genealogy of Morals* as Nietzsche orients his reflections on the genealogical provenance of morality to the scientific ears and utilitarian sensibility of what he called the "English psychologists"

(*GM* I:1), while the very Darwinian oblivion of mechanical habit and sociocultural reinforcement is exactly under fire. Here, in *GM* I:7, the text is directed to, and hence it begins by, appealing to the most typical prejudices of all-too Christian anti-Semitism.

The Christian/anti-Semite is drawn into, seduced into the text, as the first section of *GM* throughout its repeated emphasis on the meaning of words as a defense of a "lordly" or "noble" Greco-Roman past, a charge held against Jewish antiquity. Thus one reads that everything ever done against the historical phantasm or "ideal" of the "noble" must fade into inconsequentiality compared with what "the *Jews* have done against them" (*GM* I:7). The doubling of the aphoristic stylizing of this text (I have elsewhere called it the barb of Nietzsche's style referring not to Derrida's spurs but Nietzsche's "fisher of men" language as he regards his texts as so many "fish hooks") turns the reader's conviction against the reader himself or herself. The recoil is all the more effective the more deeply anti-Semitic the reader, an effect intensified in the course of reading. Indeed, as he or she continues to read, the anti-Semite will have no choice but to be caught in the middle of the text.

Identifying the Jew as the one who first inverts the "aristocratic value equation," overturning the noble self-sufficiency of strength, confidence, and joy ("good = noble = powerful = beautiful = happy = beloved of God" [*GM* I:7]) using the alchemy not of love but of the most "abysmal hatred," Nietzsche transcribes the new, slavely moral equation as it now appears in the (now-dissonantly) *Christian* litany of the indemnification of the disenfranchised, made good again, as we recognize the well-known message of the Sermon on the Mount (Matt. 5, 1:13). Nietzsche will later elaborate this new equation in terms of *ressentiment*. But first Nietzsche sets nothing other than plain Christian values into the mouth of this very same Jewish revaluation: "the wretched alone are the good, the poor, powerless, lowly alone are the good; the suffering, deprived, sick, ugly alone are pious, alone are blessed by God" (ibid.). The newly revalued equation is thus articulated as a re-weighting of the original values of strength (the "lordly" or noble values of antiquity) not for the nostalgic sake of a return to such pristine values but to identify and to trace the consequences of this same genesis: "One knows *who* appropriated the legacy of this Jewish revaluation" (ibid.). With this provocation, the reader is caught in his or her own assumptions.

The reversal of the aphorism already occurs in the double ellipsis *included* in Nietzsche's own text. Nietzsche seduces the anti-Semitic reader into the text only to turn his or her reflections against the ultimate consequences of his or her own convictions. It now transpires that the anti-Semite *is* himself or herself a Jew and thus everything turns out to be coordinately on the way to becoming "Judaized, Christianized"—and for good, socialist, and atheistic measure (that is to say: to make it worse), Nietzsche includes an allusion to the "people" as well (*GM* I:9). With regard to the title of Christian or Jew, Nietzsche asks "what do words matter" (ibid.), and as he will later remind us in his *Anti-Christian*, the Christian is nothing more than a Jew of a more catholic (broader) "confession" (*A* 44).[16]

For the sake of the reader who might be "incapable of seeing something that required two thousand years to achieve victory" (*GM* I:8), Nietzsche repeats the redoubling emphasis in his next section with an exactly overwrought or agonized reflection on the working of revenge and *ressentiment* in religion and moral values. Describing such "a grand politics of revenge"—and recollecting as we shall detail below, the spiritual danger of "grand politics" as he describes it in *Human, All Too Human*—Nietzsche argues that Israel itself has had to "deny the active instrument of its revenge before all the world as its mortal enemy and nail it to the cross" (*GM* I:8). This denial ensures that "the opponents of Israel" swallow the bait, precisely as they are defined in reactive terms by contrast with Israel. Nietzsche's text thus plays to the reader's anti-Semitism (conscious or not), just as it convicts the reader on the very same terms.[17]

The Nietzschean aphorism exceeds the stylistic rhetoric of an author who can write against the prejudices of anti-Semitic conviction exposing the Semite within, the self-loathing of prejudice against the other as it betrays us in ourselves. To read Nietzsche's aphorisms in this way requires a doubled reading, an *acromatic* or discursive reflection. Reading Nietzsche requires, as he expresses it, that the reader have "ears" for his words.[18] Nietzsche thus insinuates a dialogical dimension into the text by means of the aphorism as a saying (*Spruche*), and in order to begin to engage the text critically, the reader must advert to the resonances of this acoustic dimension.

To take a further example, to illustrate a more patent, conceptual resonance, consider what might at first glance seem the incidental aphorism that relates the contest between memory and pride. "I have done that,' says my memory. 'I cannot have done that'—says my pride, and remains adamant. At last—memory yields" (*BGE* 68). The reflex here turns on the balance of pride and memory and, in particular, on the conviction that the one belongs to a primary (and more objective) and the other to a secondary (and more subjective) mental order. Nietzsche's reflection upon the ultimate primacy of what had appeared to be the secondary faculty of pride, the corrigible, merely subjective faculty, now supplants and corrects the supposedly primary (objective) faculty of memory. Between memory and desire or pride (this is the teasing point contra objectivity), fading memory defers to desire in recollection itself. The truth to life of this reflection catches the confidence of objective self-knowledge and both memory and pride are resolved into the soul's sentiments, each on equal terms in the struggle of the self to tell itself.

It is worth noting that Nietzsche's use of the aphorism is not the same in his earlier and later writings. Even where we read Nietzsche's reflections on the art of the aphorism (reading and writing) in *Human, All Too Human* (*HH* I:35, 163, etc.), we are reading Nietzsche on the way, as it were, to what we tend to recognize as the specifically Nietzschean aphorism. For such an early example, we may consider the above cited "Grand Politics and their Costs" (*HH* 481). Weaving several threads into his account of grand politics (that is to say: war) Nietzsche finds that the greatest cost of war is not material but rather the sacrifice of spiritual "capital" (*Kopf-und Herz-Capitale*). The mode of expression in this early work is one of agonized repetition, expressing the *unsung* dangers of war for the body politic itself and on the individual level. For Nietzsche, this is "the cost involved in the removal year in, year out of an extraordinary number of its efficient and industrious men from their proper professions and occupations in order that they might become soldiers" (*HH* 481). Turning his point concerning such wasted talent, he goes on to say that from the moment a people begins to preoccupy itself with war (whether for defense or conquest), "a great number of the most leading talents are sacrificed upon the 'Altar of the Fatherland' or national honor, where other spheres of action had formerly been open to the talents now absorbed by the political" (ibid.). Thus the true cost of war is the decadence of the genial spirit. He says this in yet another complex reprise, drawing the key consequence henceforward invoked as the dangers of "reading newspapers" as a daily occupation (ibid. *GM* III:26).[19] In addition to the device of repetition, this aphorism is also articulated by what will become the more dominant rhetorical device of dialectical engagement with the reader's anticipations and subsequent recollections (projections/convictions). Both aspects of this dialectical tension have to do with the working of the text on the reader's *pathē*. The ultimate "cost" of war is thus what Nietzsche named *decadence* The literal sacrifice or degradation of a society. This devastation is the inevitable and invisible "price" of war: " . . . the sum total of all these sacrifices and costs in individual energy and work is so tremendous that the political emergence of a people almost necessarily draws after it a spiritual impoverishment and an enfeeblement and a diminution of the capacity for undertakings demanding great concentration and application" (ibid.).

The spiritual impoverishment Nietzsche deplores here is the wastage of nihilism. In complete accord with Plato (the social philosopher Jacques Ranciére has explored this in a different direction[20]), Nietzsche indissolubly links politics and greed, and he goes further in a *Nachlaß* note where he reflects on the widespread character and tendencies of his age: "Here the ghostly finger of the spiritualists, there the mathematical-magical conjurer, then the brain-wasting cult of music, there the re-awakened vulgarities of the persecution of the Jews—all mark the universal training in hatred" (*KSA* 9, 213).

Hence prior to this section, we recall, reading backward—as one must always read Nietzsche's aphorisms in resonant counterpoint: backward and forward, reading those texts that precede and those texts that follow a particular aphorism—that a few sections earlier, writing against nationalism and on behalf of the "good European" (*HH* 475, cf. *GM* III:27) Nietzsche had identified the Jews as those "freethinkers, scholars, and physicians who held fast to the banner of enlightenment and of spiritual independence while under the harshest personal pressure and defended Europe against Asia" (*HH* 475). In this way, Nietzsche asserts that Judaism is the very influence that renders "Europe's mission and history into a continuation of the Greeks" (ibid.). The context of Nietzsche's emphasis here is reviewed in his earlier reproach of Christianity in the aphorism entitled "The non-Greek element in Christianity" which concludes by describing Christianity as "barbaric, Asiatic, ignoble, non-Greek" (*HH* 114, cf. *BT* 12).

If Nietzsche began the *Genealogy* by setting Jewish values against noble values, he concludes with nothing less than a focus on Christian values, going so far as to repeat a favorite theme, his antipathy toward the New Testament itself (*GM* III:22) but also to reprise the impatient sentiments he elsewhere expressed as signs of the Jewishness of "familiarity with God" in thoroughly Christian terms (ibid.).

Nietzsche's at times convoluted expression in *Human, All Too Human* gives way so some have argued to an increased elegance or mastery of style in the later work. But this stylistic change does not transform Nietzsche's emphases. Hence, Nietzsche repeats the same grave insight in *Twilight of the Idols*: "Coming to power is a costly business: power makes stupid. . . . Politics devours all seriousness for really intellectual things, *Deutschland, Deutschland über alles* was, I fear, the end of German philosophy." From *uman, All Too Human* to *Twilight of the Idols*, Nietzsche would seem to have maintained the conviction that one cannot indulge a concern for politics, especially global politics, without a corresponding intellectual sacrifice, in other words: without losing one's soul.

The provocative quandary, damned if one does, damned if one does not, is the philosophical engine of Nietzsche's aphorism. The conclusion, like the related premises invoked by association, is enthymematic: alluded to but not given and in fact only alluded to *in potentia*: the resolution of an aphorism is not fixed and can always change. The shifting reference in part accounts for Nietzsche's apparent mutability in meaning from reading to reading. And the same mutability seems in turn to justify multifarious and even racist, fascist, dangerously criminal readings. If we attend, as we began, to Nietzsche's remonstrations, the problem of understanding Nietzsche's political sentiments as they manifestly persist must be located on the side of our own readerly "convictions:" "*adventavit asinus/pulcher et fortissimos* (the ass appears, beautiful and overweening strong)" (*BGE* 8 my translation; cf. "the great stupidity which we are" *BGE* 231), not in the dissonance of Nietzsche's texts. But a reflection on stupidity, however esoterically expressed with a reference to Ovid's mysteries (as in *BGE* 8), does not resolve our problem. We are thus returned to the question of Nietzsche's style as an effective or *working* style.

Nietzsche himself famously affirms what is now a commonly accepted assessment of his writing style: "Before me it was not known what could be done with the German language—what could be done with language in general" (*EH* "Books" 4) Yet we cannot but ask, if Nietzsche could do so much with words, given his rhetorical mastery, why then did he not secure his words against malicious appropriation?[21] This ethical question corresponds to Nietzsche's own charge against Christian stylistics, against the pastiche style and aura of the New Testament: "It was a piece of subtle refinement that God learned Greek when he wanted to become a writer—and that he did not learn it better" (*BGE* 121). As the same Nietzsche was associated, from the perspective of British politics, with the exemplification of German aggression in World War I and again in World War II (like Hölderlin's writings, Nietzsche's *Zarathustra* was published in soldiers' editions, for the "field"), perhaps we might say that Nietzsche himself should have learnt his own rhetorical polishing of his German language style much "better" than he did in the end.

Here, we can only concede that in spite of everything Nietzsche could with do words, it remains true that his achievements in this domain are as limited socially and politically, indeed exactly as limited as so many scholars have rightfully observed.[22] This is especially the case where "the art of reading" that Nietzsche repeatedly enjoins upon us as his readers, has made less, not more, progress in the interim.

In the end, seeking a point of redemptive transformation, it is perhaps worth underscoring not Nietzsche's rhetorical prowess but his relative impotence instead. Nietzsche's words failed to arrest world history (in advance), just as his longing failed to bring back the Greece of the past (even in the form of a rebirth of the tragic art in the music of his age, whether Wagner or Bizet). As much as Nietzsche endeavored to change the world in his writing (and, here more classicist than philologist, he did this from the start), it is perhaps more relevant, and certainly more human, even transcendently so, to recall that he came himself to recognize the limitations of his efforts and would express himself with increasingly impatient frustration (in letters and postcards to friends) for the rest of his life. And thus I read the anti-writerly, anti-readerly rhetoric of one of his last notes in which he declares, "I am having all anti-Semites shot."

NOTES

I owe Christa Davis Acampora special thanks for her editorial suggestions and comments. I am also grateful to Don Rutherford and the other participants in the History of Philosophy Reading Group at the University of California at San Diego for critical responses to this essay on March 17, 2006.

1. See Richard Schacht, ed., *Nietzsche, Genealogy, Morality* (Berkeley: University of California Press, 1984); Brian Leiter, *Nietzsche on Morality* (New York, Routledge, 2002), Aaron Ridley, *Nietzsche's Conscience: Six Character Studies from the Genealogy* (Ithaca, NY: Cornell University Press, 1998), and so on. Apparent exceptions seem to be: Simon May, *Nietzsche's Ethics and his War on "Morality"* (Oxford: Oxford University Press, 2002) and Werner Stegmaier, *Nietzsches "Genealogie der Moral"* (Darmstadt: Wissenschaftliches Buchgesellschaft, 1994).

2. See also Nietzsche's own comments distinguishing the kind of "aphoristic books" he writes from treatises (which are, as Nietzsche notes here, for "asses and for readers of newspapers" (*KSA* 11, 579).

3. In connection with Rée, see Robin Small's reflections on Nietzsche and the aphorism (and beyond) in Small, *Nietzsche and Rée: A Star Friendship* (Oxford: Oxford University Press, 2005), 57–65.

4. Note the subtitle of Pierre Hadot's *Philosophy as a Way of Life: Spiritual Exercises from Socrates to Foucault*, trans. Michael Chase (Oxford: Blackwell, 1995).

5. *Hippocrates, Volume III*, W. H. S. Jones, trans. (Cambridge: Harvard University Press [Loeb]: 1995 [1923]). It is Seneca's elaboration of the first two points made in the first line (cited by Seneca from the "most famed physician": "*vitam brevem esse, longam arte*") that has ensured its survival. See Seneca, *De brevitate vitae / Von der Kürze des Lebens*, trans. Josef Feix (Stuttgart: Reclam, 1977).

6. I find evidence of this effort to imitate Nietzsche in the structure (and genesis) of Heidegger's *Beiträge*. I discuss this (and its limitations) in chapter 14 of Babich, *Words in Blood, Like Flowers: Poetry and Philosophy, Music and Eros in Hölderlin, Nietzsche, Heidegger* (Albany: State University of New York Press, 2006).

7. Although one can use an aphorism as an epigraph, an epigraph need not be an aphorism but can be a poem or a motto, or a quote alluding to another text, like the epigraph found as an object example at the start of the present chapter (quoting Nietzsche's reflections on the *Genealogy* in his *Ecce Homo*), or like Nietzsche's reference to *Thus Spoke Zarathustra* in the epigraph he placed at the start of the third essay in *On the Genealogy of Morals*.

8. See, for one example, Heinz Krüger's, *Studien über den Aphorismos als philosophischer Form* (Frankfurt: Nest Verlag, 1956). Krüger's book is articulated in opposition to Kurt Besser's more properly philological, *Die Problematik der aphoristischer Form bei Lichtenberg, Schlegel, Novalis, und Nietzsche* (Berlin: Junker and Dünnhaupt, 1935). See for a more recent and very comprehensive general discussion: Detlef Otto, *Wendungen der Metapher. Zur Übertragung in poetologischer, rhetorischer, und erkenntnistheoretischer Hinsicht bei Aristoteles und Nietzsche* (Munich: Fink Verlag, 1998). Recently, English language scholars have turned their attention to the role of the aphorism in Nietzsche's thought. See Small's *Nietzsche and Rée*, cited above, in addition to further references in the notes below.

9. For a discussion of these problems as they have haunted the analytic as well as the literary tradition of philosophic scholarship, and the particular danger of mistaking an epigraph for an aphorism (never a good idea with a scholar of rhetoric such as Nietzsche was), see John T. Wilcox, "What Aphorism Does Nietzsche Explicate in Genealogy of Morals Essay III?" and Maudemarie Clark, "From the Nietzsche Archive: Concerning the Aphorism Explicated in Genealogy III." Both published in the *Journal of the History of Philosophy* 35/4 (1997): 593–633. See also Wilcox, "That Exegesis of an Aphroism in 'Genealogy III': Reflections on the Scholarship," *Nietzsche-Studien* 28 (1998): 448–62. See also Paul Miklowitz's reply to Wilcox in *Nietzsche-Studien* 29 (1999): 267–69. The issue is not a settled affair and Christoph Cox cites the epigraph as the aphorism in question at the start of his book, *Nietzsche: Naturalism and Interpretation* (Berkeley: University of California Press, 1999), 15. Still more recently, Jill Marsden likewise favors the epigraph from Zarathustra in her "Nietzsche and the Art of the Aphorism," in Keith Ansell Pearson, ed., *A Companion to Nietzsche* (Oxford: Blackwell, 2006), 22–38, esp. 32–37. Marsden herself follows Kelly Oliver's reading. See Oliver, *Womanizing Nietzsche: Philosophy's Relation to the "Feminine"* (London: Routledge, 1995).

10. In her editor's notes to the 1998 translation (with Alan J. Swenson) of Nietzsche's *On the Genealogy of Morality*, Clark observes that from "an examination of the printer's manuscript, it is clear that when Nietzsche began writing it out, the third treatise begins with what is now section 2." (Hackett, 1998), 198. Clark also adds a further reference to Christopher Janaway's independent corroboration of this point at this same locus.

11. Despite this tour through so very many forms of the ascetic ideal (and the thrice-repeated title of the third essay *What is the Meaning of Ascetic Ideals?* tells us that this variety

is crucial), in place of *GM* III:I, readers, as the above references attest, continue to identify the epigraph to the third section as the aphorism Nietzsche had in mind: "Untroubled, mocking, violent—thus will wisdom have us: she is a woman, she always loves only a warrior.—*Thus Spoke Zarathustra*" (*GM* III, *Epigraph*). Wilcox and Clark certainly had their work lined up for them, at least as Wilcox stated the problem and certainly as Clark resolved it by the expedient of taking a visit to the Nietzsche archives for a look at the original manuscript. It is important to note that neither Wilcox nor Clark disagree with the above identification of the aphorism in question. The only difference in my reading is that I offer the above identification in classically "continental" fashion, that is, by way of the traditionally hermeneutic expedient of readerly exegesis (and I submit that a hermeneutic, or "art of reading" is precisely what Nietzsche expected).

12. Aristotle located the responsibility for being understood on the plain side of the author and the lucidity of prose.

13. There are other, most notably Augustinian, loci for this image. But a fine instanciation of this textual sensibility, precisely because of the comprehension of the full range of the incarnate sensuality of the letter and the book, is Ivan Illich, *In the Vineyard of the Text: A Commentary on Hugh's* Didascalicon (Chicago: University of Chicago Press, 1993), chapter 3, esp. 54ff.

14. This is the point of departure for the late Jacques Derrida's discussion of style, using the (gallically stylistic) conceit of, "woman" in *Éperons: Les Styles de Nietzsche Spurs: Nietzsche's Styles*, Barbara Johnson, trans. (Chicago: University of Chicago, 1979). I raise this question from another perspective in terms of the Nietzsche's question of the problem of the artist in Babich, "The Logic of Woman in Nietzsche: The Dogmatist's Story," *New Political Science* 36 (1996): 7–17.

15. Krüger, *Studien über den Aphorismos als philosophischer Form*, 26.

16. It is worth noting that any Christian preacher or priest would say the same thing.

17. Apart from readerly anti-Semitism, I elsewhere follow the dynamic of this writing as it engages prejudicial convictions in reviewing the functioning of Nietzsche's critique of ascetic ideals in terms not only of religion anterior to morality but science. Babich, *Nietzsche's Philosophy of Science: Reflecting Science on the Ground of Art and Life* (Albany: State University of New York Press, 1994), see chapter 4 and, in particular, chapter 5.

18. I discuss this point in terms of Nietzsche's original philological impetus for writing his *The Birth of Tragedy out of the Spirit of Music* in Babich, "The Science of Words or Philology: Music in *The Birth of Tragedy* and the Alchemy of Love in *The Gay Science*," *Revista di estetica*, edited by Tiziana Andina 45:28 (2005): 47–78. See further, Manfred Riedel, *Hören auf die Sprache. Die akroamatische Dimension der Hermeneutik* (Frankfurt am Main: Suhrkamp, 1989) and Holger Schmid, *Kunst des Hörens: Orte und Grenzen philosophische Spracherfahrung* (Cologne: Böhlau, 1999).

19. "But aside from these public hecatombs and at bottom much more horrible, there occurs a spectacle played out continually in a hundred thousand simultaneous acts: every efficient, industrious, intelligent, energetic man belonging to such a people lusting after political laurels is dominated by this same lust and no longer belongs completely to his own domain as once he did" (*HH* 481).

20. Jacques Ranciere, *The Philosopher and His Poor*, John Drury, Corinne Oster, and Andrew Parker, trans. (Durham: Duke University Press, 2003). See also, Pierre Bourdieu et al., *The Weight of the World: Social Suffering in Contemporary Society*, Priscilla Ferguson et al., trans. (Stanford: Stanford University Press, 1999). See further *KSA* 9, 213.

21. Berel Lang raises exactly this question in his contribution to Jacob Golomb and Robert S. Wistrich, eds., *Nietzsche, Godfather of Fascism: On the Uses and Abuses of Philosophy* (Princeton: Princeton University Press, 2002).

22. See, for an example, again, Golomb and Wistrich, eds., *Nietzsche, Godfather of Fascism*. But see, too, the contributions, including my editor's introduction, "Habermas, Nietzsche, and the Future of Critique: Irrationality, *The Will to Power*, and War," *Nietzsche, Habermas, and Critical Theory*, edited by Babette E. Babich (Amherst, NY: Prometheus Books [Humanity Books Imprint] 2004), 13–46.

12

"We Remain of Necessity Strangers to Ourselves"

The Key Message of Nietzsche's *Genealogy*

Ken Gemes

INTRODUCTION[1]

The central claim of this chapter is that *On the Genealogy of Morals* is primarily aimed at gradually bringing us, Nietzsche's readers, to a potentially shattering realization that in a deep and fundamental sense we do not know ourselves.[2] I argue that Nietzsche's initial assertion in the preface of the *Genealogy* that his aim is to expose the historical origins of our morality is intentionally misleading and that Nietzsche employs uncanny displacements and subterfuges in order to disguise his real target. This is exposed only in section 23 of the third essay where the reader is faced with Nietzsche's central claim that we moderns are in fact the ultimate embodiment of the ascetic ideal. Nietzsche argues that we have mistakenly taken ourselves to have overcome this ideal in the move from a religious to a secular, scientific worldview, when in fact that move only signifies the deepest and most sublime expression of that ideal. This essay aims to expose the methods behind, and reasons for, Nietzsche's dissimulation about his true aim.[3]

A STRATEGY OF MISDIRECTION

In the first section of his preface to the *Genealogy* Nietzsche tells his readers that we are "strangers to ourselves." This beautiful and uncanny phrase is an echo of the

191

first line of the preface: "We are unknown to ourselves, we knowers: and for a good reason." In his typical elliptical fashion, Nietzsche does not tell us what that good reason is. Indeed, the whole theme of our being strangers to ourselves is quickly and quietly dropped. In the second section of the preface Nietzsche brings up what is ostensibly the focus of the *Genealogy*, the question of the origins of our morality, "that is what this polemic is about" (*GM* P:2). Certainly the first essay, with its main theme of the triumph of Judeo-Christian slave morality over the Greek/ Roman master morality, seems to bear out the claim that his polemic is about the origins of morality. And, to take us further from the opening claim that we are strangers to ourselves, Nietzsche explicitly emphasizes in the second essay that show-ing the origins of something tells us little, if anything, about its current purpose and value.[4]

But if that is so, then, how can Nietzsche's aim be to show us that we are strangers to ourselves? How can the *Genealogy* be about who we are, when it is telling us mainly about our ancestors? To see the solution to the problem we must realize that the *Genealogy*, like so many of Nietzsche's texts, divides into a manifest and a latent content. Nietzsche cannot afford to be too explicit about that latent content because it is challenging and terrifying, striking at the center of our self-conception. Like a clever psychoanalyst, he knows that a direct approach will merely awaken the patient's/reader's defenses and provoke a reflex denial and a refusal to countenance his message. Moreover, Nietzsche believes that mere intellectual knowledge can often work against deeper forms of realization that are necessary for genuine change. Nietzsche, educated by Schopenhauer, regarded consciousness as being a rather shal-low phenomenon, almost to the point of dismissing it as epiphenomenal (cf. *GS* 11, 333, 354; *BGE* 32). Prefiguring Freud, he believed that for ideas to be truly effective they must work on us at a level below consciousness. Thus, in the *Genealogy*, he chooses to approach his aim obliquely. He starts at some distance from us—with our ancestors—and even suggests that his examination of them does not have direct and immediate consequences for us. But, in fact, Nietzsche is talking about us, first indirectly and later directly. He is telling us deeply disturbing and momentous truth about ourselves, though we may not at first recognize that we are the subjects who are being damned in his polemic.

That such indirection is the method of the *Genealogy* is something Nietzsche explicitly claims in *Ecce Homo*: "Every time a beginning that is calculated to mislead. . . . Gradually . . . very disagreeable truths are heard grumbling in the dis-tance" (*EH* "*GM*"). We are for Nietzsche strangers to ourselves for the very good reason that to face who we are is a challenge requiring momentous courage, a chal-lenge that, properly undertaken, should precipitate a shattering struggle. But, as Nietzsche warns us in the first section of the preface of the *Genealogy*, such chal-lenges provoke strong resistance: "In such matters we are never really 'with it': we just don't have our heart there—or even our ear." Though, he suggests that when his true message is registered, "we will rub our ears *afterwards* and ask completely amazed, completely disconcerted, 'What did we actually experience just now?' still more: 'who *are* we actually?'" (Nietzsche's italics). The italics here are significant. The emphasis on "afterwards" is an indication of Nietzsche's belief that only after his message has slowly snuck through our defenses will we recognize what the *Genealogy* is really about. The emphasis on "are" is an indication that the *Genealogy* is ultimately about who we are and not, as it might first appear, about who our ancestors were.[5]

TRUTH AND THE ASCETIC IDEAL

What, then, is the kernel of Nietzsche's message that might lead us to question who we really are? Basically, the *Genealogy* teaches that our much prized morality of compassion, in particular, our evaluations of good and evil (essay I), our concept of conscience (essay II), and our commitment to truth (essay III) are all expressions of impotence and sublimated hostility.

In order to get his readers to appreciate this message, Nietzsche engages his readers' interest and affects by using history as a means for creating a distance between his ostensible subject, the origins of morality, and his real subject, the sickness in our current morality. It is in *GM* III:23 that we find ourselves for the first time more directly addressed. Having exposed the psychohistorical roots of our sense of good and evil, and sense of conscience, characterizing these as handymen to the life-denying ascetic ideal, Nietzsche there asks if there is not now a new counterideal in the modern ideal of truth, objectivity, and science.[6] Here he is directly engaging his readers who identify themselves as adhering to this modern ideal, which they take as being fundamentally opposed to the religiously motivated ascetic ideal.

Secular readers, inspired by Enlightenment ideals, have little resistance to recognizing that the religious founders of Judaeo-Christian morality were in fact inspired by hatred and envy. They see themselves as being far removed from that religious mentality. This provides the comforting "pathos of distance" that allows the first and second essay to do their work on the reader. But in *GM* III:23 Nietzsche provides what he hopes will be a moment of self-recognition when he responds to his question about the existence of a counterideal by claiming that the will to truth, the will to objectivity, is not the means by which we have escaped the religious world and its associated ascetic ideal. Rather, it is, in fact, the last and most complete expression of that ideal. This is the moment when we are meant to rub our ears: How is it that we who have thrown off the crutches of superstition and religious obscurantism, who have committed ourselves to embrace the truth at any cost, and thus relinquished the comforting myth of a world to come, can be accused of participating in the ascetic ideal? As Nietzsche himself says, it is our love of truth that has allowed us to realize the falsity behind the ascetic ideal, the hollowness of religious claims (cf. *GM* III:27). Now he relies on our love of truth to force us to recognize the true meaning of that love. Nietzsche, thinking primarily as a psychologist, is looking at the latent meaning of our commitment to truth. That commitment, he maintains, stems from the same motivation that fuelled commitment to religious ascetic values, namely, fear of life and feelings of impotence.

The religious person attempts to remove himself from the torments of this world, a world that largely resists his desires. He tells himself that what happens in this life is ultimately unimportant; that what matters is what is in his soul, which will determine his real, eternal, life in the world to come. The modern scholar similarly removes himself from life by telling himself that what is of ultimate value is not acting in this world, not what he does, but in understanding the world, in what he knows. Both the religious ascetic and the ascetic scholar believe "the truth will set you free." Nietzsche has realized that here to be free means to be free of the pull of this world, the tumult of earthly passions and desires. Just as the ascetic ideal demands suppression of the passions, so the scholar's emphasis on objectivity and truth demands "the emotions cooled" (*GM* III:25). Where the religious take revenge upon the world by denying that it is of ultimate importance, the scholar revenges himself by saying that passive understanding is of greater value than "mere" action. Furthermore, the scholar takes his possession of knowledge to somehow give him a sort of magical possession of the world. Nietzsche seems to countenance two ways in which knowledge can function as a form of revenge against the world. On the first account the valorization of passive knowledge over action is a way of withdrawing from the active life that a healthy nature demands (cf. *D* 42 "*Origin of the vita comteplativa*"). On the second account, through knowledge people attempt to possess the world "as if knowledge of it sufficed to make it their property" (*D* 285).

THE IDENTIFICATION OF PASSIVITY IN SCHOLARS IN NIETZSCHE'S EARLIER WORK

The scholarly mind values reasons and reasonable belief and is suspicious of passions and unreasoned desire. But life, at least genuine life, ultimately, is a world of passions and desires. Thus, claims Nietzsche, (the pursuit of) science can act as a means of withdrawal from the world: "Science as a means of self-anaesthetisation: *are you acquainted with that?*" (*GM* III:24). Nietzsche had in earlier works already claimed that such repression of passions, as exhibited in the scholar, is part of a death drive. In *The Gay Science*, in a passage that Nietzsche explicitly directs us to in *GM* III:28, he characterizes the will not to be deceived as something that might be: "a principle hostile to life and destructive—'Will to truth'—that can be a hidden will to death" (*GS* 344). In the same place he tell us, "those who are truthful in the audacious and ultimate sense that is presupposed by the faith in science *thus affirm another world* than the world of life, nature, and history." These thoughts Nietzsche first fully thematized in his early work the *Untimely Meditations*. There, in the second essay,

On the Use and Disadvantages of History for Life, he characterizes "the scholar, the man of science" as one who "stands aside from life so as to know it unobstructedly" (*HL* 10). Focusing on the use of history, Nietzsche contrasts his demand that we use history for "life and action" with the scholar's use of history for the ends of "easy withdrawal from life and action" (*HL* P). Nietzsche pictures "the historical virtuoso of the present day" as "a passive sounding board" whose tone and message "lulls us and makes us tame spectators" (*HL* 6). It is the desire to stand aside from life that links the scholar and the priest as practitioners of the ascetic ideal.

In *HL* Nietzsche uses metaphors of mirroring, castration, and impotence to capture the passivity of the scholar and, in particular, the historian. These metaphors Nietzsche repeats throughout his corpus in order to emphasize the same point. In *HL* he asks the rhetorical question: "[o]r is it selflessness when the historical man lets himself be blown into an objective mirror?" (*HL* 8, my translation). In the same essay Nietzsche asserts that the scholar's ideal of pure objectivity would characterize "a race of eunuchs" (*HL* 5). In *Beyond Good and Evil* (207) Nietzsche again captures the element of passivity and otherworldliness behind the exorbitant overvaluation of truth and objectivity by referring to "the objective person . . . the *ideal* scholar" as "a mirror: he is accustomed to submitting before whatever wants to be known, without any other pleasure than that found in knowing and 'mirroring.'" Later, in the same section, he refers to the scholar as a "mirror soul, eternally smoothing itself out." In the very next section Nietzsche tell us that, "'objectivity,' 'being scientific' . . . is merely dressed up scepticism and paralysis of the will."

These themes are repeated in *Thus Spoke Zarathustra* in the sections "Of Immaculate Perception" and "Of Scholars." In the first of these sections Zarathustra characterizes those who seek "pure knowledge" as hypocrites, on the grounds that while they are men of earthly lusts they have "been persuaded to contempt of the earthly." Again, Nietzsche has recourse to the metaphors of passive mirroring, when he expresses the voice of those seekers of pure knowledge as follows: "For me the highest thing would be to gaze at life without desire. . . . I desire nothing of things, except that I may lie down before them like a mirror with a hundred eyes." Nietzsche's repeated negative references to passive mirroring when characterizing the will to truth and objectivity are a deliberate reference to, and in contrast with, Schopenhauer who favourably spoke of the intellect "abolishing all possibility of suffering" (*World as Will and Representation* II:368) when it renounces all interest and becomes "the clear mirror of the world" (*World as Will and Representation* II:380). It is presumably Nietzsche's early struggles with Schopenhauer that first alerted him to the possibility that intellectual contemplation can function as a means for attempting escape from this painful world of becoming.[7]

Zarathustra also repeats the metaphors of impotence and castration when those who seek pure knowledge are told, "[t]ruly you do not love the earth as creators, begetters. . . . But now your emasculated leering wants to be called 'contemplation'!" (*Z*, ibid.) The metaphor of the scholar as mirror is used in the *Genealogy*. There, in describing modern historiography, which he characterises as being "to a high degree ascetic" and "to a still higher degree nihilistic," Nietzsche says modern historiography's "[n]oblest claim is that it is a mirror" (*GM* III:26). In the same section there are multiple metaphors of castration and impotence. For instance, Nietzsche, with a side reference to the famous historian Renan, characterizes certain "objective" "armchair" "contemplatives" in terms of their "cowardly contemplativeness, the lecherous eunuchry in the face of history, the making eyes at ascetic ideas, the justice-Tartuffery of impotence!" (*GM* III:26).

The core of Nietzsche's objection to both the ascetic idea, in its first religious incarnation and its last incarnation, in the objective scholar's will to truth, is that they both are a symptom of, and caused by, an "aversion to life" (*GM* III:28). Nietzsche's Zarathustra says of scholars, "they want to be mere spectators" (*Z*:II, "Scholars"). Both religious ascetic and ascetic scholar take, and try to justify, an essentially passive stance toward the world. They are passive because they are weak and scared, but they dress their passivity up as a virtue and a choice.

It might be thought that there is a fundamental difference between the powerlessness of the original Jewish slaves and the situation faced by scholars and other members of Nietzsche's audience. The latter of course belong to a dominant, successful society. While there are differences, the key point is that that success is now the success of a herd animal who is still vehemently repressing many of his individual desires pursuing an alleged common good.[8]

One of the reasons Nietzsche so highly values the (pre-Socratic) Greeks is because, while they understood that life is essentially, and inevitably, painful, they still had the strength to affirm it and act decisively, even horribly—think of Medea's terrible revenge against Jason.[9] By contrast, the Christian and modern men, in particular scholars, still are fundamentally obsessed with escaping the pain of this life: "*the absence of suffering*—this may count as the highest good" for them, hence their valorization of passivity (*GM* III:17).[10] Since all doing inevitably involves (the risk of) pain, they seek to avoid doing, hence their valorization of being over becoming. For Nietzsche, the scholar's valuing truth, like the religious person's valuing the world to come, is generally paired with a valorization of being over becoming. Even if the scholar takes truth to be truth about the world of appearance this would not abrogate Nietzsche's point. Fundamentally, in Nietzsche's work, the being/becoming dichotomy aligns with the passive/active dichotomy. This explains his rather monotonous emphasis on becoming over being throughout his corpus, which is only broken in *GS* 370. There he lets on that a valorization of becoming in certain contexts can actually be manifestation of a rejection of life, and a valorization of being can in certain contexts be a manifestation of a healthy creative attitude. This shows that his ultimate concern is with fostering creative activity rather than championing one side or the other of a metaphysical being/becoming distinction.

Nietzsche repeatedly uses the metaphors of mirroring, castration, and impotence to viscerally bring home the degree of passivity in the scholar. He is a philosopher who, more than most, uses metaphor as a marker of significance. The repetition is thus a clear marker of the importance Nietzsche attaches to this theme.

NIETZSCHE'S MIXED ATTITUDES TO
THE WILL TO TRUTH

Does Nietzsche unconditionally reject the will to truth? Clearly he sees the modern will to truth as a manifestation of a passive attitude to life and presents himself as the great advocate of life as an expansive Dionysian activity. Still, it would be surprising if this great opponent of the unconditional should unconditionally reject the will to truth. Perhaps then his objection is to the elevation of truth to an end in itself.[11] There is something to this but it misses the real focus of Nietzsche's objection.

When Nietzsche objects to a thing, for example religion or the will to truth, it is important to place that thing in its relevant context. The point here, one often made by Nietzsche himself, is that something that is dangerous, unhealthy in a given context may well be beneficial in another (cf. *BGE* 30). Nietzsche is always a local rather than a global thinker. He will not simply condemn, for instance, the will to truth, but rather will condemn it within a given context.[12] The point is what ends it serves in a given context. In the context of Christianity and the modern scholarly spirit he sees the will to truth as serving the purpose of slandering life. But this still leaves room for him to recognize that in other contexts, or for given individuals within a specific context, the will to truth can be a manifestation of a robust health. Thus, he clearly does not regard Goethe's prodigious curiosity and will to truth as a negative phenomenon. And surely in his own case his insight into human nature, though bought at a terrible personal cost, is not something he sees as a negative manifestation of the will to truth. It is a repeated theme in Nietzsche's corpus that the stronger a being is the more truth it can endure (cf. *BGE* 39; *TI* "Maxims" 8; *EH* P:3).

It would be too facile to simply say that what separates Goethe and Nietzsche's positive manifestation of the will to truth from the Christian's or the scholar's is that they, unlike the later, do not regard truth as an end in itself. Would a scholar who claims that truth is no ultimate end, say a postmodernist of today, be any less a target of Nietzsche's polemic? And would a creative, Goethe-like, figure who did indeed take truth to be the ultimate value be a fit subject for Nietzsche's attack? The will to truth, even the will to truth taken as an ultimate end, is not the object of Nietzsche's attack. Rather it is the will to truth in its now prevalent context of the Christian's and scholar's passive and negative orientation toward life that Nietzsche rejects.[13] To take the will to truth even in its most extreme case as the principle target of Nietzsche's attack is to mistake a symptom for a cause.

To understand the nature of Nietzsche's complaint against the will to truth in the context of its manifestation in modern men of science, and to contrast it with the healthier will to truth exhibited by rare individuals such as Goethe and Nietzsche himself, it is helpful to return to the second of his *Untimely Meditations.*

A key charge in the *Untimely Meditations* is that the scholar, the modern man of science, falls "wretchedly apart into inner and outer, content and form" (*HL* 4). It is for this reason that "our modern culture is not a living thing" (ibid.). According to Nietzsche, in the hands of the typical scholar knowledge is merely a personal, internal affair that does not express itself in outward action. The content of his knowledge does not express itself in outward forms. "Inner" and "content" for Nietzsche refers to man's internal world of thought; "outer" and "form" refer to the external world of action. Modern man's unbridled exhortation of the will to truth facilitates his emphasis on inner content to the exclusion of outer forms. Against this splitting Nietzsche recommends that a "higher unity in the nature of the soul of a people must again be created, that the breach between inner and outer must vanish" (ibid.). This unity is exactly the characteristic that Nietzsche so often extols in Goethe and claims to have finally arrived at himself. In them the will to truth does not express itself as a stepping back from the world in order to enter an otherworldly realm of ineffectual contemplation. Rather, it is an active part of their engagement with the world. Nietzsche and Goethe possess active rather than passive knowledge. Indeed Nietzsche's *On the Use and Disadvantage of History for Life*, which is his most sustained attack on knowledge as a means to inactivity, begins with the following quotation from Goethe, which he tells us he fully concurs with: "In any case I hate everything that merely instructs me without augmenting or directly invigorating my activity" (*HL* P). The importance of the notion of unity for a genuine person is a theme that we will return to shortly.

Of course, in *GM* and elsewhere, Nietzsche's primary example of the life-denier is the Christian, not the scholar. For him Nietzsche reserves his strongest rhetoric: "this entire fictional world has it roots in *hatred* of the natural (actuality!). . . . *But that explains everything.* Who alone has reason to *lie himself* out of actuality? He who *suffers* from it. But to suffer from it means to be an abortive reality" (*A* 15).

Yet we should recognize here a voice not unrelated to that with which Nietzsche chastises the scholar in the passages quoted above. This talk of abortive reality is of a piece with his rhetorical question in *HL* concerning the current age of "universal education": "Are there still human beings, one then asks oneself, or perhaps only thinking-, writing-, and speaking-machines" (*HL* 5). There are important differences in the way Nietzsche regards the scholar and the Christian. In the latter he sees only forces inimical to life. In the former and his objective sprit he sees much that is useful and for which we should be grateful (cf. *BGE* 207). After all, it is the scholar, with his will to truth, who helps us see through the fabrications of religion. But for Nietzsche, "[t]he objective man is an instrument . . . he is no goal, no conclusion and sunrise" (*BGE* 207). His essential passivity toward the world means that, "[w]hatever still remains in him of a 'person' strikes him as accidental, often arbitrary, still more disturbing; to such an extent he has become a passageway and reflection of strange forms and events even to himself" (ibid.). This enigmatic talk of being a passageway to strange forms and events, of the arbitrary and the accidental, hints at some profound sense of alienation. But what exactly this involves is not thematized in *Beyond Good and Evil*. To get a better understanding of what is at stake here we do well to return to the *Genealogy*.

ACCIDENTAL, ARBITRARY MODERNS VS. THE SOVEREIGN INDIVIDUAL

When Nietzsche says in the preface to *GM* that we are strangers to ourselves, that we are unknown to ourselves, it is tempting to take this estrangement as merely a matter of our lack of self-knowledge. But then we must ask the question why exactly this should be taken as a criticism? Surely it cannot be that we are under some obligation to know the full truth about ourselves; that kind of imperative looks suspiciously like a manifestation of the very will to truth that is the object of Nietzsche's critique in the third essay of the *Genealogy*. What is more, Nietzsche has often told of the need for self-deception (cf. *BGE* 2 and 4). Indeed, Nietzsche tells us that ignorance of one's deeper drives and motivations can often be a healthy phenomenon (cf. *EH* "Clever" 9). This thought goes hand in hand with his general dismissal of consciousness as a weak, irrelevant, even disruptive, force.

How can Nietzsche extol the virtues of self knowledge yet at other times praise ignorance of the self? Again, part of the answer is to be found in the different ends knowledge and ignorance can serve in different contexts. In the case of Wagner and himself Nietzsche sees ignorance as something that helps a deeper unifying drive finally reach its full active expression.[14] In the case of Christians and scholars, their ignorance merely serves to facilitate their passive attitudes and their splintering into weak fragmented personalities. This brings us to the deeper sense in which Nietzsche takes us to be strangers to ourselves. As *GM* unfolds, beyond our mere ignorance, a deeper estrangement is suggested, namely, that of having parts of ourselves that are split-off. These parts are split-off, not simply in the sense that we have no conscious access to them, but in the sense that we contain within us hidden affects and drives. These are separate movers that are not part of any integrated whole. Taken to the extreme, this notion of being strangers to ourselves actually threatens the notion of a unified self. That is to say, we have strangers *within* ourselves, so that, in fact, our self is no genuine self. We are nothing more than a jumble of different voices/drives having no overall unity.[15] Not wishing to directly threaten his audience with this frightening thought, Nietzsche brings this idea to his readers in various subtle ways throughout the *Genealogy*.

In *GM* I, Nietzsche playfully torments his audience with variations on this theme of being subverted from within. For instance, Nietzsche's claim that Christian morality is nothing but the inheritor of a Jewish slave morality based on *ressentiment* would for a contemporary German audience strongly hint at the claim that they need not be worried about being "jewified" (*verjudet*) because, with their current morality, they are already as Jewish as they could be.[16] The worry of being "jewified" was one that Germans of the 1880s were keenly aware of. Where a typical (liberal) German audience of Nietzsche's time sees "The Jew" as a foreign body that somehow needs to be cleansed and brought into the Christian-German world, Nietzsche is telling his audience that they are themselves fundamentally contaminated with Jewishness.[17] This is a direct threat to his German audiences' sense of identify. In nineteenth-century Germany one of the common means for dealing with the problematic question of German identity was by establishing a contrast to those who were clearly not Germans. Jews, in particular, were commonly denominated as the paradigm of the un-German. Nietzsche's claim that the Germans are already "jewified" brings home to his reader in an uncanny way his theme that they are strangers to themselves. It is presumably his sense of provocative playfulness that leads Nietzsche to even suggest that the Jewish elders actually gathered as a cabal and deliberately repudiated Christ as a means of enticing their enemies to swallow the poison of Christian slave values (cf. *GM* I:8).

Having in the first essay tormented his audience with the thought that they are already infected with a Jewish voice, one that they themselves would take to be thoroughly foreign, Nietzsche, in the second essay implicitly raises the question of whether such a thoroughly mixed being can be capable of genuine agency. This he does in a rather subtle way, by introducing a figure, the "sovereign individual" capable of genuine agency, and then implicitly contrasting this strong commanding figure with the weak will-o'-the-wisps of his day.

For Nietzsche, genuine agency, including the right to make promises, is the expression of a being who is a unified whole. The second essay begins with the question: "To breed an animal with the right to make promises—is this not the paradoxical task that nature has set itself in the case of man? is this not the real problem regarding man?" (*GM* II:1). The text might easily lead the unwary reader to think this is a task already accomplished, leading the reader into a sense of complacent satisfaction. The sense that Nietzsche is talking of past events is heightened when, having first raised this question of nature's task, he concentrates on the prehistory of man, and man's first acquiring of deep memory—memory burnt in by punishment. The task of acquiring memory is one that has been clearly accomplished; it is something that his audience can proudly lay claim to. Nietzsche, after raising his question, immediately refers to the breeding of an animal with the right to make promises as a problem that "has been solved to a large extent." This furthers the sense that the task is largely behind us. However, when a few pages later Nietzsche introduces "the end of this tremendous process" as the "sovereign individual," his audience should at least have a suspicion glimmering of whether they themselves are this proud, noble-sounding individual or the "feeble windbags" Nietzsche despises. He describes the sovereign individual in hyperbolic tones clearly not applicable to ordinary individuals. He describes him as one "who has his own protracted will and the right to make promises and in him a proud consciousness, quivering in every muscle, of what has at length been achieved and become flesh in him, a consciousness of his own power and freedom . . . [and who] is bound to reserve a kick for the feeble windbags who promise without the right to do so" (*GM* II:2).

It is typical of Nietzsche's caginess that it is not at first clear whether the sovereign individual is a creature already achieved or one yet to come. The terms Nietzsche uses to describe the sovereign individual—"proud," "quivering in every muscle," "aware of his superiority," "like only to himself," "bound to honour his peers"— clearly hark back to the descriptions of the masters of the first essay. Since his audience is meant to identify themselves as the inheritors of slave morality, it is clear that they cannot be identified with this sovereign individual, who, unlike them is "autonomous and supermoral," a "lord of the free will." The implicit message to his audience is that you are not sufficiently whole to have the right to make promises; you have no free will, but are merely tossed about willy-nilly by a jumble of competing drives and, hence, you cannot stand surety for what you promise. You can give no guarantee that the ascendant drive at the time of your making a promise will be effective when the time comes to honor that promise.

NIETZSCHE AND THE UNCANNY

In *GM* III:10, Nietzsche again invokes the notion of free will in an unsettling way. There he suggests a contrast between philosophers as they have occurred so far, "world-negating, hostile towards life, not believing in the senses," with a possible successor who, presumably unlike his predecessors, has sufficient "will of the spirit, *freedom of will*" (*GM* III:10). In this passage, like the earlier ones concerning the sovereign individual and free will, Nietzsche leaves the reader in some doubt as to whether he is talking about something already achieved or yet to be achieved. In both these cases Nietzsche creates a kind of uncanny effect on the reader. The uncanny here is operating in Freud's sense of something that is disturbingly both familiar and unfamiliar.[18]

Let us first consider the case of the sovereign individual and then return to that of the philosopher.

The sovereign individual is, at first, seemingly familiar to his readers as modern man, the possessor of memory and the right to make promises. But Nietzsche's text, by characterizing the sovereign individual in terms typically applied to the masters of the first essay, disturbingly suggests a gulf between the sovereign individual and modern man, the inheritor of slave morality. The sense of the uncanny comes not simply through the confusion about who exactly is the sovereign individual, but also by a certain play on temporality. Is Nietzsche talking about who we are in the present or is he talking about some past beings or some envisaged successor?

The same questions of identity and temporality produce an uncanny effect when Nietzsche describes philosophers in *GM* III:10. He begins with "the earliest philosophers": "to begin with the philosophic spirit always had to use as a mask and cocoon the *previously established* types of contemplative man . . . a religious type." The reference to the earliest philosophers suggests some distance between modern philosophers of Nietzsche's era and the subjects of his descriptions. This suggestion is furthered when Nietzsche then says, "the ascetic priest provided *until modern times* the repulsive caterpillar form in which alone the philosopher could live and creep about" (emphasis mine). Yet when Nietzsche then immediately asks the rhetorical question "Has this really *altered*?" his reader is left with the uneasy feeling that perhaps the repulsive caterpillar form is not really a thing of the past.

These temporal shifts are important for creating an uncanny sense of dislocation in the *Genealogy*. What is far away often turns out to be quite close; and what is apparently already with us turns out to be yet to come. A notable example of such dislocation occurs in his characterization of the "counteridealists" in *GM* III:24. These he accuses of unknowingly sharing the ascetic ideal they explicitly repudiate since "they still have faith in truth." Interestingly, among these counteridealists he includes "pale atheists, antichrists, immoralists, nihilists." These terms can be applied to Nietzsche himself, and, moreover, he himself has done so in various places. The rhetorical effect here is striking; Nietzsche, by his insinuating, conspiratorial tone, suggests that he and his reader have now seen things that others have completely missed, namely, the continued prevalence of the ascetic ideal. By implicitly accusing himself of still being involved with the ascetic ideal he suggests that that accusation equally falls on his reader.

The air of the uncanny hangs over the question of who is the addressee of the *Genealogy*. In the first line of the preface Nietzsche addresses "we knowers." In *GM* III:24, just before the passage quoted above where Nietzsche talks of anti-Christians, immoralists, and the like, he refers again to we knowers but this time puts quotation marks around "knowers," implicitly calling into question his and his addressees' status as knowers. And later, in *GM* III:27, when raising the crucial question of the meaning of the will to truth he talks of touching "on my problem, our problem, my unknown friends (—for as yet I have no friends)." This leaves the reader in the uncanny position of wondering if he can at all consider himself one of Nietzsche's friends, one of Nietzsche's intended readers.[19]

Uncanny effects mark Nietzsche's claims about the Jews and slaves in the first essay. Jewish slaves would at first seem a rather foreign people, especially for a nineteenth-century German audience, a people who had recently emerged as surprising victors in the Franco-Prussian war. But as the *Genealogy* progresses the distance between the psychological makeup of the Jewish slaves and modern man seems to progressively shrink so that the unfamiliar merges with the familiar, each taking on the traits of the other. The Jewish slave turns out to have conquered the whole Western world (not just France!), and modern European man turns out to have continued the Jewish slave's hostility to the real world.

Nietzsche has explicit recourse to the notion of the uncanny in *GM* when characterizing nihilism as "the uncanniest of monsters" (*GM* III:14). While that particular passage merely heralds nihilism as a possibility, in his notebooks of the same period he is much more explicit, "Nihilism stands before us: whence comes this most uncanny of all guests?" (*KSA* 12:2 [127.2]—my translation). His immediate answer, in keeping with the general tenor of the *GM*, is that it is the will to truth that, having destroyed the metaphysics that underpinned our values, is slowly bringing belated recognition that those values themselves now lack any coherent foundations. Thus we are inevitably being led to a void of values. But why does he call nihilism an uncanny guest and the uncanniest of monsters? Presumably because he realizes that for his audience nihilism is, on first approach, rather distant and unfamiliar, and yet in some deep, perhaps, as yet, unarticulated sense, profoundly close and familiar. It is unfamiliar to his audience because, valuing truth, objectivity, science, education, progress, and other Enlightenment ideals, they would regard themselves as having firm, deeply held values. It is somehow familiar because they would have an inchoate sense that the demand central to the Enlightenment ideal, the demand that all assumptions must face the test of reason, is a test that consistently applied would put those values, indeed, all values, into question.

Nietzsche, like David Hume, realized that if we were to take seriously the Enlightenment ideal of making no assumptions and subjecting every belief, every value, to the test of pure reason, we would in fact be left with a total devastation of all beliefs and values. It is just this devastation that he predicts for Europe's future—it is for Nietzsche the first step to a full appreciation of the death of God. A fundamental aim of *GM* is to allow his audience a possible self-awareness that will inevitably hasten such an appreciation. This is not to say that Nietzsche sees nihilism as a goal in itself. However, what he does believe is that Europe must first go through nihilism if it is to reach the possibilities of creating genuinely life-affirming values.[20] Thus at the end of *GM* III:27, where he heralds Christianity's will to truth finally subjecting itself to scrutiny, he predicts, "that great spectacle in a hundred acts that is reserved for the next two centuries, the most terrible, most questionable, and perhaps most hopeful of spectacles." The theme of the uncanny and uncanny themes proliferate throughout the text of the *Genealogy*. In no other text of Nietzsche's are there anywhere near as many occurrences of the term "uncanny" (*unheimlich*) and its cognates. Indeed Nietzsche himself emphasizes the importance of this notion for appreciating his text. In the first lines of the section in *Ecce Homo* dealing with the *Genealogy* Nietzsche characterizes that work as follows: "Regarding expression, intention, and the art of surprise, the three inquiries, which constitute this *Genealogy*, are perhaps uncannier than anything else written so far" (*EH* "GM").

The uncanny makes its first appearance in the *Genealogy* as early as section 5 of the preface. There Nietzsche gives, what maybe now, in retrospect, can be seen as a hint that his announced theme might not be his real theme. In section 4 of the preface he tells us that in *Human, All Too Human* he had already approached the subject that is, allegedly, central to *GM*, namely the question of the origins of morality. In section 5 he then tells us that even in that work he was really concerned with the value of our morality, rather than "my own or anyone else's hypothesizing about the origin of morality." In particular, he tells us that what he saw as "the *great* danger to humanity" was "the will turning against life, the last sickness gently and melancholically announcing itself: I understood the morality of compassion . . . as the most uncanny symptom of our now uncanny European culture."

THE UNCANNINESS OF NIETZSCHE'S "HISTORICAL" NARRATIVES

The concept of the uncanny helps us explain the function of *GM* as a history that is not really a history.

Consider various uncanny temporal displacements that Nietzsche uses: the ancient Jewish slaves who reappear as modern Christians, even as modern truth-loving atheists; the sovereign individual who appears first as something already achieved, then as a possible man of the future; the modern philosopher who has thrown off the mask of the religious type, but then is perhaps not so distant from this caterpillar form. Such displacements of identity and temporality are evident from the beginnings of the *Genealogy*. For instance, *GM* I leaves the reader in some confusion about who exactly are the bearers of master morality referred to in the text. In much of the text, especially the early sections, it seems Nietzsche has the Greeks in mind. His first explicit mention of particular nobility is that of Greek nobility in *GM* I:5, and his characterization in *GM* I:10 of the nobles as self-affirming is presented solely with reference to Greek nobility. *GM* I:11, which stresses the recklessness and life-affirming nature of the nobles, contains references to Pericles, the Athenians, Hesiod, and Homer. Indeed, Romans only get sustained mention in *GM* I:16, the penultimate section of the first essay. By contrast, the Jewish slaves of *ressentiment*, who are presumably more connected to the Romans than to the Greeks, are given substantial mention as early as *GM* I:7. The early juxtaposition between Jewish slaves and Greek masters is confusing since it was the Romans who conquered, and were eventually conquered by the Jews through their conversion to Christianity. This is captured in Nietzsche's phrase, "Judea against Rome" (*GM* III:16); Jewish slave morality directly triumphed over Roman master morality, not Greek master morality. This unheralded, confusing displacement of the reference of "nobles" from Greeks to Romans again creates an uncanny effect on the reader of not having a firm grip of what Nietzsche's target is.

We earlier noted how Nietzsche baits his audience with the ridiculous suggestion of an actual cabal-like ancient Jewish conspiracy. These and other factors—for instance, the absence of all the scholarly apparatus typical of a historical work (references, footnotes and the like), the sweeping nature of Nietzsche's various historical narratives, their lack of historical specificity, and the fact that he subtitles his work a polemic—create the unsettling feeling that Nietzsche is, despite his explicit rubric of historical interest, not really telling us about the historical origins of our morality. Furthermore, the idea of Nietzsche being devoted to getting the history right does not sit well with the central themes of the third essay, with its disparagement of the will to truth. Nor does it sit well with his animadversions about history and the scholars' search for truth in his essay *On the Use and Disadvantage of History for Life*. What he is interested in is certain psychological truths about who we are; he is fundamentally interested in making available to us the true, and he hopes life shattering, meaning of his initial passing comment that we are strangers to ourselves.

Nietzsche's genealogies use fabulous, historical narratives to show the employment of different uses, meanings, and interrelationships of various concepts over time. Crucially Nietzsche, following Hegel, believes that only by understanding the temporal layering of meanings can we really grasp the current import of our concepts. The potted nature of his actual historical narratives and his various games of temporal displacement serve to let us eventually see that his text is not what it first appears, and claims, to be. It is not in fact a simple historical narrative, but rather a narrative of psychological development and discovery, culminating for the reader in *GM* III:23. There, after having been exposed to the disgusting nature of the ascetic ideal, the reader is shatteringly brought to see that he himself is the embodiment of that ideal, so that afterward he may "ask completely amazed, completely disconcerted, 'What did we actually experience just now?' still more: 'who *are* we actually?'" Nietzsche aims at therapeutic rather than historical knowledge.

This is not to say that Nietzsche does not think that his historical narratives in their broad outline contain a good deal of truth. But the truth he is aiming for is fundamentally the truth about the psychological developments that led to our present state. Nietzsche believes our current psychology is built on and out of the sediments of past psychological developments, and that only by understanding those developments can we understand and perhaps eventually change ourselves.

The point of his historical narratives is ultimately to make us aware of certain psychological types and their possible relations. In doing this he invents historical narratives whose oversimplifications he could not help but be aware of. For instance, the *Genealogy's* characterization of the Greeks as simple, "unsymbolical," "blond beasts" contrasts remarkably with the much richer, more complicated stories he tells about the Greeks in *The Birth of Tragedy* and other places. The point of this simplification is not to paint an accurate historical picture of the ancient Greeks but to use them as a means of bringing to the fore a certain psychological type.

In *Ecce Homo* Nietzsche says "[t]hat a psychologist without equal speaks from my writings is perhaps the first insight reached by a good reader" (*EH* "Books" 5). This is one of Nietzsche's few self-assessments which I take to be absolutely correct. In reading Nietzsche we should follow the implied advice of looking for psychological, rather than philosophical or historical, insights. The fundamental insight of the *Genealogy* is that with the change from the religious to the secular worldview we may have changed our beliefs about the nature of this world; we, unlike the religious, accept this as the one and only world, but we have still fundamentally clung to the same hostile attitude toward it. It is because we fail to engage, in a cognitive and deeper sense, with the nature and the level of our resentment that we remain, so profoundly, strangers to ourselves.

We should not simply keep the model of the psychologist in mind when trying to unravel the *what* of Nietzsche's text but also in unravelling the *how* of it. By uncannily invoking the pathos of distance, deliberately confusing the temporal scope of his claims and the identity of his targets, Nietzsche has found an ingenious, subterranean method of getting his highly challenging and subversive message to slowly sink into his readers, without immediately provoking the defenses a more direct approach would surely arouse.

REFERENCES

Clark, M. *Nietzsche on Truth and Philosophy*. Cambridge: Cambridge University Press, 1990.

Gemes, K. "Post-Modernism's Use and Abuse of Nietzsche." *Philosophy and Phenomenological Research* 62 (2001): 337–60.

Freud, S. *The Standard Edition of the Complete Psychological Works of Sigmund Freud*. Translated by J. Strachey. London: The Hogarth Press, 1955.

Leiter, B. *Nietzsche on Morality*. London: Routledge, 2002.

Marx, K. "On the Jewish Question." In *Karl Marx: Early Texts*. Ed. D. McLellan. Oxford: Blackwell, 1977.

Schopenhauer, A. *The World as Will and Representation*. 2 vols. Translated by E. F. J. Payne. Indian Hills, CO: Falcon's Wing Press, 1958.

Wagner, R. "Judaism in Music" In *Richard Wagner: Stories and Essays*. Ed. C. Osborne. London: Peter Owen, 1973.

NOTES

This piece has benefited greatly from input from Dario Galasso, Sebastian Gardner, Dylan Jaggard, Chris Janaway, Jonathon Lear, Brian Leiter, Simon May, John Richardson, Aaron Ridley, Mathias Risse, and, especially, Pia Conti-Gemes.

1. Unless otherwise indicated, for citations of Nietzsche's works, I utilize Kaufmann and Hollingdale's *GM* and *WP*; Hollingdale's *A*, *D*, *HH*, *HL*, *TI*, and *Z*; Kaufmann's *BGE*, *EH*, and *GS*; and Whitside's *BT*.

2. The question of exactly who is Nietzsche's intended audience for the *Genealogy* is extremely complex. In the text he sometimes refers to "we knowers" (*GM* P:1), sometimes to "modern humans, that is, us" (*GM* II:7). If we take as our model, liberal, secular intellectuals I do not think we will be far off the mark of his "knowers" and "modern humans." The

section "Nietzsche and the Uncanny" further considers the question of who are Nietzsche's addressees in the *Genealogy*.

3. The idea that Nietzsche often intentionally misleads his readers in the *Genealogy* is presented in Maudemarie Clark's excellent chapter on the Ascetic Ideal in Clark (1990). Clark also notes the uncanny nature of the *Genealogy*. This is a fundamental theme of the last two sections of this chapter.

4. Nietzsche in *GS* 345 shows an awareness of the genetic fallacy of taking the origins of something as indicating its current value. However *D* 95, entitled "Historical refutation as the definitive refutation," shows that he is keenly aware of the polemical value of, and not averse to using, this argument form.

5. The question of how seriously Nietzsche takes the various historical narratives offered in the *Genealogy* is dealt with in greater detail in the section "The Uncanniness of Nietzsche's 'Historical' Narratives."

6. Where Nietzsche talks of "Wissenschaft" I talk of "science." However, it is important to recall that for the German speakers "Wissenschaft" does not simply refer to what we call the natural sciences (*Naturwissenschaften*) such as physics, chemistry, and biology, but also to the human sciences (*Geisteswissenschaft*) such as philology and philosophy. We do better to think of the practitioners of *Wissenschaft* as scholars rather than scientists.

7. Chris Janaway alerted me to the connection with Schopenhauer.

8. This is not to say that Nietzsche was against all repression. Rather much like Freud, he favored sublimation where the repressed desires are allowed to express themselves productively, albeit directed to new ends than those they originally sought. Cf. Gemes (2001).

9. This is a central theme in *The Birth of Tragedy*, for example, see *BT* 7–9. In that work, still under the influence of Schopenhauer and Wagner, Nietzsche takes art, in particular tragedy, as providing the Greeks with the means to affirm life despite suffering. As this influence waned art came to play a much less significant part in his account of the life-affirming spirit of the Greeks. Thus in the first essay of the *Genealogy*, where the Greeks are clearly configured as life affirming, there is no appearance of art as their means of affirmation.

10. In *GM* III:13–22 the ostensible subject is the ascetic ideal as personified by the ascetic priest. Here the ascetic priest is characterized as the sick physician to a sick herd. He attempts to combat the "dominant feeling of listlessness . . . *first*, by means that reduce the general feeling of life to its lowest point. If possible no willing at all, not another wish" (*GM* III:17). However, these sections also contain many references that go well beyond priests, including references to anti-Semites, to Nietzsche's contemporary, the philosopher Eugen Dühring, to modern European "*Weltshmerz*." These references already indicate that Nietzsche's polemic here against those who advocate passivity as a means of combating and avoiding the pains of life has a much wider target than just the priests. However, as argued above, it is only in section 23 that the full scope of his target comes clearly into view.

11. Clark (1990), while developing the idea that the philosopher's love of truth can function to devalue human existence, takes Nietzsche's fundamental objection to the will to truth as an objection to taking truth as an ultimate end; an objection to "faith in the absolute value of truth" (Clark 1990, 189). Leiter also recognizes Nietzsche's claim that the very will to truth can be a will to escape this life. However, he refers to this aspect of the asceticism of science as "only a minor theme in Nietzsche's discussion" (Leiter 2002, 265). Leiter claims the major objections Nietzsche has to the overestimation of truth is that certain truths "can be terrible, a threat to life" (ibid., 267) and that "it supposes falsely, that our knowledge could

be 'presuppositionless'" (ibid., 268). While there is merit in both these interpretations what they fail to grasp is that Nietzsche fundamentally takes the will to truth as a general symptom of a life-denying mode of relating to the world that he thinks is shared by both religious and modern secular lovers of truth.

12. This is part of the point of the somewhat digressive sections at *GM* III:2–5. There Nietzsche deals with the meaning of the ascetic ideal for artists only to conclude that for artists ascetic ideals mean "nothing whatever! . . . Or so many things it amounts to nothing whatever."

13. While generally Nietzsche discusses the *vita contemplativa* in the context of its use as a negative life-denying orientation (cf. *D* 42–43), *GS* 310 shows that Nietzsche recognizes that the *vita contemplativa* can in fact be a means to the highest form of creativity. This theme also appears in Nietzsche's discussion of the meaning of the ascetic ideal for philosophers in *GM* III:8–9.

14. In reference to Wagner, see *HL* 2; and in reference to Nietzsche see *EH* "Clever" 9.

15. The Nietzschean theme that modern men are not genuine persons but mere jumbles of drives is one explored extensively in Gemes (2001).

16. German readers of Nietzsche's day would have been familiar with the threat of "verjudung" from Wagner's notorious *Judaism in Music* (1973) and, possibly, Marx's equally appalling, though less well known, *On the Jewish Question* (1977).

17. This subversive theme is repeated in the *Antichrist* were Nietzsche says, "The Christian, that *ultima ratio* of the lie, is the Jew once more – even *thrice* more" (*A* 44).

18. In his essay *The Uncanny*, Freud characterizes the uncanny as, "something which is secretly familiar which has undergone repression and then returned from it" (*Standard Edition*, vol. 7, 245).

19. This is of a piece with Nietzsche's repeated suggestion that he has no readers, that some, presumably meaning himself, are born posthumously, implying that their proper readers are yet to be (cf. *A* P).

20. Cf. *WP* 2 for his most succinct statement of the inevitability of nihilism.

13

Nihilism as Will to Nothingness*

Wolfgang Müller-Lauter

> Man would rather will *nothingness* than not will.
>
> —*GM* II:28

Nietzsche no doubt came across the term "nihilism," which he began using in the 1880s, in a series of contemporary writers. Due to its use by the Russian anarchists, the term had acquired widespread popularity in the German-speaking region, too.[1] The picture Nietzsche formed of those anarchists was mostly determined by his reading of Dostoevsky's novels;[2] but he also read, for example, publications of Ivan Turgenev and Alexander Herzen (in Sorrento, by 1877 at the latest)[3] and perhaps excerpted Peter Kropotkin.[4] According to Charles Andler,[5] Nietzsche's use of the word "nihilism" resulted from his reading of Paul Bourget's *Essais de psychologie contemporaine.*[6]

Bourget, it should be noted, speaks of nihilism mainly with the Russian anarchists in mind. Yet he also relates this nihilism closely with other, in part very diverse, kinds of phenomena of his time, all pointing to *one* basic evil: disgust with the world. In his Baudelaire essay, Bourget seeks to discover the origin of this feeling. He identifies it as the discrepancy between the *needs* of the modern age that accompany the development of civilization and the *inadequacies* of existing reality. The universal outbreak of world-nausea in the nineteenth century was, he believed, caused by this outbreak. It manifested itself in different ways. Among the Slavs it

*Originally appeared in *Nietzsche: His Philosophy of Contradictions and Contradictions of His Philosophy*, written by Wolfgang Müller-Lauter and translated by David J. Parent (Chicago: University of Illinois Press, 1999), 41–49. Reprinted with permission of the University of Illinois Press.

was expressed as nihilism, among the Germanic nations as pessimism, and among the Romanic nations in an unusual nervous irritability.[7] In all this, however, Bourget finds the same "spirit of the negation of life, which darkens Western civilization more and more each day."[8]

Nietzsche recognized a kindred spirit in Bourget. Like Bourget he was concerned with diagnosing the "sickness" of the century and developing a "theory" of decadence. The horizon within which this happened in Bourget could, of course, not seem broad enough for him; the discrepancy between need and reality offered him no satisfactory explanation of the spirit of the negation of life. What supposedly comprised the background for that spirit, according to the "discrete psychologist" Bourget,[9] had to be accounted merely foreground by Nietzsche.

More distinctly than Bourget, Nietzsche sums up the various "symptoms of sickness" under the name of nihilism. How far back he traces the pathological history of the modern European was described in our comments on his philosophy of history. In retrospect it can be said that the birth of moral man marks the beginning of Western nihilism.

Nietzsche, then, reaches further back than others who spoke of nihilism before him. And he no longer understands nihilism primarily as the result of reason's exaggerated self-glorification, as it appeared in critiques of the philosophy of German Idealism by F. H. Jacobi, Franz von Baader, Christian H. Weisse, and Immanuel H. Fichte—of which critiques Nietzsche probably had no knowledge. Nihilism, detectable even *prior* to all reflection and speculation, cannot be refuted by merely rational arguments: "The real refutations are physiological" (*Nachlaß* XIV, 339).[10] For if reason wages war on decadence, it does not thereby extract itself from decadence. Reason can, at best, change the *expression* of decadence, as Nietzsche tries to show by the example of Socrates (*TI* "Socrates" 10; cf. *WP* 435).

All consciousness is, as the last and latest phase of the development of the organic, much too unfinished and weak (*GS* 11) to be of any avail against what it stems from. "The growth of consciousness" often does appear to be a "danger," indeed a "disease" (*GS* 354)—namely, in a genealogy of self-consciousness attempted by Nietzsche—yet he does not carry to extremes what the discussion of nihilism had discovered before him. He wants to seek the disease at its place of origin. The "weak, delicate, and morbid effects of the spirit" are for him ultimately merely *symptoms* of physiological processes (*WP* 899). In his view "the nihilistic movement is merely the expression of physiological *decadence*" (*WP* 38).

What does Nietzsche mean by the "physiological," which he tries to "draw forth" (*D* 542), not only from behind consciousness "as such" and its logical positings (*BGE* 3), but also from behind the moral (*D* 542; cf. *GM* I:17n) and aesthetic (*GM* III:9) valuations? Physiological processes are "releases of energy" (*Nachlaß* XIII, 263). But this means power struggles of will-quanta. Physiology, rightly understood, is thus the theory of the will to power (*BGE* 13), just as is psychology, rightly understood, which amalgamates with the former into a "physio-psychology" (*BGE* 29). Thus, we can here refer back to the discussions in chapter 1.[11]

Consciousness is, under such a physio-psychological aspect, still inadequately characterized as a weak late phenomenon. It is the "instrument" of a "many-headed and much divided master" (*Nachlaß* XIII, 257), a "means and tool by which not a subject but *a struggle wants to preserve itself*" (*Nachlaß* XIII, 71; cf. 164f). Quanta of will organize themselves into relatively independent units. Man is such an especially complex organization, which invests a consciousness for its service.[12]

Now the nature of this decadence, whose "logic" is nihilism (*WP* 43), can be clarified. It is a particular mode of physiological "releases of energy." The wills to power, previously held together in a unity, now strive to separate. Nietzsche describes this centripetal tendency as the "disintegration [*Disgregation*] of the instincts" *(TI* "Skirmishes" 35). The concept of *Disgregation* is already familiar to us. We have repeatedly come across the term and its problematic in the first two chapters.[13] This problematic now needs closer analysis.

Our starting point will be Nietzsche's portrayal of literary decadence. The very style of a work of art can reveal "that life no longer dwells in the whole. The word becomes sovereign and leaps out of the sentence; the sentence reaches out and obscures the meaning of the page; the page gains life at the expense of the whole—the whole is no longer a whole." Something similar applies to all modes of manifestation of decadence. "The anarchy of the atoms" and "*Disgregation* of the will" go hand in hand in them. The leading will that previously organized the unity of the whole loses its power. Subordinate forces press for independence. Nietzsche finds these signs, for example, in the moral claim for freedom of the individual, as in its expansion to political theory with the demand for "equal rights for all" (*CW* 7).

Decadence, described as *Disgregation*, is not a state but a process. To be sure, in it the dissolution of an organization is *intended*. But once this actually is completed, once a unity has disintegrated into a plurality without cohesion (which cohesion is possible only as a hierarchical structure), then we can no longer speak of decadence. This term can designate only the phases of the disintegration process of a whole, insofar as unity still remains despite all dissolution tendencies.

Therefore the question must be asked: What still holds together that which is in the process of disintegrating on the way to its actual disintegration? This is a specific process and not simply the mechanical disassembling of components. Nietzsche rules out a mechanical interpretation. Pressure and stress are "something unspeakably late, derivative, unprimeval." They already presuppose something "that *holds together* and *is able* to exert pressure and stress" (*WP* 622). This original thing is the "aggregate herd-condition of atoms"; in it "is precisely non-stress and yet power, not only of counter-striving, resistance, but rather mainly of arrangement, placement, attachment, transferring and coalescing force" (*Nachlaß* XII, 72f). Mechanics is, however, oriented on the model of the persistent thing, which stems from logic inflated into metaphysics. Its concept of force remains an empty word as long as an inner will is not ascribed to it (cf. *WP* 619).

The nihilistic disintegration process, too, is characterized by cohesion, and this cohesion too is established by an inner will. All cohesion presupposes the rule of one "drive," which subjugates a multiplicity of drives and forces them under itself. If the *Disgregation* of what was originally held together under such a rulership is to be carried out, that is possible only if the dominant "drive" gives the corresponding instruction. Otherwise the efficacy common to the subordinate drives to detach themselves from the union of the whole would be incomprehensible. *Perishing* thus takes the form of a *"self-destruction*, the instinctive selection of that which *must destroy"* (*WP* 55). The ruling will in such a whole must therefore be a *will to disintegration*, which strives for the end or nonexistence of the unity it had organized. It is the will to the end (*A* 9) or the will to nothingness or *for* nothingness (*WP* 401, cf. 55).

All drives subject to the will to nothingness promote disintegration. This common trait is, however, not uniform. Each drive has its "own law of development" that is determined by the conflict immanent within the whole. Each promotes the downfall in its particular way. The "rate of speed" of disintegration is different in each of them. Indeed, like every drive, the ruling will to nothingness arouses drives against itself among the drives ruled by it. If such a "counterdrive" is strong enough, it will seize the rulership for itself. Its function is, however, strangely discordant when it remains subject to the will to nothingness and nonetheless fights against it.

Nothing other than such discordant willing is expressed in the decadence phenomenon of *asceticism*, which Nietzsche investigates in the third essay of *On the Genealogy of Morals*. What concerns him there is the meaning of the *ascetic ideal*: "what it indicates; what lies hidden behind it, beneath it, in it; of what it is the provisional, indistinct expression, overlaid with question marks and misunderstanding" (*GM* III:23). This meaning becomes evident when Nietzsche analyzes the type of the ascetic priest: he finds on the ground of the ascetic ideal "a discord that *wants* to be discordant" (*GM* III:11).

Discord now emerges in full clarity in Nietzsche's arguments. On the one hand, life *denies itself* in ascetic practice. For asceticism serves only as a bridge to a completely different, indeed opposite kind of existence (*GM* III:11). For it employs force "to block up the wells of force" (*GM* III:11). An aversion to life is dominant here (*GM* III:28). On the other hand, the ascetic ideal is an "artifice for the *preservation* of life" (*GM* III:13). For even if life is to be merely a bridge, that bridge must be constructed and thus life must be maintained. The ascetic priest is, by the power of his desire "to be different, to be in a different place," chained to this life. Thus "this *denier* is among the greatest *conserving* and *yes-creating* forces of life" (*GM* III:13).

The ascetic simultaneously denies and affirms life. Naturally, it is not a matter of the simultaneity of a total No and a total Yes. His No and Yes are interwoven in a way that keeps in check the absolute claim of either side. The Yes restricts the No: in the ascetic ideal "the door is closed to any kind of suicidal nihilism" (*GM* III:28). And the No restricts the Yes: degenerating life that needs protection and healing (*GM* III:13) cannot be healed by ascetic practice (*GM* III:16). The ascetic priest as a "nurse and physician" (*GM* III:14) does not fight "the real sickness" (*GM* III:17), he merely tries in his way to alleviate the suffering itself. The means he uses to treat the patients are: reducing the feeling of life to impede depressive affects from taking their full toll (*GM* III:17), distraction from suffering by mechanical activity (*GM* III:18), careful dosages of petty pleasure (*GM* III:18), orgies of feeling (*GM* III:19). The last means makes the patients even sicker afterward (*GM* III:20; cf. 21). And even the prior ones merely alleviate the symptoms of the illness. Indeed, the ascetic priest, as "he stills the pain of the wound . . . at the same time infects the wound" (*GM* III:15). His practice, then, finally brings "fresh suffering with it, deeper, more inward, more poisonous, more life-destructive suffering" (*GM* III:28).

The possibilities and limits of a counterdrive dominated by the will to nothing-ness thus become clearly discernible. The ascetic priest is sick himself (*GM* III:15) yet must on the other hand still be healthy enough to be able to ward off immediate disintegration. His will must be strong enough to organize the still resistant vital instincts. In the struggle against depression, he strives for the formation of the herd (*GM* III:18). He fights "against anarchy and ever-threatening disintegration within the herd" (*GM* III:15). He seeks to vent *ressentiment*—this explosive material that threatens to blow up the herd—in such a way that it changes direction. This is done by shifting the cause of suffering into the sufferer himself (*GM* III:15). The result of all this, however, is merely that a chronic disease replaces a rapid death. The dom-inant will to nothingness still wins out at the core of the drive that is directed against it.[14] As long as it rules one *must* "go forward, which is to say step by step *further into decadence. . . .* One can retard this development and, through retardation, dam and gather up degeneration itself and make it more vehement and sudden: more one cannot do" (*TI* "Skirmishes" 43). Asceticism leads to such impediments and distur-bances. These, in turn, prepare the way for explosions of *active nihilism*, which will be discussed below.

As for the root of the ascetic ideal, the will to nothingness must be examined in terms of what originally constituted it. And since Nietzsche traces back not only this ideal, but all manifestations and forms of decadence to it, his analysis is of decisive significance for the problem of nihilism. According to the foregoing reflections, nihilism can basically be nothing else but the will to nothingness, and in fact it is always so characterized by Nietzsche (*GM* II:21, 24; *GM* III:14).

First, it must be asked: How can nothingness be *willed* at all? How must the will be constituted so as to be directed toward nothingness? Again we can refer back to remarks in chapter 1. There is no mere will that would occur as something simple, simply given, as a characteristic or as pure potency. In such a conception "the 'whither?'" has been "subtracted" (*WP* 692). The "willing whither" means "willing an end," which includes willing "something" (*WP* 260).[15] As such a willing, it can-not *not will*. Therefore Nietzsche, in the context of his investigation of the ascetic ideal, characterizes it as "the basic fact of the human will" that the will needs a goal: "And it will rather *will nothingness* than *not* will" (*GM* III:1). Can the will at all intend nothingness? For even if we concede that nothingness could be "something" in the sense of being intendable, we must observe that, for Nietzsche, to want "something" means to want power.

In striving for nothingness, however, the will is carrying on its own "self destruction" (*WP* 55). Can it, then, still be will to power? That is certainly Nietzsche's conviction. He does indeed write: "The will to nothingness has become master over the will to life, more precisely over the 'ascending instincts'" (*WP* 401; cf. *WP* 685). But the very formulation of this sentence ("has become master over") makes it clear that the will to nothingness, in so doing, acts as will to power. And in his characterization of Christianity, Nietzsche expressly states that in it "the will to the end, the *nihilistic* will . . . wants power" (*A* 9). The will to power must thus again and again be clearly distinguished from the will to life as understood by Schopenhauer. The will to life is "merely a special case" of the will to power (*WP* 692). Even this "process of decline" still stands "in the service of" the will to power (*WP* 675).

Even the will to nothingness is thus will to power. Its intention thereby merely becomes more incomprehensible. How can what wants power strive for nothingness? If Nietzsche were speaking of the will to power as a simple metaphysical basic principle that develops out of its own self and intensifies intrinsically, the assertion that there is a power-will to nothingness would be absurd. Nietzsche, however, starts with a multiplicity of wills to power engaged in conflict with one another and forming parties. In this struggle there are victors and vanquished. A victorious and dominant will is a strong will; a defeated and subjugated will is a weak will. Neither strength nor weakness belong to the wills as a property. They merely express the outcome of a struggle in which two wills have been engaged against one another. The victory of the stronger does not at first lead to the destruction but rather to the subjugation of the weaker.[16] It establishes a ranking order in which the two depend on each other; indeed, both are indispensable to one another (*Nachlaß* XIII, 170). Victory and rank are, however, never final; the struggle continues incessantly. In a reversal of the power relations, the subjugated will can become the dominant one, and the previously dominant will can be subjugated.

Of course, to speak of a conflict between a strong will and a weak will is a crude simplification of what is in truth a multiply gradated organization of will-quanta. It must always be remembered that "there is no will, and consequently neither a strong nor a weak will. The multitude and *Disgregation* of impulses and the lack of any systematic order among them result in a 'weak will'; their coordination under the hegemony of a single predominant impulse results in a 'strong will'" (*WP* 46). The simplifying way of speaking that Nietzsche employs again and again does not, however, impair his possibility to expound on the problematic of decadence and to make clear an essential concretization of an antithesis that determines his philosophical thinking. The simplification, must, however, not be carried so far that the multiplicity is traced back to one will to power. For then Nietzsche's basic idea is reversed. We can do justice to this problem only if we see at least "two 'wills to power' in conflict" (*WP* 401).[17]

Nothingness is intended by an initially defeated, weak will. This intention must be understood as a *reaction* to the strength of a victorious and at first dominant will.

Thus the *ressentiment*-morality stems from a kind of denial of the noble morality (*A* 24). Although it may be "creative," it remains in its ground a *reversal* of values that is bound to what it reverses.[18]

The will to nothingness is a counterwill. The weak do not deny for the sake of denial as such. By their denial they want to conquer the strong and rule over them. For the stronger and weaker are the same in this: "They extend their power as far as they can" (*Nachlaß* XII, 273). For the purpose of domination, denial must act as a *condemnation*. The weak condemn the will to power in the values of the strong. But the condemnatory will is itself will to power. It can absolutely not be anything else, for basically all reality is will to power. Thus the only reality is condemned. How can that happen? Only by the decadent will to power *inventing* another reality from which point of view the condemnation can be made. The fictional world must appear with the claim to be the *true world*.

The *possibility* of this fiction is given in man's biological need, in the stream of becoming, to grasp the similar as the same and fixate what moves. What is supposedly the same or constant can then be detached from becoming as something existing by itself. What is so detached, in truth "an apparent world," is constructed "out of contradiction to the actual world" (*TI* "World" 6). Man "invents a world so as to be able to slander and bespatter this world: in reality he reaches every time for nothingness and construes nothingness as 'God,' as 'truth,' and in any case as judge and condemner of *this* state of being" (*WP* 461). Thus, as Nietzsche sees it, in the Christian concept of God "nothingness [is] deified, the will to nothingness sanctified" (*A* 18).

In all this, the will to nothingness is a will to power that hides itself as such. In order to rule, it demands that the will to power that admits itself as such must abdicate. It acts as the absolute opposite of life in order to work against life within it. In reality it does not exit from life, for all opposites are *immanent in life*. We have in truth no situation "outside life," from which we could oppose it. Therefore "a condemnation of life by the living . . . is after all no more than a symptom of a certain kind of life" that is condemned to perish. The condemnation of life is a judgment made by condemned persons (*TI* "Morality" 5).

That the condemning will is a will to power may have become clear, but the question arises: Can the fiction of a "true world," the self-orientation by something nonexistent that this will performs, be equated with the will to self-destruction spoken of above? In both things, Nietzsche sees the will to nothingness at work. But whereas the latter instinctively seeks to destroy itself, the fiction established for the purpose of condemnation serves the self-preservation and power-instincts of the weak.

That the will to nothingness—in the sense of the will to self-destruction—has taken the upper hand may be all the less clear since Nietzsche himself shows that in "reality" the strong are weak and the weak are strong: "The strongest and most fortunate are weak when opposed by organized herd instincts, by the timidity of the weak, by the vast majority" (*WP* 685). Against Darwinism, which he once called "a philosophy for butcher boys" (*KSA* 8:12[22]) compared with his own theory, he writes that selection did not take place in favor of the strong; rather, it marshaled up "the inevitable mastery of the mediocre, indeed even of the sub-mediocre types." Nature "is cruel toward her children of fortune, she spares and protects and loves *les humbles*" (*WP* 685; cf. *TI* "Skirmishes" 14). Therefore Nietzsche must ask himself whether the "victory of the weak and mediocre" does not offer "perhaps a stronger guarantee of life, of the species" (*WP* 401), than the rule of the strong, who in ruinous struggles endanger not only themselves but also the very existence of the species (*WP* 864).

Everything suggests that this question must be answered in the affirmative. But is this not a grotesque reversal of what Nietzsche wanted to expound? Does not "life" condemn those who affirm it unreservedly? Does it not justify those who condemn it?

To counter such a supposed self-contradiction of Nietzsche's, we must refer back to what became evident in his analysis of the ascetic ideal. It was shown there that the weak remain weak even when they mobilize their still resistant vital forces against decline; all they can do is prolong the agony. Now it must be added that even their triumph over the strong, even their previous indispensableness for the preservation of the species must not hide the fact that they bring about their own self-destruction and hence the destruction of mankind. Their victory may be presented as a "slackening of tempo"; it may be "a self-defense against something even worse" (*WP* 401); nonetheless, the worst must happen at last, if they stay in power. They have preserved the "species" by redirecting the human aggressive instincts from outside to inside.[19] But the forces that formerly were exhausted in conflict are now dissipated. Finally they must dry up completely.

Thus neither the strong type nor the weak type seem able to prevent the downfall of mankind. But like the strength of the strong, according to Nietzsche, now the weakness of the strong, too, must in its necessity remain restricted to previous history, where chance prevailed.[20] Only a future "strong race," which will withdraw its power from chance by planning and discipline, will no longer surrender that power to the superior numbers of the weak. Such strong humans will stand in full agreement with "life," which in its genuine form is nothing other than the rule of ascendant wills to power over the descending wills to power.

As the will to the truly nonexistent "second world," which guides the weak, is a disguised will to power in the only real world, it is also a disguised will to nothingness, in the radial sense of the word. "With your good and evil," Nietzsche shouts to the weak, "you have forfeited life and weakened your wills; and your valuation itself was the sign of the descending will that longs for death" (*Nachlaß* XII, p. 262). The longing can swing into action. Then the weak destroy so as to be destroyed. Self-destruction is the consequence of condemning life.[21] The process of wasting away that leads to self-destruction is the history of nihilism. It brings to light more and more what the *ressentiment*-values really imply, at first without the knowledge of their representatives.

NOTES

1. We cannot go into details here on the history of this concept. Some hints, however, should be given. In France this history goes back to the French Revolution, where the word *nihiliste* was used to designate an attitude of political or religious indifference. The philosophical use of the term is first found in F. H. Jacobi, who in his *Sendschreiben an Fichte* (1799) labels his idealism as nihilism. From then on the term plays a role in various philosophical and political disputes. Its application to the movement of French socialism in the nineteenth century and to the "left Hegelians" (who are the heirs to the reproach of nihilism that had first been leveled against the idealist philosophies of Fichte, Schelling, and Hegel) determined the use of the word in the social and political struggles in Russia. From there it radiated back to the central European language area, so blurring the ongoing history of the term that I. Turgenev, in his *Literatur- und Lebenserinnerungen* (German edition of 1892, 105) could state that he had invented the word, an error that was repeated after him until our time (e.g., by G. Benn, *Nach dem Nihilismus*, 1932, GW I, 1959, 156f, and by A. Stender-Petersen, *Geschichte der russischen Literatur*, II, 1957, 251). Turgenev, however, was not even the first to use the word in Russia; quite a few authors used it there before him.

2. The spiritual relationship between Nietzsche and Dostoevsky has frequently been brought out since the turn of the century, especially in France, occasioned above all by the translation of D. S. Mereshkovski's book on Tolstoy and Dostoevsky (1903). A. Suarès, A. Gide, and L. Shestov have taken up this theme. On this topic cf. H. F. Minssen: "Die französische Kritik und Dostoevski." E. Benz discussed Dostoevsky's influence on Nietzsche in *Nietzsches Ideen zur Geschichte des Christentums*, 83–93, with consideration of the works of Minnssen and Ch. Andler. Benz published an expanded and partly revised version of his book under the title *Nietzsches Ideen zur Geschichte des Christentums und der Kirche* in the year 1956. He also cites works of Shestov and Tshizhevski on the Nietzsche-Dostoevsky problem (92). This problem is quite as inadequately treated in both versions of his book as in the two authors he cites. The extent of Dostoevsky's influence on Nietzsche had to remain unknown in any case, as long as there was incomplete knowledge of Nietzsche's reading of Dostoevsky. Only recently have G. Colli and M. Montinari, in Volume VIII/2 of the *KGW* (383–95), published the excerpts that Nietzsche copied from the French translation of Dostoevsky's novel *Les Possédés*. Only by taking into consideration Nietzsche's knowledge of *The Demons* can one do justice to his understanding of Dostoevsky, and moreover Russian nihilism.

3. Cf. M. Montinari, *Das Leben Friedrich Nietzsches in den Jahren 1875–1979* [sic]. Chronik, in *KGW* IV/4, 27. I additionally owe M. Montinari important references to sources inaccessible to me about Nietzsche's reading of these two Russian authors. Unfortunately they do not provide information as to whether Nietzsche read Turgenev's novels *Fathers and Sons* (1862) and *New Land* (1872), in which that author uses the term "nihilism." But I consider it highly probable.

4. F. Würzbach states this in vol. XIX of the *Musarion-Ausgabe*, 432. Cf. however O. Weiß, in *GA*, XVI, 515f. [*Ed. Note*—The abbreviation *GA* in this essay refers to *Großoktavausgabe*, edited by the Nietzsche Archive, 19 vols. in three divisions (Leipzig, 1894–1912). Citations designated as *Nachlaß* refer to this edition.]

5. Ch. Andler, *Nietzsche, sa vie et sa pensée*, 6 vols., 1920ff., III:418, 424.

6. The first volume appeared in 1883; the second, in 1885. H. Platz, "Nietzsche und Bourget," 177–86, cannot confirm Ch. Andler's assumption that Nietzsche read not only the second, but also the first volume of Bourget's *Essais* (181). But there is no doubt about it.

Among other authors, Bertram (*Nietzsche*, 231) called attention to the fact that Nietzsche's description of literary decadence is "a paraphrase of sentences" from Bourget's first volume. Proof that Nietzsche read this volume is found in a still unpublished fragment in a notebook from the summer of 1887, which information I owe to M. Montinari: "*Style of decadence* in Wagner: the individual turn of phrase becomes *sovereign*, subordination and adjustment become accidental" (Bourget, 25).

7. *Essais* I, 1887, 13ff. As an example of the "universal nausea before the inadequacies of this world," Bourget names "the murderous rage of the St. Petersburg conspirators, Schopenhauer's books, the furious arsenies of the Commune, and the implacable misanthropy of the naturalist novelists."

8. Ibid., 15.

9. Nietzsche writes thus about Bourget in *EH*, "Why I Am So Clever," 3.

10. *Ed. Note*—*Nachlaß* in this essay refers to the material published in *Großoktavausgabe* edition of Nietzsche's works; see note 4.

11. *Ed. Note*—The reference is to the chapter titled "Apparent Contradictions and Real Contradictions of the Will to Power."

12. Here we must forego a further investigation of Nietzsche's understanding of consciousness.

13. *Ed. Note*—For the first chapter, see note 11. The second chapter is titled "The Problem of Contradictions in Nietzsche's Philosophy of History."

14. As an example of how one can simplify the *antitheticalness of the real*, which Nietzsche is trying to show, into the *absurdity of his philosophical thinking*, L. Klages's statements on the "priestly will to power" can be cited: "If it were not the Christian in Nietzsche who with his doctrine of the will to power is addressing confessors of the will to power, namely, Christians, even his sparkling dialectics and incomparable art of description would hardly have sufficed to hide the self-contradiction even where it emerges very openly from within to the outside. The will to life is supposed to be life; life, the will to power. Now precisely the priest proclaims the most stubborn, relentless will to power that never fails even under the most difficult conditions, . . . becomes master over warriors, kings, over all mankind: then he would most clearly be the mode of appearance of *life* that is most worthy of respect. But he supposedly represents the power will of a sickness, indeed a power will of weakness and a will to nothingness. Is one to believe that anyone except Nietzsche himself . . . fails to notice the complete vacuity of such turns of phrase" (*Die psychologischen Errungenschaften Nietzsches*, 196).

15. See chapter 1, note 32. [*Ed. Note*—Müller-Lauter refers here to the discussion in which he notes the "difference from a concept of will marked by the idea of entelechy," citing a note "aimed against Hegel's teleologically determined idea of history. In this context [Nietzsche] writes: 'That my life has no purpose is clear from the accidentalness of my origin: *that I can set a purpose for myself is another matter*. But a state is not a purpose; rather, only we give it this purpose or that one' (*Nachlaß* X, 275).")]

16. "First conquering the feeling of power, then mastering (organizing) it—it regulates what has been overcome for its preservation and *thus it preserves what has been overcome itself*" (*Nachlaß* XII, 106).

17. The cited passage does not speak of *one* "will to power" engaged in a "struggle with itself" and thereby doubled, as E. Biser, says, interpreting it as a "principle" (*Gott ist tot*, 169ff).

18. E. Fink finds in Nietzsche's writings after *Zarathustra* an ambiguity in the use of the

terms *life* and *will to power*. Thus Nietzsche speaks of power "brilliantly . . . in the sense of ontological universality and then again in the sense of the ontological model" (*Nietzsches Philosophie*, 128). Fink accordingly distinguishes between the "transcendental value-plan of existence" and "a 'contentual,' 'material' interpretation of life" in Nietzsche. The transition from the one to the other is, for Fink, "perhaps the most disputable point in Nietzsche's philosophy." This disputableness also crept into his dual understanding of the will to power. The will to power was, first, "the basic tendency in the movement of all finite being," expressing itself, for example, as much in the heroic-tragic valuation as in Christian morality. "So understood, *everything* is will to power." Second, it was given a particular content and meaning, such as that of the heroic mode of thinking. Nietzsche did not succeed in overcoming such ambiguity. The estimation according to strength and weakness was nothing but a valuation of Nietzsche's, which represented only one possibility of *life's valuating activity of life*, of the "great player." Fink asks whether from the standpoint of the universal as the "ultimate gambler" and "player," "all values are not of equal rank"? "Are they not all equally forms in which life tries its hand for a period of time?" (122). The ontological dimension of life or of the will to power, prior to anything ontic, is a construction of Fink's. Nietzsche not only does not need the presupposition of such a universal; it contradicts his thinking, as was shown above. The ambiguity that Fink discovers in Nietzsche was inserted into the philosopher he is interpreting by Fink himself.

19. But the species did not preserve itself through them. In truth "there is no species"—in the sense of such an active subject—"but solely sheerly diverse individual beings." There is also no "nature," "which wants to 'preserve the species,'" but rather only the fact that "many similar beings with similar conditions of existence" more easily preserve themselves "than abnormal beings" (*Nachlaß* XII, 73).

20. See chapter 2, note 54. [*Ed. Note*—Müller-Lauter refers here to *Nachlaß* X, 402: "Whoever does not grasp how brutal and meaningless history is will also not understand the urge to make history meaningful." And to *KSA* 8:5[150], which treats, in part, the effort to rationalize history as motivated by religion.]

21. A logical consequence of Nietzsche's thinking is that even the act of suicide is the expression of a power-will: in his self-extinction the suicidal person wants to triumph over life.

III

CRITIQUING *GENEALOGY*

14

The Entwinement of Myth and Enlightenment*

Jürgen Habermas

Twenty-five years after the conclusion of *Dialectic of Enlightenment*, Theodor Adorno remained faithful to its philosophical impulse and never deviated from the paradoxical structure of thinking as totalizing critique. The grandeur of this consistency is shown by a comparison with Nietzsche, whose *On the Genealogy of Morals* had been the great model for a second level of reflection on the Enlightenment. Nietzsche suppressed the paradoxical structure and explained the complete assimilation of reason to power in modernity with a *theory of power* that was remythologized out of arbitrary pieces and that, in place of the claim to truth, retains no more than the rhetorical claim proper to an aesthetic fragment. Nietzsche showed how one totalizes critique; but what comes out in the end is only that he finds the fusion of validity and power scandalous because it impedes a glorified will to power that has taken on the connotations of artistic productivity. The comparison with Nietzsche makes manifest that no direction is inscribed in totalized critique as such. Nietzsche is the one among the steadfast theoreticians of unmasking who radicalizes the counter-Enlightenment.[1]

The stance of Max Horkheimer and Adorno toward Nietzsche is ambivalent. On the one hand, they attest of him that he was "one of the few after Hegel who recognized the dialectic of enlightenment" (*Dialectic of Enlightenment*, 44).[2] Naturally, they accept the "merciless doctrine of the identity of domination and reason" (*Dia-*

---

*Excerpted from *The Philosophical Discourse of Modernity*, written by Jürgen Habermas and translated by Frederick Lawrence (Cambridge, MA: MIT Press, 1987), 120–30. Excerpt published here with the permission of the author, MIT Press, and Polity Press.

lectic of Enlightenment, 119), which is to say, the *approach* toward a totalizing self-overcoming of ideology critique. On the other hand, they cannot overlook the fact that Hegel is also Nietzsche's great antipode. Nietzsche gives the critique of reason such an affirmative twist that even determinate negation—which is to say, the very procedure that Horkheimer and Adorno want to retain as the sole exercise, since reason itself has become so shaky—loses its sting. Nietzsche's critique consumes the critical impulse itself: "As a protest against civilization, the masters' morality conversely represents the oppressed. Hatred of atrophied instincts actually denounces the true nature of the taskmasters—which comes to light only in their victims. But as a Great Power or state religion, the masters' morality wholly subscribes to the civilizing powers that be, the compact majority, resentment, and everything that it formerly opposed. The realization of Nietzsche's assertions both refutes them and at the same time reveals their truth, which—despite all his affirmation of life—was inimical to the spirit of reality" (*Dialectic of Enlightenment,* 101).

This ambivalent attitude toward Nietzsche is instructive. It also suggests that *Dialectic of Enlightenment* owes more to Nietzsche than just the strategy of an ideology critique turned against itself. Indeed, what is unexplained throughout is their certain lack of concern in dealing with the (to put it in the form of a slogan) achievements of Occidental rationalism. How can these two men of the Enlightenment (which they both remain) be so unappreciative of the rational content of cultural modernity that all they perceive everywhere is a binding of reason and domination, of power and validity? Have they also let themselves be inspired by Nietzsche in drawing their criteria for cultural criticism from a basic experience of aesthetic modernity that has now been *rendered independent?*

The similarities in content are at first startling.[3] Point-for-point correspondences with Nietzsche are found in the construction by which Horkheimer and Adorno underpin their "primal history of subjectivity." As soon as humans were robbed of their detached instincts, claims Nietzsche, they had to rely on their "consciousness," namely, on their apparatus for objectifying and manipulating external nature: "They were reduced to thinking, inferring, reckoning, co-ordinating cause and effect, these unfortunate creatures" (*GM* II:16).[4] In the same stroke, however, the old instincts had to be tamed, and feelings and desires, no longer finding a spontaneous outlet, had to be repressed. In the course of this process of reversal of conative direction and of internalization, the subjectivity of an inner nature was formed under the sign of renunciation or of "bad conscience": "All instincts that do not discharge themselves outwardly *turn inward*—this is what I call the *internalization* of man: thus it was that man first developed what was later called his 'soul.' The entire inner world, originally as thin as if it were stretched between two membranes, expanded and extended itself, acquired depth, breadth, and height, in the name of measure as outward discharge was *inhibited*" (*GM* II:16). Finally, the two elements of domination over external and internal nature were bound together and fixed in the institutionalized dominion of human beings over other humans: "The curse of society and of peace" is based in all institutions, because they coerce people into renunciation:

"Those fearful bulwarks with which the political organization protected itself against the old instincts of freedom—punishments belong among these bulwarks—brought about that all these instincts of wild, free, prowling man turned backward *against man himself*" (*GM* II:16).

Similarly, Nietzsche's critique of knowledge and morality anticipates an idea that Horkheimer and Adorno develop in the form of the critique of instrumental reason: Behind positivism's ideals of objectivity and claims to truth, behind universalistic morality's ideals of asceticism and claims to rightness, lurk imperatives of self-preservation and domination. A pragmatist epistemology and a moral psychology unmask theoretical and practical reason as pure fictions in which power claims furnish themselves an effective alibi—with the help of imagination and of the "drive to metaphorize," for which external stimuli provide only the occasion for projective responses and for a web of interpretations behind which the text disappears altogether.[5]

Nietzsche brings out the perspective from which he handles modernity in a way different from that of *Dialectic Enlightenment*. And only this angle explains why objectified nature and morality sink to correlative forms of appearance of the same mythic force, be it of a perverted will to power or of instrumental reason.

This perspective was inaugurated with aesthetic modernity and that stubborn self-disclosure (forced by avant-garde art) of a decentered subjectivity liberated from all constraints of cognition and purposiveness and from all imperatives of labor and utility. Nietzsche, not just a contemporary and kindred spirit of Mallarmé;[6] he not only imbibed the late Romantic spirit of Richard Wagner; he is the first to conceptualize the attitude of aesthetic modernity before avant-garde consciousness assumed objective shape in the literature, painting, and music of the twentieth century—and could be elaborated by Adorno into an *Aesthetic Theory*. In the upgrading of the transitory, in the celebration of the dynamic, in the glorification of the current and the new, there is expressed an aesthetically motivated time-consciousness and a longing for an unspoiled, inward presence. The anarchist intention of the Surrealists *to explode* the continuum of the story of decline is already operative in Nietzsche. The subversive force of aesthetic resistance that would later feed the reflections of Benjamin and even of Peter Weiss, already arises from the experience in Nietzsche of rebellion against everything normative. It is this same force that neutralizes both the morally good and the practically useful, which expresses itself in the dialectic of secret and scandal and in the pleasure derived from the horror of profanation. Nietzsche builds up Socrates and Christ, those advocates of belief in truth and the ascetic ideal, as his great opponents; they are the ones who negate the aesthetic values! Nietzsche trusts only in art, "in which precisely the *lie* is sanctified, the will to deception" (*GM* III:25), and in the terror of the beautiful, not to let themselves be imprisoned by the fictive world of science and morality.

Nietzsche enthrones *taste*, "the Yes and No of the palate" (*BGE* 224), as the sole organ of "knowledge" beyond truth and falsehood, beyond good and evil. He elevates the judgment of taste of the art critic into the model for value judgment, for "evaluation." The legitimate meaning of critique is that of a value judgment that establishes an order of rank, weighs things, and measures forces. And all interpretation is evaluation. "Yes" expresses a high appraisal; "No" a low one. The "high" and the "low" indicate the dimension of yes/no positions in general.

It is interesting to see how coherently Nietzsche *undermines* the taking of "Yes" and "No" positions on criticizable validity claims. First, he devalues the truth of assertive statements and the rightness of normative ones, by reducing validity and invalidity to positive and negative *value judgments*. He reduces "p is true" and "h is right" (that is, the complex statements by which we claim validity for propositional statements or for ought statements) to simple evaluative statements by which we express value appraisals, by which we state that we prefer the true to the false and good over evil. Thus, Nietzsche reinterprets validity claims into preferences and then poses the question: "Suppose that we prefer truth (and justice): why not rather untruth (and injustice)?" (*BGE* 1). The responses to questions about the "value" of truth and justice are judgments of taste.

Of course, there could still be an architectonic lurking behind these fundamental value appraisals that, as in Schelling, anchors the unity of theoretical and practical reason in the faculty of aesthetic judgment. Nietzsche can carry out his complete assimilation of reason to power only by removing any cognitive status from value judgments and by demonstrating that the yes/no positions of value appraisals no longer express validity claims, but pure power claims.

Viewed in terms of language analysis, the next step in the argument therefore has the aims of assimilating judgments of taste to imperatives, and value appraisals to expressions of will. Nietzsche disputes Kant's analysis of judgments of taste in order to ground the thesis that evaluations are necessarily subjective and cannot be linked with a claim to intersubjective validity (*GM* III:6). The illusion of disinterested pleasure and of the impersonal character and universality of aesthetic judgment arises only from the perspective of the spectator; but from the perspective of the producing artist we realize that value *appraisals* are induced by innovative value *positings*. The aesthetics of production unfolds the experience of the genial artist who *creates* values: From his perspective, value appraisals are dictated by his "value-positing eye" (*GM* I:10). Value-positing productivity prescribes the law for value appraisal. What is expressed in the validity claimed by the judgment of taste is only "the excitement of the will by the beautiful." One will responds to another; one force takes hold of another.

This is the route by which Nietzsche arrives at the concept of the will to power from the yes/no positions of value appraisals, after he has cleansed them of all cognitive claims. The beautiful is "the stimulant of the will to power." The aesthetic core of the will to power is the capacity of a sensibility that lets itself be affected in the greatest possible multiplicity of modes.[7]

However, if thinking can no longer operate in the element of truth, or of validity claims in general,[8] contradiction and criticism lose their meaning. *To contradict*, to negate, now has only the sense of "*wanting to be different*." Nietzsche cannot really be satisfied with this in his critique of culture. The latter is not supposed to be merely a form of agitation, but *to demonstrate* why it is false or incorrect or bad to recognize the sovereignty of the ideals of science and universalistic morality, which are inimical to life. But once all predicates concerning validity are devalued, once it is power and not validity claims that is expressed in value appraisals—by what criterion shall critique still be able to propose discrimination? It must at least be able to discriminate between a power that *deserves* to be esteemed and one that *deserves* to be devalued.

A *theory of power* that distinguishes between "active" and merely "reactive" forces is supposed to offer a way out of this aporia. But Nietzsche cannot admit of the theory of power as a theory that can be true or false. He himself moves about, according to his own analysis, in a world of illusion, in which lighter shadows can be distinguished from darker ones, but not reason from unreason. This is, as it were, a world fallen back into myth, in which powers influence one another and no element remains that could transcend the battle of the powers. Perhaps it is typical of the ahistorical mode of perception proper to aesthetic modernity that particular epochs lose their own profile in favor of a heroic affinity of the present with the most remote and the most primitive: The decadent strives to relate itself in a leap to the barbaric, the wild, and the primitive. In any case, Nietzsche's renewal of the framework of the myth of origins is suited to this mentality: *Authentic* culture has been in decline already for a long time; the curse of remoteness from origins lays upon the present; and so Nietzsche conceives of the gathering of a still dawning culture in antiutopian terms—as a comeback and a return.

This framework does not have a merely metaphorical status; it has the systematic role of making room for the paradoxical business of a critique disburdened of the mortgages of enlightened thought. That is to say, totalized ideology critique for Nietzsche turns into what he calls "genealogical critique." Once the critical sense of saying "No" is suspended and the procedure of negation is rendered impotent, Nietzsche goes back to the very dimension of the myth of origins that permits a distinction that affects *all other* dimension: What is *older* is *earlier* in the generational chain and nearer to the origin. The *more primordial* is considered the more worthy of honor, the preferable, the more unspoiled, the purer: It is deemed better. *Derivation* and *descent* serve as criteria of rank, in both the social and the logical senses.

In this manner, Nietzsche bases his critique of morality on *genealogy*. He traces the moral appraisal of value, which assigns a person or a mode of action a place within a rank ordering based on criteria of validity, back to the descent and hence to the social rank of the one making the moral judgment: "The signpost to the *right* road was for me the question: what was the real etymological significance of the designations for 'good' coined in the various languages? I found they all led back to the *same conceptual transformation*—that everywhere 'noble,' 'aristocratic' in the social [*ständlisch*] sense, is the basic concept from which 'good' in the sense of 'with aristocratic soul,' 'noble,' 'with the soul of a higher order,' 'with a privileged soul' necessarily developed: a development which always runs parallel to that other in which 'common,' 'plebeian,' 'low' are finally transformed into the concept 'bad'" (*GM* I:4). So the genealogical localization of powers takes on a critical sense: Those forces with an earlier, more noble descent are the active, creative ones, whereas a perverted will to power is expressed in the forces of later, lower, and reactive descent.[9]

With this, Nietzsche has in hand the conceptual means by which he can denounce the prevalence of the belief in reason and of the ascetic ideal, of science and morality, as a merely factual victory (though of course decisive for the fate of modernity) of lower and reactionary forces. As is well known, they are supposed to have arisen from the resentment of the weaker and "the protective and healing instinct of a degenerating life" (*GM* III:13).[10]

We have pursued totalizing critique applied to itself in two variants. Horkheimer and Adorno find themselves in the same embarrassment as Nietzsche: If they do not want to renounce the effect of a final unmasking and still want to *continue with critique*, they will have to leave at least one rational criterion intact for their explanation of the corruption of *all* rational criteria. In the face of this paradox, self-referential critique loses its orientation. It has two options.

Nietzsche seeks refuge in a theory of power, which is consistent, since the fusion of reason and power revealed by critique abandons the world to the irreconcilable struggle between powers, as if it *were* the mythic world. It is fitting that Nietzsche, mediated by Gilles Deleuze, has become influential in structuralist France as a theoretician of power. Foucault, too, in his later work, replaces the model of domination based on repression (developed in the tradition of enlightenment by Marx and Freud) by a plurality of power strategies. These power strategies intersect one another, succeed one another; they are distinguished according to the type of their discourse formation and the degree of their intensity; but they cannot be *judged* under the aspect of their validity, as was the case with consciously working through conflicts in contrast to unconsciously doing so.[11]

The doctrine of active and merely reactive forces also fails to provide a way out of the embarrassment of a critique that attacks the presuppositions of its own validity. At best, it paves the way for breaking out of the horizon of modernity. It is without basis as a theory, if the categorial distinction between power claims and truth claims is the ground upon which *any* theoretical approach has to be enacted. The effect of unmasking is also transformed as a result: It is not the lightning flash of *insight* into some confusion threatening identity that causes shock, the way *understanding* the point of a joke causes liberating laughter; what produces shock is affirmative de-differentiation, an affirmative overthrow of the very categories that can make an act of mistaking, of forgetting, or of misspeaking into a category mistake threatening to identity—or art into illusion. This regressive turn still places the forces of emancipation at the service of counterenlightenment.

Horkheimer and Adorno adopt another option by stirring up, holding open, and no longer wanting to overcome theoretically the performative contradiction inherent in an ideology critique that outstrips itself. Any attempt to develop a theory at this level of reflection would have to slide off into the groundless; they therefore eschew theory and practice determinate negation on an ad hoc basis, thus standing firm against that fusion of reason and power that plugs all crevices: "Determinate negation rejects the defective ideas of the absolute, the idols, differently than does rigorism, which confronts them with the idea they cannot match up to. Dialectic, on the contrary, interprets every image as writing. It shows how the admission of its falsity is to be read in the lines of its features—a confession that deprives it of its power and appropriates it for truth. Thus language becomes more than just a sign system. With the notion of determinate negativity, Hegel revealed an element that distinguishes the Enlightenment from the positivist degeneracy to which he attributes it" (*Dialectic of Enlightenment*, 24). A practiced spirit of contradiction is all that remains of the "spirit of . . . unrelenting theory." And this practice is like an incantation seeking "to turn . . . to its end" the negative spirit of relentless progress (*Dialectic of Enlightenment*, 42).

Anyone who abides in a paradox on the very spot once occupied by philosophy with its ultimate groundings is not just taking up an uncomfortable position, one can only hold that place if one makes it at least minimally plausible that there is *no way out*. Even the retreat from an aporetic situation has to be barred, for otherwise there is a way—the way back. But I believe this is precisely the case.

The comparison with Nietzsche is instructive inasmuch as it draws our attention to the aesthetic horizon of experience that guides and motivates the gaze of contemporary diagnosis. I have shown how Nietzsche detaches that moment of reason, which comes into its own in the logic proper to the aesthetic-expressive sphere of value, and especially in avant-garde art and art criticism, from its connection with theoretical and practical reason; and how he stylizes aesthetic judgment, on the model of a "value appraisal" exiled to irrationality, into a capacity for discrimination beyond good and evil, truth and falsehood. In this way, Nietzsche gains criteria for a critique of culture that unmasks science and morality as being in similar ways ideological expressions of a perverted will to power, just as *Dialectic of Enlightenment* denounces these structures as embodiments of instrumental reason.

In one respect, ideology critique had in fact continued the undialectical enlightenment proper to ontological thinking. It remained caught up in the purist notion that the devil needing exorcism was hiding in the internal relationships between genesis and validity, so that theory, purified of all empirical connotations, could operate in its own element. Totalized critique did not discharge this legacy. The intention of a "final unmasking," which was supposed to draw away with one fell swoop the veil covering the confusion between power and reason, reveals a purist intent—similar to the intent of ontology to separate being and illusion categorically (that is, with one stroke). However, just as in a communication community the researcher, the context of discovery, and the context of justification are so entwined with one another that they have to be separated procedurally, by a *mediating* kind of thinking—which is to say, continuously—the same holds for the two spheres of being and illusion. In argumentation, critique is constantly entwined with theory, enlightenment with grounding, even though discourse participants always *have to suppose* that only the unforced force of the better argument comes into play under the unavoidable communication presuppositions of argumentative discourse. But they know, or they can know, that even this idealization is only necessary because convictions are formed and confirmed in a medium that is not "pure" and not removed from the world of appearances in the style of Platonic "pure" and not removed from the world of appearances in the style of Platonic Ideas. Only a discourse that admits this might break the spell of mythic thinking without incurring a loss of the light radiating from the semantic potentials also preserved in myth.

NOTES

1. Like his "new-conservative" successors, he too behaves like an "anti-sociologist." Cf. H. Baier, "Die Gesellschaft—ein langer Schatten des toten Gottes," in *Nietzsche-Studien* 10/ 11 (1982): 6ff.

2. Max Horkheimer and Theodor Adorno, *Dialektik der Aufklärung* (Amsterdam: Querido, 1947). English translation *Dialectic of Enlightenment* [trans. by John Cumming] (New York: Herder and Herder, 1972).

3. See also Peter Pütz, "Nietzsche and Critical Theory," in *Telos* 50 (Winter 1981–1982): 103–14.

4. *Ed. Note*: Translations of Nietzsche are Walter Kaufmann's and R. J. Hollingdale's.

5. J. Habermas, "Nachwort" to F. Nietzsche, *Erkenntnistheoretische Schriften* (Frankfurt: Suhrkamp, 1968), 237ff.

6. Pointed out by Gilles Deleuze, *Nietzsche and Philosophy* (New York: Columbia University Press, 1983), 32ff.

7. The mediating function of the judgment of taste in the reduction of yes/no positions on criticizable validity claims to the "Yes" and "No" in relation to imperative expressions of will can also be seen in the manner in which Nietzsche, along with the concept of *propositional truth*, revises the concept of *world* built into our grammar: "Indeed, what forces us at all to suppose that there is an essential opposition of 'true' and 'false'? Is it not sufficient to assume degrees of apparentness and, as it were, lighter and darker shadows and shades of appearance—different 'values' to use the language of painters? Why couldn't the world *that concerns us* be a fiction? And if somebody asks: 'but to a fiction there surely belongs an author?'— couldn't one answer simply: *why?* Doesn't this 'belongs' perhaps belong to the fiction, too? By now is one not permitted to be a bit ironic about the subject no less than about the predicate and object? Shouldn't the philosopher be permitted to rise above faith in grammar?" (*BGE* 34)

8. Deleuze, *Nietzsche and Philosophy*, 103ff.

9. Deleuze, *Nietzsche and Philosophy*, 112.

10. Here I am interested in the structure of the argument. Once he has destroyed the foundations of the critique of ideology by a self-referential use of this critique, Nietzsche saves his own position as an unmasking critic only by recourse to a figure of thought associated with the myth of origins. The ideological content of *On the Genealogy of Morals* and Nietzsche battle against modern ideas in general—in which the more cultivated among the despisers of

democracy, now as ever, show a conspicuous interest—is another matter altogether. See R. Maurer, "Nietzsche und die Kritische Theorie," and G. Rohrmoser, "Nietzsches Kritik der Moral," *Nietzsche-Studien* 10/11 (1982): 34ff and 328ff.

11. H. Fink-Eitel, "Michel Foucaults Analytik der Macht," in F. A. Kittler, ed., *Austreibung des Geistes aus den Geisteswissenschaften* (Paderborn: Schöningh, 1980), 38ff; Axel Honneth and Hans Joas, *Soziales Handeln und menschliche Natur* (Frankfurt: Campus Verlag, 1980), 123ff.

15

Translating, Repeating, Naming
Foucault, Derrida, and the Genealogy of Morals*

Gary Shapiro

Two cautions or warnings (at least) must be heeded in the attempt to do justice to Nietzsche's project of a genealogy of morals in the text that bears that name. While the *Genealogy* is often regarded as the most straightforward and continuous of Nietzsche's books, he tells us in *Ecce Homo* that its three essays are "perhaps *uncannier* than *anything else* written so far in regard to expression, intention, and the art of surprise" (*EH* "GM").[1] If we imagine ourselves successful in penetrating to these unsettling secrets and saying what Nietzsche's text means, once and for all, we should have to read again its lapidary although parenthetical injunction that "only that which *has* no history can be defined." When Nietzsche published the *Genealogy* in 1887, the main uses of the term arguably had to do with ascertaining family lineages to determine rights to titles, honors, and inheritances, as in the venerable *Almanach of Gotha*. But Foucault characterizes his *History of Sexuality* as a genealogy of the modern self, and Derrida describes a large part of his intellectual project as "repeating the genealogy of morals"; Nietzsche's practice and example are invoked in both cases.

How might we proceed to assess the significance of Nietzsche's "genealogy" in relation both to its mundane cousins and to such thinkers? I propose a partial, critical, and bifocal effort in that direction, consisting in a study of a few paradigmatic readings of Nietzschean genealogy. I begin with Jürgen Habermas, who assimilates

---

*Excerpted by the author from its original publication in *Nietzsche as Postmodernist: Essays Pro and Con*, edited by Clayton Koelb (Albany, NY: State University of New York Press), 39–55. Reprinted with permission of SUNY Press.

Nietzsche's project to the aristocratic attempt to demonstrate the superiority of the most ancient and archaic. According to Habermas, Nietzsche's rejection of all rational and critical criteria for assessing values leaves him no other option:

> What is *older* is *earlier* in the generational chain and nearer to the origin, the *more primordial* is considered the more worthy of honor, the preferable, the more unspoiled, the purer: It is deemed better. *Derivation* and *descent* serve as the criteria of rank, in both the social and the logical senses.
>
> In this manner, Nietzsche bases his critique of morality on *genealogy*. He traces the moral appraisal of value, which assigns a person or a mode of action a place within a rank ordering based on criteria of validity, back to the descent and hence to the social rank of the one making the moral judgment.[2]

This may be the genealogical scheme of values of the *Almanach of Gotha*, but it is not Nietzsche's. Despite his bursts of admiration for the "blond beasts" of early cultures, Nietzsche's narrative never returns us to a point at which one single, pure form of morality obtains. Contrary both to theological ethics and to the hypotheses of the English utilitarian historians of morality, the *Genealogy* insists that there is no single origin but only opposition and diversity no matter how far back we go. There are, always already, at least two languages of morality, the aristocratic language of "good and bad" and the slavish language of "good and evil." Where a Platonist would focus on the fact that "good" appears in both discourses and would search for its common meaning, Nietzsche notes that it is only the word shared by the two languages. One says "good" and happily designates its satisfaction with itself; the other reactively designates those who speak in such a way as "evil" and who define themselves as the opposites of the evil ones. Even within the aristocratic group, Nietzsche observes, there are again at least two varieties of the moral code "good and bad" which can be distinguished as the knightly and the priestly. Not myth, as Habermas would have it, but something much more like the structuralist analysis of myth is at work here.

While Habermas supposes that the rejection of the progressive and teleological enlightenment conception of history must entail a nostalgic valorization of the archaic, Michel Foucault's reading of Nietzsche and his own development of the genealogical project are vigorously committed to avoiding the temptations of both nostalgia and progress. Genealogy is the articulation of differences, of affiliations that never reduce to a system or totality and of the transformations of power/knowledge in their unplanned and unpredictable concatenations. Foucault's later writings, especially *Discipline and Punish* and *The History of Sexuality*, acknowledge their indebtedness to Nietzsche with respect to these themes. Foucault sees his own distinctive contribution as the extension of the genealogical approach to the constitution of the human sciences and their associated disciplines and practices. In tracing out the "capillary" forms of power, Foucault exhibits that taste for the documentary, gray page of the legal text which, as Nietzsche indicates in his preface to the *Genealogy*, is the laborious side of the outrageous attempt to raise the question of the value of morality. These works might be called translations of the *Genealogy* into the worlds of the prison and surveillance, psychiatry and biopower. These translations of the Nietzschean genealogy are grounded in his essay of 1971, "Nietzsche, Genealogy, History," which is both textual commentary on the *Genealogy*, and a thematization of the principles that govern Foucault's later studies.

Foucault distinguishes two words, *Ursprung* and *Herkunft*, which play important roles in Nietzsche's text.[3] To be concerned with *Ursprung*, or origin, is to be a philosophical historian who would trace morality—or any other subject matter—back to an original principle that can be clarified and recuperated. The genealogist will, however, be concerned with the complex web of ancestry and affiliations that are called *Herkunft*, those alliances that form part of actual family trees, with all their gaps, incestuous transgressions, and odd combinations. Here, Foucault tells us, the genealogist comes into his own: "Where the soul pretends unification or the self fabricates a coherent identity, the genealogist sets out to study the beginning— numberless beginnings whose faint traces and hints of color are readily seen by an historical eye" (*NGH*, 145).

Two possible points of view, two research programs, two types of inquirers are designated by these two words and concepts. If Nietzsche were misconstrued as one with a nostalgia for origins and an obsession with first principles, then his praise of "the blond beast" and the "artistic violence" of "noble races" would support something like the mysticism of racial purity for which some Nazis claimed his authority. Foucault tells us that Nietzsche's preface rules out such a reading: "One of the most significant texts with respect to the use of all these terms and to the variations in the use of *Ursprung* is the preface to the *Genealogy*. At the beginning of the text, its objective is defined as an examination of the origin of moral preconceptions and the term used is *Herkunft*. Then, Nietzsche proceeds by retracing his personal involvement with this question" (*NGH*, 141). The point of that narrative, Foucault says, is to establish that even Nietzsche's analyses of morality ten years earlier (in *Daybreak*) operated within the orbit of *Herkunftshypothesen* rather than the quest for origins.

Now isn't it a bit odd that Foucault determines the nature of this Nietzschean text by what he takes to be its transparent beginning? What that beginning announces, so it seems, are the fundamental concepts of the genealogist and, even, the birth of the genealogist, his vocation toward a certain kind of scientific work. What will not be in question in Foucault's reading of the *Genealogy* is the identity and voice of the genealogist. This search for a clear line, for a master speaker in Nietzsche's text, is suspect: first, because it apparently exempts this text from the very same genealogical, or differentiating, imperative that it finds in the text; and, second, because it does not completely read or translate everything that is to be found in the preface. In fact, Foucault starts not at the beginning of Nietzsche's beginning but with the second numbered paragraph of the "Preface." At the very beginning of the preface, that is, in its first lines, Nietzsche writes: "We are unknown to ourselves, we men of knowledge—and with good reason. We have never sought ourselves—how could it happen that we should ever find ourselves?" (*GM* P:1).

Might this not serve as a warning that the voice of the text is not to be identified simply as that of the genealogist who understands his business? Perhaps it is a warning that no single voice animates the *Genealogy* and that this text must itself be read dialogically, as what Foucault calls in another context a "concerted carnival" (*NGH*, 161). For shortly after the apparent confession of ignorance comes the bold sweep of the narrative to which Foucault directs our attention, the narrative in which Nietzsche explains the steps leading to his vocation. Yet these claims of dedication and discovery acquire an Oedipal tone in this context, suggesting a certain pride and self-assurance. This is a tragic voice. And it is not the only voice of the text, which alternates among a series of historical and fictional voices—those of the Oedipal scientist, the tragic dramatist, the buffoon of world history, the witnesses (real and imaginary) whom Nietzsche summons to testify about the manufacture of ideals—and doubtless there are others.

We might have begun reading the *Genealogy* at its subtitle, "*Eine Streitschrift*" (a polemical text). This *agon* or *polemos* is directed not only toward others, like the philosophical historian, who are on the outside of the text; we should also read the battle, the dialogue, the *prosopopoeia*, and exchange that goes on within the text itself. There are stylistic affinities between this text and some of Dostoyevsky's, especially the latter's *Notes from Underground*, which Nietzsche read just before writing the *Genealogy*. These affinities go beyond thematic concerns with such oppositions as the man of *ressentiment* and the normal man or the claim that consciousness is an illness (a productive, pregnant illness will be Nietzsche's restatement of the latter). We could note what Mikhail Bakhtin has called the dialogical character of the Dostoyevskean text.[4] The *Notes* enacts an exchange between the narrator and his others, the "normal" men. Dostoyevsky's normal man speaks for the progress of science and the utopia of the "crystal palace"; in Nietzsche's *Genealogy* the voice who introduces the narrative claims to be a scientist of sorts, but his scientific authority is called into question by the articulation of the polemic.

At one point Foucault recognizes a certain plurality in Nietzsche's text, noting that Nietzsche's challenge to origins is confined "to those occasions when he is truly a genealogist" (*NGH*, 142), but does not explain what the other occasions are. From this genealogist *qua* genealogist, Foucault draws a number of principles of reading. Two of these principles could be usefully employed in reading the *Genealogy* itself as a pluralized text:

1. To follow the complex course of descent is to maintain passing events in their proper dispersion (*NGH*, 146). [Then why not also the dispersion of voices in the text?]
2. The body is the inscribed surface of events (traced by language and dissolved by ideas), the locus of a dissociated self (adopting the illusion of substantial unity), and a volume in perpetual disintegration. Genealogy, as an analysis of descent is thus situated within the articulation of the body and history. Its task is to expose a body totally imprinted by history and the process of history's destruction of the body" (*NGH*, 148).

Does not the metaphorics of inscription, volume, and imprinting call for an application of this principle to the body of the text and, in particular to the inscribed textual body, the *Genealogy*, which would be the source of this principle? Foucault tends to localize this side of the text, confining it to the subject matter (assuming that such a subject matter can be isolated), rather than listening to its multiplication of voices. The upshot of the pluralization of voices in the *Genealogy* is the calling into question of a number of postures of inquiry, including that of the dedicated genealogist who is, insofar as he would practice a normal science of genealogy, not very different from the philosophical historian whom Foucault criticizes.

Consider for example the second volume of *The History of Sexuality*, which concerns the formation of a sexual ethos in fourth-century Greece, one that would be responsive to the apparent contradiction between contemporary sexual practices and the prevailing norms of responsible citizenship. How can the love of boys not lead to the habituation of a generation of prospective citizens to patterns of submission incompatible with their designated social roles? In the light of this question, Foucault undertakes a genealogy of the conception of the responsible subject that, as he sees it, is formed through discourses and practices that propose solutions to this dilemma. These formations of power and knowledge he distinguished as: (1) dietetics (prudential advice concerning the use and abuse of pleasure); (2) economics (the principles of the household); (3) erotics (the wise conduct of love affairs); (4) and "true love" (the philosophical transvaluation of the love affair into the mutual pursuit of truth).

The crucial evidence for Foucault's analysis of this last discursive form comes from Plato, especially from the *Symposium* and *Phaedrus*. What is surprising about Foucault's reading of these Platonic texts is the degree to which he flattens them out into a form that seems drastically to understate their internal plurality and complexity. Foucault simply opposes the false speeches on love to the true speeches (Diotima's in the *Symposium*, Socrates' second in the *Phaedrus*). Foucault constantly, and more than accidentally, uses various forms of the locutions "Plato says" or "Plato thinks."[5] Plato discovers that the truth of love is the love of the truth, even though Plato never speaks in his own voice in the dialogues. Foucault ignores the fact that Diotima's speech is distanced from Plato by several degrees: it is reported by Socrates, and the dialogue as a whole is relayed to us through a series of less than completely reliable witnesses. Similarly, in the *Phaedrus*, Socrates' speech is part of a very complex thematics of love and discourse, which raises questions about the self-sufficiency of the literary form in which it is embedded. This assimilation of the Platonic dialogues to the relatively linear development of a new ethics of love is at least as one-dimensional as the reading that sees them as nothing but preliminary versions of modern discussions of the universal and the particular.

Nietzsche, despite his anti-Platonic animus, had a more genuinely genealogical view of the matter when he distinguished between the Socratic and plebeian theme and its Platonic, aristocratic reworking and sublimation, or when he remarked that the Platonic dialogue was the vessel by which art survived the shipwreck of ancient culture (*BT* 14). This reading of Plato is continuous with Foucault's reading of Nietzsche in the founding essay on genealogy. For example, in mapping Greek discourses on love and sex into the four categories—in ascending order—of dietetics, economics, erotics, and true love, Foucault seems to be under the sway of the "Platonic ladder" of the *Symposium* or perhaps of the divided line of the *Republic*. When the uncanny dimension of the text of the *Genealogy* is neglected, genealogy itself tends to degenerate into a mere method that circumscribes its subject matter all too neatly. After remarking on the uncanniness of the *Genealogy*, Nietzsche added, "Dionysus is, as is known, also the god of darkness." Could it be that Dionysus lies in wait for the normal genealogist at the heart of the labyrinth into which he has strayed?

Earlier, Foucault and Derrida had an exchange concerning analogous issues in the reading and translation of Descartes. The questions hinge on knowing how many voices are speaking in Descartes's First Meditation.[6] The crux is the reading of the passage in which Descartes, or one of the voices of the *Meditations*, briefly entertains the possibility of doubting that he is sitting by the fire, only to elicit the reply that those with such doubts—who imagine that their heads are pumpkins or that they are made of glass—are mad and that he would be equally mad if he took them as a precedent for understanding his own case. For Foucault's representation of Descartes as juridically excluding the possibility of madness from the rational course of his meditations, it is important that there be one commanding voice that can be read as emblematic of the "great internment" of the mad in the seventeenth century. For Derrida, in contrast, it is crucial that we see a series of objections and replies within the text itself, so that the *Meditations*, far from excluding any possibility of madness, push this possibility to a hyperbolical extreme through the hypothesis that we are always dreaming or deceived by an evil demon. So the philosopher's voice would be always already juxtaposed to the voices of unreason, and his project would be one that proceeds whether or not he is mad.[7]

There are resonances of this celebrated dispute concerning the reading of Descartes in the different readings or repetitions that Foucault and Derrida offer of the *Genealogy*. Unlike Foucault, Derrida does not explicitly devote an essay to the text. Instead he describes at least part of what he is doing in *Of Grammatology* as "repeating the genealogy of morals."[8] This self-description occurs at the end of the section "The Writing Lesson," which interrogates Claude Lévi-Strauss's attempt to distinguish naturally good cultures without writing and exploitative Western societies that make use of writing. This reference is rather oblique, for Derrida inscribes on his page not the title *The Genealogy of Morals*, in italics, but simply the phrase "genealogy of morals." Yet there are reasons for taking even such an indirect reference seriously, for the reading of Lévi-Strauss has to do with the proper name and its possibilities of erasure or effacement. Why should Derrida repeat the genealogy (or *Genealogy*) in his analysis of Lévi-Strauss? In many ways Lévi-Strauss is a contemporary version of the normal scientist who appears in Nietzsche's *Genealogy* as infected by *ressentiment*, in whom the reaction against the other has turned into a dislike of himself. As a spokesman for science, Lévi-Strauss is a universalist, a democrat suspicious of the ethnocentrism of the West.

"The critique of ethnocentrism," Derrida writes, "has most often the sole function of constituting the other as a model of original and natural goodness, of accusing and humiliating oneself, of exhibiting its being-unacceptable in an anti-ethnocentric mirror." Lévi-Strauss is one of those knowers, who are unknown to themselves. He repeats the gesture of the English moralists insofar as he believes in an original, natural morality that has been forgotten or effaced but which is capable of retrieval or at least reconstruction through memory. Here the place of historical memory is taken by the experiment of the anthropologist who, by introducing writing to a people previously innocent of it, is able to observe what he takes to be its characteristic sudden infusion of violence and hierarchy into a pacific, face-to-face society. Lévi-Strauss tells this story in the chapter of *Tristes Tropiques* called "The Writing Lesson." Here the guilty anthropologist explains how the leader of the Nambikwara pretended to have learned the European's art of writing in order to manipulate others with the promise of rewards and the mysterious aura of an esoteric code. Derrida's genealogical reading of this Rousseauian confession focuses on the question of language; like the English historians of morality, Lévi-Strauss has taken it to be much simpler and more homogeneous than it actually is.

The English moralists, Nietzsche says, want to know what good is; like Plato, they suppose that it must have a single meaning. While Plato sought that meaning through transcendental memory, the English seek it through historical reconstruction of original experiences of utility. Yet there is no single language or discourse of the good that could support either project. There are at least two languages of morals, one that differentiates good from bad, another that differentiates good from evil. In the good/bad discourse, the speaker first, and affirmatively, designates himself as good. Only as an afterthought, does he call the others the bad. In the good/evil discourse the starting point is the characterization of the other (the master, the strong, or the noble) as evil, because he is envied, because he is violent or negligent in his dealings with us, the speakers of that language. "Good" is in each case part of a system of differences; not translatable from one moral language to the other while preserving its sense. It partakes of what Derrida calls the "proper name effect both demanding and resisting translation. Naming oneself and the other involve initial acts of violence and separation, which are not well served by either Platonic or utilitarian translations, for these assume incorrectly that there is only one voice, or one discourse, to translate.

Lévi-Strauss thinks of the Nambikwara, the people without writing, as good in a Rousseauian sense of primal innocence. So they must have a single language spontaneously and constantly animated by the intimacy of their daily life; their innocence can be read off from the fact that they have no writing, for writing would introduce a hierarchy of scribes and leaders, a differentiation that would disrupt an idyllic condition. In Lévi-Strauss's own narrative we find the evidence of the Nambikwara's own writing, double coding, violence, and hierarchy that the narrator would like to depict as specifically Western. There we learn that the Nambikwara language is spoken differently by men and women, who view each other as distinct species. The Nambikwara have secret proper names, disguised in most circumstances by substitutes. Revealing the proper name to inappropriate others or at inappropriate times sets off a long chain of reprisals. Similarly, Nietzsche had noticed that the spokesmen for an ethics of love often provide evidence of the desire for revenge (citing Tertullian and Aquinas on the pleasures of the blessed in the torments visited upon sinners). He observed the periodic recurrence of epidemics of revenge and scapegoating among our supposedly innocent ancestors. Lévi-Strauss would have us believe that violence arises among the Nambikwara only through the agency of the scientist who teaches writing or transgresses the law of the tribe by provoking young girls to reveal the secret names of comrades and parents.

Science will not hesitate to invoke the categorial apparatus of its own culture in order to protect the purity of the other culture that it studies. Yet Lévi-Strauss must account for their practice of "drawing lines." Lévi-Strauss translates: "They called the act of writing *iekariakedjutu,* namely 'drawing lines,' which had an aesthetic interest for them" (cited in *OG,* 124). But what is aesthetic interest? Nietzsche sketches a genealogy of aesthetics that demonstrates its complicity with the culture of the eighteenth century, exemplified by the Kantian tripartition of knowing, willing, and an aesthetic experience devoid of knowledge and will (see *GM* III). "Aesthetics" is a recent invention, a concept built on the exclusion of desire, laughter, the festive, and the grotesque. Derrida asks, conerning Lévi-Strauss's translation and aestheticization of "drawing lines": "Is not ethnocentrism always betrayed by the haste with which it is satisfied by certain translations or certain domestic equivalents?" (*OG,* 123). Does not the existence of a double system of names, and a system of marking, indicate that language is, even here, always already multiple and so characterized by the possibility of transgression, aggression, and violence that the guilty anthropologist would like to keep at a distance from these people? This first repetition discovers plurality and violence where an idealistic nostalgia had found only peace and unity.

Lévi-Strauss also reveals that the Nambikwara became adept at producing explanatory diagrams of such cultural matters as their kinship relations that were extremely useful to the party of anthropologists. Should we think of them, like Meno's slave boy, as being brought to discover a primal writing in the soul? Or as having been infected by the violence of the West? Or might we find Derrida to be the more insightful anthropologist here when he observes that "the birth of writing (in the colloquial sense) was nearly everywhere and most often linked to genealogical anxiety" (*OG,* 124)? This last suggestion, like Nietzsche's critique of the Kantian-Schopenhauerian aesthetics of pure contemplation, indicates the ties between art and life. From the time of the Homeric catalogues of heroes to the nineteenth-century novel of marriage, property, inheritance and the discovery of unexpected blood relationships, writing—in the colloquial sense—has maintained its link to genealogical anxiety.

Derrida also repeats the *Genealogy* in its critique or self-critique of science. Science, when pushed to its limit, reflects upon itself and recognizes its indebtedness to the morality of *ressentiment*; the scientist's dedication to the truth and his willingness to sacrifice himself for the truth are structurally identical with the asectic negation of one's self and one's present life for the sake of God. The scientist's final truth is one that he will never see, and its pursuit here and now requires the virtues of faith, hope, and charity: faith in the possibility that the truth will be attained, despite our present state of ignorance and error; hope that progress toward the truth will continue; charity as the willingness to abandon whatever is one's own, one's own favored hypothesis for example, for the sake of truth as an ultimate goal. "We knowers" are unknown to ourselves insofar as we fail to see these genealogical affiliations of our activity with that sacrifice of self. But when science becomes historical and genealogical it will discover these affiliations in a moment of tragic reversal and recognition. Science will become uncanny and undecidable: "The will to truth requires a critique—let us thus define our own task—the value of truth must for once be experimentally *called into question*" (*GM* III:24).

Of Grammatology repeats or translates the *Genealogy*, then, by reconsidering the project of several putative sciences that are shown to be impossible. Insofar as anthropology operates with a distinction between nature and culture, or between Rousseauian innocence and civilized evil, it founders on the impossibility of these distinctions themselves; in the act of deploying such distinctions, it provides the impetus to question and deconstruct them. *Of Grammatology* is also concerned with the impossible science of grammatology. Since writing, thought seriously and essentially, is that which escapes presence, totalization, and the ideal of science that is indebted to these concepts, there can be no science of grammatology. But the experiment of attempting to construct a grammatology will disclose the questionability of any science of language that would segregate or compartmentalize writing as well as the problematic project of *scientificity* itself.

Derrida asks a Nietzschean question of Lévi-Strauss: "If it is true, as I in fact believe, that writing cannot be thought of outside the horizon of intersubjective violence, is there anything, even science, that radically escapes it?" (*OG*, 127). To suppose otherwise is to place one's trust in "the presumed difference between language and power." At the end of Lévi-Strauss's most philosophical work, *La pensée sauvage*, there is a clear demonstration of the naiveté involved in such trust that is reminiscent of the positivist metanarratives of science that Nietzsche attacks through his *Genealogy*. In the rhetorically magnificent but ultimately unpersuasive coda to Lévi-Strauss's book, the claim is made that we are now witnessing the convergence of contemporary science and the timeless patterns of savage or untamed mythical thinking. According to Lévi-Strauss, information theory can offer a universal account of both the codes and messages of "primitive" peoples at one end of the spectrum, based as they are on the holistic, macroscopic, and sensible qualities of the perceived environment, with the general, instrumentalized study of the production and reception of biological and physical "messages" at the other end that reveal themselves only with the help of the abstracting methods of the hypothetico-deductive sciences. With such a convergence, we hear: "The entire process of human knowledge assumes the character of a closed system. And we therefore remain faithful to the inspiration of the savage mind when we recognize that, by an encounter it alone could have foreseen, the scientific spirit in its most modern form will have contributed to legitimize the principles of savage thought and to re-establish it in its rightful place."[9] This is utopian positivism because it takes the prevailing models in the sciences to be ultimately valid and because it supposes that we are on the verge of a total integration of various fields of knowledge, a "totalization" at least as extravagant as that practical, historical Sartrean totalization, which Lévi-Strauss criticizes in the same chapter. While rejecting Sartre's appeal to social and political history as modern myth, Lévi-Strauss reverts to the scientistic version of this myth, unconsciously reviving the teleologies of Comte and Spencer. Nietzsche's genealogy of such science aims at showing that it must founder as soon as its concepts and methods of inquiry are turned back upon itself, and it discovers its own genealogy in a morality that its inquiries have rendered suspicious. Derrida, a few years before Foucault's programmatic essay on Nietzschean genealogy, makes a similar point in suggesting that the human sciences cannot innocently presume the distinction between power and knowledge that fuels the structuralist eschatology.

At the end of the *Genealogy*'s first essay, Nietzsche calls for a series of prize essays by philologists, historians, and philosophers on the question: "What light does linguistics and especially the study of etymology, throw on the history of the evolution of the moral concepts?" (*GM* I:17). One answer is supplied by Nietzsche's first essay itself, with its analysis of the *gut/schlecht* moral system and the *gut/böse* moral system in terms of the social and ethnic differences of the ancient world; Foucault's genealogical study of the constitution of the discourses of psychiatry, punishment, and sexuality can be read as extensions of this linguistic genealogy. But the third essay pushes the question further, asking what consequences such investigations have for the sciences that pursue them. Can they remain above the battle or must they, as Nietzsche says, "submit to the law that they themselves have proposed" and, like all great things, "bring about their own destruction through an act of self-overcoming" (*GM* III:27)? Derrida's repetition of the *Genealogy* is a repetition of the third essay and of its uncanny ramifications for the inquiry itself. Here we might pause and read Nietzsche's question about linguistics and etymology once more. Why this apparent repetition of "history" and "evolution"? Must we not remember, especially if we are giving the close attention to language that Nietzsche demands and which is the theme of that question, that "history" is a double-barreled word, alternately designating either the subject matter studied or the activity of studying it?

In *Of Grammatology*, we are constantly reminded that the *de*, the preposition, in its title, indicates a question rather than introducing a subject matter. It is not a "toward" in the Kantian sense of a "Prolegomena to Any Future Grammatology That Will Come Forward as a Science." How should we translate the *zur* in *Zur*

Genealogie der Moral? There has been some controversy among Nietzsche's translators about how this *zur* might be rendered in English. Is it "On" in the sense of "concerning" or "about" or is it "toward"? "Toward" has been employed by those who favor a tentative reading of Nietzsche's text as a contribution toward something still in the making. But can one go toward that which can never be reached? Or should the title itself be read parodically? "On" is better in preserving an ambiguity with regard to the question of whether a genealogy of morals is possible, that is, whether we ought to take seriously the scientific rhetoric with which Nietzsche, especially in his first essay, attempts to situate his work in relation to historical and philological science. Similarly, there is, in Derrida's repetition of the genealogy while effacing its title, both a linguistic prudence and respect that hesitates to violate this undecidablility and a mimesis of that act of the concealment of the proper name, which has been identified as the characteristic act of writing. So there is a motivated absence of the very name Nietzsche in this part of the *Grammatology* that repeats the genealogy. Derrida asks how Lévi-Strauss, while acknowledging Marx and Freud as his masters, can write the idyllic scenario recording his nocturnal observation of the Nambikwara as a nonviolent people of unsurpassed tenderness and intimacy. He can do so only because Rousseau has been substituted for Nietzsche in Lévi-Strauss's trinity of names (Marx, Rousseau, and Freud rather than Marx, Nietzsche, and Freud).

Here we touch on the question of the genealogy of the text, a philological question inseparable from the genealogy of morals. Genealogy seeks out the unsuspected ramifications of proper names, whether present or absent. At the beginning of Derrida's reading of Lévi-Strauss, he suggests that "the metaphor that would describe the genealogy of a text correctly is still forbidden" (*OG*, 101). One might be tempted to say, for example, that "a text is nothing but a system of roots," but to do so would be to contradict both the concept of system and the pattern of the roots. To read Lévi-Strauss genealogically is to see the resonances of Rousseau. What we learn from genealogy is the inevitability of one's heritage, or *Herkunft*, and the impossibility of attempting to make an absolute beginning, or *Ursprung*. Lévi-Strauss assumes (as in his use of Rousseau), that one can determine and circumscribe precisely what use one will make of one's intellectual roots, ignoring the complexities of their subterranean system. Nietzsche warns that "we are unknown to ourselves" and attempts to situate the many voices of his text in relation to their roots in (for example) science, tragedy, history, and the novel. Derrida's effort to "repeat" the genealogy of morals arises within this context. It is not a question of whether he is consciously or fully aware of the Nietzschean roots, still less of his being in command of the entire array of a manifold *Herkunft*. For Derrida, it is a matter of the rigor and modesty of a confessed repetition and mimesis, one that makes no claims of origin-ality—that is, it makes no claim to restore the presence of an origin—and so helps us to think beyond the constant temptations of hope and nostalgia.

NOTES

1. Making slight emendations, I have relied upon Kaufmann's translations of *EH* and *BT*; and Kaufmann and Hollingdale's translation of *GM*.

2. Jürgen Habermas, *The Discourse of Modernity*, trans. Frederick Lawrence (Cambridge, MA: MIT Press, 1987), 125–26. [*Ed. Note*—An excerpt of Habermas's essay is included in this volume.]

3. Michel Foucault, "Nietzsche, Genealogy, History," (hereafter cited in the text as *NGH*) in *Language, Counter-Memory, Practice*, trans. Donald F. Bouchard and Sherry Simon (Ithaca, NY: Cornell University Press, 1977), 140–42.

4. See Mikhail Bakhtin, *Problems of Dostoyevsky's Poetics*, ed. and trans. Caryl Emerson (Minneapolis: University of Minnesota Press, 1984).

5. See Foucault, *The Use of Pleasure*, trans. Robert Hurley (New York: Pantheon Books, 1985), 236, 238, 239.

6. See Michel Foucault, *Folie et deraison: Histoire de la folie* (Paris: Pion, 1961). Jacques Derrida, "Cogito and the History of Madness," in *Writing and Difference*, trans. Alan Bass (Chicago: University of Chicago Press, 1978), 31–63; Michel Foucault, "My Body, This Paper, This Fire," trans. Geoff Bennington, *Oxford Literary Review* 4: 1 (1979): 9–28.

7. See Descartes: *Philosophical Writings*, trans. and ed. Elizabeth Anscombe and Peter Thomas Geach (London: Thomas Nelson and Sons, 1954), esp. 61–65. Anglo-analytic philosophers may want to take note of the fact that the translation of the *Meditations* by G. E. M. Anscombe and Peter Geach coincides in a general way with Derrida's reading of the text. Anscombe and Geach pluralize the text's voices by placing the objections concerning madness and dreaming in quotation marks. Perhaps Anscombe and Geach were aided in translating as they did by the example of the play of voices and question-and-answer style in Wittgenstein's *Philosophical Investigations*.

8. Jacques Derrida, *Of Grammatology*, trans. Gayatri Spivak (Baltimore, MD: Johns Hopkins University Press, 1976), 114 (cited hereafter in the text as *OG* followed by the page number).

9. Claude Lévi-Strauss, *The Savage Mind* (Chicago: University of Chicago Press, 1966), 269.

16

Nietzsche, Deleuze, and the Genealogical Critique of Psychoanalysis
Between Church and State*

Alan D. Schrift

> What charity and delicate precision those Frenchmen possess! Even the most acute-eared of the Greeks must have approved of this art, and one thing they would even have admired and adored, the French *wittiness* of expression.
>
> —Nietzsche, *The Wanderer and His Shadow* 214

> Reading a text is never a scholarly exercise in search of what is signified, still less a highly textual exercise in search of a signifier. Rather, it is a productive use of the literary machine, a montage of desiring machines, a schizoid exercise that extracts from the text its literary force.
>
> —Deleuze and Guattari, *Anti-Oedipus*

When encountering Gilles Deleuze's writings, I cannot help thinking back to the signs that flash warnings to Harry in Hesse's *Steppenwolf:* "Magic Theater," "Entrance Not for Everyone," "For Madmen Only," "Price of Admittance Your Mind."[1] Entering Deleuze's texts is for many people a frightening, indeed, even an overwhelming experience. Yet if we follow the trajectory of Deleuze's thought on Nietzsche, we see it moving from a more or less traditional philosophical exegesis in

---

*Edited and revised by the author from its original publication in *International Studies in Philosophy* 24:2 (Summer 1992): 41–52. Reprinted with the permission of the publisher.

his 1962 text *Nietzsche and Philosophy*[2] to a self-conscious utilization of Nietzsche for purposes other than an *explication de texte*. Appreciation for this development can make Deleuze's work much more accessible, particularly for the Anglophonic audience that is only now beginning to widely embrace his writings. In what follows, I will comment only briefly about his early text, focusing my attention instead on his later work in an attempt to show how certain Deleuzian and Nietzschean ideas intersect and work with one another. Ultimately, I will argue, the critique of *Anti-Oedipus* can be sketched in terms of the ways it follows an analytic pattern elaborated nearly a century earlier by Nietzsche in *On the Genealogy of Morals*, the text that Deleuze and Guattari called "the great book of modern ethnology."[3]

Deleuze's *Nietzsche and Philosophy* is an excellent study that played a large role in generating the interest in Nietzsche's thought in France that we see during the sixties and seventies.[4] In this text, Deleuze directs himself against what he regards as a misguided attempt to strike a compromise between the Hegelian dialectic and Nietzsche's genealogy. Where Hegel's thinking is always guided by the movement toward some unifying synthesis, Nietzsche, in contrast, is seen to affirm multiplicity and rejoice in diversity.[5] Deleuze comes to view the entirety of Nietzsche's corpus as a polemical response to the Hegelian dialectic: "To the famous positivity of the negative Nietzsche opposes his own discovery: the negativity of the positive."[6] Focusing on the qualitative difference in Nietzsche between active and reactive forces, Deleuze argues that the *Übermensch*'s mastery is derived from her or his ability to *actively* negate the slave's reactive forces, even though the latter may often be quantitatively greater. In other words, whereas the slave moves from the negative premise ("you are other and evil") to the positive judgment ("therefore I am good"), the master works from the positive differentiation of self ("I am good") to the negative corollary ("you are other and bad"). There is, according to Deleuze, a qualitative difference at the origin of force, and it is the genealogist's task to attend to this differential and genetic element of force that Nietzsche calls "will to power."[7] Thus, whereas in the Hegelian dialectic of master and slave, the reactive negation of the other has as its consequence the positive affirmation of self, Nietzsche reverses this situation: the master's active positing of self is accompanied by and results in a negation of the slave's reactive force.

Showing the impropriety of reading Nietzsche as a neo-Hegelian dialectician and offering the first French alternative to Heidegger's interpretation of Nietzsche, the text *Nietzsche and Philosophy* occupies an important place in the development of post-structural French thought.[8] While one can learn a great deal by reading this text, I find Deleuze's later texts, written in collaboration with the radical psychoanalyst Félix Guattari, more interesting, albeit more difficult, insofar as they seem to operate outside of the discursive practices of traditional philosophy. That is to say, these later texts move beyond those organizing rules that govern what can and cannot be said within philosophy insofar as they acknowledge the political and libidinal dimensions inscribed in every philosophical gesture.

In the remark that would become the closing entry in the nonbook published as *The Will to Power*, Nietzsche announced that the solution to the riddle of his Dionysian world was "This world is will to power—and nothing besides! And you yourselves are also will to power—and nothing besides!" (*KSA* 11:38[12]). He thereby issued a challenge to all future dualisms: it would no longer be possible for understanding to proceed according to a model that operated in terms of a simple binary logic.[9] Opting for a polyvalent monism, Nietzsche's announcement frustrates all subsequent dualistic attempts to divide and hierarchize the world neatly into dichotomous groups: good or evil, minds or bodies, truths or errors, us or them. The world is much more complicated than such dualistic thinking acknowledges, and Nietzsche's announcement that all is will to power suggests the radically contextual, optional, and contingent nature of even those most "obvious" determinations and distinctions that are legitimated by appeal to a rigidly hierarchized metanarrative of binary opposition. It has been one of the tasks of the twentieth century to respond to the anti-dualistic challenge announced by Nietzsche's will to power, and it is in this context that we should understand Deleuze and Guattari's attempt to show the complicity between binary opposites that stands at the heart of their "magic formula . . . PLURALISM = MONISM."[10]

This semiotically condensed formula marks out one of the points of contact between the projects of Nietzsche and Deleuze. It applies as well to the project of Michel Foucault, whose work at many points intersects the work of Deleuze.[11] When Nietzsche claimed that everything is will to power, he drew our attention away from substances, subjects, and things and focused that attention instead on the relations *between* these substantives. These relations, according to Nietzsche, were relations of forces: forces of attraction and repulsion, domination and subordination, imposition and reception, and so on. If there is a metaphysics in Nietzsche, and I am not at all sure that there is or that it is particularly helpful to view Nietzsche in these terms (as Heidegger did), then this metaphysics will be a dynamic, "process" metaphysics and not a substance-metaphysics, a metaphysics of becomings and not of beings. These processes, these becomings, will be processes of forces: becomings-stronger or becomings-weaker, enhancement or impoverishment. There is, for Nietzsche, no escaping these becomings other than death. The goal he advocates, therefore, is not to seek Being but to strive for the balance-sheet of one's life to include more becomings-stronger than -weaker, more overcomings than goings-under.

When we look to the work of Deleuze and Foucault, we can see them making double use of Nietzsche's will to power. Both Deleuze and Foucault engage in projects that reformulate traditional binary disjunctions between given alternatives in terms of a pluralistic continuum in which choices are always local and relative rather than global and absolute. Whether it be a continuum of desiring production or power-knowledge, the model they appeal to, explicitly or implicitly, takes the form of Nietzsche's "monism" of the will to power, a monism not in Heidegger's sense of will to power as Nietzsche's foundational answer to the metaphysical question of the Being of beings, but in Deleuze's sense of will to power as the differential of forces. This is to say, where Heidegger understood will to power in terms of a logic of Being, an onto-logic, Deleuze situates will to power within a differential logic of affirmation and negation that facilitates the interpretation and evaluation of active and reactive forces.[12] Will to power thus operates at the genealogical and not the ontological level, at the level of the qualitative and quantitative differences between forces and the different values bestowed upon those forces rather than at the level of Being and beings.[13] In going beyond good and evil, beyond truth and error, to the claim that all is will to power, Nietzsche attempted to think relationality without substances, relations without *relata*, difference without exclusion. And in so doing, his thought serves as a model for both Foucault's analyses of power relations in the absence of a subject and Deleuze's desiring assemblages conceived in terms of a logic of events.

In addition to using Nietzsche's formal structure as a model, Deleuze and Foucault each seize upon what we might call the "content" of Nietzsche's will to power, and together they offer expanded accounts of the two component poles: will and power. While French thought in general has been working for the past thirty years under the aegis of the three so-called "masters of suspicion" Nietzsche, Freud, and Marx, we can understand Deleuze and Foucault privileging Nietzsche over Marx and Freud on precisely this point. Marx operates primarily with the register of power and Freud operates primarily within the register of desire. Yet each appears blind to the overlapping of these two registers, and when they do relate them, one is clearly subordinate to the other. Nietzsche's will to power, on the other hand, makes impossible any privileging of one over the other, and his thinking functions in terms of an inclusive conjunction of desire and power. That is to say, for Nietzsche, "will to power" is redundant insofar as will wills power and power manifests itself only through will. In privileging Nietzsche over Marx or Freud, both Foucault and Deleuze recognize the complicity between the poles of will and power and, as a consequence, they can each focus on one of the poles without diminishing the importance of the other pole or excluding it altogether from their analyses. Thus Foucault engaged in a highly sophisticated analysis of power that, following Nietzsche's example, focused not on the subjects of power but on power *relations*, the relations of force that operate within social practices and social systems. And within this analysis, will and desire play an integral role in directing the relations of power. Where Nietzsche saw a continuum of will to power and sought to incite a becoming-stronger of will to power to rival the progressive becoming-weaker he associated with modernity, Foucault sees power relations operating along a continuum of repression and production and he sought to encourage a becoming-productive of power to rival the increasingly repressive power of the pastoral.

In a similar fashion, Deleuze, both in his own studies and especially in his work with Guattari, has focused on the *willing* of power—desire. He, too, refrains from subjectifying desire while recognizing the intimate and multiple couplings of desire and power.[14] In *Nietzsche and Philosophy*, Deleuze first linked the notion of desire with will to power, and the insight that desire is productive develops out of his reflection on will to power in terms of the productivity of both active and reactive forces. In *Anti-Oedipus*, he and Guattari introduce the desiring machine as a machinic, functionalist translation of Nietzschean will to power. A desiring machine is a functional assemblage of a desiring will and the object desired. Deleuze's goal, I think, is to place desire into a functionalist vocabulary, a machinic index, so as to avoid the personification/subjectivation of desire in a substantive will, ego, unconscious, or self. In so doing, he can avoid the paradox Nietzsche sometimes faced when speaking of will to power without a subject doing the willing or implying that will to power was both the producing "agent" and the "object" produced. To speak of desire as part of an assemblage, to refuse to reify or personify desire at the subject pole, recognizes that desire and the object desired arise together. Deleuze rejects the account of desire as lack shared by Freud, Lacan, Sartre, and many others.[15] That is to say, desire does not arise in response to the perceived lack of the object desired, nor is desire a state produced in the subject by the lack of the object. Instead, desire is, as it were, a part of the infrastructure:[16] it is constitutive of the objects desired as well as the social field in which they appear.[17] Desire, in other words, again like Nietzsche's will to power, is productive. And as Nietzsche sought to keep will to power multiple so that it might appear in multiple forms, at once producer and product, a monism and a pluralism, so too Deleuze wants desire to be multiple, polyvocal.[18] Nietzsche encouraged the maximization of strong, healthy will to power while acknowledging the necessity, the inevitability of weak, decadent will to power. Deleuze advocates that desire be productive while recognizing that desire will sometimes be destructive and will at times have to be repressed while at other times it will seek and produce its own repression. Analyzing this phenomenon of desire seeking its own repression is one of the goals of Deleuze and Guattari's schizoanalysis, and we should not fail to notice the structural similarity between desire desiring its own repression and Nietzsche's discovery in *On the Genealogy of Morals* that the will would rather will nothingness than not will.

To speak very generally, we can say that as Deleuze appropriates Nietzsche's thought, will to power is transformed into a desiring-machine: Nietzsche's biologism becomes Deleuze's machinism; Nietzsche's "everything is will to power" becomes Deleuze's "everything is desire"; Nietzsche's affirmation of healthy will to power becomes Deleuze's affirmation of desiring-production. In the remaining few pages, I would like to suggest some ways Deleuze and Guattari model their critique of psychoanalysis on Nietzsche's genealogical critique of Christian morality. The details of Deleuze and Guattari's critique of psychoanalytic theory and practice and the relations between psychoanalysis and capitalism are far too complex to be addressed in a short essay. There is a certain method to the madness of their account, however, and it is clear that the author of the *Anti-Christ* has influenced the development of the argument by the authors of the *Anti-Oedipus*.

I will begin by providing a selective paraphrase of certain moments in the second essay of the *Genealogy*, where Nietzsche turns to the origins of guilt and bad conscience. These origins lie in the economic relation of creditor and debtor. The moral concept "guilt," conceived as a debt that is essentially unredeemable, has its origin in the economic, legal notion of debt as essentially repayable. We see this in the origin of punishment, which as retribution emerges from the inability to repay the debt. *Schuld*, which translates both debt and guilt, is part of the strange logic of compensation that seeks to establish equivalences between creditors and debtors: because everything has its price and all things can be paid for, the debtors, having made a promise to repay, would offer a substitute payment of something they possessed: their body, their spouse, their freedom, even their life. Here Nietzsche locates the primitive intertwining of guilt and suffering: suffering will balance debts to the extent that the creditors get pleasure from making the debtor suffer. There is, for Nietzsche, a basic joy in the exercising of mastery, and, by making others suffer, the creditors thus participate in the pleasures of the masters.

When he turns to modern cultures, Nietzsche observes that punishment now appears no longer as the result of the human desire for pleasure and mastery but instead as the consequence of God's judgment. Ashamed of his instincts for cruelty, modern man has to invent free will to justify suffering: punishment now appears as deserved because one could have done otherwise. The "moral" function of punishment is thus to awaken the feeling of guilt, and it is supposed to function as an instrument to create bad conscience. To this account, Nietzsche offers his own "original" account of the origin of bad conscience: bad conscience is a serious illness contracted when human beings first entered into a community. It is, says Nietzsche, analogous to, or perhaps a repetition of, the fateful event that confronted sea animals when they were compelled to become land animals: in each case, all previous instincts were suddenly devalued and suspended. Anticipating the Freudian model of tension-reduction, Nietzsche claims that the inability to discharge their instincts leads these instincts to be turned inward. This "internalization [*Verinnerlichung*] of man" (*GM* II:16) says Nietzsche, is the origin of "bad conscience" as the instinct for hostility, cruelty, joy in prosecuting and attacking, the desire for change and destruction all are inhibited from being discharged and are instead turned against the possessor of these instincts. Bad conscience, that uncanniest of illnesses, Nietzsche concludes, is man's suffering of himself.

In an analytic move that clearly inspires Deleuze and Guattari's materialist psychiatry, Nietzsche links this psychological account of bad conscience to the origin of the state as he offers an account of the establishment of society from out of the "state of nature," which echoes the tale told by Hobbes much more than the myth told by Locke or Rousseau. Bad conscience does not originate gradually or voluntarily, but all at once. This change is initiated by an act of violence: the institution of the state. The state is a violent, tyrannical, oppressive machine, created by those unconscious, involuntary artists and beasts of prey—the conquerors and masters who impose form on nomadic, formless masses. Lacking bad conscience themselves, it originates through these masters making latent in others the instinct for freedom (the "will to power"), which, when repressed and incarcerated, can only be turned against itself. In other words, while masters and artists are able to vent their will to power on others, the weak can only vent their will to power on themselves.

Bad conscience, Nietzsche tells us, is an illness as pregnancy is an illness (*GM* II:19), and he concludes the Second Essay by exposing this illness's progeny to be Christian morality and the Church. As society evolved, the creditor/debtor relation took the form of a relation between the present generation and its ancestors: we pay back our ancestors by obeying their customs. Our debt to our ancestors increases to the extent that the power of the community increases. Ultimately, our ancestors are transfigured into gods and, in successive generations, this unpaid debt to our ancestors is inherited with interest. As the power of the community increases, the divinity of the ancestors also increases. With Christianity, Nietzsche sees what he calls a "stroke of genius" in the eventual moralization of debt/guilt and duty, as the Christian God, "the maximum god attained so far," is accompanied by maximum indebtedness. Christianity's stroke of genius was to have God sacrifice himself for the guilt of humanity. By sacrificing himself for the debtor, the creditor both removed the debt and made the debt eternal and ultimately unredeemable. The origin of the Christian God is this mad will to guilt and punishment, this will to a punishment incapable of becoming equal to the guilt. This new guilt before God results in the complete deification of God as holy judge and hangman, at once man's infinite antithesis and the ultimate instrument of his self-torture (*GM* II:22).

Nietzsche's *On the Genealogy of Morals* shows the ways in which the ascetic priests, in the form of the founders of Christianity and the ideologues of science, have constructed an interpretation of the modern world in which they are made to appear essential (cf. *A* 26). Deleuze and Guattari argue that the psychoanalyst is the "most recent figure of the priest"[19] and throughout *Anti-Oedipus* their analyses of the practices of psychoanalysis parallel the practices of Christianity as analyzed by Nietzsche. Like the early priests, psychoanalysts have reinterpreted the world in a way that makes themselves indispensable. The whole psychoanalytic edifice is constructed on the basis of the Oedipal drama, and the primary task of psychoanalysis is to successfully Oedipalize its public. Nietzsche showed how much of Christianity's practice requires convincing its adherents of their guilt and sin in order to make tenable its claim of redemptive power. Deleuze and Guattari take a similar approach, developing at length the ways in which the psychological liberation promised by psychoanalysis requires first that it imprison libidinal economy within the confines of the family. To Nietzsche's "internalization of man," they add man's Oedipalization: Oedipus repeats the split movement of Nietzschean bad conscience that at once projected onto the other while turning back against oneself, as the unsatisfied desire to eliminate and replace the father is accompanied by guilt for having such desire. They view psychoanalytic interpretive practices as no less reductive than the interpretations of Nietzsche's ascetic priests. Just as Nietzsche's priests reduce all events to a moment within the logic of divine reward and punishment, Deleuze and Guattari's psychoanalysts reduce all desire to a form of familial fixation. Like Nietzsche's ascetic priests, psychoanalysts have created for themselves a mask of health that has the power to tyrannize the healthy by poisoning their conscience. Where Nietzsche notes the *irony* of the Christian God sacrificing himself for humanity *out of love*, Deleuze and Guattari ironically chronicle the various expressions of the psychoanalysts' concern for their Oedipally crippled patients. The ultimate outcomes of these ironic twists also parallel one another: where Christianity's self-sacrificing God makes infinite its adherents guilt and debt, psychoanalysis creates its own infinite debt in the form of inexhaustible transference and interminable analysis.[20]

What is, I think, the most interesting transformation of Nietzsche's analysis is the way Deleuze and Guattari adapt Nietzsche's link between the rise of Christianity and the rise of the state to their discussion of libidinal and political economy. They want to introduce desire into the social field at all levels, and this prompts their critique of psychoanalysis. Freud could only view libidinal social investments as subliminal, and he interprets all social relations as desexualized representations of unconscious desire. Likewise, when sexual relations do appear in the social field, they are interpreted by Freud as symbolic representations of the Oedipal family. Deleuze and Guattari want to liberate desire from its enslavement within the theater of representation, and they reject the reductive familialism that sees the family everywhere while it obscures all relations of wealth, class, gender, race, status—in other words, all social relations outside the family. Because social production is libidinal and libidinal production is social, they claim it is a mistake to desexualize the social field.

> The truth is that sexuality is everywhere: in the way that a bureaucrat fondles his records, a judge administers justice, a businessman causes money to circulate; in the way the bourgeoisie fucks the proletariat; and so on. And there is no need to resort to metaphors, any more than for the libido to go by way of metamorphoses. Hitler got the fascists sexually aroused. Flags, nations, armies, banks get a lot of people aroused.[21]

Revising both Marx and Freud, Deleuze and Guattari conclude that insofar as desire is constitutive of the social field, "social production is desiring-production *under determinate conditions.*"[22]

Deleuze and Guattari "replace the theatrical or familial model of the unconscious with a more political model: the factory instead of the theater."[23] The question of desire is one not of dramatic familial representation but of material production, which is to say, a political question. This is the point at which they replace psychoanalysis with schizoanalysis or, as they put it, this makes clear the need to "schizoanalyze the psychoanalyst."[24] Psychoanalysis has failed to recognize that the successful Oedipalization of its public depends upon the phenomenon discussed earlier of desire desiring its own repression. For Deleuze and Guattari, the discovery of this phenomenon is associated first and foremost with Wilhelm Reich,[25] who refused to explain fascism in terms of the false consciousness of the masses. Instead, Reich formulated an explanation that takes the desires of the masses into account: "they *wanted* fascism" and it is this perverse manifestation of desire that must be explained. For Reich, the explanation comes in terms of the pleasures of exercising authority that are vicariously experienced by the "little man's" identification with the "Führer."[26] Deleuze and Guattari's account of this desire, along with their fascination with the relation of the officer to the machine in Kafka's "Penal Colony" and their analyses of psychoanalysis, leads them to Nietzsche's *Genealogy of Morals*. Here, in Nietzsche's account of the will to nothingness as preferable to not willing and in bad conscience choosing to make itself suffer rather than relinquish the pleasure in making suffer, they locate their answer to Reich's question of the link between psychic repression and social repression in the libidinal economy of fascism. Where Reich saw desire activated through a passive identification of the masses with their fascist master(s), Nietzsche saw the ascetic desire to make itself suffer as perverse but fundamentally *active* and ultimately *positive*—through this perverse desire, as he notes, *"the will itself was saved"* (*GM* III:28).

From their observations of Reich and Nietzsche, Deleuze and Guattari draw the following conclusion: desire is productive, it must be productive, and it will be productive. If a social field does not allow for desire to be productive in nonrepressive forms, then it will produce in whatever forms are available to it, even those that it recognizes to be socially or psychically repressive. Like Nietzsche's will to power, Deleuze and Guattari claim, desire must be analyzed locally, relative to the social field in which it operates. There can be no global, universal, or totalizing judgment concerning desire. As Nietzsche's *GM* III analyzed the concrete practices of the ascetic priests in terms of the enhancement and impoverishment of will to power, Deleuze and Guattari continue to question political and psychoanalytic practices in terms of productive and repressive libidinal capacities. Investigating the shared genealogy of church and state in terms of the diverse manifestations of desire and power, Deleuze and Guattari show themselves to be among the philosophers of the future to whom Nietzsche addressed his writings, philosophers who, appropriating Nietzsche's description of an earlier generation of French philosophers with whom he identified, create *"real ideas . . .* ideas of the kind that produce ideas" (*WS* 214).

NOTES

An earlier version of sections from this paper were presented in October 1988, at Northwestern University at the annual meeting of the Society for Phenomenology and Existential Philosophy, and a subsequent version was presented to the Department of Comparative Literature, University of Washington, Seattle. Most of the written text of this paper, published as "Between Church and State: Nietzsche, Deleuze, and the Critique of Psychoanalysis," in *International Studies in Philosophy* 24, no. 2 (Summer 1992): 41–52, was revised as part of the chapter on Deleuze in my *Nietzsche's French Legacy: A Genealogy of Poststructuralism* (New York: Routledge, 1995).

1. For translations of Nietzsche's works, I use Kaufmann and Hollingdale's *GM* and *WP*; and Hollingdale's *WS*.

2. Gilles Deleuze, *Nietzsche and Philosophy*, trans. Hugh Tomlinson (New York: Columbia University Press, 1983). One of the few critics to discuss this work in the context of French poststructuralism is Vincent P. Pecora, in "Deleuze's Nietzsche and Post-Structuralism," *Sub-Stance* 48 (1986): 34–50. Although largely critical of Deleuze's reading of Nietzsche, Pecora is, I think, correct in indicating the formative role played by Deleuze's replacement of "*le travail de la dialectique*" by the play of '*différence*'" in the emergence of poststructuralism (36).

3. Gilles Deleuze and Félix Guattari, *Anti-Oedipus*, translated by Robert Hurley, Mark Seem, and Helen R. Lane (Minneapolis: University of Minnesota Press, 1983), 190.

4. This can be seen in the two surveys of recent French philosophy to be translated into English from the French; see Vincent Descombes, *Modern French Philosophy*, trans. L. Scott-Fox and J. M. Harding (Cambridge: Cambridge University Press, 1980), esp. 187–90, and Luc Ferry and Alain Renaut, *French Philosophy of the Sixties: An Essay on Antihumanism*, trans. Mary Schnackenberg Cattani (Amherst: University of Massachusetts Press, 1990), 68–71. For a further discussion of Nietzsche's French reception, see my *Nietzsche's French Legacy*.

5. See Deleuze, *Nietzsche and Philosophy*, 197.

6. *Nietzsche and Philosophy*, 180.

7. *Nietzsche and Philosophy*, 50.

8. The importance of Nietzsche in Deleuze's thought and poststructuralist French philosophy is one of the leading themes of Ronald Bogue's fine introductory text *Deleuze and Guattari* (London: Routledge, 1989); see, in particular, his concluding comments, 156–63.

9. I have addressed Nietzsche's critique of binary, oppositional thinking in much greater detail elsewhere, particularly in relation to Derrida and deconstruction. See "Genealogy and/ as Deconstruction: Nietzsche, Derrida, and Foucault on Philosophy as Critique" in *Postmodernism and Continental Philosophy*, edited by Hugh J. Silverman and Donn Welton (Albany: State University of New York Press, 1988), 193–213, "The becoming-postmodern of philosophy," in *After the Future: Postmodern Times and Places*, edited by Gary Shapiro (Albany: State University of New York Press, 1990), 99–113; and the chapter on Derrida in *Nietzsche's French Legacy*.

10. Gilles Deleuze and Félix Guattari, *A Thousand Plateaus*, translated by Brian Massumi (Minneapolis: University of Minnesota Press, 1987), 20.

11. I wish to bring in Foucault at this point because I think it helps to understand the complex relations between the careers of Foucault and Deleuze in terms of their mutual alliances with Nietzsche.

12. See Deleuze, *Nietzsche and Philosophy*, 49–55.

13. Cf. Deleuze, *Nietzsche and Philosophy*, 220: "Heidegger gives an interpretation of Nietzschean philosophy closer to his own thought than to Nietzsche's. . . . Nietzsche is opposed to every conception of affirmation which would find its foundation in Being, and its determination in the being of man." I address and criticize Heidegger's interpretation of will to power in some detail elsewhere; see my *Nietzsche and the Question of Interpretation* (New York: Routledge, 1990), 53–73.

14. See, for example, Gilles Deleuze and Félix Guattari's *Kafka: Toward a Minor Litera-*

ture, translated by Dana Polan (Minneapolis: University of Minnesota Press, 1986), 56. Although I have linked Foucault with power and Deleuze with desire, I do not intend these linkages to be in any way exclusive. In fact, as further evidence of the rhizomatic connections between the careers of Deleuze and Foucault, we can here note that Foucault in 1972 credited *Deleuze* for being the first to thematize the question of power: "If the reading of your books (from *Nietzsche* to what I anticipate in *Capitalism and Schizophrenia*) has been essential for me, it is because they seem to go very far in exploring this problem: under the ancient theme of meaning, of the signifier and the signified, etc., you have developed the question of power, of the inequality of powers and their struggles." ("Intellectuals and Power: A Conversation between Michel Foucault and Gilles Deleuze," translated by Donald F. Bouchard and Sherry Simon in Michel Foucault, *Language, Counter-Memory, Practice*, edited by Donald F. Bouchard [Ithaca, NY: Cornell University Press, 1977], 213–14.)

15. This tradition goes back at least as far as Plato, who argues in the *Symposium* (200a–d) that one who desires something is necessarily in want of that thing. I discuss the Deleuzian critique of "desire as lack" in more detail elsewhere: see my "Spinoza, Nietzsche, Deleuze: An other discourse of desire" in Hugh Silverman, ed., *Philosophy and the Discourse of Desire* (New York: Routledge, Chapman and Hall, 2000), 173–85.

16. See the discussion of this point in Deleuze and Guattari, *Anti-Oedipus*, 348.

17. We might put this point another way and, using Benveniste's distinction, say that desire occupies both the place of the subject of the utterance (*sujet d'énonciation*) and the subject of the statement (*sujet d'énoncé*).

18. Cf. Deleuze and Guattari, *Kafka*, 57.

19. *Anti-Oedipus*, 108–12, 269, 332–33. See also *A Thousand Plateaus*, 154.

20. Cf. *Anti-Oedipus*, 64–65.

21. *Anti-Oedipus*, 293. (Translation altered slightly.)

22. *Anti-Oedipus*, 343.

23. Gilles Deleuze, Interview in *L'Arc* 49, 2nd ed. (1980), 99. See also *Anti-Oedipus*, 55.

24. *Anti-Oedipus*, 365.

25. See Wilhelm Reich, *The Mass Psychology of Fascism*, trans. Vincent R. Carfagno (London: Souvenir Press, 1970).

26. Cf. Reich, 63ff.

IV

ON POLITICS AND COMMUNITY

17

Nietzsche's Genealogy
Of Beauty and Community*

Salim Kemal

Nietzsche's genealogy explains value as an order of preferences constructed from some position in an underlying structure of power and domination. Rather than examine what "humanity" might mean in the actors' understanding of "individual goodness," for example, or how actors justify it as a principle of action, he explains how values such as humility and goodness become meaningful by showing that they "enact" the positions that actors have in conflictual power relations.

Consonantly with this account, Nietzsche talks of knowledge claims as interpretations,[1] of the style and creativity of values,[2] and of philosophers becoming "poets of our life" (*GS* 299). By this genealogical construal, all values, including the interpretations we valorize as knowledge, are only our own construction (e.g., *WP* 795, 1048, 816, and *GS* 299)[3] from a particular viewpoint, and cannot claim universal validity. And just as we cannot identify objects as works of art unless we acknowledge that they have been constructed, similarly for Nietzsche we may not hide all traces of the construction of values and still recognize them as values. Moreover, just as works embody or allow interpretations, whose sources and basis we can display, similarly we can analyze our knowledge and values genealogically to explain their basis in the particular perspectives and powers they serve.[4]

This account of genealogy also applies to aesthetic value, and in this chapter I shall first present some results of the genealogy of beauty. These lead to a distinctive conception of community that genealogy sustains, which we shall consider in the chapter's last section.

---

*Originally published in *Journal of the British Society for Phenomenology* 21:3 (October 1990): 234–49. Reprinted with the permission of the journal editor.

THE GENEALOGY OF BEAUTY

Nietzsche's construal of value as construct or art is double edged: by changing our conception of cognitive and moral values, he also questions our conception of beauty. The more thoroughly he develops criteria for grasping morality or knowledge *as art*, identifying the perspectives from which they originate, the more clearly we can analyze *aesthetic* values *as art*. Just as we see moral or cognitive order as interpretations and as modes of becoming rather than being,[5] similarly we can examine aesthetic value to identify its origin[6] in the needs it serves. That is, Nietzsche can now "envisage the *aesthetic problem* [*itself*] from the point of view of *the artist* (*the creator*)" and his or her *production* of value rather than of the spectator who responds to experiences of beauty (*GM* III:6; italics added).

This analysis results in a number of theses about value. First, aesthetic values are not mimetic of any being or reality beyond our present world, from whose standpoint we judge our own human existence as an "appearance."[7] For Nietzsche, there is no *other* reality that we will escape to from our "mere" appearances,[8] and when aesthetic value is effective, it "signifies [our present] reality *once more*, only selected, strengthened, corrected" (*TI* "Reason" 6).[9]

If values concern only our present reality, then we cannot justify them by showing how well they reflect or give us access to some other world—usually of fully rational beings and universal truths. In terms of "being" and "becoming" (see note 5), we do not refer our values to a state of perfect being to justify them by displaying their universality. Rather, Nietzsche emphasizes our constructive activity, our constant "becoming" in our particular human conditions.

Second, to articulate that human conception, Nietzsche focuses on the capacity of works for the fullest kind of oppositional forces because these embody construction and becoming.[10] Our feeling for life, the delight we feel in works, resides in "communicat[ing] something of the artists' victorious energy" (*WP* 802) over materials where the given form never completely masks traces of its construction. Third, to affirm a nonmetaphysical account he explains our construction of aesthetic value and order through notions of "seeing," "taste," and "style."[11]

Taste is the activity of organizing elements (*GS* 290). Because they have taste, agents have an economy in which they can give significance and order to different elements. To have taste of a particular kind, to construct an economy of a particular kind, is to have a particular style. Style constitutes the actors.[12] Actors without style lack taste and so have no sense of economy. As they do not possess a sense of order, they have no aims and so no means, and pursue the most pressing present impulses. Yet satisfaction of these impulses does not bring amelioration because there is no limit or order to their desires. Only style brings satisfaction, allowing the actors' behavior to be free rather than random or wild. And for Nietzsche "one thing is needful: that a human being should attain satisfaction with himself, whether it be by means of this or that poetry or art; only then is a human being tolerable to behold" (*GS* 290).

Nietzsche's emphasis on construction, his rejection of the need for values to be universalizable, and his use of "individual satisfaction" as a criterion for value, all these make possible only a *local* order. We cannot point to some teleology of styles or some "real" order or substance of which these styles must be a part in order to gain validity.[13] But he also maintains that the absence of a teleology does not deprive us of preferences. He writes that the "grand style originates when the beautiful carries off victory over the monstrous" (*WS* 96).[14] Some works are preferred over others because they cut deeper, in the sense of exposing even the most monstrous elements and implications of a perspective, and empower us as agents to deal with that perspective. These works implicate subjects with a greater capacity for action,[15] and let us see through to the tensions and power at the basis of each work.[16] Only through engagement with this tension can we keep the antimetaphysical, becoming, and interpretive part of our feeling for life from calcifying into being. Yet our preferences always occur from a perspective, so that no hierarchy is permanent or expands beyond its point of view.

Here we genealogically analyze works as particulars and do not seek rules we can prescribe for analyzing values generally. Genealogy discerns the particular construction, style, economy, and so on lying at its origin, and displays its critical power in reordering given aesthetic values to make clear how they arise from their basis. That is, the activity of genealogy shows itself in constituting as its object the construction implicated in what actors may wrongly think of as self-sufficient aesthetic values. This genealogical diagnosis may produce only an interpretation, but still genealogy constitutes as its object that interpretation of the value and its origins. In doing so genealogy exhibits itself in that object or provides us with an insight about the particular but yields nothing that we can generalize. Its success lies in constituting its particular values without providing rules we can extend from diagnosing one object to another.

In other words, genealogy is not a method. If it were, we would expect that a practiced genealogist could issue instructions to a novice, setting out what needs to be done to carry out a genealogical analysis. But the practiced genealogist cannot expect to issue any instructions more specific than "look for the origins of aesthetic values" that might constitute a set of methodological principles. This is because analysts may make good their claim that aesthetic values are a result of construction from a particular viewpoint only by exhibiting the construct at work in any value. Yet that construction does not occur in the same way in every case, and for the practiced genealogists to show the novice how to proceed, they would have to exhibit how that construction occurs in every case. That is, they would have to carry out a genealogical analysis in that case, knowing also that their analysis may not serve other values. And such repeated analysis does not help the novice learn any methodological rules of genealogy. When the novice does learn from the particular example, we may suggest, he gains models for his own analysis of particulars. But he does not gain any methodological principles that will instruct him in generally analyzing genealogically, for the genealogical reunderstanding of value *is* what the instructions would have to consist in—this *genealogy* is what must be done. By displaying how a value is constructed, genealogy shows that the values are only an interpretation, as it shows itself only in the interpretations it provides, these must depend on the object—the aesthetic value and construction—being considered. Therefore, from the genealogy of one object we cannot expect to derive general conclusions applicable to another: at best, the first provides a model for another genealogist; it does not yield the rules for a method.

Further, genealogy depends on a particular viewpoint and is itself an interpretation. Genealogists analyze the advent of a value by displaying its origin in a particular style and taste. And the particular analysis they construct itself has an origin. That is, not only are genealogists aware of the construction of value and the interpretative nature of value claims, but their own constitution of objects reveals the analyst's standpoint. Accordingly genealogy is always tied to its object from its present particular viewpoint, for which the constitution of the relation of origin and value in the object is arraigned.

We can illustrate this by considering another part of Nietzsche's genealogy of aesthetic values. When Nietzsche sees aesthetic value as a constructed tension, he implies that this value encompasses more than beauty alone, for ugly objects too can embody "the artist's victorious energy" (ibid. [sic]). This is part of a wider claim, whereby any attempt to make beauty the sole aesthetic value signifies something about the valuer. Having denied values any etiolated and purely rational foundation, Nietzsche treats them as criteria for their own origins, and argues that we show what conception of subject and life we favor when we choose values. Accordingly, aesthetic value is considered from the point of view of how it satisfies a need and so gains value to the extent that it is appropriate to a particular type of human being.

In *The Birth of Tragedy* Nietzsche developed this notion by linking Apollo with the "apotheosis of the *principium individuationis*" (*BT* 4). Individuals construct beauty and, by imposing form, also form themselves as agents for that beautiful illusion that redeems chaos. "And so, side by side with the *aesthetic necessity for beauty*, there occur the demands "know thyself" and "nothing in excess"' (*BT* 4; italics added). Similarly, he writes, "*the* beautiful exists just as little as does *the* good, or *the* true. In every case it is a question of the conditions of the preservation of a certain type of man."

In accepting a value, then, we also commit ourselves to an appropriate conception of man and life. In other words, our human, physiological life "itself evaluates through us *when* we establish values" (*TI* "Morality" 5). In effect, we enact values, revealing our commitment to a particular kind of life and subject. For example, a system of values that opposes humanity to a God-given goodliness and value is committed to a "declining, debilitated, weary, condemned life" (ibid.) because it is occasioned when we lose touch with our human physiological existence and can no longer act for ourselves, accepting in full how far we are from grace and divinity. That spiritualized morality, so to speak, enacts a particular conception of humanity. Its specific imperatives are oriented by an implicit assumption that humanity is inferior to the extent that it lacks the attributes of divinity. By contrast, a human morality would enact a value that conceives of us as actors capable of living with our mortal existence.[17]

Similarly, aesthetic values enact this commitment to action or its opposite. Where delight, pleasure, or happiness comes from an increase in power, from reminding us of the "artist's victorious energy," they result in beauty. "In the beautiful, man sets himself as the standard for perfection" (*TI* "Skirmishes" 19) by acknowledging the origin of this aesthetic value in our present human reality. Here, "perfection" is congruent with the physiological account Nietzsche thinks appropriate to our humanity. "A species *cannot* do otherwise than affirm itself alone in this manner [through the beautiful]. Its *deepest* instinct, that of self-presentation and self-aggrandizement, is still visible in such sublimated forms" (ibid.). Beauty exemplifies our construction and ordering of the world; it is not a matter of contemplation and understanding but of constructing and participation.

This sense of beauty as an engagement with events and values may be explained further by contrasting it with ugliness, to show how both aesthetic values depend on our activity (*BT* "Self-Criticism" 2).[18] Here what art does is not *be* beautiful, as if it were enough to have art for the sake of art. Rather, ugliness signals decline while beauty signals health, and both these claims are conclusions we arrive at as a result of tracing aesthetic values as a construct or art. Beauty and ugliness signal how successfully we act upon the world and the commitments we enact. Where we exhibit a commitment to creating and developing meanings, there we gain beauty and happiness (*A* 1). Accordingly, beautiful art is a stimulus to life because the subject who grasps beauty must be active in promoting life. A subject who fails to grasp beauty, or who is given to ugliness, shows he lacks that stimulus. Thus, "every token of exhaustion, of heaviness, of age, of weariness, every kind of freedom, whether convulsive or paralytic, above all the smell, color, and shape of dissolution, of decomposition, though it be attenuated to the point of being no more than a symbol—all this calls forth the same reaction, the value judgement "ugly" (ibid.).

Nietzsche makes this claim more forcefully later in *Twilight of the Idols*, when he criticizes *art pour l'art*. The questions to raise about art concern not its "moralizing tendency" but rather "What does art do? does it not praise? does it not glorify? does it not select? does it not highlight? By doing all this it *strengthens* or *weakens* certain valuations" (*TI* "Skirmishes" 24). And it does this necessarily, as a "prerequisite for the artist being an artist at all" because the values he creates also enact the subject's relation to the world.

GENEALOGY AND REDEMPTION

At the basis of Nietzsche's analysis of moral and other values is a conception of creativity that redeems interpretation (*GM* III:24). For philosophers of the new age, nourished by genealogy, "their 'knowing' is *creating*, their creating is a legislation, their will to truth is—*will to power*" (*BGE* 211; cf. *BGE* 203, 212, 213, etc.). Instead of a universal viewpoint from which to judge actions, for genealogy there are actors who generate appraisals; instead of a single uniform history, there are interpretations generated from diverse viewpoints; and instead of following rules, the genealogist creates values.

In his writings Nietzsche seems to think of creativity as an activity that involves producing original works rather than merely following rules; where the works have only the status of interpretations precisely because they are created, and so do not claim any metaphysical validity; where the results of the activity do not serve as rules for others but are at best instances where those others may be their own genealogists. Although there is no occasion where Nietzsche explicitly states and defends this conception of creativity, it seems intrinsic to the nature and function of genealogy. To make clearer this sense, we may develop Nietzsche's account of genealogy as redemption.

The stress on creativity is already apparent in Nietzsche's explanation of particularity. Genealogy is tied to the particular because it does not operate by following given rules but by producing order. In other words, we cannot expect to follow prescriptive rules in genealogy because to do so is less than creative. Where we have rules and know when they apply, the actor needs only to act as the rules dictate, and no issue of creativity arises. While it is possible to follow rules imaginatively or unimaginatively, to show initiative or to be hidebound, these are matters of exercizing judgment, in which we discern the appropriate rule for a given situation. Whatever flexibility is present in this judging is also present in the activity of genealogy; but the latter involves much more because it constitutes or creates the relation of power to value as an object. Indeed, in a sense genealogy is our awareness of the fact that we create moral value and rules: only when we forget this creating do rules become things that stand over us, as instructions of what to do in a given situation.

In valuing objects, Nietzsche suggests, we can ask: Is the artist's "basic instinct directed towards art, or is it not rather directed towards the meaning of art, which is *life*?" (ibid.). Artists who turn to art in the hope of discovering rules for their own behavior thwart their own ability to act for themselves. Even to follow a rule subjects must act; but in following a given rule they abnegate the ability to make themselves and have their own style. By following rules actors become no more than the obverse of artists who are unruly and wild—both exhibit a weakness of will and a lack of style because they lack the capacity to construct order. The one kind merely follows given rules and so does not make itself but is made by those rules, while the other acts randomly and so fails to construct rules. By contrast, Nietzsche suggests that the great artists make their own choices, constitute their own rules and values, providing the tension and order that cut deeper from a perspective.

Like artists genealogists are creative because they produce rules. Further, the values they produce are also an occasion for other genealogists to generate their own order. There is no room for mere appreciators in this schema, unless we mean that agents create their own interpretations when they appreciate works. In this sense, the genealogical conception of beauty as art both accepts that beauty has a value and meaning and also recognizes that the meaning is not final and that order and values are local. Meanings are open to construal and reconstrual, and our relation to works is one of constructing them in our interpretations or reconstructing them in other works and values we construct. Depending on the engagements with the feeling for life that they enact and sustain, they will be beautiful or ugly, powerful or weak; and depending on the order they give elements they will have grand or weak styles. In effect, a genealogical art constantly reminds that we are only human, that our values only wrongly take on a pious and permanent standing, and that our relation to objects is one of construction rather than communication.

Nietzsche develops this possibility of reconstruing meanings by associating art with God and laughter. If the former represents one impulse to meaning, the latter denies meaning any serious weight. And Nietzsche suggests that such laughter is perhaps "where we shall discover the realm of our invention, that realm in which we, too, can be original, say, as parodists of world history." That is, "perhaps if nothing else today has any future, our *laughter* may yet have a future" (*BGE* 223 and *Z*:IV, quoted at the end of *BT* "Self-Criticism"), because it recognizes the temporality of meaning and being—it empowers us to recognize that permanence and universality are gained only at the price of suppressing our human activity in producing meanings and values from a particular perspective. Like genealogy, like philosophy, art's "mockery of man, or the artist's mockery of himself" are crucial to keeping open the future (*GS* 379) because their orientation derides our pretension that we have created immutable truth and "real" meanings.

This mockery, as we saw, the "aesthetic" quality of novels, plays, or poems, resides in the manner in which they engage with and enact values. That is, Nietzsche's account also portends a new "aesthetic" relation in which agents participate and construct rather than simply contemplate and understand. Because of the different viewpoints that must be accounted for in this relationship between subjects and work, attention also shifts from the text itself as a purely aesthetic object to the conversation between subjects around the text as they construct meanings—to the concern for viewpoints and life that makes us human. Like knowledge and morality, aesthetic value elaborates on our health and physiology, our constructing order before an open future we do not fear.

GENEALOGY AND SOLIPSISM

However, genealogy's concern with the particular seems to lead to solipsism and incoherence. Genealogists produce values only from and for their own viewpoint, in this context, where genealogy is a creative act undetermined by rules, any product that serves it as a given rule also robs it of creativity. Even an earlier product of the genealogist could begin to serve as a rule. So it seems that genealogy is threatened with solipsism or incoherence because its creative acts can only serve as instances that other genealogists go beyond in their own creative acts. Only those unable to create will turn to the genealogist's product and treat it as a rule for themselves. Only then, it seems, will the product be attended to and redeemed from oblivion, but now it is an interpretation that has been left behind.

But to argue in this way is to misconstrue Nietzsche's stress on creating or willing. According to his arguments, to create is to produce objects in the absence of rules—especially those gained from some universal viewpoint—knowing that the objects produced have the status of interpretations. Genealogists cannot make such objects serve as rules by which they could legislate over other actors and their actions, as if the rules satisfied some universal standpoint. First, this is because, for the genealogist, as interpretations the objects have no more reality than other interpretations. Instead, second, interpretations serve as examples or as particular instances displaying what can be done from one point of view. Others may adopt that viewpoint and, by grasping that example, give scope and practice to their own desire to create. But to create they have to produce their own interpretations from their own viewpoint, at most using the examples as models rather than as repositories of rules to be followed.

Rather than yield rules for others to follow, the products of genealogy sustain the creative activity of others in that others can understand the product only by approaching it as an interpretation constructed out of a viewpoint and embodying a place in relations of power. Only another genealogist, aware of its nature and origin, can engage with the object, not by following it but by reconstructing it so as to develop his or her own creation of values. Nietzsche emphasizes the particular and its viewpoint not because he is a relativist but because he wants to maintain both the possibility of creation and knowledge that the object we already have is only a creation from some standpoint. Further, if the genealogists are to create, then they must act: their appraisals show themselves in the objects they produce, and in the absence of the latter we would fail to recognize the actor as an agent.

Thus, interpretations display the creating will. For Nietzsche, that will is inescapable. As he says at the end of *On the Genealogy of Morals*, "Man would rather will *nothingness* than *not* will" (*GM* III:28). So long as we strive to bring order by generating universal rules and moral values, and suppress the fact of their construction out of their origins, we will find every value inadequate and be forced into nihilism. Only when we live in full cognizance of the creation of values do we escape the force of nihilism; and then we redeem ourselves by creating value.

Further, even those who propose a universal viewpoint must accept the standpoint of this creative will, for although they do not often articulate its presence, and while they pretend it does not lie in the active power at the basis of the "universal" values they imitate, nevertheless without the creative will even their poor promising would remain ineffective and unfulfilled.

Moreover, by recasting the story in terms of our active construction of values, Nietzsche also raises an issue of the kind of community that is subtended by genealogy, including the genealogy of beauty. We can no longer use the standards of a will to truth. Instead we must draw out the implications of the kind of relentless creation of values that Nietzsche has suggested, showing it as a successful form of practice for genealogists. In effect, we must raise the issue of solipsism again, this time as a matter of action rather than knowledge. If we must think of *objects* and values as constructs and of individuals' *thinking of objects* as interpretations they construct from their own viewpoints, there seems little room for community or for shared interpretations and responses. And to grasp more fully the consequences our denial of solipsism has for genealogy, we must consider the relation between subjects that becomes possible—we must examine the politics of this kind of production.

THE POLITICS OF PRODUCTION

To characterize the community of genealogy Nietzsche proposes an equality of creators for whose future actions no present universalizable imperative can be binding. Genealogy makes clear that every imperative has a standpoint, and Nietzsche does not expect his present preferences to circumscribe the future that agents shall produce. Both these issues about the character of community and its normative force are deeply political. Together with his stress on the subject, these commitments are part of a more rational and free political order Nietzsche wants to promote.[19] And we can examine some of the problems associated with Nietzsche's account by examining very briefly some "typical" issues and objections. These center on two matters: first, that genealogy cannot be politically conservative; second, that it uses a distinctive and coherent political vocabulary to constitute its community of actors.

Nietzsche's politics is the politics of subjects who are agents. We saw him claim that value, including beauty, is always only a means for preserving a particular kind of subject. Genealogy does not question the basis of value in power by rejecting all conceptions of the subject; rather it reveals the conception at work in order to allow us to substitute another understanding of the subject as active agent. In other words, genealogy recognizes that "'the subject' is . . . a created entity, a 'thing' like all others," and thinks of interpretations and works of art embodying these interpretations as the affect of a will to power (*WP* 556). We misconstrue the "subject" as "something given," for it is "something added and invented and projected behind what there is" (*WP* 481). Indeed, talk of subjects is at best the result of power. Nietzsche maintains that "it is the powerful who make the names of things into law, and among the powerful it is the greatest artists in abstraction who created the categories" (*WP* 513). His suggestion is that we construct the subject in our construal, and some construals generate a subject who is open to development while other forms only calcify the power to act. The genealogy of beauty, then, lays bare the relations of power by which a work constructs its subject, thus opening a false "being" into a "becoming." Conscious now of how we invert cause into effect and can misunderstand the nature of art when we see it as the result of a subject's activity, the genealogy of beauty vivisects the power relations between subjects congealed in any work of art.

If genealogy works in this way, then it cannot be conservative. If we understand conservatism as the desire to preserve the results of our natural judgment (see, for example, Hume and Burke), then genealogy will corrode conservatism's basis in natural judgment. By analyzing values to show their origin in some underlying forms of domination or power, genealogy refuses to countenance any value's claim to being well founded in the kind of human essence that circumscribes natural judgment.[20] In other words, first, genealogy plays a critical role by maintaining both the following: where conservatives insist that natural judgment or our natural sense of beauty provides a standard for values, so that what satisfies nature is good and what is bad is unnatural, genealogy questions the origin and nature of this conception of nature. It proposes that this conception itself enacts values; and by displaying the origins of the values involved in that conception, it dissolves their justification.

Second, for example where Hume introduces an experimental method of reasoning into value to discover what causes give rise to values as effect,[21] or where Burke points out that aesthetic and social values result form countless adjustments too complex to understand or control, and so seeks to justify the claim that they should not be tampered with,[22] there Nietzsche maintains that by providing a genetic account of values these philosophers may have shown the sources of value and may even identify the values being enacted but, in doing so, they also open up, without answering, issues of justifying those enacted values.[23] As Hume and Burke do not have the resources for raising issues of the origin of values in enacted forms of life, power, and domination, they cannot even begin to examine the political implications of their own positions and genetic justification.

Indeed, Nietzsche's genealogical approach shows that their genetic explanations are inadequate because they do not consider their own bases. Thus, so far as conservatism is a politics of human judgment or nature that seeks to preserve what is "best" about a "natural" order, genealogy is progressive because it identifies the latter as a value-laden assumption and, pointing out its basis in power, dissolves its justification. No conservative claims to legitimacy will escape this kind of questioning, and any progressive theory that depends on similar accounts of human nature will also fail.[24]

Similarly, a politics based on subjects reasoning out the morality of their actions and projects, which they justify by bringing their actions under rational and universalizable rules, will not receive succor from genealogy. The latter finds such imperatives inadequately grounded; because they are not self-conscious of their own basis in power and domination, they are ineffective in action. These values depend on an implausible conception of man as a rational being and, in talk of aesthetic judgments, reduce value to an etiolated sphere separate from any engagement with reality. They suppose that all beautiful things share some common feature, regardless of the historical or political position of works, their construction, and reception, and maintain that we can cut through these latter contingencies to appreciate the work for itself, in its universal language, addressed to a universal subject, who underlies all the "contingent" historical and political forms of individual existence. Beauty thus becomes a matter of subjects' distinctive responses to only particular features of an object; and the construction of beauty, the notion of a subject that beauty subtends, the relation of power and domination implicated in this conception of beauty, all become lost to analysis. In this context, genealogy is progressive first by virtue of reminding us that values have a basis in power and second in dissolving that value by presenting its sources—by showing the incomplete notion of the subject that this conception of values implies.

A radical right fares little better. If we understand a radical right as the attempt to maintain a group or policy in power for the sake of that power, without any attendant claims to legitimacy, then genealogy rejects its claims. It does this first by denying that power any legitimacy,[25] and second where the power does not seek legitimacy, genealogy condemns it for the unhealthy form of life that that power portends. For this form of life, even if it holds on to power without apology, must still will an order, and that willing is the subject of Nietzsche's analysis. By his account, we may argue, works of beauty that serve only to keep a few in power lose their richness and complexity. Beauty becomes necessary only to legitimate a conception of a subject and power; yet because a radical right does not seek to justify itself, it has no such need for beauty, and so impoverishes our aesthetic need.[26] But the radical right cannot do without willing as such, and where it wants to reserve power for a few, it must either suppress others' ability to will or must control it. But if it suppresses others' wills, it makes its own power ineffective. It now no longer dominates other agents because there are no longer any agents possessing wills: by suppressing their wills, this naked power only thwarts itself. On the other hand, if it only seeks control of other wills, then it fails ever to gain a grand style, with the attendant sense of balancing strength and weakness that we saw, earlier, was essential to the exercise of strength in willing. Its interpretation and basis in power thus become impoverished.

Now the last rejection of power may seem futile because genealogy's condemnation of the radical right does not bring about its abolition. But that is a general condemnation of any methodology because, in the face of an irrational or unapologetic pursuit of power for its own sake, no rationalization can succeed. Yet at least genealogy is effective in bringing out the limitations of that brutal power, for this radical right grasp of power must establish and perpetuate itself in some way at least among those who exercise it. Against such a grab for power, a theorist of democracy who does not grasp the genealogy of democratic forms in domination and power will have recourse only to the democratic forms of opposition. But these, because they do not thematize the undemocratic mechanisms that can bring about democracy, can oppose a shameless exercise of power only with mere moral incantations. By contrast, Nietzsche's genealogy defends a "community of creators" because it depends on the very willing that underlies every exercise of power. Nietzsche can suggest where the defense begins to develop, for his exploration of irrationalism allows him to recognize that a community of creators must be prepared to counter violence and barbarity. That is, the community of creators may form as a counter to a despotism that limits willing. And because he recognizes the irrational sources of rational forms, Nietzsche can thematize that countering by developing his account of the community of creators.

To defend this claim for Nietzsche, we must look more carefully at the "community of creators." Given Nietzsche's descriptions of their ravishing the herd and nature (see *BGE* and *GM*), it is not clear that these creators can form a community. This difficulty arises also because Nietzsche's stress on *creativity*, given the differences in our abilities to create, seems to preclude the kind of balance between parts involved in talk of a community. But Nietzsche also uses the vocabulary of richness, health, strength of interpretation, and the like, that provides a positive reading of objects and actions *without* bringing in any metaphysics. This leads us to recognize that even if Nietzsche does not provide an analysis of political structures, he does give insight into the politics of aesthetic and other values; and if he gives us a genealogy of beauty, he also provides a politics of production so far as we must understand beauty as art.

The community of creators is not an impossibility. It only seems so from the point of view of a resentment that seeks control of every action by clamping it under already given rules. By contrast with some agents, who use categorical imperatives as a mechanism for controlling moral creativity and our exploration of the complexities of new moral situations, Nietzsche stresses the latter, showing we generate new rules in our actions. Rather than consider the fact of judging or responding to actions, he examines the matter of acting. His is a community of actors rather than a community of responders, and as we saw in relation to works of beauty, the former community develops out of a relation of actors to acts and not of responders to acts. A work or action provides an example that other actors can take up not as a rule to be followed by as an example they use to produce their own work. The community, then, is an interaction of producers and their objects, of rules generating new rules, of interpretations giving rise to new interpretations, and not a matter of including only those events that satisfy a universalizable rule. In other words, we may still talk about community even though it is a group of creators who respond to each others' works and actions by creating their own, or create their own independently.

But the last possibility raises a further difficulty. If we accept that individuals create and act by their own lights and, even if they relate to other creators, do so only to produce their own work rather than to follow a rule, then the distance between individual and community seems great. Little unity will arise from such independent behavior, and the membership of common practices and interactive forms of life that are usually involved in talk of community, seem nonexistent in the case of independent creators—so much so that community of creators seems empty of content. Yet, we may argue, Nietzsche sees no contradiction between such creative individuality and community. For example, he sees beauty as "the high point of communication . . . the source of language" (*WP* 809), and the languages of tones, gestures, and glances that art creates and depends on, the "host of conventions" that lie at the basis of mature art, all give substance to the community that shares this language and set of conventions.

Nor does such convention offend against creativity. Nietzsche sees convention as "the condition of great art, *not* an obstacle" (*WP* 809). We do not condemn artists as uncreative because they use linguistic and social conventions to construct a work. Conventions are a means for making ourselves and our creative products understood, and they no more interfere with creativity than the rules of logic prevent us from uttering truths. Indeed, in *Thus Spoke Zarathustra*, in "Thousand and One Goals," Nietzsche maintains that people are creators first and individuals second, suggesting both that an opposition between individual and community is a *result* of creativity, and not something that suppresses individuality, and that individuality depends on conventions because creativity does so. That is, far from individual creator and community being opposed, they are interdependent: creators use language and its conventions to produce their work and so enhance and develop the community.

Only the community that seeks to overpower the individual in the name of some social rule also opposes the creative individual. That oppressive community Nietzsche is happy to condemn; yet this does not deny all community, and Nietzsche also pleads the need for a creative *and* social individual. And such creative and social individualism, we may expect, will likely rebel against extraneous formal rules and such conservative values as either seek control or oppose the individual to all forms of community.

While this sense of a community based on actions can stand further detailing, even at this general level we can raise an objection that typifies others. A community of creators, a critic may argue, is an oxymoron because while a community suggests a balance and a relation of parts to the whole, where the former are all necessary to the latter and, so, equally important, this harmony is contradicted by the fact of creativity. For different subjects possess this ability to different degrees, and their ability to create works and rules will surely single out some individuals over others, making them more important to the community, and so causing inequality. And, because of this inequality, the community of creators becomes politically questionable. While genealogy may be progressive insofar as it rejects conservative claims to immutable moral judgments, truths, unequal sensibilities, and their resultant social and political hierarchies, still it only results in another arbitrary grouping of unequal actors. Yet progressive thought must surely liberate us from hierarchies and make possible a free and equitable relation between agents.[27] Progressive thought must make good its promise of equity, showing how any present imbalances in such things as wealth and creativity do not preclude equity in worth. Yet creativity does not sustain such liberation.

The reply to this kind of objection is straightforward. Possession of the ability to will and create is not a source of inequality: the democratic community no more institutionalizes individuals in hierarchies by reference to variations in their intelligence than a community of creators need exclude agents by reason of variations in their ability to create. More importantly, the criticism uses an evaluative conception of creativity, treating it as an inability to produce values that only some specially gifted agents possess. That is not Nietzsche's conception—the herd does not lack creativity, it merely fears to exercise it or prefers to control it.[28] Nietzsche explains that the "slave revolt in morality begins when *ressentiment* becomes creative and gives rise to values" (*GM* I:10); and, instead of denying that the herd is creative, he diagnoses the character of their activity. That is, he is characterizing the relation between members of the community on the axis of action rather than along the axis of judgments on actions. In other words, the community of creators is not obviously a system of inequalities.

Of course, Nietzsche does not provide any analysis of the political structures and institutions that will sustain creative activity. But not only is his sense of politics wider than such an institutional analysis, he also gives us a vocabulary for a positive reading of objects and actions. And this positive reading tells us *how* we should do, even if it does not tell us *what* we should do. It implicates a political relation between creators that not only rejects conservatism but also does not depend on a metaphysics of human nature, truth, or good judgment, and so is free of what could make it conservative.

A community of creators does not exclude any subject from this politics. And though he does not give us an analysis of political institutions as such, Nietzsche does suggest that we have a tool for excluding those who would introduce conservatism. He talks of the richness of interpretations,[29] of their health,[30] and of the strength in styles, as we saw earlier, that provide a criterion for politics through a notion of inclusiveness. We can exclude interpretations that impose limitations and exclude possible actions and actors.[31] People who promote, say, a community of only white males have a poorer ability to act, impoverishing themselves by insisting on the validity and incorrigibility of certain rules and having to suppress others because they can find no reason to oppose them. Yet the very insistence that white male society constitutes the only legitimate community already makes him redundant in the light of the richer experience, interpretations, and forms of life available from another perspective.

Without exhausting all possible viewpoints within the compass of a single moral fable or eschatology, Nietzsche can move that the richer interpretation is better because it empowers us better to act and construct healthy, future-seeing forms of life. The latter too may dissolve, but their destruction is the greater affair because they cut more deeply into our power to produce the future. Thus, they may fail under the pressure of their own inadequacies and for good reasons, which may become clearer from another perspective, but that destruction has powerful consequences because it explores our construction of values, forms of life, and becoming more deeply. For genealogists it is important to keep open the future. Here, *every* interpretation and its form of life is seen as a willing; and for sustaining the ability to act, for empowering us in a form of life, we value that creativity. Its contrast is with a form of life that imposes redundant boundaries of class, race, sex, position, and so on, on our power and will. Unlike this form of life, we prefer those works of beauty that allow us the better to enact our life forms. And so far as the genealogy of beauty makes this possibility available, it is a politics of production and creativity that does not aestheticize politics.

NOTES

1. See *GS* 353–380, and *WP* 68, 69, etc. Nietzsche's references to science and interpretation in this text are numerous. Translations of Nietzsche's works are drawn from Kaufmann's *BT*, *GS*; Kaufmann and Hollingdale's *GM* and *WP*; Hollingdale's *A*, *HH*, *TI*. [*Ed. Note*—Citations have been revised to conform with the style of this volume. In the course of making such translations, errors were discovered. They are corrected here.]

2. See, for example, *GM* III, where the ascetic is understood in a number of modes, including style, or *TI* "Untimely" 19 and 20, where the relation of style to valuations is considered, and *GS* 290, where the association of creativity, style, and valuations is again discussed.

3. Of course, any quotations from Nietzsche must be handled carefully because their context and purpose is not always clear in the aphorisms themselves. In this case, to take art seriously is for the philosopher to see objects and values as parts, as things constructed and not given, and as open to our actions.

4. This turn to art is central to Alexander Nehamas' book *Nietzsche: Life as Literature* (Cambridge, MA: Harvard University Press, 1985). However, Nehamas does not consider the issue I want to raise, of the impact this extension to cognition and value has on our conception of art, literature, and aesthetic value.

5. This also gives philosophy a critical role. See *WP* 797, *BGE* 291, and *GM* where seeing through the surface of values to their bases leads us to display the origins of values in power relations, barbarism, and violence.

6. Nietzsche conceives origins not in terms of their prehistory but of their nature and possibilities.

7. F. W. Schiller, in *The Aesthetic Education of Man*, maintains that they are. Similarly, Hegel sees works as symptomatic of a single story of the development of reason whose conclusion lies some way beyond all art and beauty.

8. Nietzsche's targets include Kant here, because he misconstrues Kant's notion of "disinterestedness." See S. Kemal, *Kant and Fine Art: Kant and the Philosophy of Fine Art and Culture* (Oxford: Oxford University Press, 1986): Nietzsche was simply mistaken to understand Kant in terms of a disinterestedness that excluded the possibility of ascribing an interest to aesthetic judgment.

9. That other world of "spirit," "reason," and a commensurate "morality," depends on "an unnatural extirpation of desires," as if human life were nothing until we escaped its physiology and passions to become moral. "But to attack the passions at their roots," Nietzsche reminds us, "means to attack life at its roots" in our present physiology (*TI* "Morality" 1). Thus we cannot trace that spiritualized morality to an origin in man (*A* 15). To oppose that spiritualization by extirpation, Nietzsche formulates an alternative principle: "All naturalism

in morality, that is all *healthy* morality, is dominated by an instinct for life"; and this human morality, this human life, "is at an end where 'the kingdom of God' *begins*" (*TI* "Morality" 4).

10. He writes that it is precisely through the pressure of opposites, and the feelings they occasion, that "the great man, *the bow with the greatest tension*, develops" (*WP* 967).

11. [*Ed. Note*—I am unable to determine Kemal's precise reference where he writes "ibid., 65." I believe he is referring to *TI* (not *WP*) "Germans" 6, but the three "needful" things listed there are: seeing, thinking, and writing.]

12. Actors "survey all the strengths and weaknesses of their nature and then fit them into an artistic plan until every one of them appears as art and reason and even weaknesses delight the eye" (*GS* 290).

13. Yet style is not all; it has wider application than aesthetic value because it has repercussions in morality and knowledge when its criteria are developed further. But this extension is not made by Derrida, who thinks of style as the basic concept of Nietzsche's thought. He does not relate the notion of style to the feeling for life that Nietzsche refers to. See Jacques Derrida, *Spurs: Nietzsche's Style*, trans. Barbara Harlow (Chicago: University of Chicago Press, 1979).

14. This suggests again that beauty or ugliness are not aesthetic categories in any traditional sense but are measured by their fullness or their strength. The will to power empowers us to generate interpretations.

15. In *GS* P 4, Nietzsche recognizes that the need to be comfortable with the superficial unities of traditional art is necessary; but that is never enough.

16. Each work holds together God and buffoon, Nietzsche says in *BGE* 223, where the first provides meaning and the second impiously refuses all permanent meaning.

17. Nietzsche's diagnosis of the conception of life and subject we enact in our values is part of his analysis of the errors of our thought, especially his famous reversal in "The Four Great Errors" in *TI*. See also *A* 1.

18. This activity, in turn, is seen from the perspective of life.

19. I have in mind Habermas and the "Frankfurt School" as a contrast to Nietzsche at this point.

20. The example I have in mind is Hume's reliance on a conception of human nature by natural judgments as the basis for our claims to knowledge and value. See for example, the *Treatise of Human Nature*, Book III.

21. See *Treatise of Human Nature*, Book II, for example, Section VII, on vice and virtue and Book III, Part II, Section II, on the origin of Justice and Property. See also D. C. Hoy, "Nietzsche, Hume, and the Genealogical Method" in Y. Yovel (ed.), *Nietzsche as Affirmative Thinker*, (Dordecht: Martinus Nijhoff Publishers, 1986): 20–38. Hoy seems to me to make too much of the analogies between the "genetic" features of both thinkers' methodologies and wrongly explains their differences only in terms of the generality of their approaches. Hume accepts that a genetic account justifies the value; it is far from clear that Nietzsche does so. Hume rests his analysis on claims about the efficacy of natural judgement; Nietzsche does not accept this but instead criticizes thinkers who rely on any conception of human nature. He argues that the mind is already ideologically committed and normative.

22. See Burke, *Reflections on the Revolution in France* and *Essay on the Beautiful and the Sublime*.

23. See, for example, *GS* 345, where he says that "even if a morality has grown out of an error, the realization of this fact would not as much as touch the problem of its value." Cited in Hoy, p. 20.

24. See, for example, Sebastiano Timpanaro, *On Materialism* (London: New Left Books, 1971), and Peter Fuller, *Art and Psychoanalysis* (London: Writers and Readers, 1979), both of which rely on a notion of human nature derived from biology to propose that universal values are available to Marxism.

25. That is, it rejects a radical right claim to legitimacy as it rejects a conservative claim to legitimacy.

26. See Nietzsche's criticisms of the "cultural philistines" and his account of aesthetic necessity cited earlier.

27. Even if there is an actual inequality—from each according to their ability and to each according to their need—these imbalances remain unimportant because the worth of agents is not decided by their wealth.

28. For Nietzsche, priests are creative and strong among the weak. See *GM* III on the particular creativity exercised by the ascetic.

29. See, for example, *GM* III:12, where Nietzsche points out the role of interpretations. *The Will to Power* contains numerous other instances of this stress.

30. See *TI* for more on Nietzsche's idea of health.

31. This is not entirely true as Nietzsche says we must narrow our perspective to produce new values (see *GM* III:12, where he talks of the narrowing of our perspective); but his whole thrust there, too, is to make progress in producing new works, and where a narrowing frustrates this production, we shall jettison it.

18

Nietzsche and the Jews
The Structure of an Ambivalence*

Yirmiyahu Yovel

This chapter is based on a study[1] that examines the image of Judaism as offered by the two most important philosophers of the nineteenth century, Hegel and Nietzsche. One was active in the first half and the other in the second half of the century; one was a major philosopher of reason and the other one of its severest critics. I confine myself to treating both of them as *philosophers*, which means concentrating on their own philosophical ideas rather than on their various users and abusers, and understanding their image of the Jews in its relation to each philosopher's ideas and overall philosophical project.

Hegel's philosophical project was a vast and ambitious one. It included the attempt to reach a philosophical understanding of the modern world, its essence and genesis, and thereby to shape modernity still further and lead to its climax. Hegel saw European culture as the core of world history, and as being essentially a Christian culture—which the philosopher must translate and elevate into concepts; Judaism was a necessary background for understanding the Christian revolution and era.

According to the Hegelian dialectic, every cultural form makes some genuine contribution to world history (and the world Spirit), after which it is sublated (*aufgehoben*) and disappears from the historical scene. Yet the Jews continued to survive long after their raison d'être had disappeared—indeed, after they no longer had a genuine history in Hegel's sense, but merely existed as the dead corpse of their extinguished essence. Now, with the French Revolution, the Jews were entering the modern world

*Originally published in *Nietzsche and Jewish Culture*, edited by Jacob Golumb (New York: Routledge, 1997), 117–34. Reprinted with permission of Routledge.

and claiming their rights and place within it. Hegel, despite his anti-Jewish bias, was perfectly disposed to grant these rights, but did not know what to do with the Jews in modernity *as Jews*, nor how to explain their survival in terms of his system.

Nietzsche too had an ambitious philosophical project, in many ways opposing Hegel's. A radical cultural revolutionary, his goal was not to bring the process of modernity to culmination but rather to subvert and reverse it or, more precisely, to *divert* it into a totally different course. The process that had started with Socrates, Moses, and Jesus, and that Hegel saw as creating truth, civilization, spirit, and even God himself (the Absolute) was to Nietzsche a story of decadence and degeneration. Nietzsche attributed this decadence to two main sources—rationalistic metaphysics and Christianity: the first stemming from the Greeks, the second from the ancient Jews. He therefore needed an interpretation of Judaism (and also of Socratism, as offered in *The Birth of Tragedy*) in order to expose and upset the decadent culture of the present. Given these projects, Hegel had seen the merit of ancient Judaism in its discovery—which led to Christianity—that God was spirit and that spirit is higher than nature; whereas for Nietzsche this was the great falsification that the ancient Jewish priests had brought about. However, as my analysis shows, Nietzsche did not recognize a single, permanent Jewish essence. He distinguished three different modes or phases in Judaism, and expressed admiration for two of them: for biblical Judaism, and for the Jews of the latter Diaspora.[2] His harsh critique pours exclusively on the middle phase, the second-temple "priestly" Judaism (as he calls it), which had started the "slave revolution" in morality—namely, Christianity. Nietzsche's true target is Christianity: so much so that often he reads the ideas and even the phrases of the New Testament directly into what he derogates under the name of Judaism.

On the emotional level, Hegel, especially in maturity, had lost interest in the Jewish theme, whereas Nietzsche's interest in it was increasingly passionate and burning. And this links into another aspect of my study: to what extent did each philosopher overcome the anti-Jewish feelings imbued in his upbringing and milieu? Those feelings were of a different kind in each case. Nietzsche came to maturity in the second half of the nineteenth century amid a wave of nationalistic and racist anti-Semitism raging in Germany, which had already a distinct secular feature. For a short time, Nietzsche says, he too "had resided in the zone of the disease" (meaning his association with Wagner), but later he performed a powerful overcoming of that "disease" and became opposed to the anti-Semites with particular energy and passion.

It has become a commonplace to say Nietzsche was "ambivalent" about the Jews. Yet the word "ambivalent" itself is ambiguous and often creates an impression of depth where there is but confusion. My aim is to analyze the *precise structure* of Nietzsche's ambivalence about the Jews and bring to light its ingredients in their mutual relations. On the one hand Nietzsche sees ancient Judaism as one of the main sources of European decadence, and on the other he assigns modern Jews, whom he admires, a leading role in creating the nondecadent, de-Christianized Europe he wishes for the future. As for modern anti-Semitism, Nietzsche repudiates it with the same passion he reserves for the proto-Christian Jewish "priests"—and for similar reasons. These two human types, apparently so opposed to each other—the anti-Semite and the Jewish priest—are actually genealogical cousins: they share the same deep-psychological pattern of *ressentiment* that Nietzsche's philosophy diagnoses at the basis of human meanness and degeneration.

METHODOLOGICAL ELEMENTS

The following are the main methodological elements of this study: (1) I examine Nietzsche's views of the Jews in relation to his actual philosophy, not as casual reflections that any intellectual, artist, or scientist may have about the Jews. (2) Taking an immanent approach, I deal with Nietzsche's own thought and not—despite their interest for the historian or sociologist—with its many popular and politically motivated usages, or with what is vaguely called "Nietzscheanism." (3) In addition to their philosophical meaning, I try also to listen to Nietzsche's words in their *rhetorical context*. (4) To a limited extent I have taken his psychological career into account—both his struggle with close anti-Semitic intimates, and his last twilight letters before he went mad, which carry a special hermeneutic value. (5) Above all, I am looking for the underlying structure of Nietzsche's complex position as indicated above.

This search has led me to distinguish, first, between Nietzsche's attitude toward *anti-Semitism* and toward *Judaism*. Second, within Judaism I had to further distinguish between three periods or modalities: (1) biblical Judaism; (2) second-temple "priestly" Judaism; (c) Diaspora and contemporary Jews.

JUDAISM AND ANTI-SEMITISM

When Nietzsche attacks the anti-Semites or defends the Jews, he aims at real people: the actual community of the Jews, and anti-Semitism as a contemporary movement. By contrast, when dealing with ancient priestly Judaism Nietzsche treats it as a psychocultural *category* that is latent in the current (Christian) culture and that Nietzsche, as the "genealogist" of this culture, has to expose. Contrary to many anti-Semites—and also to many Jewish apologetics—Nietzsche does not project his view of ancient Judaism into a political attitude toward the Jews of today. This break allowed him to be at the same time—and with the same intense passion—both an anti-anti-Semite and a critique of ancient priestly Judaism—the fountain of Christianity.

THE ANTI-ANTI-SEMITE: QUID FACTI[3]

A selection of four kinds of texts allows us to recognize the fact of Nietzsche's fierce and univocal opposition to contemporary anti-Semitism. These texts are drawn from (1) his published writings; (2) his intimate letters (to his sister, his mother, his close friends); (3) his "twilight letters" written on the verge of madness; (4) "The Fritsch Affair"—a correspondence with an anti-Semitic agitator who tried to recruit Nietzsche—and "Zarathustra" too, as Nietzsche says with disgust[4]—into his camp.

Here are a few illustrations. In the *Genealogy* Nietzsche says of the anti-Semites:

> This hoarse, indignant barking of sick dogs, this rabid mendaciousness and rage of "noble" pharisees, penetrates even the hallowed halls of science. (I again remind readers who have ears for such things of that Berlin apostle of revenge, Eugen Dühring, who employs moral mumbo-jumbo more indecently and repulsively than anyone else in Germany today: Dühring, the foremost moral bigmouth today—unexcelled even among his own ilk, the anti-Semites.) (*GM* III:14)

> "This is our conviction: we confess it before all the world, we live and die for it. Respect for all who have convictions!" I have heard that sort of thing even out of the mouths of anti-Semites. On the contrary, gentlemen! An anti-Semite certainly is not any more decent because he lies as a matter of principle. (*A* 55)

> Meanwhile they [the Jews] want and wish rather, even with some importunity, to be absorbed and assimilated by Europe; they long to be fixed, permitted, respected some-where at long last, putting an end to the nomads' life, to the "Wandering Jew" . . . to that end it might be useful and fair to expel the anti-Semitic screamers from the coun-try. (*BGE* 251)

> Since Wagner had moved to Germany, he had condescended step by step to everything I despise—even to anti-Semitism. (*NCW* "How I Broke Away From Wagner: 1)

To Overbeck:

> This accursed anti-Semitism . . . is the reason for the great rift between myself and my sister. (*KGB* III, 503)

And to his sister:

> You have committed one of the greatest stupidities—for yourself and for me! Your asso-ciation with an anti-Semitic chief expresses a foreignness to my whole way of life which fills me again and again with ire or melancholy. . . . It is a matter of honor with me to be absolutely clean and unequivocal in relation to anti-Semitism, namely, opposed to it, as I am in my writings. I have recently been persecuted with letters and anti-Semitic Correspondence Sheets.[5] My disgust with this party (which would like the benefit of my name only too well!) is as pronounced as possible . . . and that I am unable to do anything against it, that the name of Zarathustra is used in every Anti-Semitic Corre-spondence Sheet, has almost made me sick several times. (Christmas 1887, *PN*, 456–57)

The intimate texts carry special weight, because they prove that Nietzsche's opposition to anti-Semitism was not merely external and "political" (or "politically correct"), as with many liberals, but penetrated into the deep recesses of his mind. That result might have been reinforced by Nietzsche's intense relations with anti-Semites such as his sister, Wagner, Cosima, and perhaps also Jacob Burckhardt.[6] These depth-psychological relations could have served as a lever in providing the energy for overcoming his own early anti-Semitism in the intense way he did, that is, not as liberal rationalist but with all the passion of his being—that is, in a "Nietzschean" way.

THE ANTI-ANTI-SEMITE: QUID JURIS

Even without considering psychology, there are sufficient *philosophical* grounds for Nietzsche's active anti-anti-Semitism. The anti-Semitic movement contains and heightens most of the decadent elements in modern culture that Nietzsche's philosophy had set out to combat:

1. Anti-Semitism is a mass movement, vulgar, ideological, a new form of "slave morality" and of the man of the Herd.
2. As such, anti-Semitism is a popular neurosis, affecting weak people who lack existential power and self-confidence (as opposed to Nietzsche's "Dionysian" person).
3. Anti-Semitism, especially in Germany, served to reinforce the German *Reich* and the cult of *politics* and the *State*, which Nietzsche, as "the last *un*-political German," denounces as "the New Idol."
4. Anti-Semitism, in Germany, was also the lubricant of German *nationalism*, which Nietzsche opposed most insistently (though he did so "from the right").
5. Anti-Semitism also depends on *racism*; yet Nietzsche's philosophy rejects racism as a value distinction between groups (though he does admit of race as a descriptive category). Nietzsche demands the *mixing* of races within the new Europe he envisages.
6. At the ground of all the preceding points lies a common genealogical structure—fear, insecurity, existential weakness, and above all *ressentiment*—the malignant rancor against the mentally powerful and self-affirming, and the hatred toward the other which preconditions one's own self-affirmation and self-esteem. The anti-Semite's ardor conceals his/her deep insecurity: he does not start with the celebrating affirmation of his own being, but with the negation of the other's, by which alone the anti-Semite is able to reaffirm his own self—which he does in an overblown, empty, and arrogant manner. "They are all men of *ressentiment*, physiologically unfortunate and worm-eaten, a whole tremulous realm of subterranean revenge, inexhaustible and insatiable in outbursts against the fortunate and happy" (*GM* III:14)

Here are a few more quotes, illustrating his opposition to nationalism and the cult of politics and the state:

> Is there any idea at all behind this bovine nationalism? What value can there be now, when everything points to wider and more common interests, in encouraging this boorish self-conceit? And this in a state of affairs in which spiritual dependency and disnationalization meet the eye and in which the value and meaning of contemporary culture lie in mutual blending and fertilization! (*WP* 748)

> The whole problem of the Jews exists only in nation states, for here their energy and higher intelligence, their accumulated capital of spirit and will, gathered from generation to generation through a long schooling in suffering, must become so preponderant as to arouse mass envy and hatred. In almost all contemporary nations, therefore—in direct proportion to the degree to which they act up nationalistically—the literary obscenity is spreading of leading the Jews to slaughter as scapegoats of every conceivable public and internal misfortune. As soon as it is no longer a matter of preserving nations, but of producing the strongest possible European mixed race, the Jews are just as useful and desirable an ingredient as any other national remnant. (*HH* 475)

> Culture and the state—one should not deceive oneself about this—are antagonists. . . . All great ages of culture are ages of political decline: what is great culturally has always been unpolitical, even *antipolitical*. (*TI* "Germans" 4)

> *On the New Idol*

> State is the name of the coldest of all cold monsters. Coldly it tells lies too; and this lie crawls out of its mouth: "I, the state, am the people." That is a lie!
>   . . . every people speaks its tongue of good and evil . . . but the state tells lies in all the tongues of good and evil. . . .
>   Everything about it is false; it bites with stolen teeth, and bites easily. Even its entrails are false.
>   "On earth there is nothing greater than I: the ordering finger of God and I"—thus roars the monster. And it is not only the long-eared and shortsighted who sink to their knees.
>   Escape from the bad smell! Escape from the idolatry of the superfluous. . . . Only where the state ends, there begins the human being who is not superfluous: there begins the song of necessity, the unique and inimitable tune. (*Z*:I "On the New Idol")

Combined, Nietzsche's four negations—of nationalism, of racism, of anti-Semitism, and of the cult of the state—also explain why his philosophy is inherently opposed to fascism and Nazism, although these ideologies have abused Nietzsche for their purposes.

THE ANCIENT "PRIESTLY" JUDAISM

Nietzsche's attack on ancient ("priestly") Judaism is as fierce and uncompromising as his assault on anti-Semitism. The Jewish priests have spread the spurious ideas of a "moral world order," sin, guilt, punishment, repentance, pity, and the love of the neighbor. Thereby they falsified all natural values. The meek and the weak are the good who deserve salvation; all men are equal in their duties toward a transcendent God and the values of love and mercy He demands. (Nietzsche thus attributes to the Jewish priests a *direct* Christian content, and often describes them as Christian *from the start*.) Yet beneath his doctrine of mercy, the priest's soul was full of malice and *ressentiment*, the rancor of the mentally weak whose will-to-power turns into hostility and revenge against the other, which is his only way to affirm himself. Thereby the Jewish priests—pictured as early Christians—have created the "slave morality," which official Christianity then propagated through the world. Whereas the anti-Semites accuse the Jews of having killed Jesus, Nietzsche accuses them of having *begotten* Jesus.

> The slave revolt in morality begins when *ressentiment* itself becomes creative and gives birth to values: the *ressentiment* of natures that are denied the true reaction, that of deeds, and compensate themselves with an imaginary revenge. While every noble morality develops from a triumphant affirmation of itself, slave morality from the outset says No to what is "outside," what is "different," what is "not itself"; and this No is its creative deed. (*GM* I:10)

Priestly morality is the morality of the existentially impotent, in whom *ressentiment* against the powerful and the self-assured has become a value-creating force. The existential "slaves" take vengeance on their "masters" on an ideal plane, in that they succeed in imposing their own values on the masters, and even cause them to interiorize those new values, and thereby subjugate them. Henceforth the powerful person sees himself/herself as sinner not only in the other's eyes but in his/her self-perception as well, which is the ultimate form of subordination and also corruption.

Nietzsche thereby places the critique of ancient Judaism at a crucial junction of his philosophy. It is grounded in *ressentiment*, a key Nietzschean category, and is responsible for the corruption of Europe through Christianity. However, his critique does not serve Nietzsche in fighting against contemporary Jews, but against contemporary Christianity and the "modern Ideas" he sees as its secular offshoots (liberalism, nationalism, socialism, and the like). For modern Jews, after they go out of the ghetto and become secularized, Nietzsche has far-reaching prospects, whereas the modern anti-Semite is analyzed as the genealogical cousin of the ancient Jewish priest, whose properties the anti-Semite has inherited, but on a lower level still, since he lacks the value-creating power that the Jewish priests have demonstrated, and since, in order to feel that he is somebody, he requires the fake security of mass culture and the "togetherness" of a political movement.

Nietzsche's analysis, like Socrates's dialectic, ends in an ironic reversal. While the anti-Semite is the ancient Jewish priests' relative, the modern Jew is their complete opposite (or "antipode"). As such, modern Jews are candidates for helping to create a new Dionysian culture and redeem Europe from the decadence instilled by their forefathers.

Rhetorically, too, the anti-Semite learns that, at bottom he has the same psychology as his worst enemies in their worst period, and this is supposed to shock the anti-Semite into disgust—perhaps at himself. However, by using anti-Semitic images ostensibly against themselves Nietzsche is playing with fire.

It follows that Nietzsche holds two rather univocal positions: against modern anti-Semitism and against ancient priestly Judaism, which are linked by the same genealogical root, *ressentiment*. Nietzsche's ambivalence derives from the combination of these two positions, which look contradictory but are not so in effect. From a logical or systematic point of view there is no contradiction between rejecting both anti-Semitism and the moral message of ancient Judaism, yet this combination creates a strong psychological tension that ordinary people find hard to sustain. Hence the need to transcend ordinary psychology and cultivate an *uncommon*, noble character capable of holding on to both positions despite the tension they create. In other words, what is needed in order to maintain the two tense positions is not only a common link between them (the opposition to *ressentiment*) but a special personality whose mental power allows it to maintain a stance of "nevertheless" and insist on the distinction it involves.

This is nothing new. Almost every important matter in Nietzsche calls for an uncommon psychology. This is true, above all, of *amor fati*, which draws creative power from hard truths, and affirms life despite the demise of all "metaphysical consolations." In Nietzsche one needs anyway to go beyond the limits of ordinary humanity and human psychology, toward a goal that his rhetoric dramatizes under the name of *Übermensch*. Nietzsche's position on Judaism and anti-Semitism is no exception.

In a word, Nietzsche's noncontradictory ambivalence requires holding two (or more) differentiated positions that are logically compatible yet psychologically competitive and hard to maintain together for the ordinary person. This analysis can also help explain why Nietzsche's position has so widely been abused; for the mental revolution that he sought did not take place, while his ideas were generalized, vulgarized, and delivered to a public in which the old psychology prevailed.

At the same time, we noticed on several occasions that Nietzsche himself exploits anti-Semitic feelings and images that exist in other people (or whose traces persist in his own mind) and manipulates them in a dialectical technique, as a rhetoric device to insult the anti-Semites or hurt Christianity. For example:

> Consider to whom one bows down in Rome itself today, as if they were the epitome of all the highest values—and not only in Rome but over almost half the earth . . . three Jews, as is known, and one Jewess (Jesus of Nazareth, the fisherman Peter, the rug weaver Paul, and the mother of the aforementioned Jesus named Mary). (*GM* I:16)

As I said before, Nietzsche in this and similar cases is playing a dangerous game; his meaning can be twisted against his intention, his irony misunderstood, and his words may enhance that which he actually opposes. The irony of speaking ironically to the vulgar is that the speaker himself may end up the victim of an ironic reversal, by which his intent is undermined and his discourse is taken at face value. Nietzsche, as a master of the art, should have anticipated the ironic fate of ironizers.

THE THREE PHASES OF JUDAISM

We have also seen that Nietzsche does not attribute to Judaism a constant essence or genealogical pattern, but distinguished three periods or phases within it.

(1) In biblical times (the Old Testament) Nietzsche perceives Dionysian greatness and natural sublimity that arouses his reverence. He does not accept the content of the biblical figures' religious belief, but admires their attitude to life and religion because it was vital, natural, this-worldly and was built on self-affirmation rather than self-recrimination.

> In the Jewish "Old Testament," the book of divine justice, there are human beings, things, and speeches in so grand a style that the Greek and Indian literature have nothing to compare with it. With terror and reverence one stands before these tremendous remnants of what man once was. (*BGE* 52)

> At the time of the kings, Israel also stood in the right, that is, the natural relationship to all things. Its Yahweh was the expression of a consciousness of power, of joy in oneself, of hope for oneself: through him victory and welfare were expected; through him nature was trusted to give what the people needed above all, rain. Yahweh is the god of Israel and therefore the god of justice: the logic of every people that is in power and has a good conscience. (*A* 25)

(2) The second temple and its priests are the object of Nietzsche's harsh and merciless attack. Here the "slave morality" revolution was performed, the major denaturation and reversal of values that led to Christianity, as analyzed before.

> To have glued this New Testament to make one book, as the "Bible," as "the book par excellence"—that is perhaps the greatest audacity and "sin against the spirit" that literary Europe has on its conscience. (*BGE* 52)

> The concept of God falsified, the concept of morality falsified: the Jewish priesthood did not stop there. The whole of the history of Israel could not be used: away with it! These priests accomplished a miracle of falsification. . . . With matchless scorn for every tradition, for every historical reality, they translated the past of their own people into religious terms, that is, they turned it into a stupid salvation mechanism of guilt before Yahweh, and punishment. (*A* 26)

On such utterly false soil, where everything natural, every natural value, every reality was opposed by the most profound instincts of the ruling class, Christianity grew up—a form of mortal enmity against reality that has never yet been surpassed. (*A* 27)

(3) Diaspora Jews again arouse Nietzsche's admiration, because they have demonstrated the power of affirming life in the face of suffering and drawn force from it. Moreover, Diaspora Jews have the merit of having rejected Christ and served as a constant critic and counterbalance to Christianity.

In the darkest times of the Middle Ages . . . it was Jewish free-thinkers, scholars, and physicians who clung to the banner of enlightenment and spiritual independence in the face of the harshest personal pressures and defended Europe against Asia. We owe it to their exertions, not least of all, that a more natural, more rational, and certainly unmythical explanation of the world was eventually able to triumph again. (*HH* 475)

The Jews, however, are beyond any doubt the strongest, toughest and purest race now living in Europe; they know how to prevail even under the worst conditions (even better than under favorable conditions), by means of virtues that today one would like to mark as vices—thanks above all to a resolute faith that need not be ashamed of "modern ideas." (*BGE* 25)

CONTEMPORARY JEWS AND THE CLOSING OF THE CIRCLE

As a result of their hard and long schooling and invigorating experience, the Jews reached the modern era as the strongest and most stable people in Europe, and could have dominated it, though they did not wish to do so. However, once they decided to mingle with the other European nations, then because of their greater existential power they would naturally, without intending to, reach a dominant position, in the sense of determining the norms and the new values in Europe. If however, the Jews continued their seclusion, Nietzsche grimly predicted they would "lose Europe" (that is, emigrate or be expelled) as their ancestors had left or been driven from Egypt. Nietzsche advocates the first alternative. The Jews must pour their gifts and power into a new Europe that will be free of the Christian heritage: *the forebears of Christ must work today in the service of the modern anti-Christ (i.e., Nietzsche-Dionysus), and thereby pay their debt to Europe for what their priestly ancestors had done to it.*[7]

For this to happen, European society must open up to the Jews and welcome them, and the Jews must end their voluntary seclusion and involve themselves with all European matters *as their own*: in this way they will, inevitably, attain excellence and end up determining new norms and values for Europe. Nietzsche welcomes this prospect with enthusiasm, because he sees the Jews as allies and levers in the transition to a higher human psychology and culture. If the Nazis considered the Jews as *Untermenschen*, to Nietzsche they were a possible catalyst of the *Übermensch*.

Nietzsche thus assigns a major role to the Jews as *Jews* within his new Europe. He opposes a nationalist (or Zionist) solution, because he wants the Jews to mix with the other European peoples. At the same time he also opposes the usual, passive and imitative, Jewish assimilation. His solution is *creative assimilation*, in which the Jews are secularized, excel in all European matters and serve as catalysts in a new revolution of values—this time a curative, Dionysian revolution—that will overcome the Christian culture and the "modern ideas" born of it the (Enlightenment, liberalism, nationalism, socialism, and the like, and, if living to see it, fascism as well). The Jews' role is thereby a transitory one, for it will abolish itself when successful.

It should be noted that Nietzsche's admiration for Diaspora Jews is not aimed at them as bearers of a *religious* culture, but as displaying the human, existential element that he needs for his revolution. Nietzsche, of course, is as opposed to the Jewish *religious* message as he is to any other transcendent religion. The Jews' role is certainly not to "Judaize" Europe in a religious sense. But *Nietzsche seems to believe that their existential qualities can be extracted regardless of the content of their belief.* Nietzsche would rather expect them to secularize and practice creative assimilation in the framework of an atheistic Europe.

I must also emphasize that Nietzsche's pro-Jewish attitude does not derive from liberalism. Just as his attack on nationalism and racism is coming, so to speak, "from the right,"[8] so his defense of the Jews derives from Nietzsche's own (Dionysian and anti-liberal) sources. Also, the Jews are supposed to enhance that same Nietzschean philosophy of life—a task that many Jews, who were and are liberals, can hardly welcome.

Nietzsche's enthusiasm for the vocation of modern Jews is not merely theoretical; it derives also from a classic problem confronting any revolutionary: where is the lever *within* the existing system by which to revolutionize it? Who are the forces uncontaminated by the system? The existence, in the form of the Jews, of a human group he considers more powerful than the others and free of Christian culture is a practical asset that Nietzsche badly needs in order to make his revolution look less utopian in his and in others' eyes.

In any case, my study shows that the Jewish issue was far more central to Nietzsche's thought and project than is usually recognized. The former corrupters of European culture and its designated redeemers, the Jews are placed by Nietzsche at two of the critical junctures in his philosophy. It is thus noteworthy that he always attributes some decisive historical role to the Jews, whether negative or positive, corrupting or redeeming. In this ironic sense he continues to regard them as a kind of "chosen people"—or the secular, heretical Nietzschean version of this concept!

This closes the circle of our analysis. Nietzsche as anti-anti-Semite (and the "Dionysian" admirer of modern Jews) complements Nietzsche as critic of ancient Judaism, within *the same* basic conception and a *single* philosophical project. Using these distinctions, we have delineated the structure of Nietzsche's ambivalence and the relation between its ingredients. The analysis found a fairly consistent thought behind it. Beyond the contradictions, flashes of brilliancy, dubious historical examples, and arbitrary statements that Nietzsche's pen often ejects, we discovered at bottom a uniform way of thinking, applied to a central philosophical theme.

APPENDIX: NIETZSCHE AND HIS ABUSES

Here the question must arise: why was Nietzsche abused more than other philosophers? What was it that attracted his abusers? There seem to be at least four reasons for this: (1) his special mode of writing; (2) the nonordinary psychology required by his position; (3) the "right-wing" origin of his sensibilities; and (4) his political impotence.

(1) Nietzsche's mode of writing is one major reason. His rhetoric is deliberately often wild and paradoxical, intended to arouse and provoke rather than to simply argue and inform; Nietzsche is at times ironic, at times bombastic, and both tonalities are traps for the naive reader; for Nietzsche's irony is not easy to decipher and his fanfare produces overstated effects that others might take at face value. Another factor in his writing is the often deliberate use of contradiction, which he used for several reasons, including his "experimental" way of philosophizing, which shuns final, dogmatic truths and tries to undermine its own authoritative tone.

(2) Another reason for abuse is that Nietzsche's philosophy puts a strain on ordinary mentalities and often breaks the usual "packaging" of intellectual strands; it requires a person to hold on *at the same time* to positions that are usually considered psychologically incompatible. There is always some narrow path Nietzsche traces within the cruder ordinary distinctions, a path that cannot always be defined conceptually but requires, he says, a certain *personality* to locate and identify. Such narrow paths are dangerous, however, in philosophy no less than in mountaineering; one can easily take a deep fall and imagine one drags the author along.

(3) Several of Nietzsche's sensibilities, criticisms, and the like, when taken in isolation, may invoke the joy of recognition in a rightist reader. Because of this partial, local affinity he finds with a Nietzschean idea or sentiment, such a reader then sweeps the *whole* of Nietzsche into his own camp, no matter how many unsurpassable obstacles he has to jump or ignore. This is bad, intellectually corrupt, historically unjust, but very common and all too human. Today there is also a left-wing appropriation of Nietzsche, which makes him the father of pluralism (even of tolerance in a "postmodern" sense),[9] the liberator from "hierarchic" rationalism and the "oppressive" Enlightenment. This abuse is no better, intellectually, than the right-wing one, though politically it seems less ominous.

(4) Finally, Nietzsche attracted abusers because of what I call his political impotence—the vacuum he left in political theory. I know this is not the common view today, but I think Nietzsche's protests against politics are borne out by a marked lacuna in his thinking—the lack of a positive philosophy of the "multitude." Politics is not about the happy few, but about those ordinary people, the modern mass or "herd" which Nietzsche did not care about and did not make the topic of any posi-

tive philosophical reflection. This invites abuse, because when ordinary people are supposed to act in *extra*ordinary ("Dionysian") ways, or when a patrician message intended for a minority is generalized—that is, vulgarized—into a mass political movement, the result is not only intellectually grotesque but a political profanation and possible catastrophe, quite opposed to Nietzsche's aspirations, yet an outcome he should have foreseen.[10]

NOTES

Yovel utilizes the following translations: Kaufmann's *A*, *BGE*, *NCW*, *PN*, *TI*, and *Z*; Kaufmann and Hollingdale's *GM* and *WP*; and Hollingdale's *D* and *HH*.

1. *Hegel and Nietzsche on Judaism* (Tel Aviv: Schocken, 1996. [*Ed. Note*—Originally published in Hebrew. Published in English as *Dark Riddle: Hegel, Nietzsche, and the Jews* (University Park: University of Pennsylvania Press and Cambridge, England: Polity Press, 1998).]

2. In a paper published in 1988 (M. Duffy and W. Mittelman, "Nietzsche's attitude toward the Jews," *Journal of the History of Ideas* 49 (1988): 301–17) the authors attribute to Nietzsche a threefold division very much like mine, which they say they couldn't find in any former publication. Had they looked more attentively they would have seen a short paper of mine, "Perspectives nouvelles sur Nietzsche et le judaïsme," *Revue des etudes juives* 88 (1979): 483–85, which suggests almost exactly the same division. That paper was a summary of public lectures given first at the Israel Academy of Sciences and Humanities and later at the Paris Societé des Etudes Juives (materials from that summary are included in the present chapter). This oversight also has a reassuring side, because if others have independently reached the same thesis, then there must be something in the material that strongly calls for it. The threefold division suggested in my *REJ* paper is recognized and debated in another French paper by D. Bechtel, "Nietzsche et la dialectique de l'histoire juive," in D. Bourel and J. le Rider, *De Sils-Maria à Jérusalem* (Paris: Cerf, 1991), 67–69.

3. This section and the next are drastically shortened summaries. For a more complete discussion, see Yirmiyahu Yovel, "Nietzsche, the Jews, and *ressentiment*," in R. Schacht (ed.), *Nietzsche, Genealogy, Morality* (Berkeley: University of California Press, 1994), 214–36.

4. This indicates, by the way, that Nietzsche was aware of already being abused in his lifetime, hence his protests and indignation.

5. Nietzsche seems to refer to the Fritsch affair mentioned above.

6. There is no doubt Nietzsche considered Burckhardt an anti-Semite (though he was perhaps less extreme than the others).

7. This analysis is chiefly based on *D* 205, which Nietzsche considered most representative of his views about Diaspora Jews (he referred others, like the anti-Semitic Fritsch, to it). Its length does not allow quoting it in this summary.

8. From an aristocratic ethics of virtue and excellence and a Dionysian ethics of power.

9. This makes no sense, because Nietzsche does not tolerate all forms of life—some he would have abolished completely—and because there is no principle of *right* behind his allegedly "pluralistic" position (indeed no principle at all), which is incompatible with the left-wing politics.

10. I think he did, but was unable to cope with it—except by indignant protests, as in the Fritsch affair.

19

Nietzschean Virtue Ethics*

Christine Swanton

1. INTRODUCTION

In *Gorgias* (S.506) Plato claims that "all good things whatever are good when virtue is present in them."[1] Provided virtue is understood in the Greek sense of *arete*, or excellence, the claim marks the fact that goodness in things is to be understood through the idea of excellence, as opposed to quantities or amounts of, say, pleasantness or power. This is the key not only to understanding virtue ethics, in general, but to understanding Nietzschean virtue ethics, in particular.

Nietzsche's rejection of Hedonism (the idea that only pleasure is intrinsically good) is well known; what is less clearly appreciated is that despite certain ambiguities and exaggerations, for Nietzsche goodness (or value) is not to be understood through the idea of will to power (as such) either. It is rather to be understood through the idea of will to power exercised well or excellently, or (as I shall put it) undistorted will to power. Given that a virtue is a disposition of excellent or good responsiveness to items in its domain (such as threatening or dangerous situations, pleasure, friends or potential friends), a Nietzschean virtue ethics based on the idea of will to power will require that an agent not be motivated by will to power as such, but by undistorted will to power.

In providing an account of undistorted will to power, I seek to remove the major obstacle to a Nietzschean virtue ethics, namely, the specter of immoralism. It is

---

*Originally published in *Virtue Ethics: Old and New*, edited by Steven M. Gardiner (Ithaca, NY: Cornell University Press, 2005), 179–92. Reprinted with permission of the author and Cornell University Press.

interesting that in *Natural Goodness* Philippa Foot cites Nietzsche as a potential ally with respect to morality's structure (though not its content), "for what Nietzsche is denying of the supposed virtue of charity is exactly the connection with *human good that was earlier said to give a character trait that status*."[2] I shall appeal to aspects of Nietzsche's thought not emphasized by Foot, to question her view of him as an immoralist. However my primary aim is not to defend Nietzsche himself from that charge, but to develop a Nietzschean virtue ethics.

The claim of immoralism stems from two connected sources: (1) an overly narrow understanding of will to power, and (2) a failure to appreciate the aretaic (or excellence related) aspects of Nietzsche's notion of will to power. To rebut the immoralism charge, but more importantly to develop a Nietzschean virtue ethics, we need briefly to give an account of will to power. That will be done in the next section. Sections 3 and 4 discuss two forms of undistorted will to power: will to power as healthy will to power and will to power as excellent forms of life affirmation. Section 5 attempts to integrate apparent tensions between those two forms by developing a Nietzschean virtue ethics in which the notion of a virtue is relativized to excellence or goodness in "becoming," as opposed to an end-state of perfection.

2. WILL TO POWER

Will to power as a genus must be distinguished from various of its species. As a genus, it is a highly general idea, applicable to all life forms. "A living thing desires above all to *vent* its strength—life as such is will to power" (*BGE* 44).[3] As applied to humans, the need to "vent one's strength" (or expand) is connected essentially with their nature as active, growing, developing beings, rather than mere receptacles of pleasure or welfare.

On the face of it, this broad notion of will to power is almost devoid of content, and as such seems an unpromising base for a virtue ethics. Maudmarie Clark claims, for example, "that the psychological doctrine of the will to power . . . does not deserve serious consideration as an empirical hypothesis."[4] Her reason for this claim is that it does not explain anything, for will to power is "at work everywhere."[5] The will to power hypothesis can survive this objection, in her view, only if it ceases to be monistic. "Will to power" would have to be defined so that at least some possible motives are not instances of it.[6] I shall propose an account of the ethical dimensions of will to power that can survive the objection. The account has several aspects. The first is structural. Will to power is understood through the multifarious ways it can be distorted. J. L. Austin's attack on the notion of real did not eliminate the notion, or restrict the broad range of phenomena to which it could be applied. Further we had to divest ourselves of certain essentialist understandings. We had to focus on the various disparate ways things are not real if we were to secure a substantive content-ful understanding. Again, Austin argued, it is unfreedom or lack of freedom, and not freedom, that "wears the trousers." As far as will to power is concerned, the situation is more complex. We give content to "will to power" not by considering the various ways it can be absent, but by considering the various ways it can be distorted.

This brings us to the second aspect of the account: a relation between the idea of distorted will to power and its ethical dimensions. Distorted will to power underlies vice, whereas virtue is marked by an absence of such distortion. Pity as a vice can thereby be distinguished from virtuous altruism, which Nietzsche frequently calls "overflowing"; laziness as a vice can be distinguished from virtuous "letting things be"; resignation or "willessness" distinguished from sublimation, and (virtuous) solitariness; courage from self-destructive recklessness; and anxiety-ridden fear from proper prudence.

Third, and finally, will to power can have explanatory power only if the disparate forms of distorted will to power can be seen to be related in a theoretically interesting way. That requires that the notion be fleshed out within a psychological framework that gives substantive content to the various virtues and vices. Such a framework, I suggest, may be provided by the development of Nietzsche's psychology along the lines of Alfred Adler's views and those of later theorists and practitioners. Maudmarie Clark's criticism of will to power, I conclude, has bite only if will to power is seen as a simple positive motive without complex nominative dimensions.

The confusion of will to power as a genus with species of will to power (or power) as, namely, augmenting influence and power over, as well as the neglect of the aretaic, have led to immoralist interpretations of Nietzsche. For example, in Stephen D. Hales's consequentialist interpretation of Nietzsche,[7] the distinction between will to power generally, and unhealthy, distorted will to power is not drawn. On Hales's interpretation of Nietzsche, the value to be promoted is power as such, whether or not it expresses or promotes distorted forms. "It appears that his consequentialism ultimately aims at the maximisation of power."[8] By contrast, on my view, Nietzsche distinguishes between "life-affirming" and "life-denying" will to power, a distinction giving some content to the idea of distorted versus undistorted will to power. This idea is present in psychology, where, for example, Erich Fromm contrasts "malignant" and "benign" forms of aggression.[9]

I have suggested that the idea of will to power, properly understood, can provide a basis for a rich psychologically informed conception of virtue. However, if such an understanding is to be garnered from Nietzsche, some kind of unity in his theory is not easy to find. There seem to be two starting points for an account of undistorted will to power: will to power that is not unhealthy, and will to power that is not life denying. Note, however, that these notions are best understood, not as prescribing a monistic blueprint for a virtuous life, but as permitting multiple options constrained by (nonabsolute and sometimes conflicting) requirements to avoid various forms of distortion.

3. UNDISTORTED WILL TO POWER:
LIFE AFFIRMATION

It is time now to give an account of undistorted will to power, for that account makes for normativity—in short, for an ethics. However, wresting such an account from Nietzsche is difficult. For Nietzsche's (or a Nietzschean) notion of undistorted will to power has at its heart two central ideas: life affirmation and health. Unfortunately (from the point of view of presenting a unified theory) these two ideas do not appear to pull in the same direction. Of most concern is that what may count as life affirming may be said on depth psychological criteria apparently favored by Nietzsche to be sick. In short, we have two potential criteria for undistorted will to power—will to power that is life affirming or not life denying, and will to power that is healthy or not sick.

Let us now investigate the moral theoretic underpinnings of a morality that is based on life affirmation. The life affirmative aspects of Nietzsche's thought bear the hallmarks of a value-centered morality. The values in question are the "life affirming" ones of, for example, creativity, self-assertion, spontaneity, overflowing, lightness of spirit, play. Life-affirming value theory may or may not be virtue ethical. It is virtue ethical only if the life-affirming values of creativity, spontaneity, play, and so forth, are to be understood as aretaic; that is, as having excellence or virtue built into them. Nonaretaic value centered moralities rely on the provision of a set of "base-level" values (such as spontaneity, creativity, and play) specified independently of virtue. Such moralities then define virtues as dispositions to respond to these values appropriately—namely, to promote them, honor them, or (as on Thomas Hurka's view) to love them.[10] "Virtue" is thus understood derivatively in terms of certain sorts of responsiveness to, or dispositions to, act favorably toward those values.

A virtue ethics requires by contrast aretaic interpretations of the relevant values—creativity must be creativity that is free from all vice (or more weakly, some relevant vices); play cannot be, for example, mocking, or (in competitive sport) must be competitive without violating standards of fair play. Is an aretaic reading of the life-affirming values a plausible reading of Nietzsche? I think so. A unifying aretaic value central in Nietzsche's thought is the absence of something described as "the greatest ugliness"—mediocrity. The absence of mediocrity is inherently an aretaic idea; indeed, it connotes the satisfaction (to a sufficient degree) of standards of excellence. The substantive task, of course, is to provide theories about what constitutes mediocrity in, for example, music, the visual arts, politics, relationships, philosophy, and other areas of human endeavor and culture. The specification of spontaneity, play, self-assertion, as *aretaic* values cannot be given without having to hand theories of excellence in those endeavors.

If the absence of mediocrity provides the aretaic value that unifies the various "life affirming" values, may it not provide too, the central value that underpins the second understanding of undistorted will to power—that is, the healthy will to power or will to power that is free of sickness? If so, then the two understandings of undistorted will to power can be combined into a single Nietzschean virtue ethics. Unhealthy and life-denying will to power could then be seen as both expressing and promoting mediocrity, for Nietzsche. Much of Nietzsche's thought does indeed support this idea. Pity, a manifestation of "sick" will to power (for reasons to be explained), is also harmful to life-affirming values, by undermining the achievements of "man's lucky hits" (i.e., those free of sickness), and by not accepting "meaningful suffering," so needed for the finest creativity and the avoidance of mediocrity.

However, there are two problems with this unificatory move. First, not all "sickness" and life denial seems connected with mediocrity. There is no doubt that Nietzsche regarded the self-laceration of Christian saints (such as St. Teresa of Avila) as unhealthy and life denying, but it would be hard to describe such saints as mediocre. Rather, their actions and motivations are unhealthy and life denying because of their connection with a sense of individual worthlessness.

It may be replied that I have just cited self-assertiveness as a life-affirming value, and as such, as one of the values unified by the aretaic value of absence of mediocrity. Indeed this is so. But the kind of lack of self-assertiveness that is particularly associated in Nietzsche's thought with mediocrity, is the passivity of herd-like behavior condemned by Nietzsche in passages such as the following:

> For this is how things stand: the withering and levelling of European man constitutes *our* greatest danger, because it is a wearying sight. . . . Today we see nothing with any desire to become greater, we sense that everything is going increasingly downhill, thinning out, getting more good natured, cleverer, more comfortable, more mediocre, more indifferent, more Chinese, more Christian—man, there is no doubt, is "improving" all the time. (*GM* I:12)

Although in Nietzsche's view one could describe St. Teresa of Avila as suffering from a highly problematic sense of worthlessness, one could not describe her as herd-like or mediocre.

Here is the second problem with the unificatory move. In Nietzsche's view, it seems, the halting of the slide to mediocrity can be achieved by certain expressions of what, in views recoverable from Nietzsche, could be regarded as sick. Consider the apparently grandiose artist or philosopher living the ethics of creativity. Of such a person, Nietzsche claims: "[H]e is not far from the sinful wish: *pereat mundus, fiat philosophia, fiat philosophus, fiam!*" (*GM* III:3) ["Let the world perish, but let there be philosophy, the philosopher, me!"] Such a philosopher "does *not* deny existence, he rather affirms *his* existence and *only* his existence." (*GM* III:3) Even the sickness of bad conscience is lauded by Nietzsche, if it has a creative vigor: if it becomes "*active* bad conscience" and "[brings] to light much that is new and disturbing in the way of beauty and affirmation" (*GM* II:18).

So let us think of life affirmation and health as two somewhat independent aspects of undistorted will to power and move on now to health.

4. UNDISTORTED WILL TO POWER: HEALTH

Anticipating psychoanalytic theory, Nietzsche not only largely understands health through the idea of sickness, but also shares that view's general pessimism. "For man is more sick, more uncertain, more mutable, less defined, than any other animal . . . he is *the* sick animal." And, "He is . . . the most endangered, the most chronically and deeply sick of all sick animals" (*GM* III:13). The sickness that is at the forefront of Nietzsche's attention is resentment: a manifestation of what Alfred Adler was later to call the inferiority complex. In this complex, according to Adler, there is a gap between the despised self and the ego-ideal that at an unconscious level are in conflict. In the inferiority complex, the conflict results in various sorts of neurotic resolution with neurotic "symptoms." The symptom of resentment, at least in its supposed Christian form, is the topic of Nietzsche's best known discussion, but he is remarkably insightful on two other species of inferiority complex: what Karen Horney was later to call the expansionist solution or the desire for mastery (grandiosity and cruelty) and the solution of resignation.[11] The intellectualist version of the latter is the frequent target of Nietzsche's scorn. He excoriates philosophers who retreat to the world of abstraction and pure reason. I shall concentrate on the Christian version of a resentment-filled inferiority complex (called by Karen Horney the self-effacing solution of love) that is particularly important for a Nietzschean distinction between virtue and closely allied vices, as we shall presently see.

What, according to Nietzsche, is resentment? As Bernard Reginster puts it, Nietzsche's person of resentment is inhibited by a feeling of incurable impotence, while retaining "pride" or "arrogance" and a desire at some level to lead a life of nobility and strength.[12] Furthermore, the conflict between the sense of weakness and expansionist strivings is not resolved: either by a stoical elimination of desire or by a full (self-loving) acceptance of one's objectively based weakness.

The conflict between a desire to lead a life of strength, nobility, or achievement and a sense of being impotent and worthless creates a need for resolution. As a manifestation of this conflict, resentment consists in a certain sort of distorted resolution of this conflict, one that valorizes the welfare of the weak, and thereby the altruistic virtues, while at the same time failing to overcome a sense of impotence. This results in externalized self-hate. Hence the manner in which the altruistic virtues are expressed is one of repressed hostility and revenge, as is highlighted in Nietzsche's discussion of pity in *Daybreak*.

> An accident that happens to another offends us: it would make us aware of our impotence, and perhaps of our cowardice, if we did not go to assist him. Or it brings with it in itself a diminution of our honour in the eyes of others or in our own eyes. Or an accident and suffering incurred by another constitutes a signpost to some danger to us; and it can have a painful effect upon us simply as a token of human vulnerability and fragility in general. We repel this kind of pain and offence and requite it through an act of pity; it may contain a subtle self-defense or even a piece of revenge. That at bottom

we are thinking very strongly of ourselves can be divined from the decision we arrive at in every case in which we *can* avoid the sight of the person suffering, perishing or complaining: we decide *not* to do so if we can present ourselves as the more powerful and as a helper, if we are certain of applause, if we want to feel how fortunate we are in contrast, or hope that the sight will relieve our boredom. (*D* 133)

In Nietzsche, nonvirtuous altruism—pity—is characterized by self-referential comparisons masking externalized hostility. By contrast, genuine virtuous altruism is an overflowing expression of self-love, where the distorted will to power of pity is absent. This is clear in the following passage. "In the foreground stands the feeling of plenitude, of power which seeks to overflow, the happiness of high tension, the consciousness of wealth which would like to give away and bestow." (*BGE* 260; Kaufmann trans.) This sentiment, even the language, is echoed by Erich Fromm.

For the productive character, giving has an entirely different meaning. Giving is the highest expression of potency. In the very act of giving, I experience my strength, my wealth, my power. This experience of heightened vitality and potency fills me with joy. I experience myself as overflowing, spending, alive, hence, as joyous.[13]

The overflowing and, indeed, passional nature of many of Nietzsche's virtues is a phenomenon approvingly discussed by Robert Solomon.[14] But there is a problem with Nietzsche's valorizing such virtues on the grounds that they are life affirming. Grandiosity and grandiose self-destructiveness are, in Horney's view, one of the faces of the neurotic "expansionist" solution. This is what Horney calls a "streamlined" neurotic solution to the problem of dynamic conflict between the "superior" self (the "ego-ideal"—to use Adler's term) and the despised self, in the inferiority complex. In this version of streamlined solution, the inferior self is ruthlessly suppressed, in contrast to the self-effacing solution in which the superior self—the ego-ideal—is suppressed. I am not suggesting that all "overflowing" is sick as opposed to expressing a genuine "plenteousness": a Nietzschean term favored also by Fromm and C. S. Lewis to describe genuine agapeic love. But certainly some kinds of overflowing favored by Nietzsche seem, on the face of it, to be suspect. Consider the following from *Thus Spoke Zarathustra*: "I love him whose soul squanders itself, who wants no thanks and returns none: for he always gives away and does not want to preserve himself. I love him whose soul is overfull, so that he forgets himself, and all things are in him: thus all things spell his going under" (*Z*:I "Prologue" 4).

5. NIETZSCHEAN VIRTUE ETHICS: CONTENT AND STRUCTURE

In this section, I shall claim that the apparent tensions revealed in the previous two sections between ideals of health and life affirmation can be resolved by the development of a Nietzschean virtue ethics based on Nietzsche's ideas of "self-overcoming" or "becoming who you are": an ethics that does not presuppose the idea of an individual end state of perfection. In brief, in this resolution, we are not to see health and life affirmation as end-states of perfection. There are two broad possibilities for resolution. First, one could imagine that those who are to become "who they are" are a select few, for this is the means to realize the perfectionist-consequentialist goal of cultural excellence. This does not entail that *individuals* have, or should have, a definite goal in mind when they improve themselves in "self-overcoming." Second, one could reject consequentialism while maintaining the aretaic value of avoiding mediocrity. "Becoming who you are" is an injunction for all to follow, by exemplifying worthwhile achievement in one's own life and not destroying or undermining the achievements of others.

I shall adopt the second of these strategies. The central idea is that the tensions can be resolved if we conceive of Nietzschean virtue as essentially tied to self-improvement (self-overcoming) that does not presuppose an end-state of individual perfection, in contrast to Aristotelian conceptions of virtue as end-states of perfection. If both health and life affirmation are seen as end-states of perfection, and virtue as exemplifying both these ideals, then a virtue ethics based on them would appear to have an incoherent conception of virtue, since, it seems, they are conflicting ideals of perfection. By contrast, if norms of health and life affirmation are to be embedded in a virtue ethics of self-improvement, the tensions between these norms can be resolved. I shall claim that one can do this by recognizing that their function as norms is constrained by norms of development, such as "do not be virtuous beyond your strength."

Both the consequentialist and nonconsequentialist strategies for overcoming the tensions between health and life affirmation as ideals presuppose that we can speak of excellence in a process of betterment—in a process of what Nietzsche calls "overcoming." For we can attempt to improve ourselves in ways that fall short of satisfying norms of development by, for example, running before we can walk (emulating the supremely virtuous), seeing an analyst when we should not be, or not seeing an analyst when we should, being overly reflective or insufficiently reflective, and so on. However, how this idea features in the consequentialist strategy is quite different from the way it figures in nonconsequentialist views.

Before developing the nonconsequentialist alternative, let us take a quick look at the consequentialist strategy, for this has been a dominant interpretation of Nietzsche. Many commentators have understood Nietzsche as a particularly nasty exemplar of perfectionistic consequentialism. Perfectionism, whether consequentialist or nonconsequentialist, is the view that goodness or value is to be understood as "the realization of human excellence in the various forms of culture."[15] Perfectionism in this sense is virtue-theoretic, if these excellences include, in a central way, the virtues (however they are conceived in that theory). However, a virtue-theoretic form of perfectionism may be consequentialist, in which case it would not be virtue *ethical* on normal understandings. In fact, John Rawls ascribes to Nietzsche what Conant calls "excellence-consequentialism," which means "(1) that the perfectionist is concerned with optimizing the conditions which promote the achievement of excellence in the arts and sciences, and (2) that the goodness of an action is to be assessed in accordance with the degree to which it maximises such forms of excellence."[16]

There is some textual evidence that Nietzsche supports this view. An example of such evidence occurs in *Beyond Good and Evil*:

> The essential thing in a good and healthy aristocracy is, however, that it does *not* feel itself to be a function (of the monarchy or of the commonwealth) but as their *meaning* and supreme justification—that it therefore accepts with a good conscience the sacrifice of innumerable men who *for its sake* have to be suppressed and reduced to imperfect men, to slaves and instruments. Its fundamental faith must be that society should *not* exist for the sake of society but only as foundation and scaffolding upon which a select species of being is able to raise itself to its higher task and in general to a higher *existence*: like those sun-seeking climbing plants of Java—they are named *sipo matador*—which clasp an oak-tree with their tendrils so long and often that at last, high above it but supported by it, they can unfold their crowns in the open light and display their happiness. (*BGE* 258)

Insofar as this passage suggests a perfectionist consequentialism, norms of self-improvement, whether relating to health or life affirmation, are subservient to the promotion of the goal of overall cultural excellence understood in the following way. The measure of cultural excellence is given by the overall achievement of the best or most talented members of society. Tensions between ideals of health and life affirmation are resolved by understanding them in an instrumental way. If "sick" grandiosity in a talented artist enhances the realization of cultural achievement, such "sickness" is to be tolerated, even applauded. However, the consequentialist understanding does not sit well with a central theme in Nietzsche: the requirement on all of us to "become who you are"; to work at discovering and expressing the genius within you. Let us now elaborate the second, nonconsequentialist strategy for overcoming the tensions revealed in the previous section.

The dynamic features of a nonconsequentialist Nietzschean ethics are captured in the aphorism, "Become who you are" where the injunction is intended to apply to all, and virtues are understood as expressive of an individual's living this maxim in her own life as opposed to their being seen as traits whose status as virtues is wholly dependent on their systematically promoting the consequentialist-perfectionist goal. The aphorism, however, is on the face of it mysterious, suggesting that there is a final state (of perhaps perfection) that is your *true* self and that you have a duty to reach. However this reading seems un-Nietzschean: as Alexander Nehamas points out, for Nietzsche, "becoming does not aim at a final state."[17] A less problematic reading is suggested by the expanded version of the aphorism in "Schopenhauer as Educator": "The human being who does not wish to belong to the mass needs only to cease being comfortable with himself, let him follow his conscience, which calls to him: 'Be yourself! All you are now doing, thinking, desiring is not you yourself.'"[18]

As Conant puts it, "All one need do is become uncomfortable with the discrep-

ancy between oneself and one's self—between who we are at present, and the self
that is somehow ours and yet presently at a distance from us."[19] This does not entail
that there is an end-state of "arrival" where the self, or one of the selves, presently
at a distance from us, is the terminus of our endeavors. Self-improvement should be
the basis of our endeavors, but that does not mean that we should have definite
productive goals such as being a great artist, which now drive all our actions. Nor is
there an *end*-state of perfection that one can reach such that one can say on reaching
it that "I have arrived." Rather, improvement is a continuous matter of overcoming
obstacles, becoming stronger, while dealing with the world and achieving worthwhile goals. These goals may themselves change as one becomes stronger and faces
new obstacles and circumstances. John Richardson puts the point well.[20] Having
argued that "will to power," or power, is not itself an end but is constituted by
improvement, growth, or development in "patterns of effort" in achieving the various internal ends of "drives," he claims that

> [t]his makes the connection between power and a drive's internal and even less direct
> than we expected: not only does power not lie in this end's achievement, it doesn't even
> lie in progress toward it but in improving this progress. Moreover, the criteria for this
> "improvement" aren't set by the end—it's not just an improvement in the route's effi-
> ciency for achieving the end. Rather . . . it lies in an enrichment or elaboration of the
> drive's activity pattern.[21]

Although there need be no final state to which we should aspire, that constitutes a
norm of perfection, there do need to be norms of self-improvement if the idea of
becoming who you are is to make sense as an injunction for self-improvement.

How are norms of life affirmation and health constrained by developmental
norms of self-improvement? Given that improvement is something that occurs step
by step, what norms govern the steps we take? In *Zarathustra*, Nietzsche claims: "Do
not be virtuous beyond your strength!" (*Z*:IV "On the Higher Man") Clearly this
is not a recipe for complacency or timidity: it has to be given a dynamic reading.
The point of the injunction is to warn us against directly emulating the supremely
virtuous. For such emulation is not appropriate to one in a state of "convalescence."
According to this view, a conception of a virtue such as generosity may be understood not merely as a threshold notion (such that it is possible that one is both
virtuous and capable of improvement) but also as a continuum, relativized to the
strength of the agent. Hence (virtuous) generosity for the self-improver may not be
overflowing bounteousness, for attempts at such bounteousness in the relatively
weak may constitute self-destructive, resentment-filled, self-sacrifice that is ultimately harmful to others as well as oneself. A core virtue, or core component of
virtue, such as self-love, will not have the same features at different points along the
self-improvement path. Just as a truly self-confident society will be able to dispense
with punishment according to Nietzsche, so the strongest individuals will be able to
say: "Of what concern are these parasites to me?" (*GM* II:10) In other words, turn-

ing the other check is a virtue of the strong. By contrast, such behavior in the weak is likely to be a sign of regressive self-abasement. Though self-love in the strong can manifest itself in a form of forgetfulness, in the weak, forgetfulness may be a form of repression in which anger is driven inward and surfaces in various distortions: secretive revenge, bitterness, manipulativeness, jealousy. Better for the weak to display assertiveness, even of a retaliatory kind, to lessen their tendencies to be wounded. Nietzsche puts the point this way in *Ecce Homo*: "[The sick person] does not know how to get loose of anything, to become finished with anything to repel anything—everything injures. Human being and thing obtrude too closely; experiences strike one too deeply, memory is a festering wound." (*EH* "Wise" 6)

Again, to use another example of Nietzsche's, solitude as a disposition is a virtue of the strong; otherwise, it is loneliness, the escape *of* the sick as opposed to escape *from* the sick (*Z*:III "Upon the Mount of Olives"). In solitude, whatever one has brought into it grows—also the inner beast. Therefore solitude is inadvisable for the many" (*Z*:IV "On the Higher Education of Man"). In other words, though (proper) self-sufficiency is a virtue, the proper cultivation and nature of that virtue is not straightforward—it will have different manifestations according to one's level of strength. The cultivation of solitude and a desire for such is not advised for the weak.

We are now in a position to see how a dynamic, nonconsequentialist, Nietzschean virtue ethics resolves the tensions revealed in section 4. Rather than health and life affirmation being seen as somewhat independent states of perfection, norms of health and life affirmation interact in differing ways in different contexts of self-improvement or "self-overcoming." Progress is not understood simply in terms of realizing an already given end, for the end itself is re-created more or less continuously, and in a variety of ways for a variety of reasons. First, one's "pattern of activity" is enriched and modified as one reshapes one's ends in the light of circumstances and developing desires and interests. Second, improving one's strength or health is not a smooth progress, for in a sense one must be careful not to overreach one's (current) strength. However, this is not to say that Nietzsche regards this as a universal injunction as opposed to a general warning. At times he appears to admire such overreaching. It would be a mistake to regard Nietzsche's norms as absolute and nonconflicting. Finally, virtue itself is shaped by norms of self-improvement. Though virtue rather than an amount of power, say, is at least a necessary condition of goodness in human beings, goodness should not be understood in terms of realizing an end-state of perfection.

The proposed understanding of a Nietzschean virtue ethics poses a problem. For is it not the case that building self-improvement into the very fabric of virtue is an oxymoron? Is not a virtue a stable trait of character? Answering this question fully presupposes an account of character traits—their robustness and malleability. My own view, which cannot be defended here, is that virtues are more or less robust depending on where the threshold of virtue is set in different contexts. Second and more important, since practical wisdom is at least characteristically an aspect of virtue, virtue involves self-knowledge, including knowledge of where one is placed on the self-improvement path, and of how large or small are the steps one should take. Relative robustness had better not be confused with rigidity, incapacity to develop further, and imperviousness to changing contexts. However, this is not to deny that virtue, at high levels, is constituted by a solid core of incorruptible integrity, honesty, and so forth: a core of virtue not readily undermined by corrosive social forces and institutions.

Let me now summarize the main features of a Nietzschean virtue ethics. I began this chapter with the claim that Nietzsche's ethics is aretaic in the sense that goodness in things is to be understood as having excellence built into then. Where excellence in things is characteristically understood as their either being handled virtuously (say, virtuously handled money, honors, play, friendship, pleasure), or their being themselves virtuous (virtuous human beings), such an ethics is a candidate for being a virtue ethics.

The content of Nietzschean virtue ethics is to be understood in terms of undistorted will to power, which has two aspects: life affirmation and health. However, these are not to be understood as end-states of perfection, but as norms of self-improvement. The idea of undistorted will to power enables us to distinguish between virtues and closely allied vices, such as the forms of altruistic virtue and vice.

A Nietzschean virtue ethics can be seen as a nonconsequentialist version of perfectionism in the sense defined above. However, Nietzschean virtue ethics is a nonstandard form of perfectionism insofar as the road traveled seems more important than the destination. Self-improvement is a process, itself having norms of excellence, but (1) those norms do not presuppose that there is a single goal suitable for all, for we are all different in strength, threats, interests, and circumstances of life, (2) in a process of "self-overcoming" we do not necessarily have in mind a long-term destination, for the good life may involve much experimentation, and (3) virtue itself should not be understood as an end-state of perfection. Rather, insofar as "self-overcoming" is at the core of virtue, it is a dynamic process-notion, relativized to the strength of individuals as well as to their roles and circumstances.

NOTES

I owe grateful thanks to Steve Gardiner for his helpful suggestions for improvement, and for organizing the conference in Christchurch, New Zealand, for which this was originally written. Thanks also to the participants, especially Robert Solomon.

1. Cited in Michael Slote, *Morals From Motives* (Oxford: Oxford University Press, 2000), 155.
2. (Oxford: Clarendon Press, 2001), 107.
3. *Ed. Note*—For translations of Nietzsche's works the author uses Hollingdale's transla-

tions of *BGE, D*; Smith's translation of *GM*; Kaufmann's translations of *BGE* (where noted), *EH*, and *Z*.

4. "Nietzsche's Doctrines of the Will to Power," in *Nietzsche*, ed. John Richardson and Brian Leiter (Oxford: Oxford University Press, 2001), 139–49, at 140.

5. Ibid., 141.

6. Ibid.

7. "Was Nietzsche a Consequentialist?" *International Studies in Philosophy* 27 (1995): 25–34.

8. Ibid., 32.

9. Erich Fromm, *The Anatomy of Human Destructiveness* (London: Penguin Books, 1977).

10. See Thomas Hurka, *Virtue, Vice, and Value* (Oxford: Oxford University Press, 2001).

11. Karen Horney, *Neurosis and Human Growth: The Struggle Toward Self-Realization* (New York: Norton, 1970).

12. Bernard Reginster, "*Ressentiment*, Evaluation, and Integrity," *International Studies in Philosophy* 27 (1995): 117–24, esp. 118.

13. Erich Fromm, *The Art of Loving* (London: Unwin Paperbacks, 1975 [1957]), 26.

14. See his "Nietzsche's Virtues: a Personal Inquiry," in *Nietzsche's Postmoralism: Essays on Nietzsche's Prelude to Philosophy's Future*, ed. Richard Schacht (Cambridge: Cambridge University Press, 2001), 123–48.

15. James Conant, "Nietzsche's Perfectionism: A Reading of *Schopenhauer as Educator*," in *Nietzsche's Postmoralism*.

16. Ibid., 187.

17. Alexander Nehamas, "How One Becomes What One Is," in *Nietzsche*, ed. Richardson and Leiter, 255–80; at 261.

18. *SE* cited in James Conant, 197.

19. Ibid.

20. See his "Nietzsche's Power Ontology," in *Nietzsche*, 150–85.

21. Ibid., 158.

20

How We Became What We Are
Tracking the "Beasts of Prey"*

Daniel W. Conway

There is, of course, a beast hidden in every man.

—Ivan Karamozov

The beast in me
Is caged by frail and fragile bars.
Restless by day
And by night rants and rages at the stars.
God help the beast in me.

—Johnny Cash

I

Nietzsche takes as his task the "translation" of the human being "back into nature" (*BGE* 230).[1] Toward this end, he places humankind squarely within the amoral environs of the animal kingdom, which he in turn honors as nobler than the kingdoms supposedly ruled by "man" and "God." He thus acknowledges no hierarchical index—whether divine, metaphysical, or supernatural—whereby the human animal

---

*Revised by the author from its original publication in *A Nietzschean Bestiary: Becoming Animal Beyond Docile and Brutal*, edited by Christa Davis Acampora and Ralph R. Acampora (Lanham, MD: Rowman & Littlefield Publishers, Inc., 2004), 156–77. Published with permission of the author and publisher.

could be considered to be categorically superior to other animals or endowed with extra-animalistic powers and privileges. According to Nietzsche, the human animal is neither the acme of natural selection, nor the *telos* of evolutionary development, nor the lord of the beasts, nor the center of the biotic community, nor the steward of the planetary thesaurus. The human animal is distinguished from other animals largely on the strength of its unrivaled capacity to endure self- and other-induced suffering.[2]

The main problem that Nietzsche faces in pursuing this task is that in many respects, modern human beings do not resemble other, especially wilder, animals. We moderns are not obviously reliant upon unconscious drives and impulses to provide us with instinctual patterns of behavior that we then enact in pre-reflective embodiments of our native vitality. Our possession of conscience and free will, our facility with languages and complex symbolic systems, our creation of cultures and civilizations, and our premonition of our own death all seem to place us well outside the animal kingdom. To put it bluntly, the "ultramodern unassuming moral milksop who 'no longer bites'" (*GM* P:7) is not easily confused with "the splendid blond beast prowling about avidly in search of spoil and victory" (*GM* I:11). It is therefore incumbent upon the genealogist of morals to explain how it is that we became what we are. In so doing, he must account for the development of the human being from wild predator to domesticated herd animal.

Nietzsche's account of this development is well known to us in its general outline. The domesticated human animal is uniquely characterized by its "bad conscience" (*schlechtes Gewissen*), from which it suffers as a result of its enforced renunciation of the unconscious drives and impulses that formerly regulated its organic activity. In keeping with his commitment to the evolving paradigm of scientific naturalism, Nietzsche thus attempts to account for the "bad conscience" as an organic affliction that significantly restricts the human animal's capacity to exteriorize its native energy.[3] This affliction was produced, he conjectures, as a result of the involuntary inward discharge of primal aggression, which in turn invested the human animal with an unparalleled, if jumbled, expanse of interiority:

> All instincts that do not discharge themselves outwardly *turn inward*—this is what I call the *internalization* of humankind: thus it was that man first developed what was later called his "soul." The entire inner world, originally as thin as if it were stretched between two membranes, expanded and extended itself, acquired depth, breadth, and height, in the same measure as outward discharge was inhibited. (*GM* II:16)

This process of "internalization," he further conjectures, is the consequence of

> the most fundamental change [humankind] ever experienced—that change which occurred when he found himself finally enclosed within the walls of society and peace. The situation that faced sea animals when they were compelled to become land animals or perish was the same as that which faced these semi-animals, well adapted to the wil-

derness, to war, to prowling, to adventure: suddenly all their instincts were disvalued and "suspended." (*GM* II:16)

This is a powerful hypothesis, and it ranks among the most daring and influential of Nietzsche's many contributions to philosophy. As an explanation, however, this hypothesis raises at least as many questions as it answers. How, for example, did this "fundamental change" come about? Who or what is responsible for confining these wild, warlike, prowling semianimals behind the "walls of society and peace"?

Here Nietzsche finds himself in a familiar difficulty. Like Hegel, Feuerbach, Marx, Freud, and all other practitioners of philosophical anthropology, he must appeal to an event or occurrence that is fully natural (and, so, in principle empirically verifiable), despite having no direct evidence of the event or occurrence in question.[4] This means that he is obliged to *speculate* on the nature of the historical processes that delivered the human animal to its current state of domestication and, in this case, to posit an unexpected, inexplicable rupture in the development of the human animal.[5] The chief danger involved in speculations of this sort is that they encourage historians and anthropologists to rely on human conventions (e.g., founding agreements, social contracts) to account for the origins of human society. If Nietzsche's hypothesis is to avoid a vicious circularity, then it somehow must account for the domestication of the human animal without appealing to any virtues, powers, or capacities that uniquely belong to the modern human beings whose situation it is supposed to explain.

The very next section of *On the Genealogy of Morals* provides a clarification of this hypothesis. "Among the presuppositions of this hypothesis," he explains, is the following conjecture:

> The welding of a hitherto unchecked and formless populace [*Bevölkerung*] into a firm form was not only instituted by an act of violence but also carried to its conclusion by nothing but acts of violence—that the oldest "state" thus appeared as a fearful tyranny, as an oppressive and remorseless machine, and went on working until this raw material of peoples and semi-animals [*Rohstoff von Volk und Halbthier*] was at last not only thoroughly kneaded and pliant but also *formed*. (*GM* II:17)

To be sure, this "presupposition" would bear further elaboration. The original presentation of the "hypothesis" in *GM* II:16 identified no agents or culprits who might be deemed responsible for the enforced confinement of the formerly wild hominids. There, in fact, we were led to conclude that *all* formerly wild hominids suffered a common fate pertaining to the suspension and devaluation of their instincts.[6]

As Nietzsche asserts in *GM* II:17, however, this fate was not suffered uniformly by all formerly wild hominids. Here, in fact, he alludes to the fateful meeting of *two* hominid types, one less and the other more estranged from its native animality. Witness, for example, his unsentimental account of the origins of the "state":

[S]ome pack of blond beasts of prey, a conqueror and master race [*eine Eroberer- und Herren-Rasse*][7] which, organized for war and with the ability to organize, unhesitatingly lays its terrible claws upon a populace perhaps tremendously superior in numbers but still formless and nomadic. (*GM* II:17)[8]

As this passage intimates, Nietzsche's "presupposition" is apparently meant to explain how the "semianimals" described in *GM* II:16 came to find themselves involuntarily immured within civil society.[9] As it turns out, they were forcibly placed there by *other* hominids, who, for reasons as yet unknown, either possessed or retained a greater share of their native wildness and predatory spontaneity.

Nietzsche thus conjectures that the domestication of the human animal began with a sudden act of mass capture, as a "conqueror- and master-race" of hominids tyrannized a weaker (but larger) populace of nomadic hominids. The members of this weaker populace were compelled to forego the free, spontaneous discharge of animal vitality to which they had been accustomed, and they were obliged instead to resort to an internal discharge of their primal drives and impulses. They thereby acquired interiority and the "bad conscience" that marks its expanse.[10]

Nietzsche does not disclose the basis for this stipulated distinction between two types (or subspecies) of wild hominids. The "semianimals" who suddenly found themselves captive were "well adapted to the wilderness, to war, to prowling, [and] to adventure" (*GM* II:16), but they were utterly unprepared for the bewildering assault of their unknown aggressors. He observes that the aggressor type appeared on the scene much as it appears in the thick of his narrative: suddenly, unpredictably, and without adequate explanation. Relying on a familiar image of the masterly human beings whom he most admires,[11] he compares the arrival of the aggressor type to the onset of an unforeseen natural disaster:

One does not reckon with such [viz., "masterly"] natures; they come like fate, without reason, consideration, or pretext; they appear as lightning appears, too terrible, too sudden, too convincing, too "different" even to be hated. (*GM* II:17)

This sort of comparison is convenient not only for the captive hominids, who need not bother to divine the motives of their inscrutable aggressors, but also for Nietzsche, who is freed thereby from the onerous task of explaining the origins, history, and aims of the aggressor type.

What are we to make of this ingenious, albeit sketchy, account of the origins of the "state"? Perhaps Nietzsche means to appeal here to the stochastic variations that characterize any species population of sufficient size. It is probable that some identifiable subset of wild hominids would be far more aggressive than the average hominid, and it is plausible that these stochastic outliers might band together and conquer the larger (but less aggressive) subset. Alternately, we might interpret the suddenness with which the aggressor type appears on the scene as suggesting the unprecedented meeting, and subsequent clash, of two separate species of hominid development. Or perhaps he helps himself to such an obviously facile distinction in order to mock *any* attempt (including his own) to unearth the historical origins of the "state."[12]

In all fairness to Nietzsche, he advances this "presupposition," as well as the "hypothesis" it serves, in the context of the more sweeping anthropological narrative offered in *GM* II. For the purposes of developing this narrative, he may be satisfied simply to establish the *possibility* of a strictly naturalistic explanation of the origins of the "bad conscience." In that event, the historical accuracy of his "hypothesis" would be less important to him than its adherence to the evolving paradigm of scientific naturalism. Perhaps, that is, the text comprising *GM* II:16–17 is primarily concerned to speculate on the unique historical conditions under which the "beasts of prey" might have established a more settled, place-bound form of community.[13]

The rest, as they say, is history—*human* history, to be precise. Once caged, these formerly wild hominids began to explore the undiscovered country of their inner kingdom. Emboldened by the "slave revolt in morality" (*GM* I:10), captive peoples falsely claimed for themselves the freedom to *choose* their enforced domestication. To cope with the meaningless suffering of the "bad conscience," the human animal heaped one compensatory fantasy upon another, culminating in the installation of guilt as the primary motivation for its various endeavors. And, so, we became what we are: sickly animals verging precariously upon the "will to nothingness."

II

But what of the "beasts of prey" who unwittingly launched the development of the human animal along its current, deathbound trajectory? Were they in turn conquered, enslaved, or slaughtered by an even wilder pack of predators? Or did they simply vanish, perhaps as suddenly and unpredictably as they appeared? That such questions are not merely academic in nature is confirmed by Nietzsche's surmise that "the *meaning of all culture*" lies in "the reduction of the beast of prey 'man' to a tame and civilized animal" (*GM* I:11). Let us turn now to consider how this "reduction" might have been accomplished.

It is no accident that Nietzsche locates the formative activity of the "beasts of prey" in the dim prehistory of the species. Over the course of this unrecorded period, the human animal slowly acquired the ability (if not the permission) to make promises. This acquisition in turn obliged the human animal to endure the forcible investiture of memory, conscience, and the spare furnishings of interiority. Throughout this blood-soaked period of human prehistory, the creatures wielding the instruments of torture, delighting in every shriek, moan, and lamentation, were none other than the "beasts of prey."

Within the larger setting of Nietzsche's philosophical anthropology, the "beasts of prey" fill the role of a kind of permanently missing link. They are the shadowy, liminal creatures that connect the domesticated human animal to its wild ancestors in the unbroken chain of evolutionary development. Owing to this unique role, in fact, the "beasts of prey" acquire a quasi-mythic status. In what is perhaps his most dubious reference to the activity of the "beasts of prey," he describes them as possessed of attributes conducive both to wild predation *and* to civilized cultivation:[14]

> Once they [viz., these noble men] go outside, where the strange, the *stranger*, is found, they are not much better than uncaged beasts of prey. There they savor a freedom from all social constraints, they compensate themselves in the wilderness for the tension engendered by protracted confinement and enclosure within the peace of society, they go back to the innocent conscience of the beast of prey, as triumphant monsters. (*GM* I:11)[15]

As this passage suggests, we apparently are meant to think of the "beasts of prey" as partaking equally of both civilization *and* wilderness. Although indirectly responsible for the affliction of the "bad conscience" in others, the "beasts of prey" enjoy the privileges and freedoms pertaining to an "innocent" conscience.[16] They are able to postpone immediate gratification if necessary, but without forfeiting their capacity to visit their primal aggression upon unlucky captives. When they are not patrolling the enclosing walls of civil society, they scale these walls and return to the wilderness that renews their animal vitality. Although these predators govern their captives under an impressive regimen of self-imposed organization, apparently setting aside their natural "irritation" and "disquiet" with such tasks (*GM* III:18), they also retain the freedom to revert periodically to the wilding of a wolf pack. Borrowing a sentence from a related discussion, we might think of the "beasts of prey" as

> Human beings whose nature was still natural, barbarians in every terrible sense of the word, men of prey [*Raubmenschen*] who were still in possession of unbroken strength of will and lust for power . . . more *whole* human beings (which also means, at every level, "more whole beasts"). (*BGE* 257)

These paradoxical descriptions of the "beasts of prey" illuminate the conceptual problem that exercises Nietzsche in *GM* II. Put bluntly, he can find no fitting analogue in the wild animal kingdom to the organized assault that his "beasts of prey" supposedly conduct on unsuspecting, unformed tribes. Much to our surprise, in fact, his "beasts of prey" do not mercilessly slaughter (all of) their captives. Nor do they torture or play with their captives, as a cat will toy with a vole until (or while) killing it. Unlike the "great birds of prey," who insist that "nothing is more tasty than a tender lamb" (*GM* I:13), these "beasts of prey" *keep* their captives. They not only put their captives to work, but also impose upon them the order and discipline needed to work efficiently and productively. These "beasts of prey" thus exert on their formerly nomadic captives a distinctly formative influence, which is conducive to the processes familiarly known to us as "domestication," "cultivation," and "acculturation." In short, Nietzsche's supposedly terrible "beasts of prey," whose appearance he likens to the onset of a ferocious natural disaster, are *also* cultivators and nurturers. In this respect, or so it might seem, his "beasts of prey" depart most dramatically from the practices of the wild predators on whom they are modeled.[17]

Having exposed the softer, gentler side of his "beasts of prey," Nietzsche must now explain how a predatory animal, whose natural orientation to weaker animals is the dispensation of torture and death, *also* possesses a different orientation to its prey. That is, he must demonstrate that what we call "predation" and "cultivation" are in fact coeval expressions of primal animal vitality, such that the seemingly uncomplicated "beasts of prey" naturally exhibit predilections for domestication and acculturation. This is not to suggest, of course, that "beasts of prey" cannot also be organized and disciplined. The animal kingdom is replete with creatures that exhibit highly organized patterns of collective behavior, including those predators that contribute unwittingly to the domestication of other animal species. It is to Nietzsche's credit, in fact, that he opposes the popular caricature of "wildness" with an expanded and more sophisticated notion, which enables him to account for the capacities of complex natural systems for self-organization and self-regulation.

Still, it is certainly fair here to cast a suspicious eye on his evolving portrait of the surprisingly versatile "beasts of prey."[18] Does he advance his anthropological narrative only by equivocating on the beastliness of the "beasts of prey"? Has he perhaps baited his readers with his profile of a bloodthirsty, downswooping, death-dealing predator (*GM* I:13), only to switch in mid-narrative to an organized, patient, delay-gratifying nurturer? Has he cleverly trained this predator to serve its master as *brutus ex machina*?

Nietzsche's most persuasive response to this line of questioning would most likely draw upon his controversial description of the "beasts of prey" as *artists*.[19] It is their native capacity for artistry, he maintains, that enables them to engage in a kind of predation that is *also* civilizing and nurturing. As he explains,

> Their work is an instinctive creation and imposition of forms; they are the most involuntary, unconscious artists there are—wherever they appear something new soon arises, a ruling structure that *lives*, in which parts and functions are delineated and coordinated. . . . They exemplify that terrible artists' egoism that has the look of bronze and knows itself justified to all eternity in its "work," like a mother in her child. (*GM* II:17)

As this passage confirms, the "beasts of prey" practice their artistry in the preferred medium of *other human or hominid beings*. In bringing order and purpose to a formerly formless populace, the "beasts of prey" impart meaning and identity to their captives. They are, in short, givers of new life, "artists of violence and organizers who build states" (*GM* II:18).

It is difficult not to find this imagery abhorrent. Nietzsche's cavalier allusions to the "molding" and "ordering" of entire tribes and people—which by no means lack form and culture prior to their capture—are at least as disturbing as his approbatory references to the "blond beast." Indeed, many of his readers have registered their disgust with his careless glorifications of violence, and with his political naiveté in general.²⁰ Other readers have attempted to soften his praise for the "beasts of prey" by focusing on his experimental deployment of potentially defensible rhetorical strategies.²¹ Still others have attempted to separate his admiration for innovation and creativity from the retrograde political sentiments it so often serves.²²

Whatever we may think of it, however, Nietzsche's appeal to the artistry of the "beasts of prey" is the key to his account of the domestication of the human animal. By characterizing the "beasts of prey" as *artists*, he means to draw our attention to the transformative, life-bestowing effects of any outward expenditure of animal vitality. The scene of predation, he apparently wishes to claim, is not limited to the pursuit, capture, and death of the prey organism. Predation more fundamentally produces a multivalent vivification of the surrounding environment. While this vivification is most evident in the predator and prey species, which mutually encourage one another to adapt continually to their shared habitat, it is by no means restricted to them. Even those outbursts of primal aggression that culminate in the death of the prey organism succeed in refreshing the surrounding environment, contributing to the renewal of natural cycles and the maintenance of growth within the environment as a whole. Although predation invariably eliminates individual members of prey species, it also renews the prey species as a whole and thereby grants life to the interdependent configurations of species in a particular habitat.

Predators are therefore always also artists. They continuously recreate the environment that surrounds them, thereby renewing its unique and terrifying beauty. They are in fact artists in the highest sense recognized by Nietzsche, for they create and re-create new forms of life. He is quick to emphasize, moreover, that the artistic dimension of these displays of primal aggression is by no means deliberate or intentional, much less malicious or immoral: "Their work is an instinctive creation and imposition of forms; they are the most involuntary, unconscious [of] artists" (*GM* II:17). In this respect, too, they resemble the swollen river, the bolt of lightning, and the crashing boulder, inasmuch as they, too, unintentionally transfigure their surrounding environment.

This blind transformation of the surrounding environment is what Nietzsche means by the *artistry* practiced by the "beasts of prey." To be sure, they cannot help but stalk, maim, torture, and kill their victims, any more than "birds of prey" can help but seize tender little lambs (*GM* I:13). To expect or require them to do otherwise, after the fashion of the Church, would oblige one to sicken these noble creatures (*TI* "Improvers" 2). According to Nietzsche, however, the perspective adopted by the Church on the "beasts of prey" is unfortunately (and typically) narrow. In doing what they do naturally, the "beasts of prey" do not *merely* stalk, maim, torture, and kill, as if these activities could be neatly abstracted from the larger contexts in which they transpire. As predators, the "beasts of prey" also create something ordered and vital from an otherwise inconsequential mass of formless hominids.

Here, too, we must not allow ourselves to be distracted by Nietzsche's offensive imagery. His larger point is that predation in any form contributes to the renewal of life and the reanimation of otherwise moribund natural systems. In the context of his anthropological narrative, this means that the "beasts of prey" also *elevate* and *improve* the populace upon which they vent their primal aggression. Those captives who survive the form-giving wrath of the "beasts of prey" are ennobled by the assault, for they are then able to partake of "a ruling structure that *lives*, in which parts and functions are delineated and coordinated" (*GM* III:17).

The specific case of predation thus demonstrates (or reminds us) that the conventional distinction between "wild" and "civilized" is of only limited use to Nietzsche. Any prehistorical event of interest to him, like the founding of the original "state," invariably confounds our efforts to distinguish neatly between "wilderness" and "civilization." As his narrative discloses, what is generally considered "wild" is far more civilized than we initially might have thought, and what is generally considered to be "civilized" is often wilder than we are inclined to admit. In treating the "beasts of prey" as artists, that is, he does not deviate from the model of wild nature so much as he expands upon it, purging it of residual traces of moral prejudice. When viewed from the *tragic* perspective that he recommends to his readers (*GS* 370), both wilderness and civilization appear far more complex, possessed of far greater overlap and mutual interpenetration, than we otherwise might have thought. Rather than equivocate on the beastliness of the "beast of prey," he actually undertakes a more thorough investigation of what predation actually entails. In particular, he encourages his readers to understand predation as always already involving some elements of what are more regularly associated with civilization. As it turns out, in fact, predation involves killing *and* cultivating, maiming *and* nurturing, destroying *and* creating. To be a "beast of prey" is to practice a form of lethal artistry that also nurtures, informs, enriches, and civilizes.

The unintended elevation of this captive populace in turn closed the distance that originally separated it from its conquerors. As the populace improved, so, presumably, did the quality and quantity of the material products of its enforced labor, upon which the "beasts of prey" had grown increasingly dependent. When the "beasts of prey" inspected the fruits of their artistry, as mirrored back to them in the structure and definition that now informed the captive populace upon which they labored, the reflections they beheld exerted an indirectly civilizing effect on *them*. Inspired by the order, form, and beauty they had impressed upon their helpless captives, the "beasts of prey" may have unleashed similar regimens of violence against themselves. The ensuing modulations of their artistry in turn may have educed natural capacities for domestication and cultivation from their native complement of drives and impulses. In other words, the evolution of beastly predation into organized domestication may have been a natural, dialogical consequence of the formative artistry practiced by the "beasts of prey" on their captives.

The feedback loop initiated by their artistry also enables Nietzsche to account for their eventual disappearance. As we have seen, the dialogical process described above also led to the gradual, indirect, and unwitting *self*-domestication of the "beasts of prey."[23] Over the course of this process, the acculturation that attends the imposition of form onto matter fed back upon its purveyors, gradually domesticating *them* in accordance with the principles they dictated to their captives.[24] What may have begun as amoral play with their helpless captives—as a prelude, perhaps, to torture or sacrifice—eventually resulted in the "beasts of prey" *joining* the populace they had seized. Although it may be difficult to imagine these "beasts of prey" blending into the docile populace of a modern polity, it may not be so difficult to imagine them joining a populace that they had molded in their own, wild image. Perhaps, that is, the "beasts of prey" need not have fallen very far to have joined the elevated populace to which they had imparted form, shape, and identity.

Yet even the most talented of artists could not have raised a formless nomadic mass to a level commensurate with the wild "beasts of prey." Nietzsche must consequently account for a countervailing leveling influence, by means of which the "beasts of prey" were sickened, de-clawed, and thoroughly domesticated. They were victimized, he conjectures, by none other than the *ascetic priest*, who effectively poisoned the dialogical relationship that originally obtained between the "beasts of prey" and the products of their artistry. Owing to the intercession of the ascetic priest, the "beasts of prey" learned to pity their captives and to loathe the beauty that was reflected back to them by the products of their primal aggression.[25] Having become works of art in their own right, the "beasts of prey" were powerless to refuse the ascetic priest's dispensations of guilt and self-contempt.

III

But why would the noble "beasts of prey" have allowed themselves to become vulnerable to such a dangerous enemy? Nietzsche intimates that they initially may have detected more utility than danger in the priest. The priestly class originally may have been nothing more than a motley assortment of magicians, seers, shamans, prophets, and healers, from whom the "beasts of prey" sensed no credible threat to their dominion. (As we shall see, in fact, the priests became both dangerous and triumphant only as a byproduct of the way in which they were treated by the "beasts of prey.") The ascetic strain of the priestly type emerged fairly late in their reign, and only as an unforeseen consequence of the organizing disciplines they imparted to their captives.

It seems likely that at some point the "beasts of prey" would have needed to communicate their organizing principles to their captives. If so, then they also may have needed to work closely with a select group of mediators, who in turn would have been entrusted to communicate their demands to the populace as a whole. The labor of mediation may have fallen to the priests, whom Nietzsche describes as "neurasthenic" (*GM* I:6)—and, so, as naturally (if pathologically) sensitive and empathetic. These early priests, already adept at translating languages, arbitrating disputes, interpreting dreams, divining portents, unlocking prophecies, reading entrails, and generally decoding regnant symbolic systems, presumably would have been indispensable to the organizing activities of the "beasts of prey."

As Nietzsche explains, however, the priestly type also possesses a plasticity of soul that naturally produces a double agency. In political terms, the priest thrives by colonizing the interstitial spaces of a society, mediating between competing classes, strata, and castes. His mastery of lines and media of communication enables him to reverse the customary, downward flow of state power and to disrupt the acknowledged chain of command—even as he honors it. The priest gladly relays the wishes of the ruling elite, but only at great expense to its credibility and authority. With every communication of directives from above, the priest wages from below a silent, psychological war. While receiving the commands that are to be disseminated to the populace, the priest also steals secrets, sows the seeds of jealousy and distrust, manipulates language, flatters and ingratiates, and generally subverts the unity and stability of the ruling elite. Nietzsche's "beasts of prey" may have possessed a sufficiently developed inner life to organize themselves and their prey, perhaps even to provide cultivation and nurture, but they were no match for the cunning of the ascetic priest.

Nietzsche thus links the disappearance of the "beasts of prey" to their ill-fated dealings with the priestly class. As he explains, the priest

> must be the natural opponent and despiser of all rude, stormy, unbridled, hard, violent beast-of-prey health and might. The priest is the first form of the more *delicate* animal that despises more readily than it hates. He will not be spared war with the beasts of prey, a war of cunning (of the "spirit") rather than one of force, as goes without saying; *to fight it he will under certain circumstances need to evolve a virtually new type of beast of prey* [*Raubthier-Typus*] *out of himself, or at least he will need to* represent *it*—a new kind of animal ferocity in which the polar bear, the supple, cold, and patient tiger, and not least the fox seem to be joined in a unity at once enticing and terrifying. If need compels him, he will walk among the other beasts of prey with bearlike seriousness and feigned superiority, venerable, prudent, and cold, as the herald and mouthpiece of more mysterious powers, determined to sow this soil with misery, discord, and self-contradiction wherever he can and, only too certain of his art, to dominate the *suffering* at all times. (*GM* III:15, emphasis added)

In this remarkable passage, Nietzsche endeavors to fill a conspicuous gap in his larger narrative. While a conventional war of *violence* would be no contest, an unconventional war of *cunning* would place the "beasts of prey" at a distinct and unfamiliar disadvantage. In particular, he muses, a war of cunning could provoke the ascetic priest to replicate his antagonists, transforming himself into a "beast of prey" (or a credible facsimile thereof) in his own right.

Nietzsche envisions this priestly "beast of prey" on the model of a diploid monstrosity, possessed of the natures of "polar bear," "tiger," and "fox," which are combined in an assemblage both "enticing and terrifying."[26] Thus transformed, the ascetic priest infiltrates the ranks of the "beasts of prey," even "feigning superiority" over them. What is more, he battles them where they least expect to be engaged—in their beloved wilderness, where, presumably, they relax any mechanisms of self-pro-

tection cultivated to shield them from the toxic *ressentiment* of their captives. Unbe-
knownst to them, perhaps with their unsuspecting assistance, the priest poisons their
tonic wilderness and surreptitiously subjects them to techniques of domestication.
As they fall prey to his domesticating spell, they voluntarily abandon their wilderness, growing progressively inured to the peace and security of civil society. Once
disabused of their will for freedom, they forego altogether their furlough privileges
and slowly, imperceptibly, sink to the level of their former captives.

As they recruited the priestly class to propagate their form-giving directives, the
"beasts of prey" unwittingly tutored the priests in the strategic deployment of their
double agency. Those priests who were not crushed by the artistry of the "beasts of
prey" apparently learned to manipulate the suffering of others to insulate themselves
from the scrutiny of their captors and to secure the allegiance of their followers.[27]
Nietzsche's focus on the artistry of the "beasts of prey" thus enables him to issue a
balanced (if fantastic) reckoning of their enduring contributions. Just as he credits
them with unconsciously introducing order, discipline, and beauty into the world,
so he holds them responsible for legislating the conditions under which the "bad
conscience" developed.

An unintended consequence of their artistry, he speculates, was the empowerment
of some priests as "artists" of equal power and surpassing ingenuity.[28] As it turns
out, the artistry of the "beasts of prey" served as the model for the cunning of the
priests. What the "beasts of prey" achieved by means of their physical, outward,
overt discharge of animal vitality, the priest learned to achieve through psychological, inward, covert operations. In particular, the priest discovered the most powerful
organizational device known as yet to human history: the *ascetic ideal*, by means of
which he turned the tables of domestication on the "beasts of prey." Having convinced the "beasts of prey" to rely ever more heavily on his ministrations, the ascetic
priest eventually exploited this relationship of dependency and polluted the "innocent" conscience of his captors. Poisoned with guilt, afflicted by the "bad conscience" that they, ironically, had introduced into the world, the wounded "beasts
of prey" finally joined the captive populace they had formerly tyrannized.

CONCLUSION

Today, the "beasts of prey" are nowhere to be found (*GM* I:11). By the "early Middle Ages," Nietzsche observes, "the most beautiful specimens of the 'blond beast'
were hunted down everywhere" and transformed (= "sickened") into Christians
(*TI* "Improvers" 2). The "blond beast" now resides only at the "hidden core" of
noble peoples and cultures (*GM* I:11), its native wildness barely discernible beneath
a thick mantle of domestic manners and civilized politesse.

Nietzsche nevertheless resists the conclusion that the disappearance of the "beasts
of prey" necessarily spells the collapse of the human species. The animal vitality of
the "beasts of prey" continues to circulate—albeit in dispersed, disaggregated, per-

haps even entropic, form—throughout the decadent nations, peoples, and cultures of late modern Europe. Indeed, the challenge he faces is not unlike the challenge faced by the priestly class at the time of the founding of the original "state"— namely, how can he tap this seemingly inaccessible reservoir of monstrous, transformative energy and channel it toward the furtherance of his own, contrary ends? How can he contribute to the occasion of a metamorphosis that will supercede, cancel, or neutralize the mutation that ushered the ascetic priest onto the stage of human history?

Not surprisingly, his favored solution to this problem borrows heavily from his account of the ascetic priest's successful campaign to tame the "beasts of prey." He pins his dim hopes for the future of humankind on the possibility of another dialectical advance or mutation, along the lines of the one he describes in *On the Genealogy of Morals*. In particular, he envisions a counterevolution involving a similar transfer and conversion of energy from the ascetic priest to his as-yet-unknown other. This counterevolution will not produce a simple reincarnation of the "beasts of prey," but it may produce an Other whose generative role recalls in some salutary respects their form-giving artistry.

Nietzsche may have in mind some such dialectical advance when he alludes to the possible emergence of a "many-colored and dangerous winged creature" from the "repulsive and gloomy caterpillar form" of the ascetic priest (*GM* III:10). He hopefully identifies this emergent "creature" as the "'philosopher'," whom we should *not* confuse with those "philosophers" who have disguised themselves heretofore in "ascetic wraps and cloaks" (*GM* III:10). Were this new "philosopher" to take wing, borne aloft by a gust of "pride, daring, courage, and self-confidence" unknown since the heyday of the "beasts of prey," we would be in a position to regard the lengthy interregnum of the ascetic priest as an intermediate stage in the evolution of the human animal, a stage as natural and appropriate to our development as is the caterpillar to the emergence of the glorious butterfly.[29]

In that event, morality itself would appear just as Nietzsche wishes for his readers someday to be able to view it: as a necessary, nonlethal stage in the development of the human spirit. If he has his way, in fact, his preferred readers of a distant posterity will be in a position to regard the moral period of human development as a long, treacherous, comical, but ultimately successful detour to the freedom and strength of will formerly embodied by the "beasts of prey."

NOTES

I wish to thank Ralph and Christa Davis Acampora for their instructive comments on preliminary drafts of this essay.

1. With the exception of occasional emendations, I rely throughout this essay on Kaufmann's translations of *BGE*, and *TI*; and Kaufmann and Hollingdale's *GM*.

2. For an excellent commentary on *BGE* 230 see Laurence Lampert, *Nietzsche's Task: An Interpretation of* Beyond Good and Evil. New Haven, CT: Yale University Press, 2001, 226–31.

3. The "bad conscience" is, as he says, "an illness like pregnancy" (*GM* II:19), from which, presumably, the birth of something new might follow. At this point in his narrative, Nietzsche launches a new account of the origin of the bad conscience, which, as Henry Staten observes, "throws the previous account into confusion" (*Nietzsche's Voice* [Ithaca, NY: Cornell University Press, 1990], 54).

4. My discussion of Nietzsche's contributions to philosophical anthropology draws extensively from Richard Schacht, *Making Sense of Nietzsche* (Chicago: University of Illinois Press, 1995), especially chapter 10.

5. For a consideration along these lines of the difficulties involved in Nietzsche's proffered explanation, see Keith Ansell Pearson, *Viroid Life: Perspectives on Nietzsche and the Transhuman Condition* (London: Routledge, 1997), 101–3.

6. The analogy that Nietzsche pursues in *GM* II:16 is particularly misleading in this respect. Like "sea animals" compelled to "become land animals or perish," these "semianimals" were obliged to "devalue" their instincts or perish. According to this analogy, in fact, no oppressor or aggressor coerces these "semianimals" to evolve. The compulsion they experience arises, presumably, in a non-agential change in the environment, to which they must adapt.

7. Nietzsche uses this precise phrase in *GM* I:5 to describe the Aryan race.

8. Nietzsche offers a similar account of "the origins of an aristocratic society": "Human beings whose nature was still natural, barbarians in every terrible sense of the word, men of prey [*Raubmenschen*] who were still in possession of unbroken strength of will and lust for power, hurled themselves upon weaker, more civilized, more peaceful races, perhaps traders or cattle raisers, or upon mellow old cultures" (*BGE* 257).

9. He uses the term "semianimals" again in *GM* II:17, and he identifies them as belonging to the "raw material" that was worked over by the "oppressive and remorseless machine" of the original state.

10. For a detailed and insightful discussion of the emergence of the "bad conscience," see David Owen, *Nietzsche, Politics, and Modernity* (London: Sage Publications, Ltd., 1995), 56–67.

11. See, for example, *TI* "Skirmishes" 44, where Nietzsche explains that the "genius, in work and deed, is necessarily a squanderer. . . . He flows out, he overflows, he uses himself up, he does not spare himself—and this is a calamitous, involuntary fatality, no less than a river's flooding the land."

12. See Paul J. M. van Tongeren, *Reinterpreting Modern Culture: An Introduction of Friedrich Nietzsche's Philosophy* (West Lafayette, IN: Purdue University Press, 2000), 202–5.

13. It would be interesting to map Nietzsche's anthropological narrative onto the controversial thesis advanced by Paul Shepard. Shepard boldly asserts that "as a species we are Pleistocene, owing little or nothing to the millennia of urban life. . . . The radical implication of this is that we, like other wild forms, may actually be less healthy in the domesticated landscapes than in those places to which our DNA remains most closely tuned" (Paul Shepard, "Wilderness Is Where My Genome Lives," *Whole Terrain* 4 (1995/1996): 13).

14. Aaron Ridley nicely sums up the problem here by noting that "[w]hat Nietzsche is evading in all this, of course, is the recognition that the nobles need a 'bad' conscience them-

selves even before they can create the conditions required to produce it in others. . . . The nobles need a 'bad' conscience to do what they do" (*Nietzsche's Conscience: Six Character Studies from the* Genealogy [Ithaca, NY: Cornell University Press, 1998], 20–21). As I hope to show in Part III of this chapter, it is at least plausible for Nietzsche to claim that the "innocent" conscience of the "beasts of prey" creates the conditions under which the "bad conscience" arises and develops.

15. Both Staten (16–21) and Ridley (20–22) cite this passage as evidence of the internal strain exerted on Nietzsche's hypothesis by his apparent need to maintain his founding dichotomies between "noble" and "slave," "wild" and "cultivated," "active" and "reactive," and so on.

16. As Nietzsche explains, "It is not in *them* [viz., the "beasts of prey"] that the 'bad conscience' developed, that goes without saying—but it would not have developed *without them*, this ugly growth" (*GM* II:17). The "inventor of the 'bad conscience,'" he explains, is none other than the "yearning and desperate prisoner" who had no choice but to make an enemy of himself, to redirect inward the animal aggression that he would naturally direct outward (*GM* II:16).

17. Here, it would seem, Nietzsche approaches the limits of his attempt to model the "beasts of prey" simultaneously on the instinctual aggression of animal predators and on the self-organizing efficiency of well-crafted artifacts or machines. The more strongly he relies on the latter model, namely, to account for the organizational predilections of the "beasts of prey," the further he strays from his former model. For a promising account of "machine evolution" that is not restricted (as is Nietzsche's) by an anthropocentric emphasis on machines as human artifacts, see Ansell Pearson, 138–42.

18. As if to concede this point, Nietzsche later explains that the "beasts of prey" participated only reluctantly in the collective organization of their captives, and against their better judgment: "[T]he strong [*die Starken*] are as naturally inclined to *separate* as the weak [*die Schwachen*] are to *congregate*; if the former unite together, it is only with the aim of an aggressive collective action and collective satisfaction of their will to power, and with much resistance from the individual conscience. . . . [T]he instinct of the born 'masters' (that is, the solitary, beast-of-prey species of human) is fundamentally irritated and disquieted by organization" (*GM* III:18).

19. On the unique artistry of the "beasts of prey," see Ridley, 83–85.

20. See, for example, Mark Warren's catalog of the "limits" of Nietzsche's political thought, *Nietzsche and Political Thought* (Cambridge, MA: MIT Press, 1988), 207–48.

21. Richard White thus draws our attention to GM as a "performative critique," which "Nietzsche uses . . . to direct us toward a particular vision of the future" (*Nietzsche and the Problem of Sovereignty* [Champaign: University of Illinois Press, 1997], 38). One result of this "performative critique," apparently, is to free us "to go beyond the fable of a *literal* prehistory" (140). Paul van Tongeren similarly concludes that Nietzsche does not intend his "myth of descent" to "refer to a specific moment in time." The lesson we should draw from such passages is that "domination, submission, and struggle are not so much the first steps in the development of the human being as they are its continuous principle: from the beginning, human beings are characterized by this distinction" (205).

22. Lawrence Hatab maintains, persuasively, that Nietzsche's admiration for creativity and "artistry" actually militates *against* the antidemocratic animus of his political writings. The political regime that would best foster Nietzschean creativity, Hatab proposes, is in fact

democracy—provided, of course, that the democracy in question would both honor and enforce a fair, mutually elevating contest between democratic citizens (*A Nietzschean Defense of Democracy: An Experiment in Postmodern Politics* [Chicago: Open Court, 1995], 51–54).

23. Although most domesticate species have been forcibly tamed by other, "stronger" species (usually *homo sapiens* or its hominid ancestors), the occurrence of self-domestication is not unknown. Researchers have recently theorized, for example, that some canid species effectively domesticated themselves, so that they could live in closer proximity to the edible waste products created by humans/hominids (see Karen E. Lange, "Wolf to Woof: The Evolution of Dogs," *National Geographic* (January 2002): 4–6). According to this account, the human culture or home is an occasion for the domestication of wild canids, but not its cause. Could a similar conjecture provide some of the details of Nietzsche's anthropological story? Did early hominids effectively domesticate themselves in order to avail themselves of a promising food supply—perhaps, as Nietzsche apparently prefers, of the stability afforded them by farming (rather than roaming)?

24. My use of the term "domestication" is not meant to imply the kind of change in genetic structure that is produced through standard breeding techniques. As Shepard points out, "if we follow the definition of 'domestic' as a type created by controlled breeding with conscious objectives by humans, then we ourselves are genetically wild" (13).

25. The unintended self-domestication of the "beasts of prey" may have prompted Nietzsche's admonition: "[Let us] guard ourselves against the two worst contagions that may be reserved just for us—against the *great nausea at man!* against *great pity for man!*" (*GM* III:14).

26. Staten argues that Nietzsche's account of the ascetic priest as a "delicate" type of "beast of prey" exposes a tension within his own conception of power as primarily physical and outwardly directed (57). My own sense is that this passage is meant to explain the emergence of a conception of power that is rooted in an expanded understanding of the physical world. It is not the case that the slaves invented "mental" power to counter the "physical" power of their masters. If that were the case, then nothing would have happened in/to the "physical" world of the masters. What the slaves accomplished, perhaps unwittingly, was the formulation of a more comprehensive understanding of the physical cosmos, which now must be understood to comprise unseen forces. The slaves do not rule a parallel, "mental" world of their own invention, so much as they stumble upon a more complete understanding of the one world, the physical world of visible and invisible forces, over which they and their masters vie for supremacy.

27. Nietzsche thus describes this new, mutant species of priest as a "sorcerer and animal-tamer, in whose presence everything healthy necessarily grows sick, and everything sick tame" (*GM* III:15). He also likens the priest to a "shepherd" caring for his "herd" (*GM* III:15), a comparison that confirms the formative role of the "beasts of prey" in the development of the ascetic priest.

28. That the priests, too, are artists is confirmed by Nietzsche's observation that "the slave revolt in morality begins when *ressentiment* itself becomes creative and gives birth to values" (*GM* I:10).

29. In fact, if we may associate one *Flügelthier* (the butterfly; *KSA* 5, 361) with another (the honeybee; *KSA* 5, 247), then we are perhaps entitled to read the preface to *On the Genealogy of Morals* as introducing Nietzsche and his unknown friends as legitimate claimants to the title of "'philosopher.'"

Bibliography

There is an abundance of literature on Nietzsche. The suggestions below were selected not only for their quality but also for their specific *focus* on Nietzsche's *On the Genealogy of Morals*. Suggestions for further reading that coordinate with the main parts of the present text are annotated. A few more general works on Nietzsche's moral and political philosophy are included at the end.

"ON GENEALOGY"—RELEVANT WORKS

Conway, Daniel W. "Writing in Blood: On the Prejudices of Genealogy." *Epoche* 3:1/2 (1995): 149–81. Consideration of how to apply the insights of the *Genealogy* as they relate to Zarathustra's ideas "On Reading and Writing" and then to a reading of Nietzsche's activity of writing the *Genealogy* itself.

Geuss, Raymond. "Nietzsche and Genealogy." *European Journal of Philosophy* 2:3 (1994): 274–92. Distinctive in its rare treatment of relevant discussions in Nietzsche's *Antichrist*.

Guay, Robert. "The Philosophical Function of Genealogy." In *A Companion to Nietzsche*. Ed. By Keith Ansell Pearson. Malden, MA: Blackwell Publishing Ltd., 2006, 353–70.

Hoy, David Couzens. "Nietzsche, Hume, and the Genealogical Method." In *Nietzsche as Affirmative Thinker*. Y. Yovel, ed. Dordtrecht: Martinus Nijhoff Publishers, 1986, 20–38. Describes genealogy as a way of doing philosophy that is akin to Hume's notion of "experimental reasoning," personalized and evaluative in the hands of Nietzsche.

Kemal, S. "Some Problems of Genealogy." *Nietzsche-Studien* 19 (1990): 30–42. Compact explication of objections to Nietzsche's genealogical investigations, including particularity, relativism, and normativeness. Kemal grants that these are central to genealogy, and offers an account of how they are positive features (rather than negative consequences) of Nietzsche's work.

Owen, David. "Criticism and Captivity: On Genealogy and Critical Theory." *European Journal of Philosophy* 10:2 (2002): 216–30.

Schrift, Alan D. "Nietzsche and the Critique of Oppositional Thinking." *History of European Ideals* (1989), 783–90. A succinct account of Nietzsche's critique of binary reasoning and how this idea is developed in the writings of postmodern (specifically French) philosophers.

See also the later version of this work, along with related discussions applied to a wide range of "post-structuralist" thinkers in *Nietzsche's French Legacy*. New York: Routledge, 1995.

Williams, Bernard. "Naturalism and Genealogy." In *Morality, Reflection, and Ideology*. Ed. by Edward Harcourt. Oxford: Oxford University Press, 2000, 149–61. Provides interesting discussion of what is *wanted* from a naturalistic orientation in philosophy, particularly ethics. Offers the especially provocative suggestion that fictional stories generally, and Nietzsche's genealogical stories particularly, could be compatible with such aims.

"READING THE *GENEALOGY*"—RELEVANT WORKS

Butler, Judith. "Circuits of Bad Conscience: Nietzsche and Freud." In *The Psychic Life of Power: Theories in Subjection*. Stanford, CA: Stanford University Press, 1997, 63–82. Explores the "performative" dimension of bad conscience and guilt. Considers the ascetic ideal, the desire for desire, and the "sorry bind" of subjectivity, which involves subordination (to the community) as the very condition for the possibility of the affirmation of individual existence.

Clark, Maudemarie. "Nietzsche's Immoralism and the Concept of Morality." In *Nietzsche, Genealogy, Morality: Essays on Nietzsche's* On the Genealogy of Morals. Ed. by Richard Schacht. Berkeley: University of California Press, 1994, 15–34. Argues that Nietzsche's immoralism is largely limited to his critique of one particular kind of morality, which is thought to be all that morality is. Provides a reading of the second essay of *GM* that is supposed to show the possibility of a nonmoral social contract theory, which includes conceptions of justice, fairness, and other concepts associated with morality generally.

Janaway, Christopher. "Nietzsche's Illustration of the Art of Exegesis." *European Journal of Philosophy* 5:3 (1997): 251–68. Conclusively argues that the third essay of *GM* is organized according to the order outlined in the first section of the essay, and that the "exegesis" the third essay is supposed to constitute (see *GM* P:8) is of that rather than the epigraph from *Thus Spoke Zarathustra*.

Loeb, Paul S. "Is There a Genetic Fallacy in Nietzsche's *Genealogy of Morals*?" In *International Studies in Philosophy* 27.3 (1995): 125–41. Articulates Nietzsche's interest in aristocratic origins to consider whether fallacious reasoning is at the core of *GM*, and how our conception of the "genetic fallacy" has some origination with Nietzsche's book.

Newman, Michael. "Reading the Future of Genealogy: Kant, Nietzsche, and Plato." In *Nietzsche and Modern German Thought*. Ed. by Keith Ansell Pearson. New York: Routledge, 1991, 257–82. Considers the relation between *GM* and *Z*, partially through consideration of how *GM* III is an exegesis of the epigraph from *Z* (cf. Janaway). Focused on the cultivation of readership and how Nietzsche's texts relate to each other in this way.

Reginster, Bernard. "Ressentiment, Evaluation, and Integrity." *International Studies in Philosophy* 27:3 (1995): 117–24. Emphasizes that Nietzsche's discussion of *ressentiment* is rooted to his implicit conception of integrity such that the resentful person is characterized by their peculiar inability to integrate the values he or she professes.

Risse, Mathias. "Origins of *Ressentiment* and Sources of Normativity." *Nietzsche-Studien* 30 (2003): 142–70. Considers how *ressentiment*, particularly, arises given Nietzsche's "speculative anthropology." The conceptions of mind and practical identity that emerge from the account are compared and contrasted with Korsgaard's Kant and Nietzsche.

Risse, Mathias. "The Second Treatise in *On the Genealogy of Morality*: Nietzsche on the Origin of the Bad Conscience." *European Journal of Philosophy* 9:1 (2001): 55–81. Analyzes *GM* II:21 particularly to distinguish the bad conscience that is associated with guilt from an earlier stage of bad conscience. Focuses on the idea of "indebtedness to the gods," Christianity's appropriation of indebtedness, and the relation between Christianity and morality generally.

Siemens, Herman. "Nietzsche's Agon with *Ressentiment*: Towards a Therapeutic Reading of Critical Transvaluation." *Continental Philosophy Review* 34 (2001): 69–93. Develops an agonal model of transvaluation that supplies the basis for therapeutic practice, which accounts for the existing decadence Nietzsche finds in modern culture and meets his critiques of conceptions of health and healing as practiced by the ascetic priests.

Solomon, Robert C. "One Hundred Years of *Ressentiment*: Nietzsche's Genealogy of Morals." In *Nietzsche, Genealogy, Morality: Essays on Nietzsche's* On the Genealogy of Morals. Ed. by Richard Schacht. Berkeley: University of California Press, 1994, 95–126. Considers Nietzsche's discussion of *ressentiment* particularly in light of his characterization of weakness and strength.

"CRITIQUING *GENEALOGY*"—RELEVANT WORKS

Ansell Pearson, Keith. "The Significance of Michel Foucault's Reading of Nietzsche: Power, the Subject, and Political Theory." *Nietzsche-Studien* 20 (1991): 267–83. Discusses Foucault as among the first to recognize the political implications of Nietzsche's conceptions of power and freedom, particularly as they relate to thinking about the political subject as historicized and in the wake of critiques of modern metaphysics. Useful even for those lacking great familiarity with Foucault's work.

Foucault, Michel. "Nietzsche, Genealogy, History." In *Language, Counter-Memory, Practice: Selected Essays and Interviews*. Ed. Donald F. Bouchard. Trans. Donald F. Bouchard and Sherry Simon. Ithaca, NY: Cornell University Press, 1977. Challenges what he considers to be metaphysics' emphasis on origins, which supplies the basis for certain views about universal history and considerations of difference that Foucault rejects. He considers himself to be aligned with Nietzsche in rejecting such conceptions of origins and their value for helping us to understand ourselves, our history, and our future prospects.

MacIntyre, Alasdair. "Genealogies and Subversions." In *Three Rival Versions of Moral Enquiry: Encyclopaedia, Genealogy, and Tradition*. Notre Dame, IN: University of Notre Dame Press, 1990. Gifford Lectures given at University of Edinburgh in 1988. Discusses the relation of the genealogical text to canonical authority and the tradition of encyclopedia, and considers this in the case of Foucault. While genealogy appears to have an advantage in the recognition of the historical development of ideas, norms, and standards, MacIntyre doubts that the genealogist's own position escapes that which he critiques.

Owen, David. "The Contest of Enlightenment: An Essay on Critique and Genealogy." *Journal of Nietzsche Studies* 25 (Spring 2003): 35–57. Compares Kant's critical projects with Nietzsche's, leading to a comparison of the two on the issue of self-legislation. Owen argues that Nietzsche is wholly committed to enlightenment rather than abandoning it for myth as Habermas suggests.

Pippin, Robert B. "Nietzsche's Alleged Farewell: The Premodern, Modern, and Postmodern Nietzsche." In *The Cambridge Companion to Nietzsche*. Ed. by Bernd Magnus and Kathleen

Higgins. New York: Cambridge University Press, 1996, 252–78. Consideration of problems associated with linking Nietzsche with a renunciation of modernity. Includes discussion of Habermas's critique of Nietzsche with significant discussion of Nietzsche and Hegel and Nietzsche's *GM*.

Pizer, John. "The Use and Abuse of 'Ursprung': On Foucault's Reading of Nietzsche." *Nietzsche-Studien* 19 (1990): 462–78. Challenges the view that Nietzsche abandons consideration of origins and a sense of organic development in meaning.

Saar, Martin. "Genealogy and Subjectivity." *European Journal of Philosophy* 10:2 (2002): 231–45. Endeavors to pin down precisely in what genealogy consists. Defines genealogy as always concerned about the subject, as history, as critique, and as textual practice. Contrasts "stabilizing" genealogies with those that are disruptive.

"POLITICS AND COMMUNITY"—RELEVANT WORKS

Brown, Wendy. "Nietzsche for Politics." In *Why Nietzsche Still? Reflections on Drama, Culture, and Politics.* Ed. by Alan D. Schrift. Berkeley: University of California Press, 2000, 205–23. Argues for an agonistic relationship between theory and politics that moves beyond "identity and application"; genealogy plays a role in creating this alternative.

Card, Claudia. "Genealogies and Perspectives: Feminist and Lesbian Reflections." *International Studies in Philosophy* 28:3 (1996): 99–111. Offers a particularly interesting take on hatred and evil and the perspective from which Nietzsche makes his critical observations.

Diprose, Rosalyn. "Nietzsche, Ethics and Sexual Difference." *Radical Philosophy* 52 (1989): 27–33. Argues that Nietzsche supplies "a genealogy of the divided self" that could be useful for developing an "ethics of difference."

Roodt, Vasti. "Nietzsche's Dynamite: The Biography of Modern Nihilism." *South African Journal of Philosophy* 16:2 (1997): 37–43. Develops the idea that Nietzsche's texts provide conceptual resources for thinking of ourselves as having multiple biographies and genealogical lineages upon which we can draw to develop new senses of community among those who ordinarily think they have little in common.

Scott, Jacqueline. "On the Use and Abuse of Race in Philosophy: Nietzsche, Jews, and Race." In *Race and Racism in Continental Philosophy.* Ed. by Robert Bernasconi. Bloomington: Indiana University Press, 2003, 53–73. Argues that Nietzsche's notion of race is tied to his conception of decadence, purity, and health, all of which include various psychological, not simply biological features, which differs from the strictly biological conception of Nietzsche's nationalist and anti-Semitic contemporaries.

Shapiro, Gary. "Diasporas." In *Nietzsche and Jewish Culture.* Ed. by Jacob Golumb. New York: Routledge, 1997, 244–62. A personal narrative that ties reading Nietzsche to living one's life. Focuses on Nietzsche's seduction of Jewish readers, and then provides a compelling account of how the author himself was seduced.

Warren, Mark. "The Historicity of Power." In his *Nietzsche and Political Thought.* Cambridge, MA: MIT Press, 1988, 79–110. Includes an interesting discussion of "the genealogical method" in chapter 3, see esp. 102–10, challenging a number of prominent interpretations and arguing for the notion of genealogy as a mode of critique.

BOOKS WITH SIGNIFICANT DISCUSSIONS DIRECTLY DEVOTED TO *ON THE GENEALOGY OF MORALS*

Allison, David B. *Reading the New Nietzsche*. Lanham, MD: Rowman & Littlefield Publishers, Inc., 2001.

Ansell Pearson, Keith. *Nietzsche Contra Rousseau*. Cambridge: Cambridge University Press, 1991.

————. *An Introduction to Nietzsche as Political Thinker: The Perfect Nihilist*. Cambridge: Cambridge University Press, 1994.

Babich, Babette E. *Nietzsche's Philosophy of Science: Reflecting Science on the Ground of Art and Life*. Albany: State University of New York Press, 1994.

Clark, Maudemarie. *Nietzsche on Truth and Philosophy*. New York: Cambridge University Press, 1990.

Deleuze, Gilles. *Nietzsche and Philosophy*. Trans. Hugh Tomlinson. New York: Columbia University Press, 1983.

Havas, Randall. *Nietzsche's Genealogy: Nihilism and the Will to Knowledge*. Ithaca, NY: Cornell University Press, 1995.

Owen, David. *Nietzsche, Politics, and Modernity*. London: Sage Publications, Ltd., 1995.

Ridley, Aaron. *Nietzsche's Conscience: Six Character Studies from the Genealogy*. Ithaca, NY: Cornell University Press, 1998.

Scheler, Max. *Ressentiment*. Trans. William Holdheim. Ed. Lewis A. Coser. New York: The Free Press, 1961.

Schacht, Richard. *Making Sense of Nietzsche: Reflections Timely and Untimely*. Urbana: University of Illinois Press, 1995.

Schrift, Alan. *Nietzsche's French Legacy: A Genealogy of Poststructuralism*. New York: Routledge, 1995.

Schrift, Alan. *Nietzsche and the Question of Interpretation: Between Hermeneutics and Deconstruction*. New York: Routledge, 1990.

Strong, Tracy B. *Nietzsche and the Politics of Transfiguration*. Expanded Edition. Urbana: University of Illinois Press, 2000.

SELECTED BOOKS AND ARTICLES ON NIETZSCHE'S MORAL PHILOSOPHY AND MORAL PSYCHOLOGY

Bailey, Tom. "Nietzsche's Kantian Ethics." *International Studies in Philosophy* 35:3 (2003): 5–27.

Bergmann, Frithjof. "Nietzsche's Critique of Morality." In *Reading Nietzsche*. Ed. by Robert C. Solomon and Kathleen Marie Higgins. Reprint. New York: Oxford University Press, 1990, 29–45.

Danto, Arthur C. "Some Remarks on *The Genealogy of Morals*." *International Studies in Philosophy* 18:2 (1986): 3–15.

Foot, Philippa. "Nietzsche: The Revaluation of Values." In *Nietzsche: A Critical Collection*.

Edited by Robert Solomon. Reprinted in *Virtues and Vices and Other Essays in Moral Philosophy*. Oxford: Clarendon Press, 2002.

Geuss, Raymond. "Nietzsche and Morality." In *Morality, Culture, and History: Essays on German Philosophy*. Cambridge: Cambridge University Press, 1999.

Hunt, Lester. *Nietzsche and the Origin of Virtue*. New York: Routledge, 1991.

Leiter, Brian. *Nietzsche on Morality*. London: Routledge, 2002.

May, Simon. *Nietzsche's Ethics and His War on "Morality."* Oxford: Oxford University Press, 1999.

Moore, Gregory. "The Physiology of Morality." In his *Nietzsche, Biology, Metaphor*. Cambridge: Cambridge University Press, 2002, 56–84.

Parkes, Graham. *Composing the Soul: Reaches of Nietzsche's Psychology*. Chicago: University of Chicago Press, 1996.

Parsons, Katherine Pyne. "Nietzsche and Moral Change." In *Nietzsche: A Collection of Critical Essays*. Ed. by Robert C. Solomon. Garden City, NY: Doubleday, 1973.

Schacht, Richard, ed. *Nietzsche's Postmoralism: Essays on Nietzsche's Prelude to Philosophy's Future*. Cambridge: Cambridge University Press, 2000.

Schacht, Richard. Editor. *Nietzsche, Genealogy, Morality: Essays on Nietzsche's* On the Genealogy of Morals. Berkeley: University of California Press, 1994.

Thatcher, David S. "*Zur Genealogie der Moral*: Some Textual Annotations." *Nietzsche-Studien* 18 (1989): 587–99.

Williams, Bernard. "Nietzsche's Minimalist Moral Psychology." *European Journal of Philosophy* 1:1 (1993): 1–14.

Index

Abel, G., 174n9
Acampora, C., 105n24, 163–64, 173n3
Action(s), 40–41, 47, 61–62, 100, 102, 133, 137–41, 194–98, 259–60, 263, 266
activity, 133, 136–38, 141, 158
actors, 261, 264, 266–67, 270, 272, 274n12
Adler, A., 293, 296, 297
Adorno, T., 11, 223–25, 228–29
Aesop, 113
aesthetic(s), 7, 89, 224; justification, 63; values, 225–26, 229, 240, 260–63. *See also* art; values
agent(s)/agency, 40, 46–50, 54–55n13, 62, 86–88, 96, 98, 123, 131–145, 200, 249, 262–64, 267, 275n27. *See also* actors
agon, 115–16, 236
Alcibiades, 115–16
altruism/altruistic, 41, 297
amor fati, 4, 38n10, 152, 155, 176n24, 284
ancestry, 233, 235, 243
Andler, C., 209
animals, 23, 161n27, 174n12, 306; beast of prey-type, 315; beast(s) of prey, 113, 154, 251, 305, 308–17, 319n14, 319n18; blond beast, 35, 205, 234–35, 306, 308, 311; camel, 165; human animal, 6, 20–21, 105n24,

121, 153–54, 156, 158n3, 161n27, 164–65, 168, 170, 171, 305–320; child, 164, 166, 172, 176n26; domestication, 309–316; "men of prey," 310, 318n8; as sick animal, 20, 30, 164–65; "mere animals," 158–59n3, 165–67, 170, 173n5; "semi-animals," 306–7, 318n6. *See also* beast of prey; blond beast; philosophical anthropology
Anscombe, G. E. M., 54n6
Ansell Pearson, Keith, 14n7, 318n5, 319n18
anthropology, 239, 240, 241
anti-anti-Semitism, 9, 182–84, 279, 281–82. *See also* Jews. anti-Christ, 286
anti-Semitism/anti-Semites, 84, 182–84, 207n10, 278–74. *See also* Jews. aphorism, 9–10, 75n2, 182–87, 189n17
Aquinas, T., 240
Archilochus, 179
Arendt, H., 105n16
arête (excellence), 291–92, 294
Aristotle, 102, 124n2, 180
art/artists/artistry, 49–50, 55n19, 179, 180, 187, 207n9, 208n12, 225–26, 229, 251, 260, 265, 267–68, 311–16, 328n28
ascetic ideal(s), 3, 7, 11, 22, 35, 83, 114, 161n23, 180,

188n11, 191, 193, 195–96, 202, 205, 207n10, 208n12, 208n13; 212, 213, 216, 225, 316
ascetic priest, 60–61, 83, 202, 207n10, 213, 251, 253, 314, 315–17. *See also* priests. asceticism, 12, 58, 212
audience (of Nietzsche's *GM*), 177–78, 196, 202–3, 205, 206n2, 208n19. *See also* reading. Austin, J. L., 292
Aurelius, M., 178
authenticity, 101–4
autonomy, 88–89, 101, 137–38, 148, 150–51, 154–56, 163–64, 171

Baader, F. von, 210
Babich, B., 104n10, 105n27, 105n28
Bachelard, G., 76n12
bad conscience, 3–4, 26, 30–35, 113, 128n28, 143, 161n23, 164–66, 172, 250–51, 295, 306, 308–310, 316, 319n14, 319n16
Bakhtin, M., 236
beast of prey. *See* animals. beauty, 12, 259–63, 267–70, 273
becoming, 95, 153, 155, 157, 167, 173n3, 195, 196, 260
"becom[ing] who you are," 14n4, 49, 103, 151, 298–300

being, 70, 71, 74, 104n2, 196, 260
Benjamin, W., 225
Benveniste, 255n17
Bergmann, F., 110
Bergoffen, D., 37n2
Bible (citations from), 2–3, 69, 75n10, 103, 104n1, 123, 183, 186, 290
Biser, E., 218n17
Bittner, R., 125n7, 145n3, 144
Bizet, 187
blond beast. *See* animals. body, 5, 67–68, 70–74, 75n2, 75n4, 103, 134, 149, 176n25, 236. *See also* physiology. Bourget, P., 209–10, 217n6, 218n7
Burckhardt, J., 281
Burke, E., 268

causality, 131–145; *passim*, 151, 158
Christianity/Christian, 3, 4, 12, 40–49, 51–52, 67, 69, 71, 77, 100, 114–15, 119, 133, 145n1, 154, 183, 185, 186, 197–200, 203–4, 208n16, 214, 218n14, 251–52, 278, 279, 283, 286–87; Christ, 225. *See also* Jesus
Clark, M., 10, 55n13, 188n9, 188n10, 207n11, 292–93
class, 235, 252
communication, 229–30
community, 251, 259, 266f, 270–71
Comte, A., 242
Conant, J., 43–44, 55n21, 298, 299–300
Conscience, 101, 106n28, 113, 143, 150, 152, 156, 171, 252, 309, 310, 316, 319n14. *See also* bad conscience
consciousness, 72, 99, 102, 148–49, 163, 167, 175n19, 192, 199, 201, 211
consequentialist ethics, 293, 298–99
conservatism, 268, 271–72; "new conservatism," 230n1. *See also* right wing
Conway, D., 55n14
cosmology, 174n9
creativity, 7, 12, 60, 125n7,

172, 176n24, 208n13, 263–7, 270–73
credit/creditor. *See* debtor/creditor relation. critique; ideology, 229; totalizing, 11, 223–24, 226–28, 230n10

Danto, A., 54n4, 62–64, 124n2, 124n3
debtor/creditor relation, 4, 32–33, 114, 250–51
decadence, 185, 210–11, 278, 284
deconstruction, 254n9
Deleuze, 11, 228, 230n6, 230n8, 230n9, 245–53
democracy, 156, 161n24, 231n10, 269, 319n22
Derrida, 11, 189n14, 233, 238–43, 274n13
Descartes, 177, 238
descent, 4, 227–28, 234–36
desire, 75n1, 136, 184, 194, 248–49, 251–53, 255n15
dialectic, 99–100, 229
Digby, K., 117
Dionysian, Dionysus, 14n3, 24, 159n5, 197, 238, 281, 284–87, 289n8
disintegration [*Disgregation*], 211–14
domination, 30, 48, 98, 100, 224, 228
Dostoevsky, 209, 217n2, 236
drive(s), 72, 75n1, 199
Dühring, E., 84, 207n10, 280
duty, 154. *See also* responsibility.

Einstein, 174n9
Else, G., 127n19
Enlightenment, 203, 223–24, 228
estrangement, 191–93, 199
eternal recurrence, 9, 28, 36–37, 38n7, 157, 166–71, 174n8, 178n12, 175n13
ethnocentrism, 239, 240
excellence, 55n21, 55–56n24, 82, 110–11, 115
existentialism, 157, 158
expression, 48–50, 138, 144
expressivist, 49, 139–40

family, 251–52
fascism, 186, 252–53, 282, 287
fatalism, 38n7, 176n24

fate, 28–31, 37, 38n7, 55n15, 102–3, 124, 152, 155, 157, 165. *See also* amor fati. Febvre, L., 75n10
Fichte, Immanuel H., 210
Fink, E., 218n18
Foot, P., 89, 91n27, 91n28, 292
force(s), 35, 72, 96, 116, 134–35, 149, 153–54, 211; active and reactive, 35, 245, 247–49
forgetting, 9, 149, 153–54, 159n5, 160n19, 163, 165–68, 170–72. *See also* memory
Foucault, 228, 233, 234–38, 247–49
freedom, 4, 27–30, 37, 49–51, 55n15, 88, 95, 132–33, 143, 148–49, 150–51, 155–57, 158n12, 163, 165, 171, 211, 251
Freud, S., 73–74, 76n15, 93, 95, 168, 192, 201, 228, 242–43, 248–49, 250, 252
Fritsch, T., 7, 10, 280, 289n5
Fromm, Erich, 293

Gast, P., 37n1
Gemes, K., 54n8
gender, 252
genealogy, 4–5, 12, 39–40, 52, 54n9, 58–59, 68–70, 73, 75n1, 94–95, 227, 233–43, 246, 259–60, 261–62, 264–68
Germans, 186, 200
Geuss, R., 39, 52
God, 70–71, 74, 88, 93, 151, 164, 186, 215, 250–52, 265. *See also* Yahweh
Gödel, K., 174n9
Goethe, 197–98
grammatology, 241
Greeks, 185, 196, 204–5
Guattari, F., 11, 245–53
Guay, R., 49, 54n8, 55n21
guilt, 4, 30–31, 33–35, 37, 116, 143–44, 145n2, 165–66, 174n6, 250–51

Habermas, 11, 233–34, 274n19
Hadot, P., 178
Hales, S., 293
Hatab, L., 147, 151–52, 161n24, 319n22

Havas, R., 105n24, 160n16, 160n23, 161n24
health, 12, 197, 252, 265, 272, 294, 296–98, 300–301. *See also* sickness.
Hegel, 97, 98, 138–43, 205, 223–24, 229, 246, 273n7, 277–78
Heidegger, 104n7, 174n12, 179, 246–48
Heraclitus, 2, 13n3, 14n4, 179
hermeneutic (noun), 63–64, 182
Herzen, A., 209
Hesiod, 204
Hesse, H., 246
Hippocrates, 178–79
history, 4, 12, 23, 25, 58–59, 61–64, 94, 97 101, 195, 204–6, 219n20, 236, 242–43
Hitler, A., 252
Hobbes, 250
Hölderlin, 186
Hollingdale, R., 1, 148, 159n12
Homer/Homeric, 98, 105n13, 119–20, 125n6, 127n19, 204
honesty, 69, 137
Horkheimer, M., 11, 223–25, 228–29
Horney, K., 296–97
Hoy, D., 14n6, 274n24
human beings. *See* animals
Hume, 5, 14n6, 179, 203, 268, 274n24
Hurka, T., 294
Hutcheson, 38n3

Illich, I., 189n13
illness. *See* sickness. immoralism, 12, 292
information theory, 241
innocence, 143, 166, 174n6
instincts, 31, 69, 88, 94, 102–3, 116, 136, 152, 163, 165, 171
intent/intention, 49–50, 62–63, 102, 133, 135–36, 138–40
internalization (includes inpsychation), 31, 129n29, 136, 145n2, 149, 306
interpretation, 4, 6, 9–10, 12, 42, 54n4, 57–64, 67–69, 72–73, 96, 135, 142, 226,
259, 260–61, 263f, 266, 272
irrationalism, 229, 270
Israel, 119, 184

Jacobi, F., 210
Janaway, C., 10
Jaspers, 38n10
Jesus, 104n1, 283, 284. *See also* Christ
Jew(s)/Jewish, 182–83, 185, 196, 200, 202–4, 208n17, 277–89. *See also* Judaism
Joyce, J., 93
Judaism, 114–15, 185, 277–89
judgment, 225–26, 229, 250, 268
just/Justice, 70, 84

Kafka, 253
Kant, I., 29, 41, 102–4, 104n10, 105n19, 124n3, 160n21, 179, 226, 240, 273n8
Kaufmann, W., 1, 102, 148, 159n12
Kemal, S., 273n8
Kierkegaard, S., 74
Klages, L., 218n14
Klossowski, P., 175n13
knowledge, 4, 21, 26, 36–37, 45, 70, 160n19, 169, 175n18, 192, 194–99, 259–60
Korsgaard, C., 90n4
Kropotkin, P., 209
Krüger, H., 182, 188n8, 189n15

Lampert, L., 317n2
Lang, B., 190n21
Lange, Karen E., 310n23
language, 5, 67–68, 75n2, 135, 160n18, 226, 229, 239, 241–42
La Rochefoucauld, F., 80
laughter, 26, 170, 240, 265
Lee, R., 119, 122, 126n12
"leftist" readers, 288
Leiter, B., 7, 39, 54n9, 55n17, 55n21, 55n22, 82–83, 81–82, 91n27, 176n24, 207n11
Levi-Strauss, C., 11, 238–42, 243
Lewis, C., 297
liberals/liberalism, 161n24, 287
life, 24, 36, 63–64, 67, 69, 83,
95–96, 111, 137, 157–58, 165, 170, 178–80, 194–95, 197–98, 215–16, 219n18; life affirmation, 294, 297–98; life denial, 208n11
Locke, 5, 250
Loeb, P., 15n9, 158n3
love, 237, 252, 297
Luther, 75n10

MacIntyre, A., 56n27
Mallarmé, S., 224
Marshal, L., 122
Marx, 93, 97, 105n18, 208n16, 228, 243, 248, 252; Marxism, 274n24
masters/mastery/masterly human beings, 6–7, 109–13, 115–16, 120–22, 136–37, 157–58, 201, 204, 246, 250–51, 283, 308, 210n26; master morality, 97–98, 100, 120–21, 125n5, 125n9, 151, 224
May, S., 40, 163, 173n2
memory (includes remembering), 101, 103, 149–51, 154, 157, 160n19, 165–68, 184, 200–201, 239, 309. *See also* forgetting
metaphysics, 62, 74, 247
Miles, T., 160n15
Mill, J., 104
Moles, A., 174n9
monism, 247, 249
moral psychology, 131–45, 158
Müller-Lauter, W., 104n4
music, 70, 181
myth, 11, 223, 225, 227–30, 234, 241, 242

Nambikwara, 239–40, 243
nationalism/nationalist, 185, 281–83, 287
naturalism, 6–7, 15n13, 42, 44, 101, 133–34, 136, 157, 309
Nazi(s)/Nazism, 97, 105n16, 235, 282, 286
necessity, 157
Nehamas, A., 103, 299, 273n4
nihilism, 46, 101, 185, 203, 209–11, 213, 216, 217n1, 266
noble morality, 86, 110–13, 124n2, 125n5, 135, 183, 186, 310–314, 316, 318n14. *See also* master morality. normativity, 294

objectivity, 78–79, 184, 193–
96, 198–99, origins, 3–4, 6,
12, 67–69, 120, 227, 234–
35, 236, 243, 262, 273n6
overman, over-human. *See Übermensch*
Ovid, 186
Owen, D., 105n24, 152, 154–
56, 160n21, 161n24,
318n10

passions, 80, 194
past (problem of), 57–58, 61,
64, 93–94, 101, 103, 165,
173n5
pathos/pathos of distance, 84,
95, 104n7, 112, 142, 193,
206
Patton, P., 47–48, 54n10
Pearson, K., 159n6
Pecora, V., 253n2
Peirce, C., 117–18
perfectionism, 12, 55n21, 155–
56, 161n24, 298–300
Pericles, 204
perspective(s)/perspectivism, 45,
259, 261, 275n31
persuasion, 113–14
philosophers, 181, 201–2,
208n13
philosophical anthropology,
161n27, 307, 309
philosophy, 67–69, 73–75,
75n4, 180
physics, 104n7, 176n24
physiology, 68. *See also* body
Pindar, 14n4, 103
pity, 85, 91n16, 296–97, 314
Plato, 127n18, 175n13, 185,
232, 237–39, 255n15, 291;
Platonist, 234
pleasure, 213, 237, 250, 253
pluralism, 72, 247, 249, 288
poetry, 260
polemic, 236
politics, 12, 72, 101, 103, 156,
161n24, 184–86, 211, 252,
267, 270, 272–73, 281,
288–89. *See also* state
positivism, 242
Post, L., 128n26, 128n27
post-modern, 288
post-structuralism, 246–47
power, 47–49, 54–55n13, 72,
88, 96, 103, 135–36, 142,
148, 150, 152, 155–56,
165–66, 186, 210, 213–15,

219n18, 219n20, 223,
226–28, 234, 237, 241–42,
248–49, 254n14, 253,
268–69, 289n8, 293, 297,
300, 320n26. *See also* will to
power
pride, 168, 184
priest(s), 12, 114, 195, 218n14,
251, 279, 282–85, 314–16.
See also ascetic priest
progressivism, 12, 268–69, 271
promises, promising, 101–2,
137–38, 148, 150, 153–56,
158–59n3, 163, 171,
173n3, 200–201, 309
psychoanalysis, 11, 71, 75n1,
93, 249–50, 251–53
psychology, psychologist
(Nietzsche as), 21, 68,
75n1, 95, 205–6
punishment, 5, 59, 62–63,
139–40, 250–51
purity, 114–15

race/racism, 186, 235, 252,
272–73, 281, 282
Ranciere, J., 185
rationality, 99–100, 102–3. *See
also* reason
rationalism, 224
Rawls, J., 298
reading, 9, 69, 158, 178–87,
236, 245
reason, 11, 210; great, 73;
instrumental, 225, 229. *See
also* rationality
recollection, 167–68, 175n13.
See also memory
redemption, 33, 95, 100,
176n21, 251, 263–65
Reé, P., 3, 24
Reginster, B., 50, 296
Reich, W., 253
Reik, T., 75n9
religion, 164, 189n17, 198
remembering. *See* memory
Renan, 196
repression, 196, 207n8,
208n18, 228, 248–49, 253
responsibility, 28–29, 34, 37,
63–64, 88, 102, 105n24,
114, 141, 143–44, 148,
151, 153–55, 161n23,
163–64
resentment, 12, 127, 135, 137,
206, 296. *See also* ressentiment

respect, 85, 154, 156
ressentiment, 87, 109, 112–13,
116, 119, 121, 125n7, 133–
35, 183–84, 200, 204, 213,
215–16, 238–39, 241, 272,
279, 281, 283–84 320n28
revaluation of values. *See* values
revenge, 84, 112–13, 119, 136,
184, 194, 240, 283. *See also*
ressentiment
Richardson, J., 15n10, 56n23,
300
Ridley, A., 40, 53n1, 55n22,
91n21, 105n21, 105n24,
160–61n23, 318n14
"right wing" readers, 12, 269,
287–88
rights, 148, 156, 159n12
Risse, M., 105n22
Roos, R., 75n5
Rorty, R., 113
Rousseau, J., 97, 243, 250

Sartre, J., 242, 249
Schacht, R., 89, 318n4
Schelling, 226
schizoanalysis, 249
scholars, 181, 194–99, 205
Schopenhauer, A., 26, 33, 40–
42, 44, 95, 75n4, 76n14,
195, 207n9, 214
Schiller, F. W., 273n7
science, 7, 11, 45, 133–34, 138,
153, 189n17, 193–95,
207n6, 239–43, 251
self, 2, 71, 102–3, 235, 236,
241; de-selfing [*Entselbstung*], 97, 100, 103
self-deception, 136
self-knowledge, 2, 14n4, 68,
88–89, 184, 199, 205. *See
also* knowledge
self-overcoming, 26, 37, 74,
137, 154–55, 166, 171,
297–302
semiotics, 68
Seneca, 188n5
sexual ethos, 237–38; sexuality,
252
shame, 115–16
Shepard, P., 318n13, 320n24
sickness, 12, 164–65, 171, 210,
213, 296–97, 301. *See also*
health
Silberbauer, G., 121–22
slave(s), 86–87, 109–130; anti-
Semitism as, 283, 285; *pas-*

sim, 136–37, 196; slavish human beings, 320n26; slave morality, 86–87, 96–100, 112–15, 124n3, 131, 164, 183, 201, 246, 281

slave revolt, revolution, 8, 86–87, 109–10, 116, 118–21, 123–24, 125n7, 135–37, 161n23, 271, 278, 309

Socrates, 99, 114–16, 141, 153, 171, 175n15, 210, 225, 237

solipsism, 265–66, 267

Soll, I., 175n14

Solomon, R., 297

"sovereign individual," 9, 88–89, 101–3, 105n22, 147–61, 163–65, 173n2, 176n25, 199–201, 204

soul, 4, 71, 97, 102, 134, 144, 149, 184, 186, 235, 240

species, 216, 219n19

Spencer, H., 242

Spinoza, B., 34, 143

St. Teresa of Avila, 295

Stambaugh, J., 174n7, 176n21

state, the, 121, 281–82, 308–9, 313, 317

Staten, H., 173n5, 318n3, 320n26

Stegmaier, W., 105n22

Steven, J., 14n7

strength, 100, 131–32, 141, 297, 301

structuralism, 228, 234, 242

style, 27, 69, 183, 186, 189n14, 211, 260–61, 274n13

subject(s)/subjectivity, 8, 71, 131–45, 219n19, 224–25, 237, 247–48, 267, 269. *See also* actors

suffering, 31, 42, 54n4, 59–64, 85, 91n16, 98, 145n2, 196, 207n9, 213, 250, 253, 306, 309, 315

suicide, 219n20

Surrealists, 225

taste, 44, 51–52, 225–26, 230n7, 260

Taylor, C., 139

temporality, 74, 101, 166–67, 174n9, 174n10, 174n11, 202, 204–5

Tertullian, 240

Thatcher, D., 1, 14n8

Thomas, E., 128n27

time, 95–96

Tongeren, P., 318n12, 319n21

tragedy, 99, 207n9

translation, 73, 239–40

truth, 4, 7, 44–46, 70, 74, 193–97, 215, 226, 228–29, 230n7, 237, 241

Turgenev, I., 209

Übermensch/Übermenschen (includes overhumanity), 9, 33, 101, 147–48, 150, 152, 156, 158, 159n3, 163–73, 246, 284, 286

ugliness, 263

uncanniness, 2, 191–92, 200–206, 208n18, 238, 241–42

utility, 40, 45 (in quote), 79, 110

value(s), 17–18, 77, 103, 114, 131, 183–84, 203, 215, 259–68; impartial, 112, 115–18, 123–24; instrumental, 79–80, 88; intrinsic, 5, 40–41, 51, 79–88, 90n5, 90n6, 111, 116, 124n3; re-evaluation of values, 21–22, 39–52, 77–91; revaluation of values, 43, 90n1 (contrasted with "re-evaluation"), 136–37, 141–42 ; reversal of values, 285; value judgments, 225–26. *See also* judgment; revaluation of values

Veblen, T., 111

violence, 178–79, 235, 239–41, 251, 315; predation, 309–13

virtue, 80, 111, 289n8, 291–302; virtue ethics, 12, 291, 294

Wagner, R., 187, 199, 207n9, 208n16, 225, 278, 280–81

war, 35, 184–85

Warren, M., 54n13, 319n20

weakness, 131, 142

Weber, 103

Weiss, P, 225

Weisse, C., 210

White, R., 157, 161n29, 319n21

Wilcox, J., 10, 188n9, 189n11

will(s)/willing, 5, 22, 27–28, 133–34, 140, 164–65, 170–71, 176n24, 195, 211–14, 248–49, 253, 266, 269, 272; to life, 24, 37, 71, 72–73, 149, 151, 156–58, 161n23, 214, 218n14; to nothingness, 22, 34, 212–15, 218n14, 253, 309; to power, 6–7, 11–12, 30, 47–48, 50–52, 71, 73–74, 95, 135, 137, 164, 210, 214–16, 218n14, 218n17, 219n18, 223, 226, 228–29, 246–49, 253, 274n14, 291–302; quanta, 210–11, 214; to truth, 22, 36–37, 45–46, 51–52, 193, 194–96, 197–99, 203, 205, 207n11

Williams, B., 15n13, 90n5, 91n23, 138, 145n4

Wilmsen, E., 128n25

Wittgenstein, L., 11, 179

woman, 181, 189n14

writing, 9, 178–87, 238–41, 243

Yahweh, 285

Zarathustra, 3, 152, 158n12, 160n19, 164–73, 280. *See also Thus Spoke Zarathustra*

Zionist, 287

INDEX LOCORUM

Listed in order of publication using the citation formats and abbreviations indicated in the front matter.

The Birth of Tragedy (generally):
  21, 26–27, 63, 99, 103,
  159n5
  "Self-Criticism" 2: 263
  "Self-Criticism" 7: 26, 265
  4: 262
  7: 207n9
  8: 207n9
  9: 207n9
  12: 186
  13: 99
  13: 171
  14: 171, 238
Untimely Meditations (generally): 26, 59, 63–4
  *The Use and Disadvantage of
  History for Life* (generally):
  58, 62, 94, 102
  P: 195, 198
  3: 57, 94
  4: 198
  5: 195, 198
  s6: 195
  8: 195
  9: 58
  10: 195
  10: 104n7
  Schopenhauer as Educator
  (generally): 50, 55n16,
  55n21
  2: 26
  3: 104n7
  299
  We Philologists (generally): 68
Human All Too Human (generally): 40, 71, 120
  P: 25
  92: 91n15
  35: 178, 184
  36: 80
  40: 79
  94: 120
  114: 186
  163: 184
  381: 94
  475: 185, 282, 286
  481: 184–5, 189n19
  618: 59n8
  629: 91n15
Assorted Opinions and Maxims
  89: 120
The Wanderer and His Shadow
  (generally): 94

61: 38n7
96: 261
214: 245, 253
Daybreak (generally): 39–44,
  46, 51, 80, 82, 94, 235
P 3: 44
9: 40
10: 41
13: 41, 42
14: 54n3
16: 41, 120
21: 41
24: 41
23: 54n11
33: 41
38: 40
42: 194, 208n13
43: 208n13
70–2: 54n3
76–80: 41
77–8: 54n4
78: 42
84: 69
86: 41
95: 207n4
98: 54n3
99: 40
103: 80
104: 55n14
106: 42
108: 80
109: 72
112: 54n11
119: 72
131: 42
132: 41
133: 296–7
199: 42
205: 289n7
254: 54n11
285: 194
542: 210
556: 42
The Gay Science (generally): 42–
  43, 45–46, 85, 95
P 4: 274n15
11: 192, 210
13: 54n11, 85
108: 43, 175n17
109: 175n17
110: 45–46
116: 40, 46

118: 85
125: 43
127: 54n5
151: 44
270: 49, 103, 171
277: 176n23
290: 171, 260
299: 171, 259
310: 208n13
317: 95
324: 26
327: 26
328: 25
333: 192
335: 29, 171, 176n24
338: 85
340: 175n13
341: 28, 32, 168–70, 174n8,
  175n13, 176n24
342: 168, 170
343: 43–44
344: 45, 194
345: 207n4, 274n23
346: 46
349: 47
353: 47
354: 192, 210
357: 44
370: 24, 196, 313
379: 265
382: 22, 25
Thus Spoke Zarathustra (generally): 22, 64, 70, 103, 152,
  154
I: "Prologue" 4: 297
I: "On the Three Metamor-
  phoses": 164, 166
I: "On Reading and Writ-
  ing": 179
I: "Of War and Warriors":
  124n2
I: "On the New Idol": 282
I: "Thousand and One
  Goals": 271
I: "On the Gift-Giving Virtue": 175n17
II: "Blessed Isles": 171
II: "On Self-Overcoming":
  164
II: "Immaculate Perception":
  195
II: "Of Scholars": 195, 196

II: "The Prophet": 175n20
II: "On Redemption": 33,
   64, 94, 165, 171, 173n4
II: "The Stillest Hour": 171,
   175n18
III: "On the Vision and the
   Riddle": 167, 169,
   174n10, 175n13, 175n16,
   175n20
III: "On Involuntary Bliss":
   169
III: "Before Sunrise": 169
III: "Upon the Mount of
   Olives": 301
III: "On Apostates" 2: 71
III: "On the Three Evils":
   169
III: "The Convalescent":
   167, 169, 174n12,
   175n18, 175n20
III: "On the Great Longing":
   176n26
III: "The Seven Seals": 170,
   176n25
IV: "On the Higher Man":
   300, 301
IV: "At Noon": 169
Beyond Good and Evil (generally): 22, 28, 30, 43, 48,
   86, 97, 120, 152
P: 181
1: 226
2: 44, 78, 199
3: 210
4: 199
5: 44
8: 186
10: 70
13: 47, 210
16–20: 150
17: 132
19: 30, 49, 134, 140
21: 28, 134, 151, 176n24
22: 68
25: 286
29: 210
30: 197
31: 44
32: 192
39: 197
43: 49
44: 292
46: 43, 91n20
52: 285
56: 171, 182
61: 24
62: 25

68: 168, 184
121: 186
186: 23, 25, 54n7
188: 23
195: 114
202: 23, 25, 48, 59, 202–3:
   48
200: 195
207: 97, 195, 198–99
211: 264
212: 25, 97
213: 25
223: 265, 274n16
224: 225
225: 28, 48
226: 25
228: 25
229: 23
230: 46, 69, 305
231: 120, 186
232: 49
246: 69, 75n9
247: 69
251: 280
252: 25
257: 310, 318n8
258: 299
260: 98, 110–11,125n5, 297
261: 86
265: 141
295: 20, 24, 68
On the Genealogy of Morals (generally): 20–22, 30, 40,
   54n9, 58, 69, 72, 83–7,
   96–7, 101, 105n22, 111,
   115–16, 119, 123, 131,
   147–49, 154, 161n23
(on the title of): 242–3
P:1: 169, 180, 202, 206n2,
   235
P:2: 192
P:4: 204
P:5: 203
P:6: 23, 59–60, 90n2
P:7: 20, 24, 306
P:8: 24, 26, 178, 180–82
I:1: 183
I:2: 86, 110, 125n5
I:4: 126n11, 227–8
I:5: 118, 120, 126n11,
   127n19, 204, 318n7
I:6: 111, 114, 142, 314
I:7: 111–12, 114, 125n5,
   142, 182, 183, 204
I:8: 114, 182–84, 200
I:9: 23, 119, 182, 183
I:10: 86–88, 109–10, 121,

   125n5, 135, 142, 204,
   272, 283, 309, 320n28
I:11: 23, 112–13, 124n2,
   125n9, 204, 306, 309–10,
   316
I:12: 23, 295
I:13: 49, 87, 99, 112, 131–
   38, 143–44, 145n2, 150–
   51, 153, 164, 310–12
I:14: 70–1, 82
I:16: 125n5, 204
I:17: 126n11
II:1: 101, 149, 155, 164–65,
   167, 200
II:2: 88, 101–2, 147, 150,
   152–3, 156–58, 163, 165,
   201
II:3: 163, 165–66
II:4: 24
II:6: 31–2
II:7: 83, 161n27, 206n2
II:9: 125n5
II:11: 84, 135
II:12: 54n12, 84, 133, 135,
   138, 140, 142
II:13: 140
II:14: 113, 142
II:15: 143
II:16: 31–2, 60, 129n29,
   136, 164, 224–5, 250,
   284, 306–8, 318n6,
   319n16
II:17: 121, 128n28, 210,
   242, 307, 308, 311–12,
   318n9, 319n16
II:18: 32, 96, 116, 295, 311
II:19: 114, 164, 251, 318n3
II:20: 32
II:21: 165, 213
II:22: 20, 33, 137, 251
II:24: 22, 169, 213
II:28: 209
III (epigraph): 10, 15n15,
   179–80, 187n7, 188n7
III:1: 180–82, 189n11, 213
III:2: 180
III:3: 295
III:5: 208n12
III:6: 226, 260
III:7: 58
III:9: 210
III:10: 201–2, 317
III:11: 83, 212
III:12: 275n29 and n31
III:13: 212, 228, 296
III:14: 20, 203, 212–13,
   280–81, 320n25

III:15: 60, 62, 213, 320n27, 315
III:16: 204, 212
III:17: 196, 207n10, 212–13, 313
III:18: 213, 310, 319n18
III:19: 88, 213
III:20: 30–1, 61, 213
III:22: 71, 186
III:23: 191, 193, 205, 212
III:24: 194, 202, 241, 263
III:25: 194, 225
III:26: 185, 196
III:27: 22, 166, 185, 194, 202–3, 242
III:28: 22, 61, 180, 194, 196, 212, 253, 266
The Case of Wagner (generally): 27
P: 24
1: 72
7: 211
9: 21
Twilight of the Idols (generally): 24, 43, 49, 59, 69
P: 68, 70
"Maxims" 8: 197
"Socrates" (generally): 171, 175n19
"Socrates" 5: 115
"Socrates" 8: 115
"Socrates" 9: 116
"Socrates" 10: 210
"Reason" 3: 71
"World" 6: 215
"Morality" 1: 273n9
"Morality" 2: 273n9
"Morality" 5: 215, 262
"Morality" 6: 29
"Errors" 7: 29, 134, 274n17
"Errors" 8: 29, 38n7
"Improvers" 1: 75n3
"Improvers" 2: 312, 316
"Improvers" 3: 71
"Germans" 4: 282
"Skirmishes" 5: 43, 119
"Skirmishes" 14: 216
"Skirmishes" 19: 263
"Skirmishes" 24: 263
"Skirmishes" 26: 70
"Skirmishes" 38: 29, 49
"Skirmishes" 41: 48
"Skirmishes" 43: 164, 166, 213
"Skirmishes" 44: 318n11

"Skirmishes" 48: 164
"Skirmishes" 49: 164
"Skirmishes" 51: 179
"Ancients" (generally): 69
"Ancients" 4: 24
"Ancients" 5: 24
The Antichrist(generally): 250
P: 208n19
1: 263, 274n17
9: 212, 214
15: 69, 198, 273n9
16: 69
18: 215
24: 125n5, 215
26: 69, 251
44: 183, 208n16
52: 69, 71
55: 280
Ecce Homo (generally): 21, 24, 26, 40, 71–2, 94
P:3: 71, 197
P:4: 25
"Wise" 3: 94
"Wise" 6: 301
"Clever" 2: 76n13
"Clever" 9: 199
"Clever" 10: 34
"Books" 3: 26
"Books" 4: 69, 186
"Books" 5: 69, 205
"BT" 2: 36
"BT" 3: 24
"D" 1: 40
"Z" 1: 170
"Z" 2: 22
"Z" 6: 26
"GM": 20, 171, 177–78, 192, 203, 233
The Will to Power (generally): 69
2: 208n20
38: 210
43: 211
46: 214
55: 212, 214
229: 75n7
260: 213
401: 214, 216
461: 215
481: 267
484: 73
492: 76n15, 76n16
513: 267
552: 76n19
556: 267

619: 211
622: 211
675: 214
685: 214–16
692: 213–14
748: 282
795: 259
802: 260
809: 270–71
816: 259
864: 216
899: 210
967: 274n10
983: 34
1048: 259
Kritische Studienausgabe (KSA)
1, 547 (= "Socrates und die Tragoedie"): 99
5, 291 (= *GM* II:1): 148
5, 293(= *GM* II:1): 158n2
5, 337 (= *GM* II:25): 159 n12
5, 361(= *GM* III:10):: 320n29
5, 247 (= *GM* P:1): 320n29
7: 30 [15]: 104n7
9: 11 [148]: 167, 169
9: 11 [196]: 175n17
9: 11 [143]: 38n7
9: 11 [318]: 174n11
10: 1 [109]: 69
10: 4 [81]: 168
10: 4 [85]: 166
10: 18 [34]: 76n20
11: 25 [7]: 174n12
11: 34 [185]: 96
11: 35 [47]: 103
11: 37 [4]: 72–3
11: 38 [12]: 247
11: 40 [21]: 76n16
12: 2[127.2]: 203
12: 2 [190].47: 96
12: 2[82], 2[78], 2[86]: 76n15
12: 2 [148]: 96
12: 2 [82]: 74
12: 9 [91].65: 76n19
13: 11 [29]: 96
13: 11 [48]: 97
13: 14 [79]: 95
13: 14 [102]: 103
13: 14 [121]: 95
13: 14 [174]: 95

About the Contributors

Christa Davis Acampora is associate professor of philosophy at Hunter College and The Graduate Center of the City University of New York. She is coeditor, with Ralph R. Acampora, of *A Nietzschean Bestiary: Becoming Animal Beyond Docile and Brutal* (2004) and author of numerous articles on Nietzsche.

Keith Ansell Pearson holds a Personal Chair in Philosophy at the University of Warwick. He is the editor of *A Companion to Nietzsche* (2006) and coeditor, with Duncan Large, of *The Nietzsche Reader* (2006).

Babette E. Babich is professor of philosophy at Fordham University in New York City and adjunct research professor of philosophy at Georgetown University, Washington, D.C. She is author of *Words in Blood, Like Flowers: Philosophy and Poetry, Music, and Eros in Hölderlin, Nietzsche, and Heidegger* (2006) and *Nietzsche's Philosophy of Science: Reflecting Science on the Ground of Art and Life* (1994; Italian 1996). A three-time Fulbright Scholar and Nietzsche-Fellow (Weimar: 2004), she is founder and executive editor of *New Nietzsche Studies* and has edited several book collections including *Habermas, Nietzsche, and Critical Theory* (2004), *Hermeneutic Philosophy of Science, Van Gogh's Eyes, and God* (2002), *Theories of Knowledge, Critical Theory, and the Sciences* (1999), *Nietzsche, Epistemology, and the Philosophy of Science* (1999), and *From Phenomenology to Thought, Errancy, and Desire* (1996).

Eric Blondel is a professor at the University of Paris I (Panthéon-Sorbonne) where he holds the Chair in Moral Philosophy. Among his numerous writings are works on Nietzsche, Rousseau, love, and film. His *Nietzsche: The Body and Culture*, to which he refers in the excerpt reprinted in this volume, was published in English translation in 1991.

Daniel W. Conway is professor of philosophy at The Pennsylvania State University. He is the author of *Nietzsche's Dangerous Game* (1997) and *Nietzsche and the Political* (1997), and the editor of the four-volume *Nietzsche: Critical Assessments* (1998).

Ken Gemes is senior lecturer in philosophy at Birkbeck College, University of London. He has published many papers on the philosophy of science, as well as on Nietzsche.

Jürgen Habermas is a permanent visiting professor of philosophy at Northwestern University. He is emeritus from the universities of Heidelberg anmd Frankfurt, and he served as the director of the prestigious Max Planck Institute in Starnberg, Germany. He is the author of more than fifteen books, including *Knowledge and Human Interests* (1986), *The Legitimation Crisis* (1973), *The Theory of Communicative Action* (1981), *The Philosophical Discourse of Modernity* (1985), Between Facts and Norms: *Contributions to a Discourse Theory of Law and Democracy* (1992), and *The Divided West* (2006).

Salim Kemal taught philosophy and held research positions at numerous institutions, including Dundee, Princeton, The Pennsylvania State University, and Cambridge. Among his many articles and books are *Kant and Fine Art* (1986) and *The Poetics of Alfarabi and Avicenna* (1991). He was cofounder, with Ivan Gaskell, of the book series Cambridge Studies in Philosophy and the Arts.

Paul S. Loeb is professor of philosophy at the University of Puget Sound. He is the author of numerous articles on Nietzsche and is currently completing a book on *Thus Spoke Zarathustra*.

Mark Migotti is associate professor of philosophy at the University of Calgary. He works and publishes on Nietzsche's ethics, Peirce's theories of truth and science, and the interplay between epistemic and ethical evaluation.

Wolfgang Müller-Lauter was coeditor of the de Gruyter critical edition of Nietzsche's complete works and professor emeritus in the Department of Protestant Theology of the Humboldt University in Berlin. His numerous essays and books have had tremendous influence on Nietzsche studies. His *Nietzsche: His Philosophy of Contradictions and the Contradictions of His Philosophy*, a chapter of which is reprinted here, appeared in English translation in 1999.

Alexander Nehamas is Edmund N. Carpenter II Class of 1943 Professor in the Humanities, professor of philosophy, and professor of comparative literature at Princeton University. His *Nietzsche: Life as Literature* (1985) has been translated into nine languages. He has also authored *The Art of Living: Socratic Reflections from Plato to Foucault* (1998) and *Virtues of Authenticity: Essays on Plato and Socrates* (1998).

David Owen is professor of social and political theory, and deputy director of the Centre for Philosophy and Value, at the University of Southampton. He is the author of *Maturity and Modernity* (1994) and *Nietzsche, Politics, and Modernity* (1995) as well as coeditor of *Foucault contra Habermas* (1999) and two forthcoming volumes: *Recognition and Power* and *Cultural Diversity and Political Theory*. He is currently completing a book titled *Nietzsche's Genealogy of Morality*.

Robert B. Pippin is the Evelyn Stefansson Nef Distinguished Service Professor in the Committee on Social Thought, the Department of Philosophy, and the College at the University of Chicago. His latest book is *Nietzsche, moraliste français: La conception nietzschéenne d'une psychologie philosophique* (2006).

Aaron Ridley teaches philosophy at University of Southampton, United Kingdom. He teaches courses on aesthetics, Nietzsche, logic, and problems of value, and conducts research in the area of philosophy of music. His books include *Nietzsche's Conscience: Six Character Studies from the "Genealogy"* (1998) and *The Philosophy of Music: Theme and Variations* (2004).

Alan D. Schrift is the F. Wendell Miller professor of philosophy and director of the Center for the Humanities at Grinnell College, has published extensively on Nietzsche and French philosophy. His most recent books include *Twentieth-Century French Philosophy: Key Themes and Thinkers* (2006), *Modernity and the Problem of Evil* (2005) and *Why Nietzsche Still? Reflections on Drama, Culture, and Politics* (2000). He is currently overseeing an eight-volume history of Continental philosophy.

Gary Shapiro is the author of *Nietzschean Narratives* (1989), *Alcyone: Nietzsche on Gifts, Noise, and Women* (1991), *Earthwards: Robert Smithson and Art After Babel* (1995), and *Archaeologies of Vision: Foucault and Nietzsche on Seeing and Saying* (2003). He is currently working on questions of geophilosophy.

Tracy B. Strong is UCSD Distinguished Professor of Political Science at the University of California, San Diego. He is the author or editor of many articles and several books including *Friedrich Nietzsche and the Politics of Transfiguration* (third edition, 2000), and *Jean Jacques Rousseau and the Politics of the Ordinary* (second edition, 2001). He has also served as the editor of *Political Theory: An International Journal of Political Philosophy*.

Christine Swanton is a professor at the University of Auckland, New Zealand. Her book *Virtue Ethics: A Pluralistic View* was published in 2005. Her most recent article on Nietzsche, "Can Nietzsche be both an Existentialist and a Virtue Ethicist," is to appear in *Values and Virtues*.

Yirmiyahu Yovel holds distinguished chair positions in philosophy at the Hebrew University in Jerusalem and at the New School University in New York. He has written extensively on Spinoza, Kant, Hegel, and Nietzsche, including *Dark Riddle: Hegel, Nietzsche, and the Jews* (1998), which includes extended development of the text excerpted in this volume, and *Spinoza and Other Heretics* (1989). He is the editor of *Nietzsche as Affirmative Thinker* (1986).